Maximus the Confessor as a European Philosopher

VERITAS
Series Introduction

"... the truth will set you free" (John 8:32)

In much contemporary discourse, Pilate's question has been taken to mark the absolute boundary of human thought. Beyond this boundary, it is often suggested, is an intellectual hinterland into which we must not venture. This terrain is an agnosticism of thought: because truth cannot be possessed, it must not be spoken. Thus, it is argued that the defenders of "truth" in our day are often traffickers in ideology, merchants of counterfeits, or anti-liberal. They are, because it is somewhat taken for granted that Nietzsche's word is final: truth is the domain of tyranny.

Is this indeed the case, or might another vision of truth offer itself? The ancient Greeks named the love of wisdom as *philia*, or friendship. The one who would become wise, they argued, would be a "friend of truth." For both philosophy and theology might be conceived as schools in the friendship of truth, as a kind of relation. For like friendship, truth is as much discovered as it is made. If truth is then so elusive, if its domain is *terra incognita*, perhaps this is because it arrives to us—unannounced—as gift, as a person, and not some thing.

The aim of the Veritas book series is to publish incisive and original current scholarly work that inhabits "the between" and "the beyond" of theology and philosophy. These volumes will all share a common aspiration to transcend the institutional divorce in which these two disciplines often find themselves, and to engage questions of pressing concern to both philosophers and theologians in such a way as to reinvigorate both disciplines with a kind of interdisciplinary desire, often so absent in contemporary academe. In a word, these volumes represent collective efforts in the befriending of truth, doing so beyond the simulacra of pretend tolerance, the violent, yet insipid reasoning of liberalism that asks with Pilate, "What is truth?"—expecting a consensus of non-commitment; one that encourages the commodification of the mind, now sedated by the civil service of career, ministered by the frightened patrons of position.

The series will therefore consist of two "wings": (1) original monographs; and (2) essay collections on a range of topics in theology and philosophy. The latter will principally be the products of the annual conferences of the Centre of Theology and Philosophy (www.theologyphilosophycentre.co.uk).

Conor Cunningham and Eric Austin Lee, *Series editors*

Maximus the Confessor as a European Philosopher

edited by

SOTIRIS MITRALEXIS

GEORGIOS STEIRIS

MARCIN PODBIELSKI

SEBASTIAN LALLA

CASCADE *Books* · Eugene, Oregon

MAXIMUS THE CONFESSOR AS A EUROPEAN PHILOSOPHER

Veritas 25

Copyright © 2017 Wipf and Stock. All rights reserved. Except for brief quotations in critical publications or reviews, no part of this book may be reproduced in any manner without prior written permission from the publisher. Write: Permissions, Wipf and Stock Publishers, 199 W. 8th Ave., Suite 3, Eugene, OR 97401.

Cascade Books
An Imprint of Wipf and Stock Publishers
199 W. 8th Ave., Suite 3
Eugene, OR 97401

www.wipfandstock.com

PAPERBACK ISBN: 978-1-4982-9558-1
HARDCOVER ISBN: 978-1-4982-9560-4
EBOOK ISBN: 978-1-4982-9559-8

Cataloguing-in-Publication data:

Names: Mitralexis, Sotiris, editor. | Steiris, Georgios, editor. | Podbielski, Marcin, editor. | Lalla, Sebastian, editor.

Title: Maximus the Confessor as a european philosopher / edited by Sotiris Mitralexis, Georgios Steiris, Marcin Podbielski, and Sebastian Lalla

Description: Eugene, OR: Cascade Books, 2017 | Series: Veritas 25 | Includes bibliographical references and index.

Identifiers: ISBN 978-1-4982-9558-1 (paperback) | ISBN 978-1-4982-9560-4 (hardcover) | ISBN 978-1-4982-9559-8 (ebook)

Subjects: LCSH: Maximus, Confessor, Saint, approximately 580–662. | Philosophy—History.

Classification: BR65.M416 M39 2017 (print) | BR65.M416 M39 (ebook)

Manufactured in the U.S.A.   SEPTEMBER 13, 2017

To Fr. Andrew Louth,
with gratitude for his pioneering work
in the study of Maximus the Confessor

Contents

List of Contributors xi
Editorial Note on Abbreviations xiii
List of Abbreviations xv
Introduction xxi

PART I. FIRST PHILOSOPHY: ONTOLOGY/METAPHYSICS

1. "Eschatological Teleology," "Free Dialectic," "Metaphysics of the Resurrection": The Three Antinomies That Make Maximus an Alternative European Philosopher 3
Dionysios Skliris

2. A Metaphysics of Holomerism 24
Torstein Theodor Tollefsen

3. Being Moved: St. Maximus between Anaxagoras and Kierkegaard 35
John Panteleimon Manoussakis

4. The System of Relations as a Pattern of Historicity in the Metaphysics of St. Maximos the Confessor 55
Smilen Markov

5. An Introduction to Aristotle's Theory of Motion as a Precursor to Maximus' Understanding of Motion 65
Michail Mantzanas

6. Maximus' Theory of Motion: Motion κατὰ φύσιν, Returning Motion, Motion παρὰ φύσιν 73
Sotiris Mitralexis

PART II. EPISTEMOLOGY: KNOWLEDGE, APOPHATICISM, AND LANGUAGE

7. "A Greater and More Hidden Word": Maximos the Confessor and the Nature of Language 95

Maximos Constas

8. Both Mere Man and Naked God: The Incarnational Logic of Apophasis in St. Maximus the Confessor 110

Jordan Daniel Wood

9. Roots of Scientific Objectivity in the *Quaestiones ad Thalassium* 131

Michael Harrington

10. The Theo-Phenomenology of Negation in Maximus the Confessor between Negative Theology and Apophaticism 140

Natalie Depraz

PART III. ANTHROPOLOGY: HUMAN NATURE, ETHICS, AND THE WILL

11. St. Maximos' Distinction between λόγος and τρόπος and the Ontology of the Person 157

Andrew Louth

12. The Conceptual Apparatus of Maximus the Confessor and Contemporary Anthropology 166

Georgi Kapriev

13. The Face of the Soul, the Face of God: Maximus the Confessor and πρόσωπον 193

Marcin Podbielski

14. The Philosophical Basis of Maximus' Concept of Sexes: The Reasons and Purposes of the Distinction between Man and Woman 229

Karolina Kochańczyk-Bonińska

PART IV. MAXIMUS IN DIALOGUE: FROM ANTIQUITY TO CONTEMPORARY THOUGHT

15. Analogical Ecstasis: Maximus the Confessor, Plotinus, Heidegger, and Lacan 241
Nicholas Loudovikos

16. Man as Co-creator: Reflections on the Theological Insights of St. Maximus the Confessor within a Contemporary Interdisciplinary Context 255
Stoyan Tanev

17. Αὐτεξούσιος Activity as Assent or Co-actuality? Compatibilism, Natural Law, and the Maximian Synthesis 272
Demetrios Harper

18. Creation Anticipated: Maximian Reverberations in Bonaventure's Exemplarism 284
Justin Shaun Coyle

19. The Oneness of God as Unity of Persons in the Thought of St. Maximus the Confessor 304
Vladimir Cvetković

20. Seeking Maximus the Confessor's Philosophical Sources: Maximus the Confessor and Al-Farabi on Representation and Imagination 316
Georgios Steiris

Appendix: Philosophy and Theology—the Byzantine Model 333
Georgi Kapriev

Index 337

Contributors

Maximos Constas is Senior Research Scholar at Holy Cross Greek Orthodox School of Theology, in Brookline, Massachusetts.

Justin Shaun Coyle is a doctoral candidate in historical theology at Boston College, Massachusetts.

Vladimir Cvetković holds a doctorate in philosophy from the University of Belgrade and is currently an independent researcher in Göttingen, Germany.

Natalie Depraz is Professor of Philosophy at the Université de Rouen, France.

Demetrios Harper holds a doctorate in theology from the University of Winchester, UK, at which he is currently a Visiting Research Fellow.

Michael Harrington is Associate Professor of Philosophy at Duquesne University in Pittsburgh, Pennsylvania.

Georgi Kapriev is Professor of the History of Philosophy at the University of Sofia "St. Kliment Ohridski" in Bulgaria.

Karolina Kochańczyk-Bonińska is Assistant Professor of Philosophy at the Cardinal Stefan Wyszynski University in Warsaw, Poland.

Sebastian Lalla is Visiting Professor of Philosophy at the National University of Mongolia and *Privatdozent* at the Freie Universität Berlin, Germany.

Nicholas Loudovikos is Professor of Dogmatics and Chair of the Department of Theological and Pastoral Studies at the University Ecclesiastical Academy of Thessaloniki, Greece, Honorary Research Fellow at the

University of Winchester and Visiting Professor at the Institute for Orthodox Christian Studies, Cambridge, UK.

Andrew Louth is Professor Emeritus of Patristic and Byzantine Studies at Durham University, UK.

John Panteleimon Manoussakis is Associate Professor of Philosophy at the College of the Holy Cross in Worcester, Massachusetts, and Honorary Fellow of the Faculty of Theology and Philosophy at the Australian Catholic University.

Michail Mantzanas is Assistant Professor of Philosophy at the Ecclesiastical Academy of Athens.

Smilen Markov is Assistant Professor at the St. Cyril and St. Methodius University of Veliko Turnovo, Bulgaria.

Sotiris Mitralexis is Assistant Professor of Philosophy at the City University of Istanbul and Visiting Research Fellow at the University of Winchester, UK.

Marcin Podbielski is Editor-in-Chief of *Forum Philosophicum*, an international journal for philosophy, and teaches philosophy at the Jesuit University Ignatianum in Cracow, Poland.

Dionysios Skliris holds a doctorate from the Faculté des Lettres et Sciences Humaines of the University of Paris (Sorbonne-Paris IV), France.

Georgios Steiris is Assistant Professor of Medieval and Renaissance Philosophy at the National and Kapodistrian University of Athens.

Stoyan Tanev is Associate Professor at the Innovation and Design Engineering Section of the University of Southern Denmark, Odense, and Adjunct Professor at the Faculty of Theology of the University of Sofia "St. Kliment Ohridski," Bulgaria.

Torstein Theodor Tollefsen is Professor of Philosophy at the University of Oslo, Norway.

Jordan Daniel Wood is a doctoral candidate in historical theology at Boston College, Massachusetts.

Editorial Note on Abbreviations

The volume adopts a specific approach to bibliographic references, which reflects the fact that Maximian scholars diverge in their opinions regarding the authorship of works traditionally included in the Maximian corpus, and treat different editions as authoritative.

This divergence is not strange to any Maximian scholar. The modern edition of Maximus' works, to be published in the Corpus Christianorum Series Graeca, is far from completion. While many partial contributions have been offered since the 1917 edition of some Maximian manuscripts by Sergey L. Epifanovich, and while many new proposals, especially in respect of authorship and the arrangement of minor works, have been made over the last one hundred years or so, the only complete corpus we can refer to is still that reprinted by J.-P. Migne in the Patrologia graeca. As we refer, very much out of necessity, to this corpus, we are obliged to place our trust in the meticulous work of scholars of the premodern era, who, however, had limited access to the manuscripts. It is worth reminding readers here that the principal texts used by Migne with respect to Maximus were those included in the incomplete 1674–75 edition of François Combefis, which lacked the *Ambigua*, and the 1857 edition of the *Ambigua* by Franz Oehler.

All those issues concerning the Maximian corpus have had to be reflected in the bibliographic entries used, but without confusing the reader. Because of that, we show two lists of abbreviations below. The first list, formatted in line with the customs of the Cascade imprint as a short general bibliography, identifies major editions and translations of Maximus' works, as well as other authoritative works frequently referred to by contributors to the volume. The second list seeks to resolve inconsistencies pertaining to the abbreviations used for the titles of particular works by Maximus.

The same abbreviation is thus frequently used in reference to different editions of a given work by Maximus. The bibliography included after each paper explains which edition has been adopted as the main reference point for a given work by the author of the paper in question. Bibliographical entries for those works are preceded by their abbreviations, which thus have their definitive meaning only in the context of the individual papers concerned. Apart from Maximus' own works, only works quoted by the authors of the papers are shown in the respective bibliographies. If a passage by an ancient or Patristic author is not quoted in the original language, but only referred to in a paper, standard abbreviations and editions are referenced in the notes. In line with the norms of classical studies, those references are omitted from the bibliographies.

The bibliographic entries for the works of Maximus have been abridged—as far as is possible. The bibliographic addresses for the Migne and CCSG volumes, as well as for other major editions, are set out in the general abbreviations list. In Maximian citations, series titles and volumes, including the volumes of PG, are omitted.

Abbreviations introduced in the volume emulate the concision of those proposed by Polycarp Sherwood in his *Annotated Date-List of the Works of Maximus the Confessor*. Where possible, his original abbreviations have been preserved. A set of rules has been followed when abbreviating typical parts of titles of works: *A* always stands for *Ambigua*, *C* for *Capita*, *Cn* for *Centuria/ae*, *D* for *De* or *Disputatio*, *Df* for *Definitiones*, *Ep* for *Epistula*, *Ef* for the texts first published by Sergey L. Epifanovich, *Fr* for *Fragmentum/a*, *Q* for *Quaestiones*, *Sch* for *Scholia*, *TP* for *Theologica et polemica*, and *Vi* for *Vita*. There is no punctuation, and there are no spaces within the abbreviations. In the case of the texts published in Epifanovich, which may also be known by their own titles, "¦" is used to separate the two variants.

Marcin Podbielski

Abbreviations

Abbreviations of Maximus the Confessor's Works

(Some of the works shown here are of dubious authorship.)

AI	*Ambigua ad Iohannem*	Ambigua to John / Ambigua II
AT	*Ambigua ad Thomam*	Ambigua to Thomas / Ambigua I
CChar	*Capita de caritate*	Four Centuries on Charity
CDiv	*Diversa capita . . . (xxvi–d)*	
CGn	*Capita theologica et oeconomica / Capita ducenta*	Gnostic Chapters / 200 Chapters on Theology and Incarnation
CSu	*Capita de substantia et hypostasi*	Chapters on Substance and Hypostasis
DB	*Disputatio Bizyae*	The Dispute at Bizya
DP	*Disputatio cum Pyrrho*	Dispute with Pyrrhus
Ef01 to Ef36	*Addidamenta* in Epifanovich, including	
Ef11¦GnCn	*Capita gnostica*	The Moscow Gnostic Century
Ef20¦QThGFr	*E quaestionibus a Theodoro monacho illi propositis*	
Ef22¦CSu	*Capita de substantia et hypostasi*	
Ef30¦EpB	*Ad Stephanum presbyterum et hegumenum*	
Ep1 to Ep45	*Epistulae I–XLV*	Epistles 1–45
EpA	*Epistula ad abbatem Thalassium*	Fragment from a Letter to Thalassius

EpTh	*Epistula secunda ad Thomam*	*Second Letter to Thomas*
LA	*Liber asceticus*	*On the Ascetic Life*
LC	*Loci communes*	*Sententiae*
Myst	*Mystagogia*	*Mystagogy*
PN	*Orationis dominicae expositio*	*On the Our Father*
Ps59	*Expositio in Psalmum lix*	*On Psalm 59*
QD	*Quaestiones et dubia*	*Questions and Doubts*
QThal	*Quaestiones ad Thalassium*	*Questions to Thalassios*
SchD	*Scholia in corpus Areopagiticum*	*Scholia in Pseudo-Dionysius*
SchE	*Scholia in Ecclesiasten (in catenis: catena trium patrum)*	*Scholia in Ecclesiastes*
TP1 to TP 25	*Opuscula theologica et polemica*	

Editions of Works Belonging to the Corpus of Maximus the Confessor

CCSG 7 & 22   Maximus the Confessor and Johannes Scotus Eriugena. *Maximi Confessoris Quaestiones ad Thalassium una cum Latina interpretatione Joannis Scotti Erivgenae iuxta posita*. Edited by Carl Laga and Carlos G. Steel. Corpus Christianorum: Series graeca 7, 22. Turnhout: Brepols / Leuven: Leuven University Press, 1980–90.

CCSG 10   Maximus the Confessor. *Maximi Confessoris Quaestiones et dubia*. Edited by José H. Declerck. Corpus Christianorum: Series graeca 10. Turnhout: Brepols / Leuven: Leuven University Press, 1982.

CCSG 11   *Anonymus in Ecclesiasten Commentarius qui dicitur Catena Trium Patrum*. Edited by Santo Lucà. Corpus Christianorum: Series graeca 11. Turnhout: Brepols / Leuven: Leuven University Press, 1983.

CCSG 23   Maximus the Confessor. *Maximi Confessoris Opuscula exegetica duo*. Edited by Peter Van Deun. Corpus Christianorum: Series graeca 23. Turnhout: Brepols / Leuven: Leuven University Press, 1991.

CCSG 39	*Scripta saeculi VII uitam Maximi Confessoris illustrantia: una cum Latina interpretatione Anastasii Bibliothecarii iuxta posita.* Edited by Pauline Allen and Bronwen Neil. Corpus Christianorum: Series graeca 39. Turnhout: Brepols, 1999.
CCSG 40	Maximus the Confessor. *Maximi Confessoris Liber asceticus.* Edited by Peter Van Deun and Steven Gysens. Corpus Christianorum: Series graeca 40. Turnhout: Brepols, 2000.
CCSG 48	Maximus the Confessor. *Maximi Confessoris Ambigua ad Thomam una cum Epistula secunda ad eundem.* Edited by Bart Janssens. Corpus Christianorum: Series graeca 48. Turnhout: Brepols, 2002.
CCSG 69	Maximus the Confessor. *Maximi Confessoris Mystagogia: una cum latina interpretatione Anastasii bibliothecarii.* Edited by Christian Boudignon. Corpus Christianorum: Series graeca 69. Turnhout: Brepols, 2011.
CCSO 478–79	Maximus the Confessor. *Maxime le Confesseur. Vie de la Vierge.* Edited and translated by Michel Van Esbroeck. Corpus scriptorum christianorum orientalium: Scriptores Iberici 478–79 (21–22). Leuven: Peeters, 1986.
CD 4/1	John of Scythopolis and Maximus the Confessor (passim). *Corpus Dionysiacum IV/1: Ioannis Scythopolitani prologus et scholia in Dionysii Areopagitae librum De divinis nominibus cum additamentis interpretum aliorum.* Edited by Beate Regina Suchla. Patristische Texte und Studien 62. Berlin: de Gruyter, 2011.
CMofJCh	Maximus the Confessor. *On the Cosmic Mystery of Jesus Christ: Selected Writings from St. Maximus the Confessor.* Translated by Paul Marion Blowers and Robert L. Wilken. St. Vladimir's Seminary Press Popular Patristics Series. Crestwood, NY: St. Vladimir's Seminary Press, 2003.
CSC	Maximus the Confessor. *Capitoli sulla carità.* Edited by Aldo Ceresa-Gastaldo. Verba Seniorum N.S. Roma: Editrice Studium, 1963.

Difficulties	Maximus the Confessor. *On Difficulties in the Church Fathers: The Ambigua*. Edited and translated by Nicholas P. Constas. 2 vols. Dumbarton Oaks Medieval Library 28–29. Cambridge: Harvard University Press, 2014.
Ef	Epifanovich, Sergey L. *Materialy k izucheniyu zhizni i tvoreniy prepodobnogo Maksima Ispovednika*. Kiev: Tipografia Universiteta Sv. Vladimira; N. T. Korczak-Nowicki, 1917.
"EfR"	Roosen, Bram. "Epifanovitch Revisited: (Pseudo-) *Maximi Confessoris Opuscula varia*; a Critical Edition with Extensive Notes on Manuscript Tradition and Authenticity." PhD diss., Katholieke Universiteit Leuven, 2001.
MAS	Maximus the Confessor. *La Mistagogia ed altri scritti*. Edited and translated by Raffaelle Cantarella. Testi cristiani con versione italiana. Florence: Libraria Edititrice Fiorentina, 1931.
PG4	John of Scythopolis and Maximus the Confessor (passim). *S. Dionysii Areopagitae Opera Omnia quae extsant. Tomus posterior*. Edited by Balthasar Cordier. Patrologiae cursus completus: Series graeca 4. Paris: Migne, 1857.
PG19	Maximus the Confessor. *Eusebii Pamphili Cesareae Palaestinae Episcopi Opera omnia quae extant. Tomus primus*. Edited by J.-P. Migne. Patrologiae cursus completus: Series graeca 19. Paris: Migne, 1857.
PG90	Maximus the Confessor. *Maximi Confessoris Opera Omnia, Tomus primus*. Edited by François Combefis. Patrologiae cursus completus: Series graeca 90. Paris: Migne, 1865.
PG91	Maximus the Confessor, et al. *Maximi Confessoris Opera Omnia, Tomus secundus, Thalassi Abatis, Theodori Raithuensis Opera*. Edited by François Combefis et al. Patrologiae cursus completus: Series graeca 91. Paris: Migne, 1863.

RL	Rorem, Paul, and John C. Lamoreaux. *John of Scythopolis and the Dionysian Corpus: Annotating the Areopagite*. Oxford: Clarendon, 1998.
SelWrts	Maximus the Confessor. *Selected Writings*. Translated by George C. Berthold. Edited by Jaroslav Pelikan and Irénée-Henri Dalmais. Classics of Western Spirituality. New York: Paulist Press, 1985.

Other Abbreviations

ACO	*Acta conciliorum œcumenicorum*. Edited by Eduard Schwartz et al. Tomes I–IV [Series Prima] & Series Secunda I–III. Berlin: Verein wissenschaftliche Verlag; Berlin-Leipzig: de Gruyter, 1914–2013.
CD 1	Pseudo-Dionysius the Areopagite. *Corpus Dionysiacum I: Pseudo-Dionysius Areopagita, De divinis nominibus*. Edited by Beate Regina Suchla. Patristische Texte und Studien 33. Berlin: de Gruyter, 1990.
CD 2	Pseudo-Dionysius the Areopagite. *Corpus Dionysiacum II: Pseudo-Dionysius Areopagita, De coelesti hierarchia; De ecclesiastica hierarchia; De mystica theologia; Epistulae*. Edited by Günter Heil and Adolf Martin Ritter. Patristische Texte und Studien 36. Berlin: de Gruyter, 1991.
KPC	Vasiljević, Maksim [Bishop Maxim]. *Knowing the Purpose of Creation through the Resurrection: Proceedings of the Symposium on St Maximus the Confessor, Belgrade, October 18–21, 2012*. Alhambra, CA: Sebastian Press; Faculty of Orthodox Theology, University of Belgrade, 2013.
LSJ	Liddell, Henry G., et al. *A Greek-English Lexicon*. 9th ed. Oxford: Clarendon, 1968.
OHMC	Allen, Pauline, and Bronwen Neil, eds. *The Oxford Handbook of Maximus the Confessor*. Oxford: Oxford University Press, 2015.
PG3	Pseudo-Dionysius the Areopagite. *S. Dionysii Areopagitae Opera Omnia quae extant et Commentarii*

quibus illustrantur. Tomus prior. Edited by Balthasar Cordier. Patrologiae cursus completus: Series graeca 3. Paris: Migne, 1857.

PG36   Gregory of Nazianzus. *Sancti patris nostri Gregorii Theologi vulgo Nazianzeni . . . opera quae exstant omnia. Accedunt variorum commentarii et scholia. Tomus secundus*. Edited by J.-P. Migne et al. Patrologiae cursus completus: Series graeca. Paris: Migne, 1858.

PG86a   Eusebius of Alexandria, et al. *Eusebii Alexandrini episcopi, Eusebii Emeseni, Leontii Byzantini opera quae reperiri potuerunt omnia . . . accedunt Iustiniani, Imperatoris Augusti, scripta dogmatica. Leontii tomus prior, caeterorum tomus unicus*. Edited by J.-P. Migne. Patrologiae cursus completus: Series graeca 86a. Paris: Migne, 1860.

PG86b   Leontius of Byzantium, et al. *Leontii Byzantini opera omnia Leontii tomus posterior, caeterorum tomus unicus: Accedit Euagrii scholastici Historia ecclesiastica*. Edited by J.-P. Migne. Patrologiae cursus completus: Series graeca 86b. Paris: Migne, 1860.

Introduction

THE STUDY OF MAXIMUS the Confessor's thought has flourished in recent years: annual international conferences, publications and articles, new critical editions and translations mark a torrent of interest in the work and influence of perhaps the most sublime of the Byzantine Church Fathers.

It has been repeatedly stated that the Confessor's thought is of eminently philosophical interest, and his work is now often approached from a philosophical perspective. We can witness this tendency both in theological works highlighting the philosophical problems and solutions that Maximus proposes (starting from Hans Urs von Balthasar's classic monograph *Cosmic Liturgy*) and in purely philosophical works, written by academic philosophers for a similar audience (e.g., Torstein Tollefsen's *Christocentric Cosmology of St. Maximus the Confessor* and *Activity and Participation in Late Antique and Early Christian Thought*). However, no dedicated collective scholarly engagement with Maximus the Confessor *as a philosopher* has taken place—and this volume, together with the colloquium on which it is based, will attempt to start such a discussion.

Apart from Maximus' relevance and importance for philosophy in general, a second question arises: should towering figures of Byzantine philosophy like Maximus the Confessor be included in an overview of the history of European philosophy, or rather excluded from it—as is the case today with most histories of European philosophy? Latin Church Fathers such as Augustine or Thomas Aquinas are self-evidently included in the long history of the foundations of European philosophy. However, the equally self-evident omission of Byzantine Fathers like Maximus the Confessor from such historical overviews of philosophy[1] does not seem to be justified by any lack of philosophical efflorescence. In that sense, Maximus'

---

1. With notable exceptions such as, among others, Arthur Hilary Armstrong's *Cambridge History of Later Greek and Early Medieval Philosophy* (Cambridge University Press, 1967), which includes a chapter on Maximus (pp. 492–505) written by I. P. Sheldon-Williams, and Émile Bréhier's *History of Philosophy (Histoire de la Philosophie)*, which includes Basile Tatakis' *Byzantine Philosophy (La philosophie byzantine—Histoire de la Philosophie, par E. Bréhier, deuxième fascicule supplémentaire* [Paris: Presses Universitaires de France, 1949]).

philosophy challenges our understanding of *what European philosophy is*. In this volume, we will begin to address these issues and examine numerous aspects of Maximus' philosophy—thereby also stressing the interdisciplinary character of Maximian studies. And taking into account the above considerations, we will approach his thought as an important element of the history of European philosophy.

This volume is comprised of four parts: (1) First Philosophy: Ontology/Metaphysics, (2) Epistemology: Knowledge, Apophaticism, and Language, (3) Anthropology: Human Nature, Ethics, and the Will, and (4) Maximus in Dialogue: From Antiquity to Contemporary Thought.

The first part begins with Dionysios Skliris' article. This acts as the actual introduction to this volume, explaining in which way Maximus the Confessor is to be considered as a European philosopher, or rather as a philosopher that provides *alternatives* to basic tenets of his Western contemporaries as well as to later developments in European philosophy. Following this introduction, Torstein Tollefsen focuses on the relationship of "whole" and "part" in Maximus the Confessor's metaphysics, forming a distinct "Maximian holomerism" on the basis of the notion of the λόγοι. Fr. John Panteleimon Manoussakis proceeds to focus on Maximus' understanding of metaphysical motion (κίνησις) with reference to Anaxagoras and Kierkegaard—and, indirectly, Origen. In the next chapter, Smilen Markov studies the importance of *relation* in Maximus' ontology, and particularly in the relationship between creation and the uncreated in the context of history. We return to the theory of motion in the last two chapters of the volume's first part, proposing that Maximus' understanding of motion is both a continuation and a radical renewal of Aristotle's theory of motion in the context of an ontology that is markedly different from Aristotle's. Michail Mantzanas offers an introduction to the Aristotelian κίνησις, which is subsequently compared by Sotiris Mitralexis to Maximus' understanding thereof.

The second part, "Epistemology: Knowledge, Apophaticism, and Language," opens with Fr. Maximos Constas' account of the nature of language in Maximus' thought (with reference to Gregory of Nyssa), and with introductory hints concerning the possibility of a Maximian—and Christian—*philosophy of language*. This is followed by Jordan Daniel Wood's article on the dialectics of apophaticism and Incarnation, unknowability and knowledge, hypostasis and transcendence. Michael Harrington proceeds to focus on Maximus' *Quaestiones ad Thalassium* as a precursor to scientific objectivity through the notion of *natural contemplation* and its comparison to Pierre Hadot's philosophy. After this chapter on Maximus' *positive* epistemology, we once again return to his *negative* epistemology with Natalie

Depraz's treatment of Maximus' *theo-phenomenology of negation*, in which apophaticism is contrasted to negative theology.

The third part, titled "Anthropology: Human Nature, Ethics and the Will," begins with a "bridge" between theological ontology and (its consequences and implications for) anthropology, i.e., with Fr. Andrew Louth's treatment of the λόγος-τρόπος distinction (principle of nature-mode of existence) as the basis for a Maximian ontology of the person, human and divine. This is followed by Georgi Kapriev's paper, in which he expounds the basic tenets of Maximus the Confessor's anthropology in comparison to contemporary anthropological inquiry and proceeds to propose that we may find the seeds for solutions to certain contemporary philosophical problems in Maximus' works. Marcin Podbielski provides us with a close textual approach to the meaning of πρόσωπον, a key Maximian term. Karolina Kochańczyk-Bonińska studies Maximus' understanding of sexual differentiation, of the distinction—and division—of the sexes in the case of human beings and of its philosophical preconditions.

The final part of the present volume, "Maximus in Dialogue: From Antiquity to Contemporary Thought," is dedicated to discussions of the Confessor's philosophy in comparison to other philosophers and currents of thought, be they Maximus' predecessors, Maximus' contemporaries, or philosophers that appeared later in history. Most articles in this volume take into account a number of philosophers, thinkers, and theologians, but this part is dedicated to deeper comparative approaches, even if most chapters could easily fit in the other parts of this volume as well.

Fr. Nicholas Loudovikos employs the notion of *analogical ecstasis* in order to proceed to a discussion of Maximus in contradistinction to Plotinus, Martin Heidegger, and Jacques Lacan. Stoyan Tanev attempts an interdisciplinary approach to Maximus' insights, also proceeding to a comparison of Maximus' notion of man as a co-creator to the modern actor-network theory. Following this, Fr. Demetrios Harper studies the αὐτεξούσιον in reference to contemporary developments in ethics. In the next chapter, Justin Shaun Coyle compares certain Maximian ideas from the *Ambigua* to Bonaventure's theory of exemplarism. Vladimir Cvetković studies the oneness of God as a unity of persons in Maximus' thought with the aid of modern theological inquiry, while Georgios Steiris compares the Confessor and al-Farabi on representation and imagination, tracing possible common philosophical sources.

Some contributors give the latinized form of the Confessor's name, *Maximus*, while others prefer its Greek original, *Maximos*: we have respected each scholar's choice, as we have also done with their preferences concerning the various editions of primary Maximian sources. As there is an important semantic difference between Λόγος with a capital Λ, i.e., the second person of the Trinity, and λόγος/λόγοι, the principles of beings, the latter will be written with a small λ even at the beginning of sentences or in titles. Unattributed translations of quotations indicate that the respective author translated them.

The international colloquium entitled "Maximus the Confessor as a European Philosopher," which took place at the Freie Universität Berlin's Institute of Philosophy from the 26th to the 28th of September 2014, formed the basis of this volume—which, however, has since been enriched with further studies relevant to its research focus. Georgi Kapriev's appendix to the volume is a discussion deriving from the colloquium's round table on the theology-philosophy divide and possible reconsiderations concerning its importance today. The chapters by Boston College's doctoral candidates Justin Shaun Coyle and Jordan Daniel Wood were first produced as seminar projects for the Graduate Student Conference on Saint Maximos the Confessor's *Ambigua to John*, organized by Fr. Maximos Constas at the Holy Cross Greek Orthodox School of Theology in Brookline, Massachusetts, during the fall semester of 2014. We are grateful to both Fr. Maximos Constas and the authors of the two papers for the opportunity to include them in the present volume. We would like to use this opportunity to note the immeasurable importance of Fr. Maximos' translation—the first in English—of the complete *Ambigua*, as well as of his forthcoming English translation of the complete *Quaestiones ad Thalassium*, for the future of the study of Maximus the Confessor's thought. We extend our gratitude to doctoral candidates Athanasia Theodoropoulou and Ioanna Tripoula (University of Athens) for their aid in the initial stages of formatting and proofreading

This volume is dedicated with great gratitude to Fr. Andrew Louth, the renowned patristics scholar and Maximian studies pioneer. Together with the late Hans Urs von Balthasar, Lars Thunberg, and Polycarp Sherwood, Fr. Andrew Louth's arduous work with St. Maximus the Confessor's texts (including the first-ever English translations of substantial parts of Maximus' *Ambigua*), thought, and historical presence opened a way, in which initiatives like the present one cannot but claim to be small steps forward. In this flourishing era for Maximian studies, it is certain that future scholars will look with much gratefulness to Fr. Andrew Louth's ongoing Maximian legacy.

Sotiris Mitralexis
Georgios Steiris
Sebastian Lalla

PART I

First Philosophy: Ontology/Metaphysics

1

"Eschatological Teleology," "Free Dialectic," "Metaphysics of the Resurrection": The Three Antinomies That Make Maximus an Alternative European Philosopher

Dionysios Skliris

Is Maximus "European"? Is Maximus a "philosopher"? The two questions of the present volume also entail the concomitant questions "What is Maximus' contribution to Europe?" and "What is his contribution to philosophy?" They might equally presuppose the questions "Is Maximus something else than just a 'Byzantine'?" and "Is Maximus something else than just a theologian?" These are not new questions, and they have actually mobilized research in the last decades. It is to be remembered that Hans Urs von Balthasar, who is considered to be a sort of "founder" of a new period of interest in Maximian scholarship, regarded Maximus as a great European thinker who struggled against the "asianic" spirit and its despotism. He considered Maximus a precursor of Hegel and linked him to the latter's dialectical thought.[1] Roman Catholic specialists from 1970 onwards have tried to interpret Maximus as a precursor of Thomas Aquinas. They have insisted on Maximus' sojourn in the province of Africa, that is in the same places where Augustine of Hippo was active, as well as in Rome, and they have highlighted Maximus' conflict with the Byzantine state. Jean-Miguel Garrigues, in particular, has portrayed Maximus as a fugitive and a "refugee," who was fleeing Persians and Arabs, but also, in a certain sense, struggling against Byzantines. In the experience of this clash with the world

---

1. He even thinks that Maximus provides us with tools by which we could transcend the undesirable conclusions of the Hegelian dialectical thought. See Balthasar, *Cosmic Liturgy*, 163.

of Late Antiquity, Maximus supposedly discovered historical contingency[2] and formulated in his thought what has come to be a major problem of Western modernity. On the contrary, Orthodox scholars often consider Gregory Palamas as Maximus' true heir.[3] But for Orthodox scholars as well, the vindication of Maximus was related with all the important *enjeux* of European philosophy, both old and new. For example, Maximus' theories on the person, λόγος and τρόπος were linked to the modernist philosophical program of existentialism, as well as with personalism. The idea was to promote Maximus as an alternative thinker of the person that is not in an occidental modernist sense, but in an alternative version that is nevertheless equally European.[4] That was combined with an equal effort to regard Maximus as a more authentic continuator of Aristotle.[5] In recent decades, we have witnessed an important turning to Maximus' "psychology" and a comparison with contemporary psychology and psychoanalysis, for example in its Lacanian version,[6] or with other schools.[7] All these bold interpretations have of course coexisted with patristic, philological, and historical studies, feeding one another, and reaching the great interest in Maximus that we witness today.

The fact remains that Maximus has not found a prominent place in the history of philosophy—for example, a place alongside Augustine, or the place of an "alternative" Augustine. Maximian scholars have nevertheless pointed to specific philosophical achievements that could justify such a claim: to Maximus' theory of the will, for example, which is mainly the fact that he conceived of the will as an indispensable faculty of the human soul[8] and nature that accompanies intellection as an equally primordial drive. This could arguably be regarded as a sort of "Oriental voluntarism" that is an alternative to the Augustinian one, whence started all the adventure of Western voluntarism. One could also point out Maximus' treatment

---

2. See Garrigues, *Maxime le Confesseur*, 35–82. For a criticism to this line of interpretation, see Doucet, "Vues récentes."

3. To take just one example, see Karayiannis, *Maxime le Confesseur*. For the reception of Maximian thought by Gregory Palamas, see also Savvidis, *Lehre von der Vergöttlichung*.

4. For example, see Yannaras, *Τὸ ρητὸ καὶ τὸ ἄρρητο*, and Yannaras, *Person and Eros*.

5. To take just one example, see Betsakos, *Στάσις ἀεικίνητος*. The different reception of Aristotle in East and West is discussed in Bradshaw, *Aristotle East and West*.

6. For example, see Loudovikos, *Ψυχανάλυση καὶ ὀρθόδοξη θεολογία*.

7. See, for example, Tympas, *Carl Jung and Maximus the Confessor*.

8. See Bathrellos, *Byzantine Christ*, 128. Bathrellos is also referring to an evaluation of Maximus by the philosopher Richard Sorabji.

of Aristotelian teleology, his theory of time and the eon, his very original philosophy of history, and, in general, a restructuring of Greek metaphysics.

In my paper, I will not endeavor to prove that Maximus deserves such a place—even though I believe that he does indeed deserve it. I will focus on the preliminary questions, "Who is Maximus?" and "What is his philosophical gesture or, more widely, his existential gesture?" That is, I will first try to examine Maximus as a historical subject and to identify his project and only then to estimate his importance for European philosophy or his relevance in a contemporary context. The rich history of Maximian studies provides us with a great number of Maximus' portraits: A Hegelian Maximus, a Heideggerian Maximus, a Thomist Maximus, a Palamite Maximus, an Aristotelian Maximus, a Freudian, Jungian, or Lacanian Maximus. Maximus the unyielding, Maximus the rebel against imperial power, Maximus the refugee, Maximus who died bearing the stain of the heretic, before he was resurrected as an orthodox authority claimed by East and West alike. In answering the question "Who is Maximus?" I will draw from this great variety of portraits, trying to see them in a fresh manner that is beyond any confessional or traditional vindication.

We will witness a Maximus of the verge, a Maximus of antinomies. One should bear in mind that Maximus lived in the period of the definitive fall of the Roman ecumene under the attacks of the Persians and, finally, the Arabs, in the era when the Mediterranean was divided into a Christian and an Islamic part. He is therefore the last thinker of late antiquity and, at the same time, a voice that echoes through the Middle Ages reaching up to the beginning of Modernity. The political *enjeu* of his age was to save the multiplicity of cultural centers within the Roman Empire (for example Alexandria, Antioch, and, in general, Egypt, Palestine and Syria). The emperor will attempt this by a politics of compromise, in which differences will be violently silenced due to the need of a consensus that is imposed from the outside. Maximus will react to this imperial priority as a heresy that corrupts the integrity of Christian faith. At the same time, he is trying himself to integrate the polyphony of the late Roman Empire in one open contemplative "system" or rather worldview that would also represent the "lost" voices. Due to this care to save the "defeated" voices, Maximus' thought will become very synthetic but also eclectic. By the latter, I mean that Maximus often picked heterogeneous elements, without always reaching a definitive synthesis. On the contrary, his thought is characterized by the tension between the former great centers of the Roman Empire—for example, between Alexandrinian metaphysics, Antiochian historicity, Cappadocian trinitarian theology, Roman anti-Caesarism, and more widely between Hellenism and Judaism, nature and history, and, what concerns us here, philosophy and theology. Besides, throughout his life Maximus was erring between borders. He was a Greek-speaking participant of Hellenic culture but also a theological ally of Rome. By his contemplative nature he was inclined to a life of theory, quietism, and wisdom. Yet he led the life of an erring Ulysses without a final Ithaca,[9] travelling in all the corners of the Mediterranean, fleeing the East, reaching Africa and Italy, until he was exiled in Thraca and finally Lazica, where he died bearing the stigma of the heretic before his theology triumphed as orthodoxy *par excellence* after his death. I shall therefore consider *antinomy* as a main key to understanding Maximus; or rather what I would call an "asymmetrical antinomy," i.e., an antinomy in which the two parts are not equal, but the one is preponderant, preserving nevertheless the other in an interior tension with it.[10] I shall examine three fundamental antinomies of Maximian thought, namely "eschatological teleology," "free dialectic," and "the metaphysics of the resurrection," in order to observe in which ways Maximus was a European philosopher.

Eschatological Teleology

As the last thinker of late antiquity, Maximus might be observed from two different angles. He might be observed in relation to the past. We could then regard him as a bold reformer of Aristotelianism, or rather of a synthesis between Neoplatonism and Aristotelianism that is characteristic of the Greek-speaking East after Porphyry, as well as as a thinker who repeated Plotinus's existential gesture in a different way. And he might be observed in relation to the future. I could then say that some innovative elements of his thought, such as his theory of the will and his historical dialectic, entail a Christian transformation of the Platonic and Aristotelian legacy in the direction of its greater historicization and interiorization. In this sense, Maximus could be regarded as a precursor to the subjective dialectical idealism of modernity.

I will start by analyzing the first angle, namely Maximus' relation to the past. In what concerns Maximus' repeating of the Plotinian gesture, I would say that Maximus is characterized by the same fundamental optimism as Plotinus. He shares the belief that what exists is good to the degree that it exists. Plotinus has turned against Gnosticism in his claim that every being is good to the extent that it is a being, whereas what is not good is not a

---

9. I develop this view of Maximus in Skliris, "Θεολογώντας πάνω σὲ συντρίμμια."

10. My use of the term "asymmetrical" obviously refers to the asymmetrical Neo-chalcedonian Christology (starting in the sixth century), where Christ's two natures are full but not symmetrical, because his hypostasis is divine. The term was established by Fr. Georges Florovsky.

being.¹¹ Maximus claims a total valorization and salvation of nature against heresies that threatened to divide it into parts that are capable and incapable of salvation. The heresies that were thus "mutilating" human nature were Apollinarism, for which the human intellect cannot coexist with the divine one in Christ, as well as the different versions of Monophysitism, which were assimilating the human nature to the divine one in various degrees. In his own age, Maximus struggled against Monothelitism and Monoenergism, which he interpreted as continuations of both Apollinarism and Monophysitism. Thus, in a manner reminiscent of Plotinian optimism, he claims that will and energy belong to nature that is good to the extent that it is and should thus be saved in its entirety. What is more interesting for our subject is the new form that Plotinian optimism takes. Both thinkers, Plotinus and Maximus, have tried to solve the problem of theodicy by equating good with being and by thus forming an inverse equation where evil is proven not to exist by being equated with non-being and something else, which would serve as an explanation for why evil has some influence even though it does not really exist. For Plotinus, the latter is matter.¹² The equation is thus

"evil = non-being = matter"

We thus have a vertical metaphysical schema, where what is, is good to the extent that it has some distance from the non-being of matter. What is common with Maximus is a certain optimistic existential stance where being as being is good, whereas to the extent that something is not good it is also not a being. Nevertheless, Maximus' own equation marks a drastic entrance into the historical field. I would formulate it as

"evil = non-being = missing the end"¹³

Here I enter teleology, but also eschatology. For Maximus, true being is not what we observe inside history, but what will be manifested in its end. All beings are created in order to reach this end. History is, thus, the field of the "not-yet-being," or, in theological language, of the "image" of being (*AI* 37, 1293BC, 1296CD). True being is inversely located in eschatology after the end of history. Evil is thus active in history, but without acquiring the status of a being, because true being will only be revealed in the ἔσχατα, where evil will no longer be active. Inside history, if we call something a

---

11. See, for example, *Enneads* 1.8.10–11, II.4.13. Cf. O'Brien, "Plotinus and the Gnostics"; Gerson, *Plotinus*, 197.

12. See *Enneads* 1.8.11.2–4, 2.4.13.23, 16.3, 2.5.4.5, 3.6.7. Cf. Rist, "Plotinus on Matter and Evil"; O'Brien, "Plotinus on Matter and Evil"; Schäfer, "Matter in Plotinus's Normative Ontology."

13. See *QThal* epistol.209–226 = PG90, 253AB.

being, it is because it is good and because it is an image of true eschatological being. If something "is" evil, it "is" a non-being because it will fail to survive in the ἔσχατα. It is rather a parasite, a παρυπόστασις (*TP1* 24B) in Neoplatonic terms,[14] or a "pest" in biblical ones, which draws its force from the good being, until being expelled during the eschatological harvest of the grain (Matt 13:24–30).

Maximus thus formulates the fundamental themes of Judeo-Christianity in a philosophical way. In my view, he re-actualizes Plotinian optimism, this time not against the Gnostics, but against Monothelitism and Monoenergism. At the same time, just as Plotinus vindicated a "philosophy inside the good" against the Stoics that viewed evil as a necessary shadow that highlights the good, in a very similar way Maximus differentiates himself from Gregory of Nyssa, who sometimes considered evil as an important experience that led to maturity.[15] Maximus equally presents some similarities with Proclus, probably through Ps.-Dionysius, in that he does not attribute evil to a principle—even a non-being principle such as Plotinian matter—but to a *field*.[16] That is, Proclus had chosen not to *reduce* evil to a principle, but to *detect* it, to *trace* it to a field, thus completing Plotinian monism. And he did manage to detect it in the field of partiality, where different causal chains, which are good in themselves, meet thus provoking evil as an accident. Maximus is also avoiding reducing evil to a principle, and, just like Proclus, he is trying to detect the field where it arises. For Maximus, this field is history as a way (δρόμος, *AI* 7, 1084) towards eschatological goodbeing (ἀεὶ εὖ εἶναι). But this way might be lost. Evil thus consists in losing the way; it is something like an error (in the etymological sense from the Latin verb *errare*), a se-duction, an ab-erration, a de-viation, a loss of orientation. Even though it might, and it does indeed, happen inside history, it does not possess ontology since true being is to be found only at the end of this journey. Maximus thus coordinates on the one hand with Plotinian optimism and, on the other, with the Proclean effort to detect the field of evil rather than reducing it to a principle; but at the same time he modifies them drastically by posing evil inside the "dromic" dialectic between history and eschatology.

In order to formulate the latter, Maximus is also using Aristotelian metaphysics. Maximus is thinking of the end (τέλος) just like Aristotle, as entailing a passage from potentiality (δυνάμει) to actualization (ἐνεργείᾳ).

---

14. See Lloyd, "Parhypostasis in Proclus."

15. For the differences between Maximus and Gregory of Nyssa on this point, see Sherwood, *Earlier Ambigua*, 198–204.

16. Opsomer and Steel, "Introduction."

In my opinion, his thought could be qualified as "teleological." Maximus does observe finalities in nature, which are realized through a passage from potentiality to actuality. Just like in Aristotle, this passage is movement in a metaphysical sense, and it is measured by time leading to the "maturation" of being. Maximus also has a particularly Aristotelian sense of retroactive final causation, namely the fact that we can understand a being only from its end. He also uses a notion of "attraction" (ἕλξις, CDiv 1389A); that is, causation and motion take place mainly through attraction and not through impulsion as in mechanistic philosophies. (Just like Aristotle, Maximus does not exclude impulsion; he rather subordinates it ontologically to attraction).

But here begins Maximus' originality. After having deeply assimilated Aristotelianism, he transforms it radically by putting it in historical and eschatological terms.[17] The field of passage from potentiality to actuality is not biology or nature, but history. And the end that attracts is not natural maturity, but the ἔσχατον, which presents nevertheless a gap of radical discontinuity in relation to natural evolution. But this means that the passage from potentiality to actuality is not linear but dialectical. Eschatology at one and the same time confirms teleology and "frustrates" it (in a psychological idiom), or "crucifies" it (in a theological one). Eschatological teleology is thus an antinomy, which introduces us to Maximus' dialectical way of thinking.

Free Dialectic

By placing the passage from potentiality to actuality inside history, Maximus is introducing it to the latter's contradictions. This is equally provoking a great tension due to the fact that the end of nature is not natural but eschatological, that is supernatural (ὑπέρ φύσιν). Nature is mobilized by a longing for something outside its own powers. This dialectic is expressed by Maximus through triple schemas. The latter were also popular in Neoplatonism—one has only to think of Proclus. But with Maximus they form a real historical dialectic. In this sense, Maximus is close to the later adventure of the dialectic in the West, which constitutes anyway a secularization of Christian thought. It is worth seeing some of the most important triple schemas in order to understand what is meant by dialectic.

One of the most important is the triple schema λόγος–τρόπος–τέλος (reason–mode–end). What is characteristic of these "concepts" is that none of them can be defined by itself. It is in absolute need of the others and it

---

17. For an analysis of how Maximus' eschatological ontology incorporates elements of natural finalities, see Loudovikos, *Eucharistic Ontology*.

somehow "breaks" and is led into them. Λόγος is a will of God for a being,[18] its nature but also its historical evolution through divine providence. It is not identified with nature in itself. The λόγος is divine, and for this reason it could be interpreted as uncreated[19] or as a "divine proposition"[20] for a being, whereas the being in itself is created. Conventionally, I would say that the λόγος refers to the "protology" of being, since it is given in its origin. But such a view does not seem to render Maximian thought faithfully. The λόγος is rather a marker towards the end. It points to the being's eschatological future. Thus the λόγος "breaks" into the "concept" of the end, without which it does not have any meaning. Besides, the λόγος does not have an existential value in itself. It awaits to be realized by a historical τρόπος, the latter being the λόγος's actualization, its τρόπος τῆς ἐνεργείας[21] through which the λόγος becomes manifest. The λόγος is thus not a "thing," as in philosophical realism; it is in absolute need of the mode of existence and energy in order to become an actualized existence.[22] In the same way, the τρόπος is not a thing. It is a modification of nature. But the nature is not given in its origin. (And in this sense neither the nature is a thing strictly speaking, at least not in its historical version.) The nature is in a constant state of fluidity, changeability and restlessness even though it is also in dialogue with its uncreated λόγος. This dialogue takes place through the personal hypostases that bear and modify nature. In created being, τρόπος is a mode of existence that is a personal mode by which nature is hypostasized, just as in the Trinity, but also a mode of energy or activity that is a mode through which the nature is actualized and activated.[23] This personal mode is neither a thing nor a being; it is the personal modification and stabilization of the flux of nature that has a meaning only as a response to the λόγος-will of God. In other words, τρόπος is a hypostatic response in a dialogue. This mode takes place in view of the eschatological end, where it will find its truth in the mode of the incarnated Son the Λόγος who receives the λόγοι of nature but integrates them

---

18. *QThal* 13.8 = PG90, 296A; and *AI* 7, PG91, 1085A.

19. See *AI* 7, 1080–85, and the corresponding analysis in Loudovikos, Εὐχαριστιακὴ ὀντολογία, 90–96, 151–58.

20. See Loudovikos, Κλειστὴ πνευματικότητα, 191.

21. See *QThal* 27.27–35 = PG90, 353A; 34.22 = PG90, 377A; 40.267–271 = PG90, 396–7; *AI* 42, 1341D–45C; *TP*10 136D–7A.

22. The fact that natural potentiality and will need the person in order to be actualized is developed in the *AI* 24, 1261C.

23. See *AI* 42, 341D: "Λόγος δὲ φύσεως ἀνθρωπίνης ἐστὶ τὸ ψυχὴν καὶ σῶμα καὶ ἐκ ψυχῆς λογικῆς εἶναι τὴν φύσιν καὶ σώματος, τρόπος δὲ ἡ ἐν τῷ ἐνεργεῖν καὶ ἐνεργεῖσθαι φυσικῶς τάξις ἐστίν, ἀμειβομένη τε πολλάκις καὶ ἀλλοιουμένη, τὴν δὲ φύσιν ἑαυτῇ παντελῶς οὐ συναμείβουσα."

in the uncreated mode of the eternal Son (*AI* 15, 1220AC). The notion of τρόπος thus "breaks" in those of λόγος and end. In what concerns the latter: the end of the whole of creation is the incarnated Christ who receives the totality of the created nature in realizing its λόγοι through the supernatural mode of His existence.[24] The end is not merely an end; it is also present in the beginning in order to attract creation towards itself. It is a "mystery that has been hidden throughout the ages and generations" (Col 1:26 NRSV)[25] by God as the meaning of the world. In this sense, the end is present in the notion of λόγος,[26] since the λόγος is a *final* cause, a *raison d'être*. The end also "breaks" in the notion of τρόπος, since the end is a novel mode of existence and actualization of nature, or, in the words of Christos Yannaras, it means that "the created exists with the mode of the uncreated."[27] This end bursts into history by the Incarnation and the Resurrection of Christ, but will be manifested in all its truth after the end of history with the common Resurrection. In the person of the Christ meet all the three parts of the dialectic. The Christ is the divine Λόγος of the λόγοι; he is the divine mode of existence of the Son which incorporates all the personal modes of existence of the multiple children of God; and he is the end of the hypostatic union of the created and the uncreated. This is the meaning of the salvation of teleology: the finalities that exist inside nature concern the mode by which the natural attributes are integrated in and modified by the hypostasis of Son the Christ.[28] For example, natural attributes such as the intellect, the irascible faculty, desire, or life itself, all have a teleological reason that is, correspondingly, prayer,[29] love,[30] divine eros,[31] and fertility in the Spirit.[32] But not independently: in an eschatological twist of teleology, the reason is the mode by which Christ is integrating these attributes as, correspondingly, prayer to the Father in the Spirit, love, eros and communion of life through the sacrifice of the Crucifixion.

24. *QThal* 60.5–62 = PG90, 620C–621C; *AI* 7, 1097; 1072C–1073C.
25. See *AI* 7, 1097B.
26. See *AI* 42, 1345A: "Ὅτι πᾶσα φύσις τῷ οἰκείῳ λόγῳ διαπαντὸς ἔχει τὸ τέλος."
27. See Yannaras, Ἀλφαβητάρι τῆς πίστης, 166.
28. According to the Metropolitan John of Pergamon (Zizioulas), the fact that the multiple λόγοι are integrated in the unique Λόγος means that they are hypostasized by the divine hypostasis of Son the Λόγος through the Incarnation, the latter constituting a personal reception of the totality of created being. See Zizioulas, *Communion and Otherness*, 63–68.
29. *CChar* 1.79, 977C; 4.15, 1052A; 4.42–3, 1057B, 1068C.
30. *CChar* 3.4, 1017C; 4.15, 1052A; 4.43, 1057B; 4.74–5, 1068C.
31. *CChar* 1.79, 977C.
32. *AI* 21, 1245BC.

There is thus a conjunction of philosophy and theology in the thought of Maximus, where philosophy leads to theology but at the same time preserves its own specific character. Maximian thought can thus be qualified as dialectical in the sense that each notion "breaks" in the other, between history and eschatology. There are nevertheless at least two important differences between Maximian dialectic and a modern dialectic of the Hegelian type: (1) There is no absolute logical necessity in the Maximian dialectic. The τρόπος is historically contingent. (2) The Maximian dialectic could arguably be considered as a dialectic inside the good. But this means that evil could possibly be put outside of the dialectic or rather that it could be considered as not being *a priori* and necessarily a part of it. On the other hand, evil can become a contingent part of the dialectic. Evil is not considered exactly as a "felix culpa," as in a part of the Western tradition. At least not in the sense that it is unavoidable or that it is itself part of salvation. The Fall is a contingent event, and like all contingent historical modes it takes place in the context of dialogue between God and man, where God proposes, man responds freely and God can counter-respond to man. The modes of this divine counter-response are termed as "modes of the Economy" (τρόποι τῆς οἰκονομίας),[33] because they do not belong to the primordial divine plan, but constitute a novel miraculous modification.[34] For this reason, the modes of economy can comprise death, pain and passion, as is evident in Christ's Crucifixion, which do not constitute primordial divine λόγοι—wills for the world—but wills "according to concession" ("κατὰ συγχώρησιν," QD 83.65–6 = PG90, 801AB)—which assume the results of the human response to this dialogue. I should conclude nevertheless that Fall and evil do eventually become parts of the Maximian dialectic, even if they are contingent and not logically necessary. The distinction between God's primordial plan according to the good will (εὐδοκία) of the λόγος and the modified plan due to the dialogue with man is expressed by the terms προηγουμένως and ἐφεπομένως, which form a dialectical relation (QThal 63.414–438 = PG90, 681D–684A). It is to be noted that for Maximus Fall, even though a contingent historical event, happens almost simultaneously with man's creation (AI 42, 1321B). Thus, there was no "prelapsarian" state that has lasted for a significant period of time. But this means that the division brought about by the Fall and linked with what Maximus terms as γνώμη is something that exists almost from the beginning of humanity. According to the eschatological theology of Metropolitan John of Pergamon (Zizioulas) that is based on Maximus,

33. See QThal 37.23 = PG90, 384B; AI 42, 1317D–1320A; TP8108BC.
34. Of course, God is outside time, and thus nothing is novel for him. What I mean is that despite his atemporality, God enters into a dialogue with man in which Economy is equally determined by man's answer.

the Fall is not a Fall from a perfect prelapsarian state that has lasted in the past, but rather "a Fall from the future" that is a "Fall from the end" that man could have reached if the Fall had not taken place.[35] Secondly, the Fall leads to a counter-response on the part of God that is "more paradoxical and divine" ("τρόπος παραδοξότερος" and "θεοπρεπέστερος," *AI* 7, 1097C). There is thus in Maximian thought a sense of "felix culpa." Not in the sense that Fall is a part of the salvation, but in the sense that the human Fall provokes a free divine response, which is more miraculous and paradoxical than the primordial λόγος. There are two possible interpretations as to what is meant by this "more paradoxical and divine" answer. It can mean either the Incarnation itself or the fact that Christ had to assume death in order to save man. I will not enter here this difficult issue of Maximian scholarship. I will remark that in any case, Maximus is building his thought on the Paulinian principle that the "fullness of sin" ("πλεόνασμα τῆς ἁμαρτίας") has brought about an "overabundance of grace" ("ὑπερπερίσσευμα τῆς χάριτος," Rom 5:20). This is another striking similarity with Augustine. Yet, for Maximus, the dialectical relation between sin and grace is completely free. It is rather dialogical than dialectical (in the strict sense), or "free dialectical" if we choose to formulate it as an antinomy.

The dialogue between sin and grace is also expressed by the triple schema *according to nature-contrary to nature-above nature* (κατὰ φύσιν-παρὰ φύσιν-ὑπὲρ φύσιν). The κατὰ φύσιν can be seen as referring to the λόγος of nature. In other words, it does not mean a naturalistic essentialism, where man is called to adapt himself to a pre-existing natural norm. In order to understand the Maximian sense of "according to nature," we should interpret it as "according to the λόγος of nature" that is according to the eschatological finality of nature which tends towards its hypostatic union with God.[36] And just like the λόγος does not have an existential value of its own, in the same way the κατὰ φύσιν is actualized and realized not by itself but either by falling into the παρὰ φύσιν, or by being assumed by the ὑπὲρ φύσιν. To take an example: The will for life is "according to nature." But inside history it does not exist in a bare state. It will either "fall" into the egoistic (φίλαυτος, in Maximian terms) will for living at the detriment of others in a sort of "live and let die," or it will be assumed by the will to share life "above nature" through the Crucifixion and the Resurrection. The historical mode of the παρὰ φύσιν does not have an ontological value, but it also has to render itself to the ὑπὲρ φύσιν, the latter denoting the hypostatic union

---

35. For the eschatological character of personhood in the theology of the Metropolitan John of Pergamon, see Zizioulas, *Being as Communion*, 53–65.

36. See Zizioulas, *Communion and Otherness*, 64.

with God for which there is no λόγος of nature.³⁷ The παρὰ φύσιν is just a historical episode as a part of the dialogue with God. This schema lets us understand the Maximian dialectic as follows: The "protological" κατὰ φύσιν cannot be actualized existentially in itself; it therefore "breaks" either to the παρὰ φύσιν, which constitutes a Fall in relation to its future finality, or to the ὑπὲρ φύσιν, which is a counter-response to this Fall as an "overabundance of grace" in dialogue with man's contingent historical modes. Maximus is thus flirting with a "dialectization" of evil, without however reaching it. His thought remains what I would term as antinomical. Similarly, the actualization of the λόγος by the historical mode in view of the eschatological future constitutes not only a realization of the λόγος of nature, but also a frustration of nature's autonomy in a very antinomical way. The divine end calls us for a historical mode that would at the same time actualize nature in relation to its λόγος and frustrate its autonomy. To take the fundamental example, the will for life that is part of the human λόγος is actualized by Christ through a historical mode that both affirms the λόγος (when he expresses his will not to die in Gethsemane) and frustrates the natural autonomy of this will by the self-sacrifice of the Crucifixion.³⁸ The same is true for all other natural λόγοι.

This antinomy is also expressed by the triple dialectical schema *sixth-seventh-eighth day*. In oversimplifying Maximus' very rich and polysemous allegorical interpretations, I would claim that the sixth day is the day of creation and historical preparation, during which nature is actualized, the seventh day is the Sabbath of repose, where natural autonomy is frustrated after the Crucifixion and the Entombment of Christ's human nature, and the eighth day is the first day of the eschatological resurrection, where nature is resurrected in another mode that is after the crucifixion of its historical actualization.³⁹ By this triple schema Maximus realizes but also transcends or even frustrates Aristotelian teleology. In this he is performing an *imitatio Christi*. Just like the Christ in the Gospel is at the same time realizing the Judaic Law and transcending it or even frustrating its absolute claims, Maximus is trying to confirm Hellenic teleology by negating its unconditional

---

37. See *TP1* 33C: "Οὐκ ἔστι δὲ τῶν παρ' ἡμῶν κατὰ δύναμιν γίνεσθαι πεφυκότων ἡ θέωσις, οὐκ οὖσα τῶν ἐφ' ἡμῖν· οὐδεὶς γὰρ ἐν τῇ φύσει, τῶν ὑπέρ φύσιν λόγος."

38. For an analysis of Maximus' interpretation of Christ's prayer in Gethsemane, see Léthel, *Théologie de l'agonie du Christ*; Bathrellos, *Byzantine Christ*, 140–47.

39. Out of the numerous definitions and interpretations of the three days that exist in the Maximian corpus, the most concise is found in *CGn* 1.51, 1101C: "Ἡ ἕκτη κατὰ τὴν Γραφὴν ἡμέρα τὴν τῶν ὑπὸ φύσιν ὄντων εἰσηγεῖται συμπλήρωσιν, ἡ δὲ ἑβδόμη τῆς χρονικῆς ἰδιότητος περιγράφει τὴν κίνησιν, ἡ δὲ ὀγδόη τῆς ὑπὲρ φύσιν καὶ χρόνον ὑποδηλοῖ καταστάσεως τὸν τρόπον."

demands.⁴⁰ This is a radical "dialectization" of Hellenic teleological metaphysics that paves the way for Hegelian dialectics in avoiding the latter's monist and "Sabellianist" character.

In concluding this chapter, I would like to mention that Maximus' triple schemas usually have a "horseshoe" form—that is, the two extremes meet while the center has a function of mediation, (either before or even after the meeting of the extremes). In this, Maximus is closer to Proclus. For example, the λόγος and τέλος meet, as the λόγος points directly to the end, whereas the τρόπος constitutes a mediator. In the same way, the κατὰ φύσιν points to the ὑπέρ φύσιν whereas the παρὰ φύσιν is but a historical contingency. Similarly, the intellect and the desire are two extremes that meet in their object, namely God or the world, while the irascible part (θυμός) is a center that channels the results of this meeting to the fellow man.

Metaphysics of the Resurrection

By being faithful to the Aristotelian legacy, Maximus remains a great metaphysician. Of course there are many different definitions of metaphysics. What I mean is a particular way of doing theology, where one begins by taking a natural event and then tries to explain it by recurring to a cause above nature. For example, one begins from the natural reality of love, intellection, rationality, desire or anger and in trying to explain it one arrives at its metaphysical truth or in Maximian terms to its λόγος. Metaphysics is a theological mode that differs from others. For example, in a theology of Revelation, one starts from the otherworldly surprise provoked by the event of revelation and then one poses questions that depend themselves on this event and were not there beforehand. In dogmatic theology, one begins from above—that is, from dogmatic formulations—and then draws

---

40. Maximus tries to reformulate both Hellenic teleology and the Judaistic theology of the Law. The way in which he understands the τέλος in relation to both is epitomized in CGn 1.35, 1096C: "ὅσα μὲν ἐν χρόνῳ κατὰ χρόνον δημιουργεῖται, τελειωθέντα ἵσταται, λήγοντα τῆς κατὰ φύσιν αὐξήσεως. Ὅσα δὲ κατ' ἀρετὴν ἐπιστήμη Θεοῦ κατεργάζεται, τελειωθέντα πάλιν κινεῖται πρὸς αὔξησιν. Τὰ γὰρ τέλη αὐτῶν ἑτέρων ἀρχαὶ καθεστήκασιν. Ὁ γὰρ καταπαύσας ἐν ἑαυτῷ διὰ τῶν ἀρετῶν κατὰ τὴν πρᾶξιν τὴν τῶν φθειρομένων ὑπόστασιν, ἑτέρων ἀπήρξατο θειοτέρων διατυπώσεων· παύεται γὰρ οὐδέποτε τῶν καλῶν ὁ Θεὸς ὧν οὐδὲ ἀρχὴν ἔσχεν. Ὡς γὰρ φωτὸς ἴδιον τὸ φωτίζειν, οὕτως ἴδιον Θεοῦ τὸ εὖ ποιεῖν. Διὸ τῷ μὲν νόμῳ τὴν κατὰ χρόνον τῶν ἐν γενέσει καὶ φθορᾷ σύστασιν ἀφηγουμένῳ, τιμᾶται δι' ἀργίας τὸ Σάββατον· τῷ Εὐαγγελίῳ δὲ τὴν τῶν νοητῶν εἰσηγουμένῳ κατάστασιν, δι' εὐποιίας καλῶν ἔργων τοῦτο φαιδρύνεται· κἂν ἀγανακτῶσιν οἱ μήπω γνόντες ὅτι διὰ τὸν ἄνθρωπον τὸ Σάββατον γέγονεν, ἀλλ' οὐ διὰ τὸ Σάββατον ὁ ἄνθρωπος· καὶ ὅτι κύριός ἐστι καὶ τοῦ Σαββάτου ὁ Υἱὸς τοῦ ἀνθρώπου."

conclusions. In modern forms of theology, such as phenomenology, one starts from the experience of the finite mortal subject.

To take one example, in what concerns the question what it is to be a person, the aforementioned theological modes would lead to different approaches. A metaphysician would start from the natural and intra-historical reality of personhood and would then try to elevate it to its metaphysical meaning gathered from the fact that God is personal and bestows his image on man. A theologian of Revelation would start from the event of the revelation of personhood in the historical Christ. A dogmatician would start from the relations of the persons of the Trinity and would then draw conclusions as to what this image on man means. A phenomenologist would begin from the mortal finite person in order to pose the question of what it is that transcends it. Of course an airtight division of these modes would be too pedantic. Most theologians use more than one of them in order to counter for different needs. The reason I insist on it is that Maximus is mainly a contemplator of metaphysical relations—that is, of relations between nature and what lies beyond it. In this he is, in my opinion, a faithful heir of Aristotelianism and other forms of Hellenic teleology. Maximus is interested in beings and their λόγοι. He starts from the remark that there is, for example, intellection, rationality, love, desire, anger, and then he searches the reason for which they exist. In this quest he reaches a metaphysical and teleological explanation offered by their respective λόγοι in God.

Until here, we are still in the frame of a metaphysics of Hellenic type that is preserved in the Maximian way of thinking. But here starts the antinomy as to what lies beyond not only of Physics, but also of Metaphysics. For Maximus, λόγοι are not just external forms as in classical Platonism. They are also (1) interiorized forms inside God, just as in Neoplatonism; (2) not only forms, but also λόγοι, that is words; they are thus more like God's expressions and not just his "thoughts" or "ideas"; (3) God's wills, just as in Ps.-Dionysius;[41] and (4) what is more important, they lead to the reception of their respective natural attributes by Christ the Λόγος thanks to the Incarnation (AT 2 = PG91, 1037), as well as to the Crucifixion of their natural autonomy and to their Resurrection in another mode. This means that every natural attribute firstly needs to be explained in a metaphysical way, just like in ancient Greek thought. But this is only the beginning. The

---

41. The identification between λόγος and will is declared by Maximus in QThal 13.8 = PG90, 296A, and in the AI 7, 1085A. In the latter, Maximus names his sources as Dionysius Areopagite and "the circle around Pantenus" ("περὶ Πάνταινον"). In what concerns the Areopagitic writings, cf. De diuinis nominibus 5.8, CD 1, 188.6–10 = PG3, 824C. As to the reference to the circle around Pantenus, see Sherwood, Earlier Ambigua, 175–76.

Christian contemplator will examine how this natural attribute was received by Christ, how it was crucified and, what is the most important, how it is resurrected.

Some examples: the will for life (a subject similar to the one that has preoccupied philosophers of the nineteenth century such as Arthur Schopenhauer and Friedrich Nietzsche) is a natural event that demands a metaphysical explanation. Maximus does have a very rich theory for this natural will and he is equally linking life to the Spirit as a Trinitarian but also metaphysical source of life (*AI* 10, 1136C; 21, 1245BC). But then a Christian thinker, if she is to pursue a Maximian way of thinking, will endeavor to examine how Christ receives this will for life. She will analyze for example how Christ had "affirmed" life (to use a Nietzschean term) at his prayer in Gethsemane, in contradistinction to the Socratic contempt for the will to live. But Christ then crucifies this will for life and resurrects it as accordance to the will of the Father in the Spirit, which establishes eternal life for men as adopted sons by grace. Similarly, the intellect is affirmed as capable of knowledge of God in simple prayer, being for Maximus nothing less than an image of the primordial simplicity of God the Father (*AI* 7, 1088A; 24, 1264B). But at the same time it is "buried" since "all intelligibles need to be buried" ("τὰ νοούμενα πάντα χρήζει ταφῆς," *CGn* 1.67, 1108B) and resurrected in the eschatological knowledge by which all humanity is coordinated in a same act and state of intellection (ὁμόνοια). The irascible part of the soul is affirmed as a "spiritual fervor"[42] in order to love and to protect our defenseless fellow men as well as to get "angry" (Maximus distinguishes here between the natural θυμός and the sinful ὀργή that constitutes the former's passion) against injustice and idolatry, by imitating Christ who took the scourge. At the same time, the Christian is called to crucify the self-assurance of his anger, since the latter is leading us, according to Maximus, to a vicious circle of grief, wrath and then again resentment and grief (*CChar* 3.90–1, 1044CD–1045A). Anger is then resurrected in the form of eschatological love (*CChar* 4.22, 1052D). Desire finds its metaphysical explanation as a christological drive for infinity that is crucified for the world and is resurrected as divine eros (*QThal* 1.18–33 = PG90, 269BC). The body equally finds its metaphysical explanation in God's will for the existence of matter and for its reception by Christ. But the Christic body is "broken" in the Eucharist ("κλώμενον εἰς ἄφεσιν ἁμαρτιῶν") in order to be eschatologically shared.

By all this, I would like to point out that Maximus starts his line of thinking as a contemplator of metaphysics worthy of the great Greek metaphysicians with whom he shares a common way of doing theology. But

---

42. The Greek expression is "ζέσις πνευματική." See *QThal* 55.314 = PG90, 548D.

metaphysics is just his point of departure. The end of his itinerary is the Christology of the Resurrection that presents a gap in relation to metaphysics, a gap that is only bridged by the Crucifixion and Resurrection of Christ.

Maximian Antinomies in a Contemporary Context

I have tried to show Maximus as a thinker of antinomy. It is mostly an "asymmetrical" antinomy, where the point of departure is a teleological metaphysics that is then "crucified" (in a theological idiom) or "frustrated" (in a psychological one), the solution being given in the christological level. This solution is "asymmetrical,"[43] because the two parts, namely metaphysics and Christology, are not equal, but Christology has the final word—but also the first one according to the eschatological principle that the end is already present in the beginning. At the same time, the antinomy is not abolished, since metaphysics are preserved even if "crucified," and Maximus is thus saved as a philosopher even if in the way he is transformed into a theologian. And metaphysics are saved exactly because Maximus is an antinomical thinker who wants to save both Hellenism and Judaism, teleology and historicity. He wants to save all the "lost" voices of the fragmented Roman Mediterranean of the seventh century. I would like to conclude this portrayal of Maximus as an antinomical thinker by expressing his philosophical significance in a contemporary context.

As we have seen, Maximus belongs to a long process of Christianization of Neoplatonism and Aristotelianism. In this regard, it would be very interesting to study even more the similarities and differences between the Maximian and the Augustinian project. For example, how they both inaugurate a new sort of voluntarism, but each in his own very peculiar way, or how they try to historicize Neoplatonism. Maximus interiorizes the forms, perceives them as volitional expressions and integrates them in dialectical relations between history and eschatology. I therefore believe that Hans Urs von Balthasar is right to exalt Maximus as a precursor of Hegel who contributed to European philosophy as a whole. For the same reason, Maximus can be considered as timely in a postmodern context, where the interest in dialectics has revived in another form. In such an actualization of the Maximian dialectical thinking, we could focus not only on the dialectic between (uncreated) λόγος, τρόπος and τέλος, but also on the dialogue between the

---

43. My expression "asymmetrical antinomy" is inspired by George Florovsky's term "asymmetrical Christology." The latter is used to characterize "Neochalcedonian Christology." For a discussion of an asymmetry of a Neochalcedonian type between hypostasis and nature, see Bathrellos, *Byzantine Christ*, 110.

uncreated λόγος of God and the created λόγος of man as well as the ensuing dialogue between the created λόγος and the novel created (or even uncreated) τρόπος. What I mean is that in the dialogue with the divine λόγος, the created human λόγος often has the tendency to become independent in the form of an idol. There is then a need for new historical modes, which will be inspired by the eschatological end in order to undermine the idolized created λόγος and lead to novel modifications that are more faithful to the eschatological hope. The lesson from Maximus is that the personal subject is not founded in an ontological void, but only as a response to the divine λόγος. This could be compared with the way in which in Lacanian psychoanalysis, in order to become subjects we need the "Symbolic Order."[44] It would be interesting to make such a correspondence, where the Lacanian Symbolic would correspond to the Maximian λόγος, the Imaginary to the τρόπος by which the human βούλησις is projected towards the future through imagination, and the Real to the end. What is more, in considering a dialogue of the created idolatrous λόγος with the novel historical modes, I could say along with Louis Althusser, but from a Maximian perspective, that the subject is formed through a dominant discourse that constitutes it,[45] just as in Maximus there is no mode if it is not preceded by an eminent λόγος. And I could continue, along with Judith Butler, to stress that even though the subject is constituted by the λόγος, it can then negotiate and undermine this dominant discourse, through what Butler terms as trope,[46] and Maximus formulates through the similar term τρόπος. But this undermining happens in the interior of the λόγος, and, as I might add as a theologian, in view of a surprising and miraculous eschatological end.

This comprehension of the Maximian τρόπος might prove fruitful in relation to questions of our postmodern condition. I am referring to the unified humanity of our globalized postmodern world, where there is no longer the possibility of an alternative from the outside, but only of transformation from the inside. According to a Neomaximian dialectic of uncreated λόγος–created λόγος, τρόπος (created or uncreated) and τέλος, the Church can become again a community that will put in doubt both the idolatrous λόγοι of the world and her own ossified λόγοι that alienate the living λόγος of God. In the light of such a dialectical thinking on historical modality, we could approach some timely issues. For example, we could perceive of the nation as a *mode*, in a Maximian sense in which it is neither an essence

---

44. For a very interesting comparison between Maximus and Jacques Lacan, see Loudovikos, Ψυχανάλυση καὶ ὀρθόδοξη θεολογία, 15–42.

45. See Althusser, "Idéologie et appareils idéologiques d'État."

46. See Butler, *The Psychic Life of Power*.

according to nationalistic primordialism, nor a nominalist construction, according to those who deny every national particularity. In Maximian terms, the nation could be viewed as a modal gnomic will, which arises through a gnomic rupture, and is called to transcend this gnomic division in saving at the same time its modal particularity (ἰδιοτροπία) inside the ecclesial event. Something similar could be valid about questions of gender. Gender too could be seen as a *mode*, in a Maximian sense in which it is neither an essence, nor something totally inexistent either in an apophatic theological way or in a nominalist discourse. On the contrary, it could be seen as a historical modification and modality, what of which will survive in the ἔσχατα is unknown. Maximian thought can thus enter in dialogue with contemporary feminist and other theories of gender that perceive of gender as a tropic negotiation of a dominant discourse.

It is arguably possible to make such actualizations of Maximian thought. But the question of what is the value of this thought *per se* remains. Maximus possibly has to gain from some actualization of his thought. But is the same true for our age? What could Maximus offer to it? In this, I would remark that Maximus mainly has to offer the end of the dialectic: An end beyond any "Hellenic" essentialism but also beyond any neo-nominalist constructionism,[47] as well as any iconoclastic apophaticism of a Judaistic kind, like those that we observe in thinkers pertaining to a "Judaistic" tradition such as Jacques Derrida and Ludwig Wittgenstein.[48] An end that—as a synthesis of responses to both Hellenic and Judaistic demands—is identical to the Person of the Resurrected Christ, who saves European philosophy precisely through its crucifixion and its resurrection.

---

47. See Balthasar, *Cosmic Liturgy*, 262.

48. In his work *God Without Being* (*Dieu sans l'être*), Christian philosopher Jean-Luc Marion tries to avoid the problems of the ontotheology of traditional metaphysics. I think that Maximus would agree with Marion's title "God without Being," or rather "God above Being," since he himself states explicitly in the *Mystagogy* that non-being is somehow closer to God than being, due to God's transcendence of being: "Θεὸς . . . τὸ μὴ εἶναι μᾶλλον, διὰ τὸ ὑπερεῖναι ὡς οἰκειότερον ἐπ᾽ αὐτοῦ λεγόμενον, προσιέμενος" (*Myst* proem.103–11 = PG91, 664AB). Nevertheless, Maximus would equally qualify the negation "God without Being" by a christological affirmative expression "Christ with Being." See, for example, the beginning of this same phrase in the *Mystagogy* proem.103–6 = PG91, 664A, where God is said to be "πᾶσι πάντα καὶ ὢν καὶ γινόμενος" (1 Cor 9:22). In other words, in Maximus a theology ("Θεὸς δι᾽ ἑαυτόν") of negation and transcendence is completed by a Christology ("Χριστὸς διὰ τὰ ὄντα") of affirmation and presence.

Bibliography

Althusser, Louis. "Idéologie et appareils idéologiques d'État (Notes pour une recherche)." *La Pensée* 151 (1970) 3–38. Reprinted in *Positions (1964–1975)*, 67–125. Paris: Éditions sociales, 1976.

Balthasar, Hans Urs von. *Cosmic Liturgy: The Universe According to Maximus the Confessor*. Translated by Brian E. Daley. A Communio Book. San Francisco: Ignatius Press, 2003.

Bathrellos, Demetrios. *The Byzantine Christ: Person, Nature, and Will in the Christology of Saint Maximus the Confessor*. Oxford Early Christian Studies. Oxford: Oxford University Press, 2004.

Betsakos, Vasilios. *Στάσις ἀεικίνητος. Ἡ ἀνακαίνιση τῆς Ἀριστοτελικῆς κινήσεως στὴ θεολογία τοῦ Μαξίμου Ὁμολογητοῦ* [Ever-Moving Repose: The Renewal of Aristotelian Movement in the Theology of Maximus the Confessor]. Athens: Armos, 2006.

Bradshaw, David Houston. *Aristotle East and West: Metaphysics and the Division of Christendom*. Cambridge: Cambridge University Press, 2004.

Butler, Judith. *The Psychic Life of Power: Theories in Subjection*. Stanford: Stanford University Press, 1997.

Doucet, Marc. "Vues récentes sur les métamorphoses de la pensée de saint Maxime le Confesseur." *Science et Esprit* 31 (1979) 269–302.

Garrigues, Jean-Miguel. *Maxime le Confesseur: La charité, avenir divin de l'homme*. Théologie historique 38. Paris: Beauchesne, 1976.

Gerson, Lloyd P. *Plotinus*. London: Routledge, 1994.

Karayiannis, Vasilios. *Maxime le Confesseur: Essence et énergies de Dieu*. Théologie historique 93. Paris: Beauchesne, 1993.

Léthel, François-Marie. *Théologie de l'agonie du Christ: La liberté humaine du Fils de Dieu et son importance sotériologique mises en lumière par saint Maxime le Confesseur*. Théologie historique 52. Paris: Beauchesne, 1979.

Lloyd, Antony Charles. "Parhypostasis in Proclus." In *Proclus et son influence: Actes du Colloque de Neuchâtel, juin 1985*, edited by Gilbert Boss et al., 145–57. Zurich: Éditions du Grand Midi, 1987.

Loudovikos, Nikolaos. *A Eucharistic Ontology: Maximus the Confessor's Eschatological Ontology of Being as Dialogical Reciprocity*. Translated by Elizabeth Theokritoff. Brookline, MA: Brookline Holy Cross Orthodox Press, 2010.

———. *Εὐχαριστιακὴ ὀντολογία* [A Eucharistic Ontology]. Athens: Domos, 1992.

———. *Ἡ κλειστὴ πνευματικότητα καὶ τὸ νόημα τοῦ ἑαυτοῦ. Ὁ μυστικισμὸς τῆς ἰσχύος καὶ ἡ ἀλήθεια φύσεως καὶ προσώπου* [Closed Spirituality and the Meaning of the Self: Christian Mysticism of Power and the Truth of Personhood and Nature]. Athens: Ellinika Grammata, 1999.

———. *Ψυχανάλυση καὶ ὀρθόδοξη θεολογία. Περὶ ἐπιθυμίας, καθολικότητας καὶ ἐσχατολογίας* [Psychoanalysis and Orthodox Theology: On Desire, Catholicity and Eschatology]. Athens: Armos, 2006.

Marion, Jean-Luc. *Dieu sans l'être*. Collection "Communio". Paris: Fayard, 1982.

Maximus the Confessor. *Ad Marinum Cypri presbyterum (Theologica et polemica x)* [Copy of a Letter Sent to Sir Marinus, Priest of Cyprus]. Edited by François Combefis. PG91:133A–7C. Abbreviated as *TP10*.

———. *Ad Marinum presbyterum (Theologica et polemica i)* [To Marinus the Very Pious Priest]. Edited by François Combefis. PG91:9A–37D. Abbreviated as *TP1*.

———. *Ambigua ad Iohannem*. Edited by Franz Oehler. PG91:1061–417C. Abbreviated as *AI*.

———. *Ambigua ad Thomam*. Edited by Bart Janssens. CCSG 48:3–34. Abbreviated as *AT*.

———. *Capita de caritate* [Four Centuries on Charity]. Edited by François Combefis. PG90:960A–1080D. Abbreviated as *CChar*.

———. *Capita theologica et oeconomica* [Gnostic Chapters]. Edited by François Combefis. PG90:1084A–173A. Abbreviated as *CGn*.

———. *Exemplum epistulae ad episcopum Nicandrum de duabus in Christo operationibus (Theologica et polemica viii)* [Copy of an Epistle Addressed to the most Sacred Bishop, Sir Nikander, by Saint Maximus, on Two Operations in Christ]. Edited by François Combefis. PG91: 89C–112C. Abbreviated as *TP8*.

———. *Mystagogia*. Edited by Christian Boudignon. CCSG 69:3–74. Abbreviated as *Myst*.

———. *Quaestiones ad Thalassium*. Edited by Carl Laga and Carlos Steel. CCSG 7:3–539; 22:3–325. Abbreviated as *QThal*.

———. *Quaestiones et dubia* [Questions and Doubts]. Edited by José H. Declerck. CCSG 10:3–170. Abbreviated as *QD*.

O'Brien, Denis. "Plotinus and the Gnostics on the Generation of Matter." In *Neoplatonism and Early Christian Thought: Essays in Honour of A. H. Armstrong*, edited by Henry J. Blumenthal and Robert Austin Markus, 108–23. London: Variorum, 1981.

———. "Plotinus on Matter and Evil." In *The Cambridge Companion to Plotinus*, edited by Lloyd P. Gerson, 171–95. Cambridge: Cambridge University Press, 1996.

Opsomer, Jan, and Carlos Steel. "Introduction." In Proclus, *On the Existence of Evils*, 1–53. London: Duckworth, 2003.

Pseudo-Dionysius the Areopagite. *Corpus Dionysiacum I: Pseudo-Dionysius Areopagita, De divinis nominibus*. Edited by Beate Regina Suchla. Patristische Texte und Studien 33. Berlin: de Gruyter, 1990. Abbreviated as CD 1.

Pseudo-Maximus the Confessor. *Diuersa capita ad theologiam et oeconomiam spectantia deque uirtute et uitio (xxvi–d)*. Edited by François Combefis. PG90:1188A9–392A. Abbreviated as *CDiv*.

Rist, John. "Plotinus on Matter and Evil." *Phronesis* 6 (1961) 154–66.

Savvidis, Kyriakos. *Die Lehre von der Vergöttlichung des Menschen bei Maximos dem Bekenner und ihre Rezeption durch Gregor Palamas*. Veröffentlichungen des Instituts für Orthodoxe Theologie 5. St. Ottilien: EOS, 1997.

Schäfer, Christian. "Matter in Plotinus's Normative Ontology." *Phronesis* 49 (2004) 266–94.

Sherwood, Polycarp. *The Earlier Ambigua of Saint Maximus the Confessor and His Refutation of Origenism*. Studia Anselmiana, philosophica theologica. Rome: "Orbis Catholicus"/Herder, 1955.

Skliris, Dionysios. "Θεολογώντας πάνω σὲ συντρίμμια . . . μαζὶ μὲ τὸν Μάξιμο." *Synaxi* 123 (2012) 4–14.

Tympas, Grigorios Chrysostom. *Carl Jung and Maximus the Confessor on Psychic Development: The Dynamics between the "Psychological" and the "Spiritual"*. London: Routledge, 2014.

Yannaras, Christos. *Person and Eros*. Translated by Norman Russell. Brookline, MA: Holy Cross Orthodox Press, 2007.

———. Ἀλφαβητάρι τῆς πίστης [Alphabet of Faith]. Athens: Domos, 1983.

———. Τὸ ρητὸ καὶ τὸ ἄρρητο. Τὰ γλωσσικὰ ὅρια ρεαλισμοῦ τῆς μεταφυσικῆς [The Effable and the Ineffable: The Linguistic Boundaries of Realism in Metaphysics]. Athens: Ikaros, 1999.

Zizioulas, John. *Being as Communion: Studies in Personhood and the Church*. Contemporary Greek Theologians 4. Crestwood, NY: St. Vladimir's Seminary Press, 1985.

———. *Communion and Otherness: Further Studies in Personhood and the Church*. Edited by Paul McPartlan. London: T. & T. Clark, 2006.

2

A Metaphysics of Holomerism

Torstein Theodor Tollefsen

This idea of the balance and reciprocity of universal and particular is perhaps the most important in the whole of Maximus' thought.

—Hans Urs von Balthasar[1]

In the first part of the first chapter of his *Mystagogia*, St. Maximus, in a rather dense way typical of him, sketches the architecture of the cosmos as the interrelatedness of all creatures with one another and with their cause, God (*Myst* 1, 132–53). The terminology is dynamic. Maximus says God made all things, and that he encloses, gathers, and limits them (συνέχει, συνάγει, περιγράφει). He binds (ἐνδιασφίγγει) the intelligible and the sensible providentially to one another and to himself. As cause he is the beginning and end (ἀρχὴ καὶ τέλος) of all things. These divine activities are manifestations of a *power* (δύναμις) that leads all things into an unconfused identity of movement and subsistence. The system manifested on the basis of this power reveals all things "as the whole reveals its parts or as the whole is revealed by its cause by which the whole and the parts of the whole came into appearance and being" (*Myst* 1, 147–48; I will return to an interpretation of these words below). Towards end of the chapter, Maximus introduces the image of the circle, its centre, radii, and circumference, as a means to illustrate how God is the centre of the principles of beings ("τὰς ἀρχὰς τῶν ὄντων") that, figuratively speaking, stretch forth from him for the

---

1. Balthasar, *Cosmic Liturgy*, 161.

constitution and direction of beings in the world system (*Myst* 1, 189–98). In this way God encloses like a circumference the whole of creation in his providence. These *principles* are, in all probability, identical with the divine λόγοι that are central to Maximus' *Christocentric cosmology*.

For St. Maximus there are two fundamental metaphysical structures that secure the unity of being. One of these is causative of the other. The one that is causative is strictly divine, while the other, which is the result of this, is a certain *internal cosmic arrangement* in created being. According to Maximus, all aspects of the whole drama of the world are unified in Christ, the second hypostasis of the Trinity, the Word or the Λόγος of God. Both cosmology and soteriology are somehow unified in him. This is the background for the term "Christocentric cosmology": the unifying divine bond of all created reality is the Λόγος himself, who is the origin of all creative and structural principles or λόγοι:[2] The one Λόγος is many λόγοι. The second metaphysical structure, which is the primary subject of this article, is the *whole and part arrangements* that are established on the basis of these λόγοι.

In *Ambiguum* 7, the λόγοι are divine acts of will that define creatures essentially:

> From all eternity, he contained within himself the preexisting λόγοι of created beings. When, in his goodwill, he formed out of nothing the substance of the visible and invisible creation,[3] he did so on the basis of these λόγοι. By his *word (λόγος) and his wisdom he created* and continues to create *all things*—universals as well as particulars—at the appropriate time. We believe, for example, that a λόγος of angels preceded and guided their creation; and the same holds true for each of the beings and powers that fill the world above us. A λόγος of human beings likewise preceded their creation, and—in order not to speak of particulars—a λόγος preceded the creation of everything that has received its being from God.[4]

> For in their essence and generation all created things are defined by their own λόγοι, and by the λόγοι of the beings that are external to them and surround them.[5]

---

2. Cf. *AI* 7.15 = PG91, 1077C.

3. Constas has "worlds" here. I prefer "creation." Cf. *Difficulties*, 2:95.

4. *AI* 7.16 = PG91, 1080A, Constas' translation slightly modified (*Difficulties*, 2:95–96).

5. *AI* 7.19 = PG91, 1081B. This is my translation, which comes close to the sense of *CMofJCh*, 57. Here I think Constas is a bit less satisfactory (cf. *Difficulties*, 101).

Here the λόγοι are presented as the divine principles for the institution of *particulars and universals* in the created world. We shall now shift our focus to the *whole and part arrangements*. In modern philosophy we have the discipline called *mereology*, which is the philosophy of parthood relationships.[6] In connection with Maximus it would be more proper to talk of *holomerism*, the *philosophy of whole and part*, from the Greek words ὅλον and μέρος. This is a part of Maximus' thought that seems never to have been treated properly by any scholar, if treated at all.[7] Before we move on, one should keep in mind three rather curious sayings in the quotations above: (*a*) in the *Mystagogia* Maximus says that the whole reveals its parts, and "the whole is revealed by its cause by which the whole and the parts of the whole came into appearance and being." (*b*) In the first quotation from *Ambiguum* 7 Maximus speaks of *universals* as *created beings*, these universals are most probably *species and genera*, and (*c*) in the second quotation from the same text he seems to suggest that an entity is defined both by its own λόγος and by the λόγοι of beings that surround it. We need to ask what all this could mean.

Historically the topic of whole and part relationships is connected with Platonic divisions like the ones we find in the Sophist, and the so-called *Porphyrian tree* and its derivatives. While Porphyry would not address the questions of whether universal genera and species subsist or only depend on thought, and if they exist whether they are bodily or incorporeal, and further whether they are separable or in sensible things, later Neoplatonists definitely considered such subjects.[8] In Simplicius we find a quite typical Neoplatonic doctrine in this regard.[9] Species and genera have a threefold existence: (1) first there are the intelligible genera that are wholes that comprise several intelligible species as parts. These genera are causative of another kind of universals, viz. (2) those species that are immanent in sensible beings. (3) Then we have the universal that is the abstraction made by an intelligent being. What we find in Maximus differs in some important

---

6. Here one could consult, e.g., Varzi, "Mereology."

7. The only exceptions I know of is von Balthasar, who, in his *Cosmic Liturgy*, 66–73, 159–65, touches upon some aspects of such an arrangement of the cosmos, and Zachhuber, "Universals in the Greek Church Fathers," 447–50, who, in an interesting article on the universal in the church fathers, has written a few pages that touch upon the topic. Zachhuber also points out that Maximus probably develops for his own purposes a concept of the universal worked out by St. Gregory of Nyssa, which seems very probable.

8. The famous saying by Porphyry, *Isagoge* 4,1.1.

9. Simplicius, *In Aristotelis categorias commentarium* 82–83, trans. de Haas and Fleet, in *On Aristotle's "Categories 5–6,"* 24.

respects from this, and, one could claim, he develops the subject into an interesting cosmology that also suits his soteriological concerns.

We should first notice that while a Neoplatonist system contains several levels of being between the first principle and sensible beings, there are no traces of such levels in the metaphysics of Maximus. On the one hand we have the Creator–Λόγος who contains all the λόγοι as principles of beings, and on the other hand we have the created world with its immanent order of being. Here we should remember what was said in the quotation above, viz. that God created and creates all *particulars and universals*. Universals, we should keep in mind, are created beings.

In an important text from *Ambiguum* 10, Maximus says that essence is moved hierarchically from the most universal genus through intermediate genera to the species. The movement terminates with the most specific species, which are the lowest species in a system of division, under which are the particulars.[10] Particulars, however, are not mentioned in the context (*AI* 10.89 = PG91, 1177BC). What is the ontological status of these universal species and genera? It is obvious that they are neither the contents of the divine mind, since they are subject to motion, nor are they intermediate entities between God and particular entities, which would be quite strange in a Christian system. It is also obvious that they are not abstract universals in the human mind. This leaves us with the solution that they are immanent genera and species in creatures, and that their "movement," which is qualified as *expansion* (διαστολή), is the systematic and orderly distribution of essence in the cosmic system. However, there are two "movements," the first is expansion, the second is *contraction* (συστολή). While the expansive distribution is from unity to plurality, the contractive is from plurality to unity.

What is described in this text seems to have two aspects: on the one hand, Maximus describes the dynamics of procession and conversion of being in relation to God, i.e., the creation and salvation or fulfilment of being in God. On the other hand, what is described is a permanent feature of created being, viz. the internal, ontological dynamics. Both these aspects shows that God made a structured cosmos, in which universals and particulars are internally, hierarchically arranged. The question is *how should this internal dynamics be understood*? We shall look at another quotation from *Ambiguum* 10:

> For if the universals subsist in the particulars, and do not in any way possess their λόγος of being and existence by themselves, then it is quite clear that, if the particulars were to disappear,

---

10. This is at least how these species are understood by Porphyry, cf. *AI* 10.89 = PG91, 1177BC 4,1.4, trans. Barnes, in Porphyry, *Introduction*, 5.

> the corresponding universals would cease to exist. For the parts exist and subsist in the wholes, and the wholes in the parts, and no argument can refute this.[11]

It is, of course, tempting to say purely *a priori* that particular beings are the primary entities in a Christian metaphysics, but what Maximus says in this quotation confirms such a preconception: universals exist in the particulars and if particulars are eliminated universals disappear as well. The universals do not "possess their λόγος of being and existence by themselves (καθ' αὐτά)," which probably means that they do not possess them independently of their "localization" in the particulars. There are λόγοι for species and genera, but these would be λόγοι for species and genera situated immanently in particulars.[12] On the other hand, we are not warranted to diminish the importance of the universal, for even if universals disappear with the particulars, "parts subsist in the wholes." There is a mutual dependence here: wholes on parts and parts on wholes.

What, then, does the relationship between part and whole amount to? We may turn to a passage from *Ambiguum* 41:

> For all things that are distinguished from each other by virtue of their individual differences are generically united by universal and common identities, and they are drawn together to one and the same by means of a certain generic λόγος of nature, like genera that are united with each other according to essence, and consequently have something one and the same and indivisible. For nothing that is universal, or which contains something else, or which is a genus, can be divided in any way by what is particular, contained, and individual. For that which does not draw together things that are naturally separated is no longer able to be generic, but rather divided up together with them and so departs from its own individual unity. For every generic item, according to its own proper λόγος, exists as a whole indivisibly and really in the whole of those things subordinate to it, and with respect to the particular it is viewed as a whole in general. (*AI* 41.10 = PG91, 1312CD)

This is what I call *holomerism*. What does this mean? Let us return for a moment to the first chapter of the *Mystagogia* where Maximus makes a sketch of a dynamic cosmic system as arranged by God. The divine power, manifested in activities, institutes a created totality where "the whole reveals

---

11. *AI* 10.101 = PG91, 1189CD, Constas' translation, slightly modified (*Difficulties*, 2:313).

12. Cf. *AI* 41.10–11 = PG91, 1312B–13B.

its parts." The cosmos is a whole containing parts. In this text the parts, we might guess, are the particulars and universal species and genera created by God. If the cosmos is viewed as a whole, then all other creatures, irrespective of how they relate to one another, are parts. These parts are revealed in so far as they are contemplated in light of the powerful divine activity of being enclosed, gathered, delimited, and directed in an orderly movement in their relation to one another, and in their relation to God as cause, i.e., as the beginning and end of the whole. Each item in the world becomes intelligible within the system as a whole, and the whole system itself becomes intelligible with a view to the cause that is its beginning and end. One might ask: to whom does this cosmic order become intelligible? Maximus' answer would probably be that this intelligibility is revealed in so-called *natural contemplation*, which is the second of three stages of spiritual development. In natural contemplation the cosmos is conceived of in its divine principles. Somehow the cosmos is viewed not from below, but from above: beings are not grasped in their confused manifold through sensible perception, but rather grasped in their unified condition in their λόγοι, gathered together in the one Λόγος.[13] This conception of the cosmos may be supplemented with the doctrine of expansion and contraction that we found in the 10th *Ambiguum*: a hierarchical order of being is instituted in the cosmos, but not in the way that a realm of intelligible universal structures is instituted between God and the particular creatures, rather there is an immanent dynamics in the particulars as such.

How does what is put forward in the quotation from *Ambiguum* 41 above fit into this picture? Maximus describes a dynamics in which essences are kept apart as parts while they at the same time are unified on the level of the whole. Species, for instance, are kept apart since each species is constituted by its own specific difference that makes it different from other species, like human being compared with horse: animal nature combined with "difference a" is "human being," while animal nature combined with "difference b" is "horse." (It seems obvious that all differences, in the system of Maximus, are conceived of as potentially, not actually, contained in the genus in order to preserve the ontological bond between all beings.) On the other hand, there are generic identities so that two different species have a common generic identity. A simplified example would be that "human being" and "horse" are as species parts of the genus animal. The identity of the species is secured by the λόγος of the particular species and the identity of the genus is secured by the λόγος of the particular genus. Species have

---

13. For Maximus' conception of spiritual development and natural contemplation, see Thunberg, *Microcosm and Mediator*, and Tollefsen, *The Christocentric Cosmology*.

a common identity in the genus as a whole: a human being is animal in the whole of its being, and it is an animal in the *one and identical way* that a horse is an animal. The genus exists as a whole in the whole of each of its species. According to what Maximus says in the above quotation, parts (*in casu* species) do not divide the genus into a non-relational and non-communal plurality. What is obvious from this is that it is *essence* that is the principle of communion in Maximus, essence, however, *as instantiated in particular beings*. The same principle applies throughout the whole distribution of essence as was described in *Ambiguum 41*.

There is one more thing, mentioned above, that deserves comment. Maximus says that an entity is defined both by its own λόγος and by the λόγοι of what surrounds it.[14] This is not quite easy to explain. Maybe we could say that since the essence of each particular is holomeristically related to the essence of all other particulars, it is defined by its own λόγος, but also by the λόγοι of what surrounds it. For example, there is a λόγος of human being, of, let us say further, a particular species of angelic being, and of a particular species of animal. The λόγος of human being defines the particular human being, but since human beings also have something in common with angles and with animals, the essence of human being is defined or delimited by the divine intentions (λόγοι) of other creatures as well. Man's nature partakes both of the intelligible and the animal essence. This is how the system of the cosmos as a whole is constituted. Figuratively speaking the essential constitution of any given particular is like a Chinese box. Each part of the cosmos mirrors each other part because all parts belongs to wholes that are similarly related, but each "mirror" mirrors what is essentially in it in a way that is genuinely unique.

Before I try to draw some conclusions from what has been put forward here, I shall make some comments on the particulars within this system of part and whole. Particulars, Maximus says, "who share common features with each other according to their species become completely one and the same with each other, since by virtue of their common origin and nature they are indistinguishable and free of all difference."[15] Each human individual, that is, is essentially "human being," so that each particular *mirrors* the whole species or *is* the whole species.[16] There is even more here: the human

---

14. Cf. *AI* 7.19 = PG91, 1081B.

15. *AI* 41.10 = PG91, 1312D, transl. Constas, in *Difficulties*, 2:117. That beings are one and the same by their origin comes close to one of the senses of "genus" put forward by Aristotle in *Metaphysics* Δ, chapter 28 on genus. This should probably be investigated further.

16. Here it is temping to quote St. Basil's *Contra Eunomius*: "For this reason, we are the same as one another in most respects, but it is only due to the properties

particular, by mirroring its whole species, mirrors the whole genus to which the human essence belongs: the human being is animal in the whole of its being. However many generic levels there are in the holomeristic system of the cosmos, they are all mirrored in man.[17] What makes entities into particulars is the sum of accidents that accrue to the subject. In *Ambiguum* 41, Maximus comments on how a given entity is related to its species and how, on the other hand, it is constituted as a genuine particular by its collection of accidents:

> Individuals who share common features with each other according to their species become completely one and the same with each other, since by virtue of their common origin and nature they are indistinguishable and free of all difference. Accidents, finally, also possess unity, on the level of the subject, where they are in no way scattered.[18]

This description is, of course, strictly ontological and nothing more.

It might be said that this metaphysical description of the dynamics of being is constructed from a soteriological concern. When Maximus in *Ambiguum* 41 describes human nature as microcosm and mediator one should first notice that it is nature or essence that is the focus, not the hypostasis or person as some kind of primary fabric of communion. The hypostasis of human beings can only be the source of communion if it is a species within the system of part and whole. Since every human person is an expression of a whole that is carried immanently, and since the human species is a part of the genus animal carried immanently, and since animal is a part of a still "higher" genus carried immanently until we arrive at the most universal genus of essence carried immanently, Maximus claims that humanity can be the cosmic centre, the microcosm and mediator. It could be claimed that Maximus does not construct this system of being from a purely religious concern, but rather that he found the key to the cosmic arrangement in

---

contemplated in connection with each one of us that we are different, each from the other" (2.4). Cf. Basil of Caesaraea, *Contre Eunome*, 2:18.

17. Here I should like to make a comment on an issue where there seems to be some disagreements among scholars, viz. as to which beings there correspond λόγοι. I think it can be argued from the texts that there are λόγοι for all creatures: angels, human beings, all kinds of animals, plants, and minerals. Cf. for instance *AI* 7.16 = PG91, 1080A which in the context of the doctrine of λόγοι speaks of God as creator of all things (τὰ πάντα), universals as well as particulars. I suppose "all things" means "all things." Maximus further says a λόγος preceded the creation of everything that has received its being from God ("παντὸς τῶν ἐκ θεοῦ τὸ εἶναι λαβόντων," 7.16.9). Are there any entities that have not received their being form God? Cf. also *AI* 42.13 = PG91, 1328AB.

18. *AI* 41.10 = PG91, 1312D, transl. Constas, *Difficulties*, 2:117.

soteriology, and that it is his philosophical conviction that this is the way the cosmos is structured. Despite its Christian character, the system is well situated within late antique philosophy. But it is a distinctly Christian worldview.

One might ask, since all beings are within the web of ontological relatedness and the whole-part mirroring, is not every creature a microcosm and a potential mediator? First we should accept that all differences are present in the generic unity *potentially*, not actually, and secondly that the emergence of the species implies the actualization of one distinctive difference for each species, not of the whole range of generic potentialities. Most of these remain latent whenever a species is established. Further, since the human being is the only one among creatures that comprise actualized essential elements from both of the main parts of the created totality, viz. both an intellectual and an animal nature, human nature is a microcosm and a potential mediator to the fullest degree possible. This is not to deny that other creatures are microcosms potentially, but their microcosmic nature remains a potential that is not actualized within the order of being.

The idea that human nature is the mediating bond of the cosmos turns out to accommodate a basic Christian idea: the renewal of creation from its human centre. But then it becomes clear that the centrality of human nature is divinely designed for the Incarnation of the Λόγος in the world-system.[19] In the Incarnation the Λόγος as source and centre of all structural principles, the λόγοι, incarnates in the nature that has been made to be cosmic mediator, and from there effects the universal regeneration of all holomeristically arranged being. In this way the Christian theology of Incarnation and soteriology has been formulated as a piece of late antique Christian metaphysics.

One might ask, is this a typical late antique system of thought or does it have a more lasting value? One may at least say that from the point of view of Christian philosophy what is presented is a metaphysical doctrine, not a piece of physics or biology. If one believes that God made the world, it might be reasonable to think that he did so according to a certain plan. It is therefore reasonable to claim that the one Λόγος contains the many λόγοι that constitute the metaphysical background on which the natural development of the world, physically and biologically, takes place. From a theological but also from an ethical point of view, the claim that basically all being is objectively related, should be of great practical value as well: a world in which all particulars are parts interrelated with each other in essential wholes, should be a world that we should be concerned with. How should we relate to one another, to the different species of animals, to the vegetation that surrounds

---

19. *Ambiguum* 41 shows how Maximus conceives of this.

us, and to the mineral resources of the earth? The first of these questions is easily answerable on Christian and Maximian principles, the rest, however, is more of a challenge. If one should want to address them, something the whole drive of Maximus' thought seems to invite to, then one should have to apply Maximian principles out of their mainly anthropological context. I suggest that this both could and should be done, even if it is beyond the scope of this paper to do it.

Maximus' metaphysics of λόγοι and of whole-part relationships culminates not so much in a vision of humanity as master of the cosmos as it does in a vision of humanity as the *servant* of the whole. And this servitude is demonstrated in the work of Christ himself who lived his incarnate life completely in accordance with the divine purpose of the world, "recapitulating all things, both in heaven and on earth, in himself, in whom they also had been created."[20]

Bibliography

Balthasar, Hans Urs von. *Cosmic Liturgy: The Universe According to Maximus the Confessor*. Translated by Brian E. Daley. A Communio Book. San Francisco: Ignatius Press, 2003.

Basil of Caesaraea. *Contre Eunome*. Translated by Bernard Sesboüé. Edited by Bernard Sesboüé et al. 2 vols. Sources chrétiennes 299, 305. Paris: Cerf, 1982–83.

Maximus the Confessor. *Ambigua ad Iohannem*. Edited and translated by Nicholas P. Constas. In *Difficulties*, 1:62–450; 2:2–330. Abbreviated as *AI*.

———. *Mystagogia*. Edited by Christian Boudignon. CCSG 69:3–74. Abbreviated as *Myst*.

———. *On Difficulties in the Church Fathers: The Ambigua*. Edited and translated by Nicholas P. Constas. 2 vols. Dumbarton Oaks Medieval Library 28–29. Cambridge: Harvard University Press, 2014. Abbreviated as *Difficulties*.

———. *On the Cosmic Mystery of Jesus Christ: Selected Writings from St. Maximus the Confessor*. Translated by Paul Marion Blowers and Robert L. Wilken. St. Vladimir's Seminary Press Popular Patristics Series. Crestwood, NY: St. Vladimir's Seminary Press, 2003. Abbreviated as *CMofJCh*.

Porphyry. *Introduction* [Isagoge]. Edited and translated by Jonathan Barnes. Clarendon Later Ancient Philosophers. Oxford: Clarendon, 2003.

Simplicius. *On Aristotle's "Categories 5–6"*. Edited and translated by Frans A. J. de Haas and Barrie Fleet. Ancient Commentators on Aristotle. London: Duckworth, 2001.

Thunberg, Lars. *Microcosm and Mediator: The Theological Anthropology of Maximus the Confessor*. 2nd ed. Chicago: Open Court, 1995.

Tollefsen, Torstein. *The Christocentric Cosmology of St. Maximus the Confessor*. Oxford Early Christian Studies. Oxford: Oxford University Press, 2008.

---

20. Cf. Col 1:16 and *AI* 41.6 = PG91, 1308D.

Varzi, Achille. "Mereology." *The Stanford Encyclopedia of Philosophy* (Spring 2016 Edition). Edited by Edward N. Zalta. http://plato.stanford.edu/archives/spr2016/entries/mereology/.

Zachhuber, Johannes. "Universals in the Greek Church Fathers." In *Universals in Ancient Philosophy*, edited by Riccardo Chiaradonna and Gabriele Galluzzo, 425–70. Pisa: Edizioni della Normale, 2013.

3

Being Moved: St. Maximus between Anaxagoras and Kierkegaard

John Panteleimon Manoussakis

For Fr. Maximus Constas

It can be safely stated that the greatest contribution of St. Maximus' thought, when appreciated purely from a philosophical point of view, was the ontological vindication of κίνησις with all the far-reaching implications that such a position had for the Christian metaphysics that had operated hereto with the categories, assumptions, and limitations of the Greek thought. For this reason, Fr. Polycarp Sherwood's assessment of St. Maximus' thought finds its sharpest articulation as a refutation of Origenism.[1] By Origenism, of course, we should understand not only the work and thought of Origen himself but also of any Christian who was still the prisoner of Greek metaphysics, that is, of Neoplatonic and Platonizing thought.

The question, then, becomes that of the criteria by which one is to make such an accusation. The philosophical language and the technical vocabulary were inevitably common for both the Christian Athens and the Hellenized Jerusalem and thus it is not a safe ground for judging an author's true affinities. Maximus' thought offers us precisely the demarcating line. When in question as to where a certain work's or a certain author's allegiance lies, then the question to be asked should be that of κίνησις.

---

1. Sherwood, *Earlier Ambigua*, 92–116. Maximus' contribution on the conception of κίνησις has been summarized in the reversal of the Neoplatonic (and Origenistic) triad στάσις-κίνησις-γένεσις into γένεσις-κίνησις-στάσις. The reversal takes place in Maximus' *Ambiguum 7* of which more below.

This question is not as easy as it might sound. For it involves a complex conceptual cluster as well as a broad spectrum of topics: the metaphysics of κίνησις covers the problem of be-coming, of whether the world is eternal or not, of genesis and creation, of multiplicity, of individuality and of the will, human and divine. It is also the question of history and, above all, of the enigma of time. In other words, κίνησις is a nodal point where cosmology, anthropology, and theology converge.

Given this importance, to which we have just alluded in the most general terms, it is pertinent to try to situate St. Maximus' contribution within the history of philosophy (a history which, it should be said from the outset, is Western and specifically European).[2] Is Maximus' revolutionary affirmation of κίνησις an ἅπαξ λεγόμενον, so to speak, in philosophy's history? Does his thought have any predecessors with whom he might share, if not the exactness of his articulation, at least an affinity of views? And do we find echoes, however distant, of his groundbreaking refutation in the subsequent course in the history of ideas? This is, in short, the task at hand of the present essay.

In what follows I would attempt to establish bridges with St. Maximus' philosophical past and future. Looking back in time, I single out the figure of Anaxagoras of Clazomenae, one of those original thinkers whom our need for classification, already since Aristotle's first book of *Metaphysics*, groups under the category of Presocratics. Looking ahead in time, we meet the idiosyncratic writings of Søren Kierkegaard, whose thought, as I hope to show here, and as others have already argued,[3] was obsessed with the topics of movement and becoming. I should make clear that I do not suggest that St. Maximus was directly influenced by Anaxagoras nor that Kierkegaard was a reader of St. Maximus. Even though there is evidence that St. Maximus was at least familiar with Anaxagorean thought, and although one could make the case that one of Kierkegaard's aims was, like St. Maximus, to free Christianity from the burden of Origenism, nevertheless, the connection I am exploring here between these three thinkers is one that belongs to the genealogy of ideas, to the affinity of minds, and not to the tedious facts of historicism.

My thesis is that Anaxagoras's cosmology anticipates Maximus' more elaborate treatment of κίνησις in the same way that Kierkegaard's appropriation of κίνησις in the life of the individual—that is, in the task of becoming oneself—is anticipated by Maximus' theology of the will. As Anaxagoras

---

2. See Heidegger, *What Is Called Thinking?*, 224; Derrida, "Violence and Metaphysics," 81.

3. See, for example, Carlisle, *Kierkegaard's Philosophy of Becoming*; Kangas, *Kierkegaard's Instant*; Nason, "Motion, Change, and Activity."

rebelled against the Eleatic conception of a static being, so Kierkegaard launched a "polemic against truth as knowledge"[4]—that is, against a closed speculative system that had excluded the movement of personal will and, therefore, of faith.

Thinking Moves: St. Maximus and Anaxagoras

That something is what is not (what it appears) or that it is not what seems to be was the conclusion at which both Heraclitus and Parmenides arrived albeit from different ways. It is important that both philosophical positions were ultimately motivated by how each philosopher positioned themselves vis-à-vis the problem of κίνησις. Philosophy at this early and crucial moment of time became a question of denying or affirming κίνησις. In this sense one could make the claim that all of the so-called Presocratic philosophy is a philosophy of movement. Indeed, this is the case inasmuch as each of the Presocratic philosophers attempted to articulate an answer to the problem of be-coming: Thales saw the unity of many in the one element or origin. Anaximander saw the dispersion of the one into multiplicity as both the crime and punishment of becoming; Anaxagoras, as we shall see, saw in becoming a process of perfection, and so on. Furthermore, the repercussions of either the Eleatic or Ionian school assumed a meaning that gives philosophy as a whole the voice which we still recognize today when she speaks. The problem of κίνησις was much more than denying or affirming a simple statement, for philosophy was now saying this: *what is is not*. For Parmenides this meant that sensory, empirical evidence of movement and change was a lie. For Heraclitus, on the other hand, this meant that the sensory, empirical evidence of constancy and permanence was a lie. How either of them read this statement is not important as long as we allow ourselves to stand in front of this decisive moment where a disjuncture, the non-coincidence of itself with itself, between the "apparent" world and the "real" world was first pronounced. Suddenly, the world became twofold. *All* spirituality, whether Christian or Platonic, finds its root and origin, its very foundation in this bifurcation of the world at which philosophy arrived, or rather, at which philosophy led us, when it contemplated the problem of κίνησις.

Parmenides's argumentation in his Way of Truth seemed to have decided the question of κίνησις once and for all. At the heart of that argumentation lies the principle of identity—the Parmenidean *is* (the being) simply and most emphatically is—and that's pretty much all. Parmenides's thought reaches its highest moment in the articulation of the briefest utterance:

---

4. Kierkegaard, *Concluding Unscientific Postscript*, 253.

ἔστι γὰρ εἶναι—*that which is* (what is usually translated as "being") *is*.[5] The implication of this flash of light is to illuminate the entire region of being. Parmenides should be credited for being the first to take note of the far-reaching consequences of his thought: what is, he says,

> neither came to be nor could pass away,
> [it is] simple, immovable and without end.
> Nor was it ever, nor will it ever be; for now *it is*,
> all at once, one, and continuous.
> For what kind of origin should you search for it?
> How and where from could it ever increase?
> I shall not let you say nor think that it came from what is not;
> for one can neither think nor say that *what is* is not.[6]

Thus it becomes immediately clear that one could not walk *The Way of Truth*—that this is a way that leads nowhere, for there is nowhere to go, nor could anything ever move. Movement is not only impossible (Zeno's famous paradoxes of the impossibility of movement offered the layperson's version of Parmenidean ontology) but also erratic: it wanders away from the truth and thus into error.

Anaxagoras's response to Parmenides's description of a being in *rigor mortis* was nothing short of a stroke of genius. Parmenides had himself identified being and thinking ("τὸ γὰρ αὐτὸ νοεῖν ἐστίν τε καὶ εἶναι"[7])—after all, it was by means of his brilliant argumentation that he had reached the asphyxiating summit of the immovable One. And it was this very "reaching" that Anaxagoras had noticed: Parmenides denies movement *by moving* from one position to the next, from premise to conclusion. *Thinking moves*: this was Anaxagoras' way of saying *solvitur ambulando*.[8] And it moves not just itself (as in discursive reasoning) but thinking moves the world. Thus, this corrective to Eleatic metaphysics becomes the cornerstone of Anaxagorean cosmology where the νοῦς, the mind, becomes a creative force of be-coming and in-forming by being precisely the principle of κίνησις.[9]

5. Parmenides, DK 28 B6.1.
6. Parmenides, DK 28 B8.3–9 (my translation).
7. Parmenides, DK 28 B3.
8. "And motion is truth and not semblance, as Anaxagoras proves in spite of Parmenides by the indubitable succession of ideas in our thinking." Nietzsche, *Philosophy in the Tragic Age*, 92.
9. "Νοῦς is the cause of motion [τῆς δε κινήσεως αἴτιον εἶναι τὸν νοῦν]. For Anaxagoras says this: 'When Νοῦς began to move [things], there was separation off from the mutlitude that was being moved, and whatever Νοῦς moved, all this was dissociated;

Subject to the well-known limitations of Greek metaphysics, Anaxagoras's vision of *genesis* is not a radical one—that is to say, it is not a becoming which presupposes nothing other than nothing itself (*ex nihilo*). The idea of creation, properly understood, does not fall within the scope of his system. Nevertheless, his brilliant cosmogony provides a description to the question of the world's transformation from chaos to cosmos. His ontology is inexorably connected with such a "cosmetic" understanding of the world, where τὸ καλόν (the beautiful) is, quite literally, *moving*: for it propels the world toward its future perfection. Here ontology meets teleology under the auspices of aesthetics as we find them again in certain passages of Plato, in the Greek Fathers, including St. Maximus and, finally, one last time, albeit in a much weaken form, in Kant's *Third Critique*.

This is at least what the attentive reader intimates from the celebrated passage in Plato's *Phaedo*, when Socrates offers, by a way of a long answer to Cebes' question after "the cause of generation and corruption" (95e), a surprising autobiographical account of his philosophical beginnings:

> One day I heard someone reading, as he said, from a book of Anaxagoras, and saying that it is Mind [νοῦς] that directs [ὁ διακοσμῶν] and is the cause [or reason] of everything. I was delighted with this cause and it seemed to me good, in a way, that Mind should be the cause of all. I thought that if this were so, the directing Mind would direct everything [κοσμοῦντα πάντα κοσμεῖν] and arrange each thing in the way that was best. If then one wishes to know the cause [or reason] of each thing, why it comes to be or perishes or exists, one had to find what was the best way for it to be, or to be acted upon, or to act. One these premises then it befitted a man to investigate only, about this and other things, what is best . . . As I reflected on this subject I was glad to think that I had found in Anaxagoras a teacher about the cause of things [τῆς αἰτίας περὶ τῶν ὄντων] after my own heart . . . Once he had given the best for each as the cause for each and the general cause of all, I thought he would go on to explain the common good for all, and I would not have exchanged my hopes for a fortune. I eagerly acquired his books and read them as quickly as I could in order to know the best and the worst as soon as possible.[10]

---

and as things were being moved and dissociated, the revolution (περιχώρησις) made them dissociate much more'" (DK 59 B13.6–10, trans. Curd, in *Anaxagoras of Clazomenae*, 25). "Νοῦς in Anaxagoras's theory is a source of motion and change, and the principle of intelligibility in Anaxagoras's universe" (ibid., 144).

10. Plato, *Phaedo* 97b–98b. Cf. the translation of Grube, 84–85.

Socrates understands that Anaxagoras had offered two revolutionary answers. To the fundamental ontological question, "*Why* is there something at all?" he had replied, "Because it is best": this means it is best for it and for the best's sake. To the question, "*How* does something come to be?"—which now can be translated as "how does something become what is best for it"—Anaxagoras had replied, "by being moved." Let us hear once more Socrates' interpretation: "If then one wishes to know the cause (or reason) of each thing, why it comes to be or perishes or exists, one had to find what was the best way for it to be, or to be acted upon, or to act." Let us, then, follow Socrates' advise and ask what state of being was considered by Anaxagoras as being the best for the world? Remember that Anaxagoras's concern was to offer an account of the world's transformation from chaos to cosmos. It is, therefore, of the utmost importance to note that "the best" as cause and reason of the world's existence was not, nor could have been, the *original* state of the world, but only a *future* state which, as future was still to come and the occasion of a be-coming, namely, of the world's movement toward it. At every given moment, therefore, the world exists because it is moved to a perfection ("the best") and by this perfection (the Νοῦς). This perfection, τὸ τέλειον, cannot be but a feature of the end, τὸ τέλος.

Thinking moves: but this movement is not random nor spasmodic; rather, it is purposeful and all the more so as it is excercised by νοῦς, that is, as far as it is an *intelligible* movement. It is, therefore, always a movement-toward, a movement directed to an end, for otherwise the inception of movement would have remained unaccountable and the world would have been unknown.[11] Contrary to Heraclitean flux, Anaxagorean κίνησις is a movement with a beginning and an end—and above all a movement with a direction. Nevertheless, insofar as it remains restricted to the natural order, it is a movement that operates only within necessity; a movement for which the concept of freedom has yet to emerge.[12] And it is a movement still underway, for if it had reached its goal, movement would have already ceased and history would have already ended. Anaxagoras calls this movement by

---

11. In spite of Anaxagoras's support of the ἄπειρον regarding the ingredients of the original mix (their number?), nevertheless, νοῦς knows them—or perhaps it would be better to say that they are known in the directedness of νοῦς. "For he [i.e., Anaxagoras] makes it clear that he thought that they [the things being separated off] were limited in form when he says that Νοῦς knows them all. And indeed if they really were unlimited, they would be altogether unknowable; for knowledge defines and limits the thing that is known" (DK 59 B 7.3–8, trans. Curd, in *Anaxagoras of Clazomenae*, 21).

12. What is still missing is what one finds in Kierkegaard later on: not merely the movement of time that carries with it the world (and humanity), but the self-movement of a will in becoming oneself. See Carlisle, *Kierkegaard's Philosophy of Becoming*, 62. More on this distinction below.

a term that should be familiar to the student of theology: περιχώρησις. It is such a reading of Anaxagoras's vision which a youthful Nietzsche finds compelling and to which he gives the following gloss, so much reminiscent of Maximian eschatology:

> The end can only be striven toward in an enormously long process; it cannot be created all at once by a mythological magic wand. When someday, at an infinitely remote time, it is accomplished, when all the likes are gathered together and the primal essences lie side by side, undivided and in beautiful order, when each tiny particle has found its companion and its home, when the great peace enters the world after the great divisions and splits of the substances and no more split or divided material is left—then νοῦς shall return to its self-movement, no longer roaming the world, itself divided, at times into greater, at times into smaller masses, as vegetative or animal spirit, indwelling in alien materials. Meanwhile the task is not yet at an end, but the kind of motion that the νοῦς has figured out, in order to accomplish its end, demonstrates marvellous efficiency, for by it the task is nearer completion with each passing moment.[13]

Here two related ideas emerge simultaneously but also for the first time: first, a natural etiology that is teleological—what will be named in Aristotle's system as final cause and entelechy; and secondly, the ontological vindication of κίνησις, where movement is not a falling away from some primordial perfection, nor the result of the One's dispersion into multiplicity (cf. Plotinus), but rather, to use one of Heidegger's phrases, *the event of being*. From the Parmenidean being to the Anaxagorean be-ing is, indeed, a long way.

Did Plato lose sight of Anaxagoras's insight? As the quoted passage from the *Phaedo* suggests, on the contrary. Albeit his expressed disappointment with Anaxagoras, Plato's Socrates intentionally inscribes his own philosophical project within the Anaxagorean context, inviting us to think the one in light of the other. This becomes all the more apparent when Socrates suggests that his own philosophical methodology was precisely the attempt to construct what was the second best—the famous "second sailing" (99d)—to the high expectations which Anaxagoras's philosophy had raised in him.

This is nothing else than the theory of the λόγοι: ἐν τοῖς λόγοις σκοπούμενον τὰ ὄντα (100a). It is a common mistake to take Socrates's turn to the λόγοι as signaling the abandonment of his youthful inquisitions into

13. Nietzsche, *Philosophy in the Tragic Age*, 107.

the nature of things by becoming instead the ethical interlocutor interested in such things as the definition of virtue, etc.[14] In fact, there is a connection between Socrates the naturalist disciple of Anaxagoras and Socrates the ethicist: namely, κίνησις, the desire to affirm the reality of change which both Parmenides *and* Heraclitus had denied.[15] The metaphor of the "second sailing" suggests a change of plan, not a change of destination. Socrates remains interested in the "cause of generation and corruption" of beings, only now this investigation is carried by means of the λόγοι, that is, by what is better known as the Platonic ideas or forms. If that theory became somewhat unintelligible in modern times it was precisely because it was understood outside of the Anaxagorean context that we have described. That is, the relationship between the forms and their participants was seen as static. But to deny the dynamism of this relationship is to leave it unexplained. Thus, Socrates insistence that "the beautiful becomes beautiful by the beautiful" (100d) sounds like an oracular riddle. What is missing in making sense of such a statement is the way one understands (or, alternatively, fails to understand) the form's capacity for production—literally for producing, i.e., for bringing forward, what it in itself possesses preeminently. If the Platonic forms are some mysterious, outworldly entities, their fecundity in making things the kind of things they are remains inexplicable—or else we are forced to come up with some magical explanation of "participation." On the other hand, if the forms are understood as perfections—that is, as both formal and final causes in the sense that God is portrayed in St. Thomas' Third Way—then participation is both the attraction which the form exercises on the thing by "moving" it (that is, by moving it to achieve its purpose) as well as the thing's striving to become more and more like its future perfection.

In short, what is missing from the explanation of the so-called theory of forms is the dimension of *time*, or more properly, the element of *time difference* between the two poles of participation or (trans-)formation. What forms, the idea, and what is formed are never contemporaneous. In a sense, what makes a thing the kind of thing it is is nothing else than the thing itself

---

14. Representative of this mistake is Vlastos, "Reasons and Causes in the *Phaedo*." So also Curd in *Anaxagoras of Clazomenae*, 136n20, commenting on Socrates's reference to Anaxagoras in the *Phaedo*: "Socrates is convinced that all good explanations are teleological, but he does not explain why this must be so.... Moreover, insofar as it lack a teleological element, Socrates's hypothesis about Forms as causes or explanations in the *Phaedo* is introduced as a 'second best' theory."

15. That, in spite of all his talk of movement, Heraclitus's view falls short of affirming change, I find Clare Carlisle's following remark particularly insightful: "Because the aesthete has no passion, his inner world resembles Heraclitus's κόσμος: without any fixed points or solid ground, everything is true and so nothing is true; everything is in motion and no*thing* is in motion." Carlisle, *Kierkegaard's Philosophy of Becoming*, 56.

in its future perfection. That the "cause" or "reason" (the λόγος) of every beautiful thing is nothing else than the beautiful seems to be still remembered in an author writing long after Plato such as Dionysius:

> The beautiful [καλόν] that is beyond all being is called beautiful [κάλλος] on account of its own beauty that it transmits to each and every thing and for being accountable for the harmony and brilliance of all as the light that shines to every thing its radiating rays and for calling [καλοῦν] everything to itself and gathering everything and in every respect, for which reason it has been called beautiful [κάλος].[16]

The Dionysian trajectory leads us to St. Maximus and in particular to the Maximian elaboration of the λόγοι τῶν ὄντων.[17] There is much more here than the seemingly coincidental borrowing of the Socratic λόγοι. In fact, St. Maximus in explaining a passage from St. Gregory the Theologian's oration *On Love for the Poor* (*Ambiguum 7*) confirms the Anaxagorean provenance of the Platonic λόγοι for he identifies them with the Anaxagorean μοῖρα.

> It follows, then, that each of the intellective and rational beings, whether angels or men, insofar as it has been created in accordance with the λόγος that exists in and *with God*, is and is called a "portion of God" (μοῖρα Θεοῦ), precisely because of that λόγος, which, as we said, preexists in God.[18]

Μοῖρα is unambiguously part of the main Anaxagorean vocabulary (occurring some seven times in the few lines of the preserved fragments). Its employment by Gregory Nazianzen is not surprising for there is textual evidence of other Anaxagorean references in his work.[19] Speaking of his

---

16. Pseudo-Dionysius the Areopagite, *On the Divine Names* 4.7, PG3, 701C (my translation).

17. Prior to Dionysius, St. Gregory of Nyssa had borrowed Plato's analogy and terminology from the second sailing in *Phaedo*. Thus, whereas Socrates thought that "ought to be careful that I did not lose the eye of my soul; as people may injure their bodily eye by observing and gazing on the sun during an eclipse, unless they take the precaution of only looking at the image reflected in the water, or in some similar medium" (*Phaedo*, 99e), Gregory advises us that "man does not possess a nature that would be able to look steadily into the God Λόγος as into the sun-disk; rather he looks at the sun in himself as in a mirror. The rays of that true and divine virtue shine forth from his purified life by the riddance of passions, which emanates from them, and make the invisible visible to us and the inaccessible comprehensible by displaying the sun in the mirror that we are" (*In Canticum canticorum* 3, 90.10–16).

18. *AI* 7.10 = PG90, 1080B, transl. Constas, in *Difficulties*, 1:97.

19. One such instance is found, for example, in his autobiographical poem *De Vita Sua* 1153–54, in which Gregory refers to "those who acknowledge nothing divine but

friendship with Basil, Gregory uses the Anaxagorean language of "everything in everything."[20] The anonymous scholiast finds the opportunity to explain briefly Anaxagoras's views (see, fragment B10). On another occasion, Elias of Creta commenting on Gregory's *Oration 31* identifies the Anaxagorean νοῦς with God's Λόγος through which the world was created.[21] I cannot prove that Maximus had read Anaxagoras's work, but it is clear that he knew intimately Gregory's work and, therefore, I cannot deny him what other commentators of Gregory's orations have demonstrated. What remains uncontested is the fact that in Maximus' thought on κίνησις we find a worthy successor of Anaxagoras' cosmology.

Κίνησις as a Leap of Faith: St. Maximus and Kierkegaard

I propose now to examine the importance of the concept of κίνησις for Kierkegaard's thought,[22] by paying close attention to the relevant passages from three works that are connected by their common treatment of κίνησις, namely the *Philosophical Fragments*, *The Concept of Anxiety*, and *Repetition*.[23] I would like to suggest that Kierkegaard's treatment of this concept constitutes a largely unprecedented development in the history of philosophy, insofar as it re-evaluates movement/motion and, by extension, time and history as positive ontological categories against a prevalent model that favored immobility and immutability—the latter usually being credited to the Plotinian (and ultimately Platonic) triptych of στάσις-κίνησις-γένεσις where movement (κίνησις) is only a falling away from στάσις. Furthermore, what is of particular interest in Kierkegaard's refutation of that metaphysical

---

movement alone, / by which this universe comes into being and is set in motion" (trans. White, in *Gregory of Nazianzus*, 95–97).

20. *Funebris oratio in laudem Basilii Magni* (Orat. 43) 20.2.4–5: "πάντα ἐν πᾶσι κεῖσθαι." The anonymous scholiast traces the phrase as well as the cosmological doctrine expressed by it back to Anaxagoras (*Basilii aliorum scholia* fr. 149, PG36, 911).

21. "And Anaxagoras by saying that mind [νοῦς] is the cause of order and harmony for beings he was not far from our [i.e., Christian] beliefs. What else did the Prophet David indicate than this when he said 'by the word of the Lord were the heavens made; and all the host of them by the breath of his mouth' [Ps 33:6 NRSV]?" Elias of Crete, *Commentarii in S. Gregorii Nazianzeni Orationes 19*, PG36, 826B.

22. That importance is testified by Kierkegaard himself in *The Concept of Anxiety*, 242 (hereafter abbreviated as KrCA).

23. The connection between *Philosophical Fragments* and *The Concept of Anxiety* is made on several occasions by these two texts. In KrCA Kierkegaard alludes to *Repetition* by writing, "[h]ere the category that I maintain should be kept in mind, namely, repetition, by which eternity is entered forwards" (note to page 90). Thus, a trilogy of sorts is formed by *Philosophical Fragments*, *The Concept of Anxiety*, and *Repetition*.

hierarchy is that he is not treating the problem at hand abstractly but rather through the concrete prism of salvific history, coming thus in confrontation with what can be called the lingering specter of Origenism over Christianity. *In fact, Kierkegaard's contribution on the subject of motion can be fully understood only as a refutation of Origenism.* In making this claim, I would like to compare Kierkegaard's treatment of the concept of κίνησις with the thought of St. Maximus the Confessor who undertook, as demonstrated above, a similar refutation of Origenism by giving priority to κίνησις over γένεσις.

Turning to Kierkegaard should also allow us to take notice of the differences between Maximus' theology of motion and Anaxagoras's cosmology of movement—despite the similarities that have been described already above. The chief difference between the Greek philosopher and the Christian theologian lies in the concept of *freedom*. Anaxagoras's worldview is ultimately aesthetical—note, for example, the emphasis on the νοῦς as the decorating force of the cosmos—while Maximus' theology, even though sensitive and appreciative of cosmic beauty, sees in movement a force of *ethical* consideration as well. There is a certain automatism in the Anaxagorean march toward teleological perfection that disregards the volatile force of volition. On the other hand, for Maximus reaching the eschatological end is not something that either nature or history could ever achieve on their own, that is, apart from humanity's constant and free consent to God's plan. How this is so becomes clear by calling our attention to Kierkegaard's insistence on the philosophical importance of movement, to his understanding of the instant, and to his ethics of becoming.

Furthermore, Kierkegaard's critique of Hegel's speculative system is precisely motivated by his suspicion that Hegel's philosophy of motion, although it takes the form of an unfolding through a sequence of historical moments, remains ultimately merely aesthetic—the dance of the *Geist* through history as it was for the Anaxagorean Νοῦς. Kierkegaard seems to argue that Hegel's system falls short of grasping motion's full potential as an agent of ethical agency. What is missing is, in Kierkegaard's vocabulary, *interiority* which here means nothing more than taking into account the movements of the subject's will or, better yet, the will as movement. In his engagement with the Monothelitic controversy, Maximus was afforded the opportunity to develop a detailed anthropology of the human will (for him always based on and corresponding to Christology) that becomes complementary to the macroscopic role that movement plays in history.[24] There-

---

24. For a discussion of Maximus' contributions to the philosophy of the will, see Manoussakis, "The Dialectic of Communion."

fore, any account that fails to pair Maximus' theology of the will with that his cosmic understanding of motion is bound to remain incomplete.

Discovering Origen in Kierkegaard's Works

References to Origen in Kierkegaard's works are sparing and cryptic. The only explicit reference to Origen in the published works is found in the *Concluding Unscientific Postscript*.[25] Given, however, the close affinity between the *Postscript* and the *Philosophical Fragments* (an affinity further reinforced by the author's note connecting the very argument by means of which Origen's name is invoked to the *Fragments*), we could trace Origen's specter through the pages of that latter work. And, indeed, we find, I believe, an allusion to Origen in a note at the beginning of the *Fragments* that criticizes the idea of the soul's preexistence. Such a doctrine was a commonplace in pagan philosophy, yet, there was only one Christian author closely associated with it—and later condemned for it—namely, Origen.[26] With regard, then, to this "Greek idea" (and notice that it would make little sense to accuse a Greek philosopher for holding a Greek idea; therefore, the author's target here could not have been Plato or any of the later Neoplatonic thinkers), Kierkegaard writes,

> This Greek idea is repeated in ancient and modern speculation: an eternal creating, an eternal emanating from the Father, an eternal becoming of the deity, an eternal self-sacrifice, a past resurrection, a judgment over and done with. All these ideas are that Greek idea of recollection, although this is not always noticed.... The contradiction of existence [*Tilværelse*] is explained by positing a "pre" as needed.[27]

---

25. Kierkegaard, *Concluding Unscientific Postscript*, 96.

26. For Origen's adaptation of the theory of the soul's preexistence, see his *De principiis* 3.3 Karpp (English trans. of Koetschau's edition by G. W. Butterworth, in Origen, *On First Principles*, 228). However, Origen adopts the pre-existence of the souls with some modifications due to his Christian sensibilities, thus, the souls are not unbegotten but created by God (1.3.30), yet they predate the human body and they can go through a succession of embodiments not all of which are necessarily in human form (1.8.72–74); it was on account of such pre-existence that the souls fell away from God, a falling described as a process of losing their old fervent love, thus growing cold (ψυχισταί), from which they derived their names (ψυχή) (II.8.123–4). These views of Origen, and perhaps even Origen himself, were condemned by the Fifth Ecumenical Council convoked by Justinian in Constantinople in 553 (see Alberigo et al., *Oecumenical Councils*, 161, 183).

27. Kierkegaard, *Philosophical Fragments*, 10 (hereafter abbreviated as KrPF).

The explicitly Christian context of the passage (creation, self-sacrifice, resurrection, judgment) helps us locate the reference to "ancient speculation" to a specific *time* in history. A note from Kierkegaard's *Journals and Papers* provides further evidence as to the *place* as well. There, the proposition of a pre-existence (of the Λόγος, of matter, of the soul, of evil) is more explicitly attributed to the "Alexandrian."[28] The same idea is repeated later on in the *Journals and Papers*, in the context of the same passage from the *Philosophical Fragments*: "The contradictions of existence are explained by positing a 'pre' as needed (the Alexandrians)."[29] The plural reference to the Alexandrians allows us the possibility of suggesting that Kierkegaard is thinking in this second note of Origen and Clement of Alexandria[30] and that the earlier reference to "the Alexandrian" must refer exclusively to Origen.

Of equal significance for our purposes is a lengthy note on the genealogy of the concept of the moment in Greek philosophy from *The Concept of Anxiety*: "This category" writes Kierkegaard, "is of utmost importance in maintaining the distinction between Christianity and pagan philosophy, as well as the equally pagan speculation in Christianity" (KrCA, 84). It is this "pagan speculation in Christianity" that becomes the target of both the *Philosophical Fragments* and *The Concept of Anxiety*. The expression "pagan speculation *in Christianity*" excludes Plotinus, but it allows us to include the Neoplatonic influence on a range of theological thinkers who write "in Christianity," from Origen to Schelling.

Kierkegaard's Refutation of Origenism

Having established, however cryptically, an allusion that connects the idea of pre-existence with Origen in Kierkegaard's published works, it is now time to examine the place that this idea occupies in his thought.

Origenist metaphysics had, in effect, denied the reality of becoming, of this coming-into-existence in freedom and in the *moment* which

---

28. Journal note made on 29 May 1839, quoted in the "Supplement" to KrPF 181 = *Journals and Papers*, 2:2088 = *Søren Kierkegaards papirer*, 2A:448.

29. Passage translated in Kierkegaard, KrPF, 187 = *Søren Kierkegaards papirer*, 5B:404, 8.

30. It is tempting to suggest Plotinus as one of the Alexandrians. Plotinus did, indeed, spend some time in Alexandria where, together with Origen, he studied with Ammonius Saccas, but his association with that city was interrupted on account of many journeys and his final sojourn in Rome where he taught. On the other hand, the two Christian Alexandrians, Origen and Clement, are both named in a list found in Kierkegaard's notes from Henrik Nicolai Clausen's "Dogmatic Lectures." See Martens, "Origen: Kierkegaard's Equivocal Appropriation," 117.

Kierkegaard so passionately defended. Origen's position was captured in his vitiation of the beginning, especially an absolute beginning such that the creation of the world *ex nihilo* implied.[31] For Origen, not only did all souls pre-exist their primordial fall into the material realm but also—horrified as he was by the idea of an idle God that an absolute beginning of the creation in time seemed to suggest[32]—he had posited a continuous act of divine creation. That is, to the question, "What was God doing before the creation of the world?"—a question that is now famous by means of St. Augustine's eleventh book of the *Confessions*, but which was first posed by the Alexandrian[33]—Origen had given an answer consistent with his metaphysical vision, that is, of a God who continually creates (and presumably destroys) a succession of worlds.[34] Therefore, even if *this* world is not eternal, as some of the ancients had believed, and, consequently, must have had a beginning (but, note well, *only in its material aspect*[35]), God's creative act, on the other hand, has no beginning.

The presupposition of Origen's system lies in the devaluation of κίνησις (change, movement) and, as a consequence, it effects the vitiation of becoming insofar as an absolute becoming for the Greek theologies of Plotinus and the Platonizing Fathers was tantamount with some kind of fall, a falling away from an initial perfection (represented by various ideas of Paradise) that was also, philosophically speaking, the καταστροφή (the term originates precisely in this context as the "turning downward") from the One to many and from immutability to change. It is this Alexandrian (Origenistic and Plotinian) patrimony that Kierkegaard sought to refute by emphasizing the *moment*, precisely as κίνησις, the change of becoming of the eternal into the temporal.[36] Thus, in an entry from his *Journals and Papers* which the editors

---

31. On that *nihil*, Kierkegaard writes, "The Christian view takes the position that non-being is present everywhere as the nothing from which things were created, as semblance and vanity, as sin, as sensuousness removed from spirit, as the temporal forgotten by the eternal; consequently, the task is to do away with it in order to bring forth being" (Kr*CA*, 83).

32. For Origen, God does not *begin* to create at any point, for that would imply a period prior to that point during which God remained idle (ἀργήσας ποτέ), see *De principiis* 1.4 (trans. Butterworth, in Origen, *On First Principles*, 43).

33. "If the word had a beginning in time, what was God doing before the world began?" *De principiis* 3.5.238.

34. Origen, *De principiis* 3.5 (trans. Butterworth, 239).

35. Origen restricts the creation "at a definite time" to only "all *visible* things" (*De principiis* 3.5, trans. Butterworth, 237, my emphasis).

36. "What is the change [κίνησις] of coming into existence?" Is not the whole argument of the Kr*PF* in defense of the possibility for such change of a coming-into-existence, of a be-coming? Especially since "this change . . . is from not existing to

of *The Concept of Anxiety* call "a significant notation," Kierkegaard writes, "The category to which I intend to trace everything, and which is also the category lying dormant in Greek Sophistry if one views it world-historically, is motion (κίνησις), which is perhaps one of the most difficult problems in philosophy" (KrCA, 242).

It is for this reason that the "companion piece"[37] to the *Fragments*, namely, *The Concept of Anxiety* takes hereditary sin as its point of departure, and, in doing so, it questions the Paradisiacal innocence and the concept of a prelapsarian perfection, both of which would have rendered the *moment* (or the becoming of history) harmful and disadvantageous, for movement would have signified a moving away from such an alleged perfection and a degeneration into imperfection. For the positing of such a time of perfection before history amounted to nothing else than what Origen had felt the need of doing when he introduced into his Christian dogmatics this *pre* of pre-existence, which, like a metaphysical *deus ex machina*, sought to explain away the paradox of historical existence. "When thought met with difficulties," Kierkegaard writes, "an expedient was seized upon. In order to explain at least something, a fantastic presupposition was introduced, the loss of which constituted the fall as the consequence" (KrCA, 25). This "fantastic presupposition" is precisely the idea of Paradise. "The understanding" he continues later in the same text, "talks fantastically about man's state prior to the fall, and, in the course of the small talk, the projected innocence is changed little by little into sinfulness, and so there it is" (KrCA, 32). But the current state of man is left all the same unexplained. "The more fantastically Adam was arrayed [in his pre-existence before the fall], the more inexplicable became the fact that he could sin and the more appalling became his sin" (KrCA, 36).

Instead, Kierkegaard insisted on his paradoxical proposition that "the first sin is the sin"[38]—underscoring that, by failing to assume responsibility insofar as no man is tempted except by himself—for the serpent in Paradise,

---

existing" (KrPF, 73). On the importance of the "moment" see Heidegger: "What we here designate as 'moment of vision' (Augenblick) is what was really comprehended for the first time in philosophy by Kierkegaard—a comprehending with which the *possibility* of a completely new epoch of philosophy has begun for the first time since antiquity. I say this is a possibility; for today when Kierkegaard has become fashionable, for whatever reasons, we have reached the stage where the literature about Kierkegaard, and everything connected with it, has ensured in all kind of ways that this decisive point of Kierkegaard's philosophy has not been comprehended." See Heidegger, *Fundamental Concepts of Metaphysics*, 150.

37. See the historical introduction to KrPF by the editors, xvi–xvii.

38. Kierkegaard, KrCA, 30. "Through the first sin, sin came into the world" (ibid., 31); "*Sin came into the world by a sin*" (ibid., 32, emphasis in the original).

like the Sphinx at the gates of Thebes in *Oedipus Rex*, was the externalization of man's *concupiscentia*[39] (self-temptation, there is no other!)—one falls prey to the seduction of the seduction (KrCA, 43, 48), that is to the *ad infinitum* regression (preexistence) of evil and, at the same time, the elimination of the decisiveness of the moment.

Similarly, the Origenist assumption of pre-existence makes "any point of departure *in time* . . . something accidental, a vanishing point, an occasion."[40] In the endless regression of eternity no point in time—nor, indeed, time itself—makes any difference. For, *sub specie aeternitatis*, the only vantage point for the Greek philosopher, time is indifferent:

> The temporal point of departure is nothing, because in the same moment I discover that I have known the truth from eternity without knowing it, in the same instant that moment is hidden in the eternal, assimilated into it in such a way that I, so to speak, still cannot find it even if I were to look for it, because there is no Here and no There, but only an *ubique et nusquam*. . . . If the situation is to be different (than the Greek paradigm represented by Socrates), then the moment in time must have such decisive significance that for no moment will I be able to forget it, neither in time nor in eternity, because the eternal, previously nonexistent, came into existence in the moment. (KrPF, 13)

And again,

> Let us recapitulate. If we do not assume the moment, then we go back to Socrates, and it was precisely from him that we wanted to take leave in order to discover something. If the moment is posited, the paradox is there, for in its most abbreviated form the paradox can be called the moment. Through the moment, the learner becomes untruth; the person . . . instead of self-knowledge . . . acquires the consciousness of sin. (KrPF, 51)

It is sin that is the difference between man and God[41] and it is that concept, the concept of sin, that Socrates, in spite of all his erudition on human

---

39. Kierkegaard, KrCA, 40. "Furthermore, the difficulty with the serpent is something quite different, namely, that of regarding the temptation as coming from without. This is simply contrary to the teaching of the Bible, contrary to the well-known classical passage in James, which says that God tempts no man and is not tempted by anyone, but each person is tempted by himself" (ibid., 48).

40. Kierkegaard, KrPF, 11, my emphasis.

41. "As sinner, man is separated from God by the most chasmic qualitative abyss. In turn, of course, God is separated from man by the same chasmic qualitative abyss when he forgives sins. If by some kind of reverse adjustment the divine could be shifted over to the human, there is one way in which man could never in all eternity come to be like God: in forgiving sins." See Kierkegaard, *Sickness unto Death*, 122.

nature, lacked (KrPF, 47)—and lacking it, the Greek philosophy remained innocent of the importance of time. As Socrates lacked the consciousness of sin, so Origen, by remaining within the Socratic, lacked the moment. It is under this light that Kierkegaard's "condemnation" of Origenism at the beginning of the *Philosophical Fragments* makes sense.

All of the above assumes a particular force in Kierkegaard's discussion of *objective* anxiety (KrCA, 56–60). The very distinction between objective and subjective anxiety would make little sense if it was not clear that sin is as much a cosmic as it is a moral category that pertains not only to the individual but to nature in general. In its cosmic consideration—applied, as it were, on the macroscopic scale of the whole creation—sin's entanglement with time (for what else do we call now to mind if not history?) becomes extremely significant. The significance is underlined in Kierkegaard's gloss on Romans 8:19. "Inasmuch" he writes, "as one can speak of an eager longing, it follows as a matter of course that the creation is in a state of imperfection" (KrCA, 58).

What is this "longing" if not direction, movement, desire that stretches out (ἐπέκτασις) to its ultimate goal at the end of time? Thus, movement becomes the indication of perfection insofar as this perfection has not been reached yet, *and* the means by which this perfection is carried out. The catastrophic aspect that Origen had attached to history and time is here reversed and annulled.[42]

Kierkegaard and St. Maximus

I would like now to draw very briefly and by a way of a conclusion, a comparison between Kierkegaard's refutation of Platonizing Christianity, as it has been sketched in the foregoing material, with a similar attempt undertaken by St. Maximus the Confessor. Maximus' main argument, according to the pioneering work of one scholar, was "grounded in the doctrine of motion."[43] One sees already here what prompted me to bring these two thinkers together. Maximus' positive re-evaluation of motion turned becoming, γένεσις, and, by extension, history into instruments of teleological perfection that, in his theological language, translates more specifically into

---

42. Kierkegaard's remarks in 58 and 59 (especially vis-à-vis the dangers of Pelagianism's return "from a different side") concern the error of making the Fall a normative state of man and nature—it should be stated clearly that, by denying a prelapsarian perfection we do not accept that the creation was created fallen, for otherwise salvation and redemption would have been ab-normal.

43. Sherwood, *Earlier Ambigua*, 92.

salvation and deification. From the outset of his seventh *Ambiguum*, Maximus sets with the force of a metaphysical principle the fact that everything that moves does so as enabled by the power (δύναμιν) of its movement (κινήσεως) that is according to its desire (κατ' ἔφεσιν). This is a circumlocution to say that everything that is moved is moved by a desire seeking its fulfillment in the desideratum (ὀρεκτόν) that has been set by its nature. That history is still in progress is for Maximus, as it was for Anaxagoras before him and for Kierkegaard after him, evidence that things have not yet reached the fulfillment of their desire.[44] A little later, St. Maximus will clarify that to be created amounts to be moved and to be given being implies also the gift of motion. Thus, both the Origenist idea of a pre-existence outside time, as well as its corollary of the first man's existence in a paradisiacal perfection, are denied. Rather, humanity moves in steps that one of Maximus' famous triads defines as being, well-being, ever-well-being. The first and the last of this trinity of concepts is given only by God, since it *is* God: "For the end of the motion of things that are moved is to rest within eternal well-being itself, just as their beginning was being itself, which is God, who is the giver of being and the bestower of the grace of well-being, for he is the *beginning and the end*."[45] The middle term, however, that is, "voluntary motion," depends upon us. In von Balthasar's words, motion "consists in allowing oneself to be carried by another in the depths of one's being and to be borne toward the ocean of God's rest."[46] And yet so much is at stake at this "allowing"—the whole drama of history is condensed here so much so that it might give the false impression of an almost effortless abandonment to its vagaries. On the contrary, "to be carried by another in the depths of one's being" consists in a life-long struggle punctuated with moments of dramatic anxiety, the kind which Kierkegaard often described in his works.

By this I do not suggest a Maximian influence on Kierkegaard. I simply draw attention to the curious convergence of these two critiques that stand apart in centuries, yet they are brought together by a common target, the Platonizing Christianity of Origen, by a common solution, the vindication of κίνησις and, perhaps, by a common orientation in thought that takes the incarnation seriously enough as to place Christ in its center.

---

44. *AI* 7.3, 7.7 = PG91, 1069B, 1072C.

45. *AI* 7.10 = PG91, 1073C, trans. Constas, in *Difficulties*, 1:87. Italics denote Maximus' reference to Rev 21:6.

46. Balthasar, *Cosmic Liturgy*, 130.

Bibliography

Alberigo, Giuseppe, et al., eds. *The Oecumenical Councils from Nicaea I to Nicaea II (325-787)*. Corpus Christianorum. Conciliorum Oecumenicorum Generaliumque Decreta 1. Critica ed. Turnhout: Brepols, 2006.

Anaxagoras. *Fragmenta*. Edited by Hermann Diels and Walther Kranz. In Diels and Kranz, *Die Fragmente der Vorsokratiker*, 6th ed., 2:5-45. Abbreviated as DK 59.

Balthasar, Hans Urs von. *Cosmic Liturgy: The Universe According to Maximus the Confessor*. Translated by Brian E. Daley. A Communio Book. San Francisco: Ignatius Press, 2003.

Carlisle, Clare. *Kierkegaard's Philosophy of Becoming: Movements and Positions*. Albany: State University of New York Press, 2005.

Curd, Patricia. *Anaxagoras of Clazomenae: Fragments and Testimonia*. Toronto: University of Toronto Press, 2010.

Derrida, Jacques. "Violence and Metaphysics." In *Writing and Difference*, translated by Alan Bass, 97-192. Chicago: University of Chicago Press, 1978.

Diels, Hermann, and Walther Kranz. *Die Fragmente der Vorsokratiker: Griechisch und Deutsch*. 3 vols. 6th ed. Berlin: Weidmann, 1951.

Gregory of Nazianzus. *Funebris oratio in laudem Basilii Magni*. Edited by Fernand Boulenger. In *Grégoire de Nazianze: Discours funèbres en l'honneur de son frère Césaire et de Basile de Césarée*, 58-230. Paris: Alphonse Picard et Fils, 1908.

Gregory of Nazianzus. *Sancti patris nostri Gregorii Theologi vulgo Nazianzeni ... opera quae exstant omnia. Accedunt variorum commentarii et scholia. Tomus secundus.* Edited by J.-P. Migne et al. Patrologiae cursus completus: Series graeca. Paris: Migne, 1858. Abbreviated PG 36.

Heidegger, Martin. *The Fundamental Concepts of Metaphysics: World, Finitude, Solitude*. Translated by William McNeill and Nicholas Walker. Studies in Continental Thought. Bloomington: Indiana University Press, 1995.

———. *What Is Called Thinking?* Translated by Fred D. Wieck and J. Glenn Gray. Religious Perspectives 21. New York: Harper & Row, 1954.

Kangas, David J. *Kierkegaard's Instant: On Beginnings*. Bloomington: Indiana University Press, 2007.

Kierkegaard, Søren. *The Concept of Anxiety*. Edited and translated by Reidar Thomte, in collaboration with Albert B. Anderson. Kierkegaard's Writings 8. Princeton: Princeton University Press, 1980.

———. *Concluding Unscientific Postscript to Philosophical Fragments*. Edited and translated by Howard V. Hong and Edna H. Hong. 2 vols. Kierkegaard's Writings 12. Princeton: Princeton University Press, 1992.

———. *Philosophical Fragments*. Edited and translated by Howard V. Hong and Edna H. Hong. Kierkegaard's Writings 7. Princeton: Princeton University Press, 1985.

———. *The Sickness unto Death: A Christian Psychological Exposition for Upbuilding and Awakening*. Edited and translated by Howard V. Hong and Edna H. Hong. Kierkegaard's Writings 19. Princeton: Princeton University Press, 1980.

———. *Søren Kierkegaard's Journals and Papers*. Edited and translated by Edna H. Hong et al. 7 vols. Bloomington: Indiana University Press, 1967-78.

———. *Søren Kierkegaards Papirer*. Edited by Peter Andreas Heiberg, Victor Kuhr, and Einer Torsting. 16 vols. Copenhagen: Gyldendal, 1909-78.

Manoussakis, John P. "The Dialectic of Communion and Otherness in St. Maximus' Understanding of the Will." In *KPC*, 159–80.

Martens, Paul. "Origen: Kierkegaard's Equivocal Appropriation of Origen of Alexandria." In *Kierkegaard and the Patristic and Medieval Traditions*, edited by Jon Stewart, 111–22. Kierkegaard Research: Sources, Reception and Resources 4. Burlington, VT: Ashgate, 2008.

Maximus the Confessor. *Ambigua ad Iohannem*. Edited and translated by Nicholas P. Constas. In *Difficulties*, 1:62–450; 2:2–330. Abbreviated as *AI*.

———. *On Difficulties in the Church Fathers: The Ambigua*. Edited and translated by Nicholas P. Constas. 2 vols. Dumbarton Oaks Medieval Library 28–29. Cambridge: Harvard University Press, 2014. Abbreviated as *Difficulties*.

Nason, Shannon M. "Motion, Change, and Activity in the Thought of Søren Kierkegaard." PhD diss., Purdue University, 2008.

Nietzsche, Friedrich. *Philosophy in the Tragic Age of the Greeks*. Translated by Marianne Cowan. Washington, DC: Regnery, 1962.

Origen. *On First Principles: Being Koetschau's Text of the De principiis*. Translated by G. W. Butterworth. London: SPCK, 1936.

Parmenides. *Fragmenta*. Edited by Hermann Diels and Walther Kranz. In Diels and Kranz, *Die Fragmente der Vorsokratiker*, 1:227–46. Abbreviated as DK 28.

Plato. *Phaedo*. Translated by G. M. A. Grube. In *Complete Works*, edited by John M. Cooper, 49–100. Indianapolis: Hackett, 1997.

Sherwood, Polycarp. *The Earlier Ambigua of Saint Maximus the Confessor and His Refutation of Origenism*. Studia Anselmiana, philosophica theologica. Rome: "Orbis Catholicus"/Herder, 1955.

Vlastos, Gregory. "Reasons and Causes in the *Phaedo*." *The Philosophical Review* 78 (1969) 291–325.

White, Carolinne, trans. and ed. *Gregory of Nazianzus: Autobiographical Poems*. Cambridge: Cambridge University Press, 1996.

4

The System of Relations as a Pattern of Historicity in the Metaphysics of St. Maximos the Confessor

Smilen Markov

For St. Maximos the Confessor, Incarnation is the ontological optimum of all creation.[1] Not merely the return of creation to God is at stake, as is the case in the Areopagite writings, but a new mode (τρόπος) of being, by which all creation enters into the hypostasis of Christ. Constitutive for this christological *transcensus*, which shapes the metaphysical synthesis of St. Maximos, is the historical transition between three modes of creation, namely emergence-movement-repose. The category of "relation" plays a decisive role in this process.

Definition of "Relation"

In his *Epistle 13*, Maximos writes that unlike difference (διαφορά), relation always presupposes division (διαίρεσις); for him division is a result of doing (ποιεῖν) or suffering (πάσχειν). Essences are divided according to the extent to which they realize their potency to do or to suffer; the measure for this is the category quantity (ποσόν). "Relation" is a community of members, differing in quantity. Each of the indicators, applied in forming such communities, has two aspects: a constant connection between the members, on the one side, and a dynamic vector, on the other, denoting the movement towards unification or towards further division (*Ep13*, 513B). Obviously for Maximos, relation does not pertain simply to the predication of a quality, but to the disposition of the relatives to each other, resulting for each relative from different levels of realization of what is potential in the essence.

---

[1]. I am obliged to Scott Ables for editing the English version of this text.

This model differs from the Aristotelian concept: Aristotle would not apply the category "relation" to the first or to the second essence, as these exist independently and are not defined with regard to something else.[2] He associates "relation" not with the essence, but with its accidents. This is why for him habitus (ἕξις) and disposition (διάθεσις) are relations only in a secondary sense, because rather than denoting accidental constellations, they refer to the existence of the essence. Whereas for Maximos, relations pertain to the way of being of the essence (τρόπος). Porphyry divides relations into (*a*) asymmetrical and (*b*) reciprocal; he explains further the reciprocal ones are not always simultaneous, as their members are not supposed to be in contact with each other all the time.[3] For Plotinus, on the other hand, relations are truly present in each of the members at any time, i.e., relations are *polyadic*.[4] The concept of St. Maximos would be closer to a *polyadic* model, with the qualification that the common *substratum*, which is really present in all members and enables the relation, has a dynamic nature and is guaranteed by the communion between God and creation.

Being indicative of the process of overcoming all ontological divisions, Maximos' concept of relations serves as a matrix, according to which the complex metaphysical structure of a created being could be reconstructed. In this matrix the relations among the created essences are seen as a precursor for the historical *transcensus* towards the union with God, without imposing any notion of automatism on the transformative event. In what follows the ontological, epistemological, and anthropological aspects of Maximos' concept of relation will be studied.

Creation and Relation

Not according to an automatism of self-reflection (as by Origen) does Got bring creation in being.[5] Creation results from his free will: God wants to reveal himself to what he has created and to prepare it to freely answer his invitation for union, i.e., for deification. The connection between God and creation does not impose any necessity whatsoever to the divine being. Nevertheless, God is intimately engaged in his revelation—he is anxiously

---

2. Marmo, "Theories of Relation," 196.

3. He repeats the examples, given by Aristotle. The relation "wing of a bird," for instance, is not reciprocal, as it cannot be given in the form: "bird of a wing." Reciprocal is only the relation "wing of a winged." Cf. Evangeliou, *Aristotle's Categories and Porphyry*, 83.

4. Plotinus, *Enneads* 6.1.6 (42).

5. Origen, *De principiis*, 1.2.2, 1.4.3–5. Cf. Köckert, *Christliche Kosmologie*, 299–302.

waiting for the answer of creation. What enables creation to give an answer is it is not the mere sum of things, but a transparent totality, in which things "do not belong to themselves, but to each other" (*Myst* 7, 685B). When Maximos states God creates and keeps creation in being through a "unifying relation" ("κατὰ τὴν ἑνοποιὸν σχέσιν," ibid., cf. *Myst* 2, 669A), he means God is immanently active in bringing things together and the relations among created beings are determined by divine energy. The dynamic interrelatedness of beings is not of merely accidental character, but pertains to the essences, becomes clear from the above mentioned definition of "relation." The explanation in *Mystagogia* further clarifies the definition of relation given above from *Epistle 13*, in that created beings are in a *multiple, reciprocal and multidimensional relation to God, whose scope varies in the course of history* (*Myst* proem., 664AB).The dynamic vector of the relation has a historical trajectory, which means through relations God is acting in the world's history, man being his co-worker.

The reciprocity of the relation between God and the world might seem puzzling, taking into consideration Maximos' insistence God is non-relational ("ἄσχετος") (which is a *locus communis* in the patristic tradition) and he takes the initiative to reveal himself to the world. But instead of the Aristotelian model of one-sided or reciprocal relations, we are confronted with a complex model of many-to-many relations. Created beings are in constant movement towards their own ontological end. As they are moving to different ends, collision is inescapable, if it were not for divine energy to hold all created things in a simple and unitary course. Divine action is one and simple ("κατὰ μίαν ἁπλῆν δύναμιν"), but it forms multiple and reciprocal relations to each being, just as the center of the circle is in a relation to each of the radii. Maximos calls this reciprocal and multiple pattern of the relation between God and creation "a wise totality of goodness" ("ὁ πάντα τῆς ἀγαθότητος ἀπειρόσοφον"—see *Myst* 1, 668A).

The relational community, conceptualized as an expression of the divine call for union, is not a counterpoint to movement, with the task to keep the stability of beings according to the hierarchy of natures. This community is initiated by the hypostasis of Jesus Christ and it takes place through his personal existence ("διὰ Χριστοῦ"). The unifying existential activity of Christ addresses the principles of essences through their existential dimensions. Christ's economy is not about manipulating the essential core of created beings, it affects the content of their energetic interaction. Not the λόγος but the τρόπος of essences is being changed. In the perfect union with God through Jesus Christ, a new τρόπος of being is formed, a τρόπος which is radically different from all other τρόποι accessible to created natures. Being the Λόγος of all natures, hypostases, and accidents, Christ guarantees unity of all extremes of creation ("κατὰ τὸ πέρας τῶν ἄκρων ἀλλήλοις συναπτομένων," *QThal* 48.185-6) and shares (*Myst* 1, 668AB) his own supernatural way of being with creatures (*QThal* 48.187-9). The latter observation indicates for Maximos the principle of "relation" is not an object, present in the relatives as in subjects. "Relation" is the measure of the union among beings, and in the final analysis with God; this union, dynamically realized is a fundamental task of the ontological constitution of creation.

Created beings are called by God out of nothing (*DP* 288C-D, *Ep12* 488D) and they are constantly at risk of moving towards nothingness. When Maximos speaks of a "unifying relation," he means a movement of the essences according to the teleology of their natural λόγος. However, the violation of the natural order (παρὰ φύσιν) means orientation to non-existence (ἀνυπαρξία).[6] This is not annihilation, since no essence, once created by God, could ever disappear; Maximos means rather a turning back to the source of natural being and in this sense he uses "μή," connoting a "weak form of non-being."[7] Maximos denotes the totality of existence, achieved through participation in the divine unifying act as a new form of being/good being, as opposed to ill-being, or being-in-vain. The category "relation" does not express these metaphysical states—they are realized through the hypostatic modulation of essential energy. Relation denotes only the historical movement towards these states, as well as the distance between them. In this sense, relatives cannot be subjects of the relation, they are its borders that bridge the gap between the extremes. By "extremes," Maximos means not only the extreme values of a quality, but also the real and potential divisions, inequalities, and contrasts in the contingent world. The partakers of these relations are often remote in time or in place. By connecting divided sectors of the thinkable world, relations realize divine providence in history, leading creation to the dynamic peace of deification (cf. *AI* 15, 1217A-C).

The anthropological implication of the Maximian theory of relations is exemplified by Christ, in whom the personification of the intimacy of divine engagement with the world is realized as self-sacrifice, resurrection, and salvation. The common *fundamentum* of all relations is Christ himself, in whose Person all principles of unity are contained ("ἐφ' ὧν οἱ καθόλου τῶν μερῶν προφανέντες λόγοι ποιοῦνται," *QThal* 48.185-6). Each relation within the created world has a principle corresponding to Christ as Cause and End of all creation. To be sure, the system of relations is not a contingent projection of a transcendent plot, it shows the existential authenticity of the encounter with God. This encounter is the mode in which man is an

---

6. Cf. Mitralexis, "Ever-Moving Repose," 73.

7. *Myst* 1, 668. Cf. Mitralexis, "Ever-Moving Repose," 73.

ontological center of relations—it represents the ontological potential of the union. St. Maximos underlines that the resurrection of all human persons guarantees the resurrection of the whole world (*Myst 7*, 684D–687B). All other relations in the world are derivative of this fundamental relational structure, even if it is not directly noticeable for those with unpurified cognitive ability. In this sense, all relations, uniting created things, are symbols of this paradigmatic relation.[8]

The realization of this complex ontological content of "relation" requires a certain disposition of human cognitive powers and of the human person in general.

Epistemological Dimension

World history aims at union with God. The movement towards this purpose is conceptualized through relations ("ἐν σχέσει θεωρουμένη κίνησις," *TP1* 233A) that are accessible for discursive knowledge or "natural contemplation" as Maximos calls it. The striving for God as Good is innate in the human soul and is realized through the activity of human reason (λόγος). The synchronization of human knowledge with divine Truth is the task of the intellect (νοῦς). When reason interacts with the intellect, rational understanding (φρόνησις) opens up to truth (ἀλήθεια), and the faith of reason approximates certain knowledge. This optimization of human cognitive powers traces out the epistemological dimensions of deification (θέωσις).[9]

"Reason" and "intellect" are not simply two functions of cognitive intentionality—they are correlated in correspondence to the metaphysical structure of the world, as well as to the personal encounter with God. By grasping the relations in the created world, human reason recognizes the divine Goodness, which shines in the plurality and in the order of beings. Through discursive analysis reason comes into relation with every being, which is after the First Cause, and enters into the "great achievement of being" ("μεγαλουργία," *AI* 42, 1328A).

According to this model, soul is for Maximos a medium between the thinking agent (intellect) and that which is thought. The activity of this medium transcends the dynamic plurality of the world, without negating it. The soul never reflects again on what was once thought. Grasping an object is a unique noetic movement. From the moment this movement is completed, the object of thought is always at the disposal of the person's

---

8. For the status of symbolic knowledge in Maximos the Confessor cf. *Myst* 2.

9. For the deification of human nature in Maximos cf. Kapriev, "Die menschliche Natur."

cognition. The intellect is able to contemplate this noetic content at any time without any external activation. In other words, as Maximos puts it, what is once thought of, enters the repose of thought forever. Due to everything exists in relation to something else, thinking makes the soul an interval (*intervalum*) between all relations in the world: in this sense it is the borderline of all relations.

The structure of this rational analysis of relations and the content of the detected commonness between beings are so designed, as to enable human cognition to encompass (διάστασις) all relations of the current αἰὼν and to turn to participation of the Truth of being. This is the level of intellect. The metaphysical pattern of relations has an adequate cognitive counterpart, which reflects the dynamic nature of relations. Noetic contemplation is based on the internalization of relations in the soul, itself being an endless movement towards union with God the Truth ("μὴ εὑρίσκων πέρας ἔνθα μὴ ἔστι διάστημα," *Myst* 5, 677A). St. Maximos underlines God is not intelligible, so the soul cannot possibly grasp him cognitively, except for the case of the so called "simple union," when the person's existence transcends all discursive thinking. In order to reach this contemplative state, the soul must gain a "limitless movement." It should be noted at stake is not a solipsistic self–improvement of human intellect, nor some kind of interpersonal relation between God and man, providing an exit from the fragmented world. On the contrary, human intellect is invited to achieve the dynamic union with God through grasping all relations of the created world in their finality, i.e., in their constant repose. This is possible, because the epistemological content of all relations is divine love, transforming the world. From these perspective relations grasped by reason receive another meaning, they are symbols of the economy of Christ, who constructs a new existential scope for dialogue between Creator and creation. The dynamic character of this relation precludes man's having God as an object of knowledge. At the same time, man is the decisive agent, whose activity enables creation in every segment of history to touch divine life and to experience it as joy ("τὴν δὲ ἀγάπην ὡς ὅλης τοῦ Θεοῦ κατὰ διάθεσιν ὅλην μετέχουσαν τῆς τερπνότητος," *Myst* 5, 680B).

The process depicted by Maximos does not merely exemplify an ontology of the intellect. The dynamic repose in the ἔσχατον is a state of creation, which is confirmed within the borders of individual human existence. In human mental and corporeal existence the extreme values of the world are preserved and overcome: through Christ borders penetrate each other ("περιχώρησις τῶν ἄκρων," *TP16* 189D) and the being of creatures is validated on a new level. There is no discrepancy between intra—and extra-mental aspects of relation as the dynamism of these relations expresses the encounter with God ("φέρει καὶ φέρεται"). Thus human thought is transformed in a unifying relation, encompassing everything, which is after God, and bringing everything to God (*AI* 17, 1228D–1229A).

Anthropological Aspects

Relation is a determinant of human existence, namely of human knowledge and of human will.[10] Maximos underlines, the silence (σιγή) of God can be experienced only because of the sacred connection (κοίτη) of believers within the Church (*Myst* 5, 680D). During his earthly life, and especially on Tabor, Christ gave instructions as to what could be grasped "after him" and "concerning him" (*AI* 10, 1156B). In order to participate in the christological event, men of all times should be on the border and be a border between God and what is after him, i.e., His living presence in the world (*AI* 15, 1217C). Christ is not only actualized as a paradigmatic principle (be it also a divine, a living and a personal one), but his living presence, i.e., His grace and energy, truly dwells in the communion of believers and is manifested through the relations of love. Christ's church is the place of divine knowledge, because in it men experience unity to each in every moment of history (*AI* 15, 1216B).

In order to really experience divine love, man should cognitively achieve all things (*Ep2* 401A–404B). At the same time, the soul should overcome the relations with the sensible, otherwise it would be ruined by the passions (*Ep1* 392D). This shows knowledge of the divine presence through the created world is not objectifying, but it is regulated by a personal readiness for communion. Its prerequisite is the curing of passions that are resistant to rational control. Thus, the activity of the soul is diverted from seeming goods that do not have a true ontological base, i.e., from evil. The corporeal relations of man with the world, providing sense perception, are not negated. However, from a passive recipient, sense perception turns into a positive power, unifying the "divided extremes."[11] Imagination becomes subservient to reason, whereas reason, in turn, opens up to the benevolence of God for creation. God himself, who acts in creation, is now revealed to be the extreme of each relation. The realization of this transition as outlined is the task of practical philosophy. In practical philosophy the human person

---

10. Cf. "τῶν ἄκρων σχέσις," *TP16* 188B; "Φρόνησις μέν ἐστιν σχέσις," *TP1* 21B; "ἐν σχέσει γνωμικὴν ἐπρεύσβευον ἕνωσιν" *TP15* 172D.

11. *AI* 18, 1233A. Of crucial importance is imagination. Although it should be eventually overcome, it plays a crucial role in tracing unifying relations in the fragmented world.

cultivates virtues through the exchange of energies between the opposing poles of the world, which follows the pattern of relations. Purification of the soul is needed, whereby the intellect ought to be deified by the Holy Spirit. Maximos warns the process is not regular (Maximos uses the term "στοχαστικός"), and is not manageable by algorithms (*AI* 18, 1233A).

Marriage could serve as an example. Man has the task to overcome sexual division and through marriage he bridges the gap between manhood and womanhood (*AI* 18, 1233A; 41, 1304D–5A). Marital virtues strengthen this unifying relation and protect it from destructive passions. Thus concrete marriage becomes part of the hypostatic life of Christ. At stake is not a mere natural relation, resulting from the desire of Eros. Ἀπάθεια, seen as the optimum of marital virtuousness, guarantees the internalized relation of sexual attraction is not subordinate to natural necessity, to the functions of the senses, or to a mere cognitive intentionality. The relation must be designed to express the divinizing energy, characteristic of a stable Christ–like hypostatic existence. This state is called by Maximos "theological contemplation." This change corresponds to the biblical motif of the third heaven. Whereas, St. Paul witnesses it is not possible for man to be lifted there, Maximos dares to claim man himself has the capacity to become a "heaven" (*AI* 20, 1237D).

Maximos develops a similar explanatory model for the historical validity of relations, when commenting on the volitional dimensions of participation in Christ's revelation. Addressing the will towards its objects means constructing an internal relation in the soul, a relation bridging the extremes and realizing the natural desire for Good. Men intentionally transform their own existence in a relation, which confirms a certain individual position ("προαιρετικὴ ἕξις," *AI* 20, 1237A). This intentional relation develops into a stable state with the co-operation of divine grace, which is beyond the borders of human nature. This is a divine gift to Man.

Maximos' concept of relation does not imply the human person negates his or her nature or is emancipated from it. At stake is a transformation of creation, which takes place in each moment of history through him, who wants that it lives with him. That is why Maximos does not conceptualize this type of relation according to any hierarchical scale of being, as Dionysios does.

A Comparison with Dionysios

A comparison will be instructive with the function of interpersonal relations in *Ecclesiastica hierarchia* by (Pseudo-)Dionysios, and a view to its anthropological relevance. As the purpose of the Dionysian hierarchy is to manifest divine presence, the historical dynamism of man's position in it is determined by the imperative of more authentic and more complete participation in the divine theurgy. Dionysios explains the devotion of the single man to Christian life as entering into a new network of interpersonal relations, which correspond to and express the new status of Man.[12] Dionysios enumerates the relations with the sponsor, the priest, and the bishop, which construct the new pattern of self-identification of the baptized Christian.

For Dionysios, this scope consists in ascending the ecclesial hierarchy. Dionysios sees the hierarchical structure of the church, which is a path towards participation in divine revelation, as a new pattern of relations, (to the patron, to the priest, to the bishop, etc.), through which the proselytes discover their proper self.[13] Relations are much richer in content for Maximos, in whose metaphysical model the "proper self" and the "hidden uniqueness of each thing" (*Myst* 1, 665B) are re-discovered, preserving all principles, but realizing a completely new ontological mode of existence in accordance with the christological event.

Conclusion

Commenting on the Aristotelian categories, Byzantine philosophers insist habit and disposition are not relations in the proper sense, although they bear the characteristics of relations, i.e., they manifest existential dynamic and hypostatic uniqueness. However, the internalization of relations of the created world, realizing union with God, described by Maximos, does form a stable hypostatic disposition. It does not presuppose any multiplicity of hypostatic selfhood, nor a building up of personal identity. When internalized, relations form a constant disposition of the entire human being, which transforms the individual existence into a historical event. Relations do not construct humanity or personhood, but add historicity to human hypostases. With this dimension of the history of revelation human existence is able to come into dialogue with God and to take part in the divinized τρόπος of human nature. This concept is not a precursor to a metaphysics of the person. The internalization of relations does not lead to proclaiming an absolute personal subject: it is seen as an indication that the profound base of each relation is God's love for creation.

---

12. Dionysius the Areopagite, *De ecclesiastica hierarchia* 2, cont. 5, 401B.
13. Ibid. 2, cont. 4, 409C.

Bibliography

Dionysius the Areopagite. *De ecclesiastica hierarchia*. PG3:369A–569A.

Evangeliou, Christos. *Aristotle's Categories and Porphyry*. Philosophia antiqua 48. Leiden: Brill, 1988.

Kapriev, Georgi. "Die menschliche Natur in Christus nach Maximus Confessor und Iohannes Damascenus." In *Christus bei den Vätern*, edited by Ysabel de Andia and Peter Leander Hofrichter, 224–34. Pro Oriente 27. Innsbruck: Tyrolia-Verlag, 2003.

Köckert, Charlotte. *Christliche Kosmologie und kaiserzeitliche Philosophie. Die Auslegung des Schöpfungsberichtes bei Origenes, Basilius und Gregor von Nyssa vor dem Hintergrund kaiserzeitlicher Timaeus- Interpretationen*. Studien und Texte zu Antike und Christentum 56. Mohr Siebeck: Tübingen, 2009.

Marmo, Costantino. "The Theories of Relation in the Medieval Commentaries on the *Categories* (Mid-13th to Mid-14th Century)." In *Aristotle's Categories in the Byzantine, Arabic and Latin Traditions*, edited by Sten Ebbesen, John Marenborn, and Paul Thom, 195–215. Scientia Danica. Series H, Humanistica 8. Copenhagen: Det Kongelige Danske Videnskabernes Selskab, 2013.

Maximus the Confessor. *Ad Marinum presbyterum (Theologica et polemica i)* [To Marinus the Very Pious Priest]. Edited by François Combefis. PG91:9A–37D. Abbreviated as *TP1*.

———. *Ambigua ad Iohannem*. Edited by Franz Oehler. PG91:1061–417C. Abbreviated as *AI*.

———. *De duabus unius Christi Dei nostri uoluntatibus (Theologica et polemica xvi)* [On the Two Wills of the One Christ Our God]. Edited by François Combefis. PG91:184C–212B. Abbreviated as *TP16*.

———. *Disputatio cum Pyrrho* [Dispute with Pyrrhus]. Edited by François Combefis. PG91:288A–353B. Abbreviated as *DP*.

———. *Epistula i* [Epistle 1, To the Eparch George on Sailing for Constantinople]. Edited by François Combefis. PG91:364A–92D. Abbreviated as *Ep1*.

———. *Epistula ii* [Epistle 2, To John the Chamberlain]. Edited by François Combefis. PG91:392D–408C. Abbreviated as *Ep2*.

———. *Epistula xii* [Epistle 12, To John the Chamberlain]. Edited by François Combefis. PG91:460A–509B. Abbreviated as *Ep12*.

———. *Epistula xiii* [Epistle 13, To Peter the Illustrious]. Edited by François Combefis. PG91:509B–33A. Abbreviated as *Ep13*.

———. *Mystagogia*. Edited by François Combefis. PG91:657C–717D. Abbreviated as *Myst*.

———. *Quaestiones ad Thalassium*. Edited by Carl Laga and Carlos Steel. CCSG 7:3–539; 22:3–325. Abbreviated as *QThal*.

———. *Spiritualis tomus ac dogmaticus . . . ad sanctissimum Dorensem episcopum Stephanum (Theologica et polemica xv)* [Spiritual and Dogmatic Tome . . . Addressed to Stephen the Most Holy Bishop of Dora]. Edited by François Combefis. PG91:153B–84C. Abbreviated as *TP15*.

Mitralexis, Sotiris. "Ever-Moving Repose: The Notion of Time in Maximus the Confessor's Philosophy through the Perspective of a Relational Ontology." PhD diss., Freie Universität Berlin, 2014.

5

An Introduction to Aristotle's Theory of Motion as a Precursor to Maximus' Understanding of Motion

Michail Mantzanas

The notion of *motion* (and change) is prominent in the philosophical toolbox of antiquity. However, it is to Aristotle's genius that we owe one of the most comprehensive treatments of κίνησις (and μεταβολή) as a major ontological category and as a prism, through which cosmology and ontology can be intelligibly framed and articulated. Maximus the Confessor is, without doubt, an heir of the rich philosophical heritage that lies behind him *as a whole*. However, his works demonstrate a particular affinity to a markedly Aristotelian *attitude* towards the use of philosophical vocabulary: Maximus' theory of motion is not merely a continuation and radical renewal within a new ontological frame of theories of motion *in general*, but rather an implicit engagement with Aristotle's mode of philosophical enquiry, an implicit Christianized dialogue with the Stagirite.

This chapter, as well as the one following it, are dedicated to an exploration of Aristotle's and Maximus' theories of motion and to a comparison between them. I will provide a brief introduction to Aristotelian motion from the perspective of ontology (and, in certain instances, cosmology), along with some preliminary hints concerning Maximus' seminal contribution, while the next chapter by Sotiris Mitralexis will be comprised of an exposition of Maximian motion. The reader should be aware of the fact that this short introduction aims to merely serve as a frame for comparison of Maximus to Aristotle, not as a deep and comprehensive enquiry into the exhaustively researched subject of Aristotelian motion, i.e., not as a contribution to Aristotelian studies *as such*.[1]

Aristotle's theory of κίνησις and μεταβολή[2] is mainly exposed in his *Physics*, in books III–VIII. One aspect of Aristotle's theory of motion consists of the analysis of change in substance (genesis and decay), change in size (increase and decrease), the change in quality (alteration) and displacement, etc.[3] Motion is one of the fundamental principles of nature: "nature is the beginning of motion and change."[4] In the words of the Stagirite himself,

> Since nature is a source of motion and change, and the source of our enquiry concerns nature, we must not neglect the question of what motion is, since if we are ignorant about what this is so too are we ignorant about nature. Once we have determined what motion is, we must endeavor to tackle in like manner what follows in its appropriate order. Change seems to be continuous, and the first thing manifested in the continuous is the infinite. This is why it so often falls to those defining the continuous to attempt an account of the infinite: being continuous is being divisible into infinity. In addition to these matters, change is impossible without place, void, and time. It is clear, then, because of these relations, and also because of their being common and universal to all, that we must inquire into each of these,

---

1. For further studies of Aristotle's theory of motion and change, as well as for the differences between these two, the reader would do well to consult Kosman, "Aristotle's Definition of Motion"; Bostock, *Space, Time, Matter, and Form*; Brague, "Aristotle's Definition of Motion"; Graham, "Aristotle's Definition of Motion." For a comparison with later philosophers see Kaulbach, *Der philosophische Begriff der Bewegung*. See also the habilitation thesis by Aichele, *Ontologie des Nicht-Seienden*. See also Stein, "Immanent and Transient Potentiality"; Gourinat, "Origine du mouvement"; Tuozzo, "Aristotle and the Discovery"; Marmodoro, "The Union of Cause and Effect." These references are merely indicative of a staggeringly vast secondary literature on the subject. For a general introduction to Aristotle with useful elucidations concerning motion, see Shields, *Aristotle*.

2. *Phys.* 218b20: "At the moment, we do not need to distinguish between movement [κίνησις] and other kinds of change [μεταβολή]." The translation of all quotes used here derives from Wicksteed and Cornford, in Aristotle, *Physics, Books I–IV*, unless otherwise noted. Aristotle identifies these notions in Book III of his *Physics*, but he proceeds to differentiate between them later.

3. "The fulfillment of what exists potentially [ἡ τοῦ δυνάμει ὄντος ἐντελέχεια], in so far as it exists potentially, is motion; namely, of what is alterable in so far as it is alterable, alteration; of what can be increased and in opposition of what can be decreased (for there is no common name for both), increase and decrease; of what can be created and what can deteriorate, creation and corruption: of what can be carried along, locomotion" *Phys.*(201a10–15).

4. *Phys.* 200b12: "ἡ φύσις μέν ἐστιν ἀρχὴ κινήσεως καὶ μεταβολῆς."

arranging them in advance, since a study of more specific topics is posterior to a study of the more common topics. But first, as we have said, our enquiry is into motion.[5]

This points to the fact that the Aristotelian theory of motion cannot be separated from the concept of nature, since, according to Aristotle,[6] a lack of motion entails an absence of nature, as movement is life itself and life implies movement (*Metaph.* 1014b21–22). Motion, in Aristotle, is an ongoing process in nature[7] and both genesis and decay occur in nature.[8] Although Aristotle does accept certain elements of the natural philosophy of the Pythagoreans, the Presocratics, as well as Plato, he questions the theory of the multiplicity of beings and criticizes them for supporting the notion of the indivisible magnitude. Moreover, Aristotle is strongly opposed to the fact that these philosophers made no distinction between substance and a lack of substance. According to Aristotle, movement is the capacity of natural beings[9] themselves and is not prompted by any exterior force that is independent from them.[10]

Furthermore, motion does not exist independently from beings and by itself, but is manifested through beings. Motion exists when it is realized in its specific manifestations:

> Apart from things being changed, there is no change. For what changes always changes either in substance or quantity or quality or in place and we claim that it is not possible to identify anything common to these, which is neither a particular thing nor a quantity nor a quality nor any of the other things categorized. Consequently, there is no motion or change apart from the things mentioned, since there is in fact nothing beyond the things mentioned. In each of these cases everything is in one of two ways. So, for example, in the case of a particular thing, it has either a form or a privation; in the case of quality, the light or the dark; in the case of quantity, the complete or the incomplete. Similarly, in the case of local motion we have up or down, or light or heavy. Consequently, the kinds of motion and change are as many as the kinds of being.[11]

---

5 *Phys.* 200b12–25. For the translation see Shields, *Aristotle*, 198.
6. Shields, "Mind and Motion in Aristotle."
7. Bodnár, "Movers and Elemental Motions in Aristotle."
8. *Phys.* 200b14. Cf. Kelsey, "Aristotle Physics I 8."
9. Hankinson, "Natural, Unnatural, and Preternatural Motions."
10. *Phys.* 192b12–13.
11. *Phys.* 200b32–201a 9. For the translation see Shields, *Aristotle*, 199.

Presocratic physiologists engaged in the generation, synthesis, division and the quantitative difference of material elements. According to Aristotle, the problem of motion goes hand in hand with creation (ποίησις) and condition (πάσχειν). While the theory of *creatio ex nihilo* is not to be traced in the thought of earlier philosophers,[12] Aristotle at least addresses the issue of the possibility of non-being by introducing the idea of deprivation.[13] For him, non-being is the absence of form. Additionally, Aristotle disconnects the concepts of comparison and mood from creation and deterioration and dissociates creation and decay from motion.[14] Consequently, movement is neither creation nor decay, while creation (γένεσις) is something different from the notion of the qualitative change of beings (alteration).

Aristotle's *Physics* constitutes an attempt on the part of the philosopher to prove that nature and the world are in unison and all movements of the natural world have a common structure[15]—while spatial motion plays the most important role. If it would be possible to present the Aristotelian idea of motion in the form of a pyramid, on the top of this pyramid would be the first principle that guides all others, while it remains immovable (the first motionless movement-initiator), to which every change in nature is attributed.[16] The significance of the Aristotelian theory related to the notion of motion lies on the philosopher's support of the idea of continuity.

In the Aristotelian teachings regarding continuity, the philosophical theory of possibility appears to be prominent, since motion is the capacity natural beings themselves and is not triggered by some external force that is independent from them. Nevertheless, the priority of the soul is also prevalent in the Aristotelian teachings related to continuity, which according to Aristotle is the cause of motion, since it creates its own movement.[17]

Maximus the Confessor[18] based his own course of thinking on Aristotle's aforementioned views, but attempted to proceed further, as his ontological *Weltanschauung* was a radically different one. The reader will find a treatment of his theory of motion in the next chapter, but an outline with certain elucidations will be provided here as well. According to Maximus,

12. See, e.g., Curd, "New Work on the Presocratics."
13. Cf. Moravcsik, "What Makes Reality Intelligible?"
14. Shields, "Aristotle on Action."
15. Cf. Coope, "Aristotle's Account of Agency"; Coope, "Change and its Relation."
16. Cf. Kelsey, "Aristotle *Physics* I 8"; Kelsey, "The Place of I 7 in the Argument of *Physics* I"; Kosman, "Aristotle's Definition of Motion."
17. Judson, "Heavenly Motion and the Unmoved Mover."
18. It is to Louth's *Maximus the Confessor* that we owe not only an excellent introduction to Maximus the Confessor but also some of the first substantial translations of parts of the *Ambigua* in English.

motion exists in the world since the creation of cosmos. The absence of motion implies the absence of salvation. This is thus for, according to the theistic theory, the unity of God, i.e., the three hypostases, projects the same energy and motion because of this very common substance.[19] Human movement is a result of will, passion and love, and it can lead man to salvation. In the same way that God moves towards man and offers them the so-called *transmission*, i.e., the capability to approach his energies rather than his essence, man must move towards God in order to be saved.

For Maximus, motion is a primary characteristic of both creation and man, but it can be actualised either as a motion κατὰ ψυχήν, i.e., according to nature, or παρὰ φύσιν, i.e., contrary to nature, nature as defined by the λόγοι of nature.[20] The very act of creating the creation is a continual and eternal *creative motion* from the uncreated Godhead towards a κόσμος that is now, in its Christian frame, disclosed as a personal κτίσις. An overview of the overall κατὰ ψυχὴν motion of creation and man, the personal mediator of creation, would disclose it as a *returning* motion, as a motion of the created world back to the communion with its uncreated Creator and source of existence. However, a motion contrary to this return to uncreated communion, a motion *contrary* to nature, results in the dissociation of creaturehood from its continuing and timeless source of existence, and thus results in death, decay, inexistence.

Maximus' dialogue with Aristotle is implicit, as the Confessor merely uses the Aristotelian *toolbox* in order to formulate a *different* ontology and cosmology. However, his refutation of Origen's theology is a much more explicit one. Maximus maintains that Origen was influenced by Plato when he argued that the perceptible universe and rational beings in authority were in a unison with God through Λόγος. However, souls were saturated because of this situation, so they moved away from the original consubstantial unity with God, after their grief caused by their stillness within the boundaries of this oneness (*AI* 7, 1089). This led God to create the material world, as well as bodies, in order for them to be imprisoned in those souls that sinned, so as to begin seeking to return to their original unity. God, according to Origen,[21] imprisoned souls in bodies as a punishment and with a view to creating a desire to return to God, after being released from the prison of the body. In this case, motion separated souls from God. Both bodies and

---

19. For example, see *QThal* 60, 624.

20. For an excellent treatise on the λόγοι as a foundational notion of Maximus' ontology, see Loudovikos, *Eucharistic Ontology*.

21. Crouzel, *Origen*.

the perceptible world resulted from this sin. Thus, according to Origen,[22] motion was created before the physical world and bodies. The world and the bodies are the consequences of the movement or the sin that was committed by souls in the condition of a disembodied preexistence. First, there was motion, then the creation of the world and bodies took place, and the stagnation of the physically released souls within God followed. The following pattern is another version of the above mentioned phenomenon presented by Origen: stable primary unit-stagnation, movement, genesis, i.e., the created being, the arrival to the physical world (*AI 7*, 1069A). So, according to Origen,[23] who has catalytically influenced by Plato, movement is the reason for the constant distancing of souls from God.

Maximus changes and reverses the order of motion in Origen[24] into generation–motion–fixity, as the reader will see in the following chapter, thereby "correcting" ontological preconditions that he regarded as problematic. There is also a mystical side to this understanding of κίνησις. In this new Maximian rendering of the order of motion, motion is a natural characteristic of God's creation, a means for creation to reach its full participation in divine life. No creature can approach the energies of God's essence without constantly activated movement. Motion is thus a means to experience God, and man reaches the point of eternal fixity within him, in order to achieve the Aristotelian final end, which in Maximus' case is deification—a radically changed form of Aristotelian entelechy, and the highest possible purpose (τέλος).

Contrary to my brief introduction to Aristotle's theory of motion, which hopes to serve as an adequate frame of a preliminary comparison with Maximus, these final elucidations on the Maximian understanding of motion aim to merely serve as *hors d'oeuvres* for the treatment of the Maximian κίνησις that will now follow.

Bibliography

Aichele, Alexander. *Ontologie des Nicht-Seienden: Aristoteles' Metaphysik der Bewegung*. Neue Studien zur Philosophie. Göttingen: Vandenhoeck & Ruprecht, 2009.

Aristotle. *Metaphysics*. Edited by William D. Ross. 2 vols. 2nd ed. Oxford: Clarendon, 1953. Abbreviated as *Metaph*.

———. *Physica*. Edited by William D. Ross. Oxford: Clarendon, 1950. Abbreviated as *Phys*.

22. Kannengiesser and Petersen, *Origen of Alexandria*.
23. Jonas, "Origen's Metaphysics."
24. Janowitz, "Theories of Divine Names."

———. *Physics*. Vol. 1, *Books 1–4*. Translated by Philip H. Wicksteed and Francis Macdonald Cornford. Loeb Classical Library 228. Cambridge: Harvard University Press, 1957.

Bodnár, István M. "Movers and Elemental Motions in Aristotle." *Oxford Studies in Ancient Philosophy* 15 (1997) 81–118.

Bostock, David. *Space, Time, Matter, and Form: Essays on Aristotle's Physics*. Oxford: Oxford University Press, 2006.

Brague, Rémi. "Aristotle's Definition of Motion and Its Ontological Implications." *Graduate Faculty Philosophy Journal* 13 (1990) 1–22.

Coope, Ursula Charlotte Macgillivray. "Aristotle's Account of Agency in *Physics* III.3." *Proceedings of the Boston Area Colloquium in Ancient Philosophy* 20 (2004) 201–21.

———. "Change and Its Relation to Actuality and Potentiality." In *A Companion to Aristotle*, edited by Georgios Anagnostopoulos, 277–91. Chichester: Wiley-Blackwell, 2009.

Crouzel, Henri. *Origen: The Life and Thought of the First Great Theologian*. Translated by A. S. Worral. Edinburgh: T.& T. Clark, 1989.

Curd, Patricia. "New Work on the Presocratics." *Journal of the History of Philosophy* 49 (2011) 1–37.

Gourinat, Jean-Baptiste. "Origine du mouvement (ὅθεν ἡ ἀρχὴ τῆς κινήσεως) et cause efficiente (ποιητικὸν αἴτιον) chez Aristote." In *Aitia I. Les quatre causes d'Aristote: Origines et interprétations*, edited by Cristina Viano et al., 91–121. Aristote: traductions et études. Leuven: Peeters, 2013.

Graham, Daniel W. "Aristotle's Definition of Motion." *Ancient Philosophy* 8 (1988) 209–15.

Hankinson, Robert James. "Natural, Unnatural, and Preternatural Motions: Contrariety and Argument for the Elements in *De caelo* 1.2–4." In *New Perspectives on Aristotle's De caelo*, edited by Alan C. Bowen and Christian Wildberg, 83–118. Leiden: Brill, 2009.

Janowitz, Naomi. "Theories of Divine Names in Origen and Pseudo-Dionysius." *History of Religions* 30 (1990) 359–72.

Jonas, Hans. "Origen's Metaphysics of Free Will, Fall, and Salvation: A 'Divine Comedy' of the Universe." In *Philosophical Essays: From Ancient Creed to Technological Man*, edited by Hans Jonas, 305–23. Englewood Cliffs, NJ: Prentice-Hall, 1974.

Judson, Lindsay. "Heavenly Motion and the Unmoved Mover." In *Self-Motion: From Aristotle to Newton*, edited by Mary Louise Gill and James G. Lennox, 155–71. Princeton: Princeton University Press, 1994.

Kannengiesser, Charles, and William L. Petersen. *Origen of Alexandria: His World and His Legacy*. Notre Dame: University of Notre Dame Press, 1988.

Kaulbach, Friedrich. *Der philosophische Begriff der Bewegung. Studien zu Aristoteles, Leibniz und Kant*. Cologne: Böhlau, 1965.

Kelsey, Sean. "Aristotle Physics I 8." *Phronesis* 51 (2006) 330–61.

———. "The Place of I 7 in the Argument of *Physics* I." *Phronesis* 53 (2008) 180–208.

Kosman, Aryeh L. "Aristotle's Definition of Motion." *Phronesis* 14 (1969) 40–62.

Loudovikos, Nikolaos. *A Eucharistic Ontology: Maximus the Confessor's Eschatological Ontology of Being as Dialogical Reciprocity*. Translated by Elizabeth Theokritoff. Brookline, MA: Holy Cross Orthodox Press, 2010.

Louth, Andrew. *Maximus the Confessor*. The Early Church Fathers. London: Routledge, 1996.

Marmodoro, Anna. "The Union of Cause and Effect in Aristotle: *Physics* 3.3." *Oxford Studies in Ancient Philosophy* 32 (2007) 205–32.

Maximus the Confessor. *Ambigua ad Iohannem*. Edited by Franz Oehler. PG91:1061–417C. Abbreviated as *AI*.

———. *Quaestiones ad Thalassium*. Edited by François Combefis. PG90:244–785B. Abbreviated as *QThal*.

Moravcsik, Julius M. "What Makes Reality Intelligible? Reflections on Aristotle's Theory of *Aitia*." In *Aristotle's Physics: A Collection of Essays*, edited by Lindsay Judson, 31–48. Oxford: Clarendon, 1991.

Shields, Christopher J. *Aristotle*. Routledge Philosophers. London: Routledge, 2007.

———. "Aristotle on Action: The Peculiar Motion of Aristotelian Souls." *Aristotelian Society Supplementary Volume* 81 (2007) 139–61.

———. "Mind and Motion in Aristotle." In *Self-Motion: From Aristotle to Newton*, edited by Mary Louise Gill and James G. Lennox, 117–33. Princeton: Princeton University Press, 1994.

Stein, Nathanael. "Immanent and Transient Potentiality." *Journal of the History of Philosophy* 52 (2014) 33–60.

Tuozzo, Thomas M. "Aristotle and the Discovery of Efficient Causation." In *Efficient Causation: A History*, edited by Tad M. Schmaltz, 23–47. Oxford: Oxford University Press, 2014.

6

Maximus' Theory of Motion: Motion κατὰ φύσιν, Returning Motion, Motion παρὰ φύσιν*

Sotiris Mitralexis

The *theory of motion* is very prominent in Maximus the Confessor's thought.[1] Following Aristotle,[2] Maximus interprets existence as a perpetual becoming (γίγνεσθαι), an aggregate of continuous changes that are recapitulated in the word "motion" (κίνησις). Following Aristotle, Maximus discerns several different type of motion: *locomotion* (φορά, μετάστασις ἐκ τόπου εἰς τόπον), *change and alteration* (ἀλλοίωσις), *corruption/decay* (φθορά), *origination* (γένεσις), *return* (ἐπιστροφή), *change into something else* (ἑτεροίωσις); growth, *increase* (αὔξησις), *decrease* (φθίσις); *spiral movement* (ἑλικοειδής),

---

* This chapter on Maximus' understanding of motion is based on pp. 109–124 of Mitralexis, *Ever-Moving Repose*.

1. On various aspects of Maximus' theory of motion, see Tollefsen, "Causality and Movement"; Cvetković, "St Maximus on Πάθος."

2. We must once again remark here that Maximus does not see himself as a commentator of Aristotle or Plato or anything similar: Maximus does not write *about* the Aristotelian philosophical language, but his writings *echo* this language—without necessarily repeating its original contents. Betsakos, in his comparative study of Aristotle and Maximus, writes that Maximus is integrated into the Aristotelian tradition of thought (into the Aristotelian philosophical language) in the way that native speakers are integrated into their mother tongue: they appropriate it, without it belonging to them; they are speaking it, not *about* it; they use it to articulate formulations concerning truth, but truth always remains beyond language; they use language as a means for their expression, not as an agent imposing limitations in content. Maximus uses the Aristotelian *language* in order to denote a truth other than that of Aristotle's. See Betsakos, Στάσις ἀεικίνητος, 261–62. As we have remarked previously, we cannot know for certain if Maximus has studied the writings of Aristotle and the ancient Greek philosophers in their original form or if his thorough familiarization with them is a result of the study of *florilegia* and, generally, channels of transmission of the ancient Greek thought incorporated into Christian education.

cyclical movement (κυκλική),³ etc.—in short, every conceivable type of change or movement. Ensuing Michail Mantzanas' introduction to Aristotle's theory of motion, I intend to present here the basic tenets of Maximus' understanding of motion as both a continuation and a renewal of the Aristotelian one.⁴

For Maximus' philosophy of motion,⁵ to exist *is* to be in motion: "according to Maximus, the created character of things entails their being in motion."⁶ Everything in creation is in motion,⁷ nothing can be described

---

3. E.g. *SchD*, in *Diu. nom.*, 257A–D, 381B–D.

4. Such a comparison has been attempted by Betsakos in Στάσις ἀεικίνητος. This book constitutes an attempt which is comparable to this article, and which I will repeatedly cite in my analysis.

5. The phrase is Sherwood's, from the introduction to his translation of *The Ascetic Life* and *The Four Centuries of Charity*, 49.

6. Loudovikos, *Eucharistic Ontology*, 165.

7. Note von Balthasar's remarks: "Maximus took up Gregory of Nyssa's axiom that finite being is essentially characterized by *spatial intervals* (διάστημα) and, therefore, by *motion*" (*Cosmic Liturgy*, 138); "Time and space are, for Maximus and Gregory of Nyssa, the expression of finitude itself; they are pure limitation. Space is not fundamentally a physical or astronomical reality but an ontological category: 'the limitation of the world through itself'" (ibid., 139); "The ontology of created being is a study of motion. More precisely, it is the study of the relationship between rest and motion, whose balance is what defines the essence of finite being" (ibid., 154). We must here remark that, while Maximus draws from diverse sources in order to achieve his unique synthesis and considers himself a natural continuator of the patristic tradition, Gregory of Nyssa must have been a particularly strong influence on his thought, especially on matters concerning motion and time. Maximus' explicit and implicit use of the notion of spatial, temporal and generally ontological *distance* (διάστημα, often translated as interval or extension), which among other things is a key difference between creation (which possesses it and which is defined by it) and the uncreated (where there is no *distance*), is based on Gregory of Nyssa's conception thereof. And it is on this notion that a great number of interconnected Maximian concepts depend. While there are a number of paradoxical phrases concerning motion prior to Maximus' στάσις ἀεικίνητος (such as Proclus' κίνησις ἀκίνητος; cf. Gersh, *Κίνησις Ἀκίνητος*), it is also on this matter that Gregory's influence (whom Maximus had certainly read) must have been most decisive. For Gregory of Nyssa's eschatological identification of eternal movement with fixity ("This is the most marvelous thing of all: how the same thing is both a standing still (στάσις) and a moving (κίνησις)"), which must have served as a predecessor and influence for Maximus' "ever-moving repose," see Blowers, "Maximus the Confessor, Gregory of Nyssa," 157–65, where this is demonstrated. On Gregory of Nyssa's thought on distance, time and the Aeon, see also Plass, "Transcendent Time and Eternity"; Plass, "Transcendent Time in Maximus"; Bradshaw, "Time and Eternity in the Greek Fathers," 335–42. See also Plass's account of the Maximian στάσις ἀεικίνητος in "Moving Rest." It would be outside the scope of our study to provide an exhaustive comparison of Gregory and Maximus on *distance*, motion, time and the Aeon, but we must nevertheless note that Gregory's influence on Maximus on these matters is much, much more discernible in comparison to that of other church fathers prior to the Confessor.

as motionless, beyond movement, change and alteration: "nothing that has come into being is motionless, not even something inanimate and tangible."[8] For Maximus, this motion "does not have to do with the mutability or change or corruption of things, but is an ontological property belonging to them."[9] This motion is not opposing the true nature of things, it is not to be interpreted as a "consequence of the Fall," as the ecclesial language would formulate it. The source and cause of this motion resides beyond createdness: "the beginning of every natural motion is the origin (γένεσις) of the things that are moved, and the beginning of the origin of whatever has been originated is God, for he is the author of origination."[10] "Everything that comes from God and is subsequent to him undergoes motion, inasmuch as these things are not in themselves motion or power. So they do not move in opposition (to their nature), as it has been said, but through the λόγος creatively placed within them by the cause which framed the universe."[11]

Motion, an ontological property of beings, is a result of *relation*. "All beings are absolutely stable and motionless according to the λόγος by which they were given subsistence and by which they exist."[12] However, it is from the beings' *relation* to one another that their motion emerges—which, in turn, signifies the presence of God's dispensation (οἰκονομία) for the universe: "by virtue of the λόγος of what is contemplated around them, they (the beings) are all in motion and unstable, and it is on this level that God's dispensation of the universe wisely unfolds and is played out to the end."[13] The *relationality* of beings is a prerequisite for the emergence of motion, this most fundamental ontological property of theirs: without this relationality, they are "stable" and "motionless," they do not participate in being. Motion is the signifier of a being's existence, and this signifier emerges in the beings' relationship to other beings, to "the λόγος of what is contemplated around

---

8. *AI* 7.6 = PG91, 1072B: "οὐδὲν γὰρ τῶν γενομένων ἐστὶ . . . ἀκίνητον, οὐδ' αὐτῶν τῶν ἀψύχων καὶ αἰσθητῶν." Since Constas' critical edition (*On Difficulties in the Church Fathers: The Ambigua*) names Migne's PG column of each respective passage, while many scholars still depend on PG's *Ambigua*, we will use Constas' critically edited text while simply citing *Ambigua* with PG91 columns for the reader's convenience, as PG91 columns can be easily traced back to Constas' edition, while the opposite is naturally not the case. When directly using Constas' translation, we will cite Constas' page numbers.

9. Loudovikos, *Eucharistic Ontology*, 166.

10. *AI* 15.7 = PG91, 1217C (trans. Constas, in *Difficulties*, 1:369).

11. *DP* 352AB (trans. Elizabeth Theokritoff, in Loudovikos, *Eucharistic Ontology*, 65).

12. *AI* 15.5 = PG91, 1217 AB (trans. Constas, in *Difficulties*, 1:367).

13. Ibid. (trans. Constas, in *Difficulties*, 1:367).

them," as has been actively willed by God. The very notion of λόγος contains this relationality.[14]

Origination-Motion-Fixity

Maximus reverses the order of the Origenist triad of *fixity-motion-generation* (στάσις-κίνησις-γένεσις) into *origination-motion-fixity* (γένεσις-κίνησις-στάσις), which he sees as the "uniquely possible order."[15] The Confessor explains this by stating that "if motion naturally presupposes origin, and rest presupposes motion, it is obvious that origin and rest cannot possibly be among those things which are simultaneous in existence, since between them stands a natural obstacle that separates them: motion."[16] According to this substantial revision, which changes the Origenist triad completely, (*a*) birth and origination also mean the setting-in-motion, the beginning of motion; (*b*) the whole of existence and life, as well as each particular existence, is characterized by motion from the moment it exists up to its definitive end; and (*c*) everything moves towards an end, the motion of everything aspires towards its end and repose. We must here note that the Greek word τέλος denotes both the temporal end and the causal end, the purpose and consummation—while ἀρχή can mean both temporal beginning and source as well as origin and cause.[17] (With this semantic frame, God cannot but be described as both the cause, the purpose, the beginning, the end and the middle ground of all). Motion is an ontological property that "applies to all created beings without exception and not only to rational beings."[18]

---

14. On this, see Mitralexis, "Maximus' 'Logical' Ontology: An Introduction and Interpretative Approach to Maximus the Confessor's Notion of the Λόγοι."

15. See Sherwood, "Introduction," 47, where this particular subject is treated. However, Sherwood has erroneously cited the Origenist triad as having the following order: generation-fixity-motion (γένεσις-στάσις-κίνησις), something which also seems to be the case in Louth's treatment of the subject in *Maximus the Confessor*, 64. Andrew Louth has recently pointed out to me that the Origenist position is an explanation of γένεσις, according to which the λογικοί originally existed eternally in a state of rest (στάσις)—their "beginning" is not to be traced in their becoming, but in them being at contemplative rest. In *moving from* this state of rest (i.e., in proceeding from στάσις to κίνησις) and initiating the realm of becoming, which they came to occupy, they initiate γένεσις. As such, the correct Origenist triad is *fixity-motion-generation* (στάσις-κίνησις-γένεσις), the order of which is reversed by Maximus.

16. *AI* 15.7 = PG91, 1217D (trans. Constas, *Difficulties*, 1:371).

17. As well as principle, power, authority, element, sovereignty, empire, realm etc., according to the LSJ and Lampe's Lexicon.

18. Loudovikos, *Eucharistic Ontology*, 165.

Motion κατὰ φύσιν, Returning Motion, Motion παρὰ φύσιν

However, motion is not only and always of the aforementioned type. Motion has two "directions" or "tendencies,"[19] one "according to nature" (κατὰ φύσιν) and, secondly, its deviation and failure, i.e., motion "contrary to nature" (παρὰ φύσιν).[20] Note that the word *nature* is here used with the meaning it bears in the context of the λόγοι τῶν ὄντων: "according to nature" means according to the end and purpose (τέλος) of nature and in God, according to "pre-fallen" nature, and "contrary to nature" means contrary to this end and purpose, according to the mode of existence of nature in its "fallen" state.[21] Motion "according to nature" is motion towards the fuller communion with the uncreated person of God, the *returning motion*[22] to the

---

19. We are not referring here to the three motions of the soul in *AI* 10.9–13 = PG91, 1112D–17A, but to a distinction of a different type.

20. Cf. *AI* 8.2 = PG91, 1104A, on the movement towards passions, corruption, and death. *AI* 10.7 = 1112AB: "Every human mind has gone astray and lost its natural motion, so that its motion is determined by passion and sense and things perceived by the senses, and it cannot be moved anywhere else as its natural motion towards God has completely atrophied"; *AI* 10.8 = 1112 C: "The soul, when it is moved contrary to nature through the means of flesh towards matter, is clothed in an earthly form, but when, in contrast, it is moved naturally by means of the soul towards God . . ." (trans. Louth, in *Maximus the Confessor*, 96). Note that these two tendencies/directions of motion correspond to man's two wills, his natural will (θέλημα φυσικὸν) towards motion according to nature and his gnomic will (θέλημα γνωμικὸν) towards motion contrary to nature: *TP14* 153 A: "Θέλημα φυσικόν ἐστιν, οὐσιώδης τῶν κατὰ φύσιν συστατικῶν ἔφεσις. Θέλημα γνωμικόν ἐστιν ἡ ἐφ' ἑκάτερα τοῦ λογισμοῦ αὐθαίρετος ὁρμή τε καὶ κίνησις." Cf. *TP16* 192 BC.

21. That is, "according to nature" means "according to the λόγος of nature," according to God's *intention* for his creature. See *AI* 42.15 = PG91, 1329AB: "It is according to these (the λόγοι) that all things are, and have come to be, and remain always drawing closer to their own predetermined λόγοι through natural motion, and ever more closely approximated to being by their particular kinds and degrees of motion and inclination of choice. They receive well-being through virtue and through their direct progress toward the λόγος according to which they exist; or they receive ill-being through vice and their movement contrary to the λόγος by which they exist. To put it concisely, they move in accordance with their possession or privation of the potential they have naturally to participate in him who is by nature absolutely imparticipable, and who offers himself wholly and simply to all—worthy and unworthy—by grace through his infinite goodness, and who endows each with the permanence of eternal being, corresponding to the way that each disposes himself and is. And for those who participate or do not participate proportionately in him who, in the truest sense, is and is well, and is forever, there is an intensification and increase of punishment for those who cannot participate, and of enjoyment for those who can participate" (trans. Constas, *Difficulties*, 2:149).

22. *AI* 10.99 = PG91, 1188C, quoting *Diu. Nom.* 4.4, 148.13–15: "εἰς αὐτὸν τὰ πάντα ἐπιστρέφεσθαι, καθάπερ εἰς οἰκεῖον ἕκαστα πέρας"—"Everything will return to (God), as each to its own goal" (trans. Louth, *Maximus the Confessor*, 141). Note that the Neoplatonic notion of return/conversion (ἐπιστροφ;h) is substantially different to Maximus'

Creator and the source of creation: "for the whole world (the) cause is God, in relation to whom it naturally moves."²³ Motion has the tendency to "be directed toward the unmoved, uncreated God, who is unmoved in the sense that he is not subject to precisely the passivity characteristic of creaturehood's motion, because there is nothing higher than himself toward which he could move."²⁴ This *returning motion* is not described as an automatically actualized tendency, but as an intense longing for communion with the Creator, as an ἔρως for him that must be affirmed freely and willingly—an ἔρως that constitutes the answer to God's ἔρως for the world, the answer to God's call for communion.²⁵ For Maximus, to *know* God is to be *in communion* with God and vice versa; knowledge signifies a personal encounter, not a transmission of information; knowledge equals participation²⁶—and relationship and communion grants and constitutes the *knowledge* of the Other's otherness. This *returning motion* to God is described as the fullness of hope and the created beings' driving force for striving forward.²⁷ Fragmented reality, the many, are summoned back to the one, and this union with the one, this communion-in-otherness, this participation in the cause, constitutes the true and primary knowledge.

The deviation from "motion according to nature" is the tendency of created beings to exist for themselves and in themselves, without the communion with the source of their existence that gives them life and being, without the communion with the absolute otherness that manifests and actualizes them as othernesses and hypostases. It is a motion that aspires to actualize non-relation as a mode of existence, and as such it is a motion towards death. This tendency of creation and created beings towards individual onticity, non-relation, corruption, decay and death is a motion "contrary to nature";²⁸ it does not reflect the true nature of createdness. In the

ἐπιστρεπτικὴ ἀναφορά, cf. Cvetković, "St Maximus on Πάθος," 99.

23. Balthasar, *Cosmic Liturgy*, 138.

24. Loudovikos, *Eucharistic Ontology*, 167.

25. *Myst* 11.2–4: "τὴν ἐμφαντικὴν δηλοῦν ἔφασκε τῶν θείων ἡδονὴν ἀγαθῶν, πρὸς μὲν τὸν ἀκήρατον τοῦ Θεοῦ καὶ μακάριον ἀνακινοῦσαν ἔρωτα"—"The delight (ἡδονή) that discloses the divine blessings moves (the souls) towards the clear and blessed ἔρως of God." Cf. *QThal* 54.154–163.

26. This knowledge-through-participation is a standard theme in Maximus' mentions of a cognitive becoming. E.g., *AI*, 7.13 = PG91, 1077B: "γνώσεως . . . μόνης καὶ μετεχομένης" ("knowledge . . . singular and subject to participation"). Cf. Loudovikos, *Eucharistic Ontology*, 176.

27. *QThal* 49.48–51: "ἑρμηνεύεται ἐπιστροφή, σαφῶς μηνύουσα δι' ἑαυτῆς τὸν πληρέστατον τῆς θείας ἐλπίδος λόγον, οὗ χωρὶς οὐδαμῶς οὐδενὶ καθοτιοῦν πρὸς θεὸν ἐπιστροφὴ γίνεσθαι πέφυκεν."

28. As this motion "contrary to nature" is, according to Maximus, a result of man's

case of the human person, motion contrary to nature is manifested through the "passions"[29] and, eventually, evil.[30]

To conceive of evil and of the "passions" in such a way is to transfer these concerns from the moral level (the level of ethical *behavior* or lack thereof) to the ontological level, the level of the question concerning the existence (and, by extension, man's existence) *as such*. For Maximus, it is not a matter of *behavior*, but a matter of *motion*, a matter of one of the primary ontological properties, paving the way for an "ontological ethics," not one based on authority or convention.[31] As Nicholas Loudovikos remarks regarding these two types of motion,

> Maximus distinguishes sharply between the "irrational impetus towards non-being" which he calls "unstable behavior and a terrible disordering of soul and body" and again "deliberate inclination towards the worse" ([*AI* 7.23 =] PG91, 1084D); and

---

Fall, of man's inability to exist in communion with his Creator, God's incarnation—and as such, the renewal of nature through the bridging of the gap between createdness and the uncreated—has been necessary in order to remedy this and to enable man's return to the motion "according to nature." Cf. *AI* 41.6 = PG91, 1308CD: "Since then (since the Fall) the human person is not moved naturally, as it was fashioned to do, around the unmoved, that is its own beginning (I mean God), but contrary to nature is voluntarily moved in ignorance around those things that are beneath it, to which it has been divinely subjected, and since it has abused the natural power of uniting what is divided, that was given to it at its generation, so as to separate what is united, therefore 'natures have been instituted afresh,' and in a paradoxical way beyond nature that which is completely unmoved by nature is moved immovably around that which by nature is moved, and God becomes a human being, in order to save lost humanity. Through himself he has, in accordance with nature, united the fragments of the universal nature of the all, manifesting the universal λόγοι that have come forth for the particulars, by which the union of the divided naturally comes about, and thus he fulfils the great purpose of God the Father, to recapitulate everything both in heaven and earth in himself (Eph 1:10), in whom everything has been created (Col 1:16)" (trans. in Louth, *Maximus the Confessor*, 156–57). The focal point of this *renewal* is, of course, corruption: *QThal* 42.18–20: "Therefore our Lord and God, rectifying this reciprocal corruption and alteration of our human nature by taking on the whole of our nature" (trans. Blowers in *CMofJCh*, 119).

29. *CChar* 2.16.1: "Πάθος ἐστὶ κίνησις ψυχῆς παρὰ φύσιν."—"Passion is a movement of the soul contrary to nature" (my translation).

30. Cf. Betsakos, Στάσις ἀεικίνητος, 177–86. *CChar* 4.14: "Οὐ περὶ τὴν οὐσίαν τῶν γεγονότων τὸ κακὸν θεωρεῖται, ἀλλὰ περὶ τὴν ἐσφαλμένην καὶ ἀλόγιστον κίνησιν."—"Evil is not to be regarded as in the substance of creatures but in its mistaken and irrational movement" (trans. Berthold, in *SelWrts*, 77). According to Maximus, evil is the result of motion contrary to nature, and more precisely an ἀλόγιστος κίνησις (*QThal* epist. 220–23).

31. On a discussion concerning this matter in relation to the whole of the patristic era and not exclusively to Maximus, cf. Yannaras, *The Freedom of Morality*.

on the other hand "positive movement" as a property of the inner principle of the creature's nature. The latter is the creature's "ascent and restoration" (due precisely to the natural operation and power of things consequent upon their essential principle) to its "divine goal" ([AI 7.17 =] PG91, 1080C). And precisely by reason of the supreme goal of this movement, "nothing originate has ever halted in its motion, nor has it attained the lot appointed to it according to the divine purpose" ([AI 7.28] = PG91, 1089A).[32]

As a consequence, man's striving is an ontological one: it is not only to restore his motion as *motion according to nature*, but to freely answer God's call to himself and to the whole of creation. It is not to be content with the returning motion of createdness (next to its deviation, motion-as-corruption) but to actualize this return and strive for the repose[33] (στάσις) and the ever-moving repose in God (στάσις ἀεικίνητος) that is the "ever well-being" (ἀεὶ εὖ εἶναι), the fullness of the communion with the wholly Other.

The Motion of the Uncreated

Maximus' uncompromisingly apophatic stance is apparent when he is treating the subject of God's motion. According to Maximus, God is both motionless/immovable,[34] moving *and* beyond movement and fixity.[35] Lo-

32. Loudovikos, *Eucharistic Ontology*, 166.

33. AI 7.3 = PG91, 1069B: "Nothing that is in motion has stopped before arriving at its object of desire."

34. Everything that is created has a cause and is in motion, but God has not been created and has no cause but is himself the cause of everything; as a consequence, God is motionless. AI 23.2–3 = PG91, 1260A: "Now if every being which is moved (which also means that it has been created) exists and is in motion and has been created in consequence of a cause, then whatever does not exist in consequence of a cause is obviously neither created nor moved. For that which does not have a cause of being is not moved at all. If, then, the uncaused is necessarily also unmoved, it follows that the Divine is unmoved, insofar as it does not owe its being to a cause, being itself the cause of all beings. How, then, someone perhaps might ask, does this marvelous teacher, in the passage cited above, introduce a Divinity in motion?" (trans. Constas, *Difficulties*, 2:5).

35. AI 15.11 = PG91, 1221AB: "And if someone should ask, 'How can rest be attributed to God without it having been preceded by motion?,' I would answer first by saying that the Creator and creation are not the same, as if what is attributed to the one must by necessity be attributed likewise to the other, for if this were the case the natural differences between them would no longer be evident. I would, in the second place, state the principal objection: strictly speaking, God neither moves nor is stationary (for these are properties of naturally finite beings, which have a beginning and an end); he effects absolutely nothing, nor does he suffer any of those things which are conceived or said of

comotion requires space and change manifests in time, and as a consequence to speak of motion in the case of the uncreated, of God, would be illogical: the uncreated is by definition beyond categories entailing spatiotemporality. However, under different perspectives and contexts we can describe God as both motionless and being in motion, if we remain conscious of language's unavoidably relative and apophatic character—especially in signifying the uncreated (which, residing "beyond the limits of our world," is "beyond the limits of our language"). Even if we do employ concepts such as motion or fixity in relation to God, Maximus warns us that we cannot think of them in terms of the motion of created beings.[36]

To ask whether God *is moved*, whether he *suffers* motion or change, would be irrational. God is motionless and infinite, he is by definition beyond change and beyond motion,[37] beyond beginning and end, beyond substance, activity or potency.[38] As God's intentions (pre)existing in him, the λόγοι of beings are motionless as well, in contrast to the beings of which they are the λόγοι.[39] Therefore, the *potentiality* and *capability* to arrive at a repose and to attain fixity is innate in the λόγος of each being and manifests itself as a tendency and longing to achieve this fixity, to arrive at this repose. This is clearly stated by Maximus: God attracts his creations and moves them towards a spiritual union of ἔρως with him in order to be longed for and loved by them; he is the cause of motion in that he moves his creations through their λόγος in order to return to him. Our tendency towards the divine person(s) is foremostly a tendency of radical self-transcendence and full communion, an erotic motion (ἐρωτικὴ κίνησις) without beginning or end.[40] It is this ἐρωτικὴ κίνησις that can restore the human person's full communion with the divine persons: "love is the ἔκ-στασις which makes the rational creature a person, i.e. deifies it, according to Maximus, identifying it in the perfection of its movement with the 'divinely perfect λόγος according to which it is and has come into being' ([AI 21.10 =] PG91, 1249B), a

---

him among ourselves, since by virtue of his nature he is beyond all motion and rest, and in no way is subject to our modes of existence" (trans. Constas, *Difficulties*, 1:375–76).

36. SchD, in *Diu. nom.*, 381B: "Ἀκούων κινεῖσθαι τὸν Θεόν, μηδέποτε νοήσῃς κίνησιν τὴν ἐπὶ τῶν κτιστῶν νοουμένην καὶ μάλιστα τῶν αἰσθητῶν."

37. *AI* 7.3 = PG91, 1069B: "εἰ γὰρ τὸ θεῖον ἀκίνητον, ὡς πάντων πληρωτικόν, πᾶν δὲ τὸ ἐκ μὴ ὄντων τὸ εἶναι λαβὸν καὶ κινητόν, ὡς πρός τινα πάντως φερόμενον αἰτίαν." See also *CGn* 1.2, 1084A.

38. *CGnCGn* 1.4, 1084BC.

39. *AI* 15.5 = PG91, 1217AB.

40. SchD, in *Diu. nom.*, 268B: "Ἡ ἐρωτικὴ κίνησις, τοῦ ἀγαθοῦ προϋπάρχουσα, ἐν τῷ ἀγαθῷ ἁπλῆ καὶ ἀκίνητος οὖσα καὶ ἐκ τοῦ ἀγαθοῦ προϊοῦσα αὖθις ἐπὶ τὸ αὐτὸ ἐπιστρέφει ἀτελεύτητος καὶ ἄναρχος οὖσα, ὅπερ δηλοῖ τὴν ἡμῶν ἔφεσιν πρὸς τὸ θεῖον."

λόγος or principle that by nature goes outside itself so as to be deified."⁴¹ God is the prototype, projector and generator of ἀγάπη and ἔρως; these permeate existence and constitute its link to its cause, making God also the *object* of ἀγάπη and ἔρως, to whom the motion is directed—according to each human person's access to reality and longing for ever well-being.

While God is by his "substance" motionless, Maximus testifies that he is in motion: "The Divine by essence and nature is completely unmoved, insofar as it is boundless, unconditioned, and infinite, but not unlike a scientific λόγος that exists within the substances of beings, it is said to be moved, since it providentially moves each and every being (in accordance with the λόγος by which each one is naturally moved)."⁴² We could say that, as God's relationship with creation and created beings is a relationship of activity (ἐνέργεια) and not of substance (οὐσία), God's motion is merely acknowledged from our perspective, not in actual reality. However, Maximus' texts would not encourage such a purely relativistic approach: God's existence as a Trinity of persons and hypostases is testified as a motion, as a perpetual movement; God "has moved atemporally and out of love in order to arrive at the distinction of hypostases."⁴³ While the "substance" of God is described as motionless, the Trinity of his hypostases (actual existences) is described as being but in perpetual interpenetration.⁴⁴

If we are to employ the concept of motion to denote God's relationship with creation, we can only say that he *moves*, not that he *is moved* (not that he 'receives the motion').⁴⁵ To say that God is moved would only make sense in the context that he is thirsty for being the object of thirst, that he longs to be the object of longing, that he loves being the recipient of love: "Being love and ἔρως, the divine is in motion, while being the object of love and longing it draws towards itself everything that is receptive to love and ἔρως."⁴⁶ According to Maximus, we, and not God, receive the motion (πάθος κινήσεως, πάσχειν τὴν κίνησιν). And the motion of God is his disclosure to us (or, vice versa: God's disclosure to us is his motion). We are moved in order to know God:⁴⁷ God's motion constitutes the knowledge of God's ex-

---

41. Loudovikos, *Eucharistic Ontology*, 175–76.

42. *AI* 23.5 = PG91, 1260B (trans. Constas, in *Difficulties*, 2:5–6).

43. SchD, in *Diu. nom.*, 221A: "ὁ Θεὸς καὶ Πατήρ, κινηθεὶς ἀχρόνως καὶ ἀγαθοπρεπῶς καὶ ἀγαπητικῶς προῆλθεν εἰς διάκρισιν ὑποστάσεων."

44. SchD, in *Myst. theol.*, 425A:"Φησὶν οὖν ὅτι καὶ ἐν μονῇ ἀκινήτῳ ἀεὶ οὖσα ἡ θεία φύσις, δοκεῖ κινεῖσθαι ἐν τῇ ἀλλήλοις χωρήσει."

45. *AI* 10.119.7–11 = PG91, 1204D. Note that the generation and motion of beings emerges from the will, βούλησιν, and activity of God, not from his substance.

46. *AI* 23.3 = PG91, 1260C. Cf. Betsakos, Στάσις ἀεικίνητος, 97.

47. *QD* 105.12–19: "τῆς ἁγίας θεότητος κινούσης ἡμᾶς εἰς ἐπίγνωσιν ἑαυτῆς . . .

istence and God's mode of existence (τὸν τοῦ πῶς αὐτὴν ὑφεστάναι τρόπον) *for those that are receptive to this knowledge.*[48] To discern God's personal activity (ἐνέργεια) in creation, to acknowledge creation as a motion originating from God, is a *choice*. One must be *receptive* to encountering existence as the mediation of a personal relationship—as it is a *choice* to acknowledge a painting as a λόγος of its artist that founds a relationship with his otherness and not as mere sum of paint and canvas, as we have noted in our exposition of the prerequisites for a critical ontology. As a consequence, the human person's motion back to God is also a matter of *choice* and *freedom*, a motion according to man's free will: "man's movement toward spiritual communion with God is the expression of this freedom and consciousness of his: as Maximus says, it is a 'movement of free will,' and the capacity of free will (αὐτεξούσιον) is identified in his writings with man's will."[49]

Ever-Moving Repose, Stationary Movement

When using the language of *motion* and *fixity* to describe God, we must bear in mind that we are describing a relation and communion *par excellence*, as the divine hypostases exist as *persons*, i.e., insofar as they are in communion with each other: the person of the *Father* is an existential and ontological reference to the person of the *Son*, not an individual onticity, the person of the *Breath/Spirit of God* is the breath of the *Father*, etc.: "The name of 'Father' is neither the name of an essence nor an activity, but rather of a

---

Λέγεται οὖν κινεῖσθαι ἢ δι' ἡμᾶς τοὺς ἐπ' αὐτὴν κινουμένους ἢ ὡς αἰτία τῆς ἡμῶν πρὸς τὴν γνῶσιν αὐτῆς κινήσεως. Ἐκίνησεν οὖν ἑαυτὴν ἐν ἡμῖν πρὸς τὸ γνῶναι ὅτι ἔστιν τις αἰτία τῶν ὅλων· ὅπερ ἐστὶν μονάδος κινηθείσης." "The holy divinity itself moves us into an acknowledgement of itself . . . And so, it is said to be set in motion either because of us, who are set in motion towards it (the Trinity), or as the cause of our movement toward the knowledge of it. It moved itself in us toward the knowledge that some cause of all things exists. That is 'the Monad having been moved'" (trans. Prassas, in Maximus the Confessor, *Questions and Doubts*, 99).

48. *AT* 1.32–38: "But if, having heard the word 'movement,' you wonder how the divinity that is beyond eternity is moved, understand that the passivity belongs not to the divinity, but to us, who first are illuminated with respect to the λόγος of its being, and thus are enlightened with respect to the mode of its existence, for it is obvious that being is observed before the mode of being. And so, movement of divinity, which comes about through the elucidation concerning its being and its mode of existence, is established, for those who are able to receive it, as knowledge" (trans. Lollar, in Maximus the Confessor, *Ambigua to Thomas; Second Letter to Thomas*, 51). Cf. Betsakos, Στάσις ἀεικίνητος, 95.

49. Loudovikos, *Eucharistic Ontology*, 168. Cf. *DP* 301 A–C.

relation, and of the manner in which the Father is related to the Son, or the Son to the Father."⁵⁰

So, the question arises: is *motion* or *fixity* a more accurate term in order to describe such an existence-in-communion? The fact that relation is a dynamic event, not a static one, the fact that it constitutes a perpetual becoming and not a coordinated given, would advocate for the word *motion* as a more accurate term. However, *motion* implies *distance*, a *distance* that has not been covered as of yet. (Once again: these words suggest a spatio-temporality that is not characteristic of the uncreated; but they are the only *words* we have, for they emerge from the only *world* we have—and they are to be understood apophatically). And *distance* implies that a *fuller* relation and communion would be possible, for it measures *nonrelation*: distance measures the degree and extent to which the immediacy of relation has not yet been achieved, it measures how *far away* you are from something or someone. The fullness of communion and of existing-in-communion (of which the Trinity is the prototype) would not allow for any distance to be covered (through motion), as the existence of that distance would indicate that the fullness of relation and communion has not yet been achieved. This makes *motion* an unfit word.

However, *fixity* or *repose* is an equally unfit word to denote the "state" of God. A God whose hypostases, whose uncreated actualizations are described as being in perpetual interpenetration cannot be accurately described as a being in fixity and repose. The notion of a constant dynamic communion and an actualization in relation and radical referentiality is contrary to the notion of fixity, of repose, of being static and motionless. Interestingly, Maximus employs the notion of the absence of *distance* in order to declare motion as never-ending, not as inexistent: "For God is the truth toward which the mind moves continuously and enduringly, and it can never cease its motion: since it cannot find any distance (διάστημα) there, no cessation of motion can take place."⁵¹

Maximus transcends these limitations of language by writing about the "ever-moving repose" (στάσις ἀεικίνητος) and the "stationary movement" (στάσιμος ταυτοκινησία) that characterizes the communion with God.⁵² It is to be noted that this paradoxical phrase is not merely a rhetorical device or a standard phrase denoting apophaticism: it is an attempt at a *most accurate*

---

50. *AI* 26.2 = PG91, 1265D (trans. Constas, in *Difficulties*, 2:21).

51. *Myst* 5.100–102.

52. According to Maximus, nature restored in its full communion with God will arrive at an "ever-moving repose," in perpetual motion around God; *QThal* 65.544–547:"ἐν δὲ τῷ θεῷ γινομένη . . . στάσιν ἀεικίνητον ἕξει καὶ στάσιμον ταυτοκινησίαν, περὶ τὸ ταὐτὸν καὶ ἓν καὶ μόνον ἀϊδίως γινομένην."

use of language. If we are to speak about *motion* or *fixity* concerning God, concerning the "motionless" God and the "perpetually interpenetrating" Trinity of divine persons, we have to acknowledge that it is both *the fullness of motion* and *the fullness of fixity*, an understanding that transcends even the designation of being 'beyond motion.' Maximus' genius formulates this in language by speaking of the "ever-moving repose" and the "stationary movement" of those that have restored the fullness of the communion with God.

Creative Motion

As we have noted, the existence of creatures denotes simultaneously their being in motion and their birth and origination is the beginning of this motion. Apart from God's "internal motion," i.e., the interpenetration of the divine hypostases, God's creative activity is his "external motion": the creation of the world can be described as God's motion, and it is this motion that grants life and existence. Maximus does not describe this as a movement that occurs once, at the generation of the world or of each being: God's motion to the world is a continuous one, and to be separated from this motion, from this perpetual becoming, is to risk to return to the state of non-being, to risk perfect inexistence.[53] Beings exist insofar as they are moved by God[54]; nothing moves on its own, everything receives the movement from God.[55] *Being* and *being in motion* are identical; the cause of being is also the cause of motion. Everything that exists and is in motion has a cause for moving and existing, a cause that is inherent in its origination and which is also its purpose and end[56]: God is the beginning, end, origination

---

53. *Myst* 1.67–72.

54. And this motion constitutes a relation, meaning that beings exist insofar as they are in relation with God. To say that God is the source of motion (that the origin of motion lies beyond createdness) and that everything that exists is in motion (and, of course, that everything that is in motion *exists*, participates in being) is to define existing as being in some sort of relation, either a fuller relation or an inadequate one, with God, with the person(s) that is the uncreated source of being. Therefore, to sever this relationship completely is to cease to exist.

55. *AI* 7.9 = PG91, 1073B: "πάντα γὰρ ὅσα γέγονε πάσχει τὸ κινεῖσθαι, ὡς μὴ ὄντα αὐτοκίνησις ἢ αὐτοδύναμις."

56. *AI* 23.2 = PG91, 1257 CD: "Everything which is moved according to nature is necessarily moved in consequence of a cause, and everything moved in consequence of a cause necessarily also exists in consequence of a cause; and everything that exists and is moved in consequence of a cause necessarily has as the beginning of its being the cause in consequence of which it exists and from which it was initially brought into being; likewise, the end of its being moved is the same cause in consequence of which

and motion of created beings[57]; they are in motion due to him and thanks to him, and it is in him that they will be in repose. "The end and purpose of the activities according to nature is the repose at the cause of the created beings' motion."[58]

Fixity and Repose: στάσις

The fact that the beginning and cause of created beings is their origination in motion entails that their end and purpose is their repose and fixity. Maximus elucidates this by stating that nothing is in motion without a reason and a cause; the beginning of natural motion (κίνησις φυσική) is generation (γένεσις), and the beginning and cause of the generation of beings in motion is God. The end and purpose is also God; and this end and purpose entails the attainment of fixity and repose (στάσις), the annihilation of "any spatial or temporal distance"[59] (διάστημα)—i.e., the immediacy of

---

it is moved and toward which it hastens. Now everything which exists and is moved in consequence of a cause is necessarily also created, and if the end of whatever is moved is the cause in consequence of which it is in motion, this cause is necessarily the same cause in consequence of which it was created and exists. From this it follows that the cause of whatever exists and is moved, in any way at all according to nature, is one single cause encompassing both the beginning and the end, to which everything that exists and is moved owes its existence and motion" (trans. Constas, in *Difficulties*, 2:3).

57. For example, see the the interrelationship of cause, end, motion, repose and God in *AI* 15.6–7 = PG91, 1217B–D: "For no being is completely self-actualized, since it is not self-caused, and whatever is not self-caused is necessarily moved by a cause, which is to say that it is actualized by being naturally set in motion by its cause, for which and to which it continues in motion. For nothing that moves does so in any way independently of a cause. But the beginning of every natural motion is the origin (γένεσις) of the things that are moved, and the beginning of the origin of whatever has been originated is God, for he is the author of origination" (trans. Constas, *Difficulties*, 1:369).

58. *AI* 15.7–8 = PG91, 1220A: "For it was for activity that created things were brought into being, and every activity exists in relation to a particular goal, otherwise it is incomplete. For whatever does not have a goal of its natural activities is not complete, but the goal of natural activities is the repose of creaturely motion in relation to its cause. So that from one example we might understand the form of motion that obtains among all beings, take, for instance, the soul, which is an intellectual and rational substance, which thinks and reasons. Its potentiality is the intellect, its motion is the process of thinking, and its actuality is thought" (trans. Constas, *Difficulties*, 1:371). See also *AI* 7.10 = 1073C: "Τέλος γὰρ τῆς τῶν κινουμένων κινήσεως αὐτὸ τὸ ἐν τῷ ἀεὶ εὖ ἐστίν."

59. *AI* 15.7 = PG91, 1217C: "The end of the natural motion of whatever has been originated is rest (στάσις), which, after the passage beyond finite things, is produced completely by infinity, for in the absence of any spatial or temporal interval (*distance*, διάστημα), every motion of whatever is naturally moved ceases, henceforth having

relation and communion. According to nature, generation precedes motion and motion precedes repose. However, repose is not a natural activity of beings in motion, stemming from the fact that they have been generated; it is their purpose and end, which remains a mere potentiality until it is finally achieved.[60] We gather that there are two different ways of understanding fixity: (*a*) when motion, i.e., being, consummates in repose, i.e., ever being, in man's approach to God (and in ever-moving repose, i.e., ever well-being, in the full communion with God), and (*b*) its deviation, when a creature is separated from God's life-giving motion and risks slipping into non-being. Instead of coming to be κατὰ φύσιν, repose is achieved only κατὰ γνώμην, only as a free choice; the striving towards ever being (εὖ εἶναι) and ever well-being (ἀεὶ εὖ εἶναι), towards God, can only be a deliberate path, an act of freedom.[61]

Deification is the consummation of motion in repose, but this repose is described as an "ever-moving repose" (στάσις ἀεικίνητος), as we have seen and as we will further examine. In deification, the divine state of motion is iconized, as man's and God's activity (ἐνέργεια) are united, are as one: "so that through all there is only one sole ἐνέργεια, that of God and of those worthy of God, or rather of God alone, who in a manner befitting his goodness wholly interpenetrates all who are worthy."[62] Deification circumscribes an eradication of the differentiation between human and divine activity, as man is "acting in accordance with the λόγοι."[63] However, this

---

nowhere, and no means whereby, and nothing to which it could be moved, since it has attained its goal and cause, which is God, who is himself the limit of the infinite horizon that limits all motion" (trans. Constas, in *Difficulties*, 1:369).

60. *AI* 15.7 = PG91, 1217D: "Thus the beginning and end of every origin and motion of beings is God, for it is from him that they have come into being, and by him that they are moved, and it is in him that they will achieve rest. But every natural motion of beings logically presupposes their origin, just as every condition of rest logically presupposes natural motion.... For rest is not a natural activity inherent within the origin of creatures, but is rather the end of their potentiality or activity, or whatever one might wish to call it" (trans. Constas, *Difficulties*, 1:369–71).

61. *AI* 7.10 = PG91, 1073C: "If then rational beings come into being, surely they are also moved, since they move from a natural beginning in 'being' (εἶναι) toward a voluntary end in 'well-being' (εὖ εἶναι). For the end of the movement of those who are moved is 'eternal well-being' (ἀεὶ εὖ εἶναι) itself, just as its beginning is being itself which is God who is the giver of being as well as of well-being. For God is the beginning and end. From him come both our moving in whatever way from a beginning and our moving in a certain way toward him as an end" (trans. Blowers, in *CMofJCh*, 50–51).

62. *AI* 7.12 = PG91, 1076C: "ὥστε εἶναι μίαν καὶ μόνην διὰ πάντων ἐνέργειαν, τοῦ Θεοῦ καὶ τῶν ἀξίων Θεοῦ, μᾶλλον δὲ μόνου Θεοῦ, ὡς ὅλον ὅλοις τοῖς ἀξίοις ἀγαθοπρεπῶς περιχωρήσαντος" (trans. Constas, in *Difficulties*, 1:91).

63. *AI* 7.22 = PG91, 1084C.

eradication of the activities' differentiation does not entail an eradication of man's (or existence's) otherness, quite the contrary: in perfect communion, the perfect otherness of the beings-in-communion emerge. *Inconfusedly*, as they remain distinct othernesses and partners in communion and are not "swallowed up" by the divine. *Unchangeably*, as deification is not a change in nature or substance, but in mode of existence: man is deified in every sense "except of the identity of substance,"[64] as we have remarked. *Indivisibly* and *inseparably*: once attained, this new mode of existence is not to be abandoned and this fullness of communion is not to be ceased; the "ever-moving repose" will not lapse into ordinary motion any more.

Motion in Maximus and Aristotle

According to Betsakos, the philosophy of motion is, for both Maximus the Confessor and Aristotle, a potent tool for examining reality: both philosophers discern a comprehensive overview of existence in it, as motion is seen as one of the definitive components of the world, one of the modes of its existence. For both Aristotle and Maximus alike, φύσις denotes a *becoming*, not a static reality: this does not only apply to φύσις as a whole, but to the particular beings' nature as well, which is led to its end and purpose (τέλος), to its consummation. Both philosophers distinguish *potentialities* from *actualities*, the δυνάμει from the ἐνεργείᾳ, and thoroughly employ this distinction in order to interpret reality.[65] Beings exist *in relation* to other beings, and the categories of time and space are components of motion; the existence of motion is seen as their *precondition*, while they act as the *dimensions* of that motion.

To recapitulate the crucial difference of Maximus' theory of motion to that of Aristotle's would be to highlight the fact that motion, according to Maximus, is primarily a *returning* motion,[66] a motion of creation and created beings back to their Creator, back to their source. Elements of the *returning* character of motion (albeit of a mechanistic, automatic and inanimate nature) can be found in Aristotle as well, but in Maximus the returning motion is the dimension (the "horizon") of a relationship be-

---

64. *Ep1* 376AB. See also *QThal* 22.40–44.

65. As Betsakos remarks in Στάσις ἀεικίνητος, 105, the Aristotelian distinction of potentiality and actuality (δυνάμει–ἐνεργείᾳ) is also employed by Maximus: the κατὰ δύναμιν motion is included in the substance of beings, but it is the πρὸς ἐνέργειαν κίνησις that gives actuality to this potential motion. Cf. *CGn* 1084B.

66. A thorough overview of the *returning* motion with a focus on its anthropological side is to be found in Betsakos, Στάσις ἀεικίνητος, 143–209.

tween persons, a longing for communion, an ἔρως for the annulling of the distance (διάστημα) between the persons. Man's returning motion to God circumscribes the consummation of this relationship, and through the human person as a cosmic mediator, the whole of createdness, the whole of the κτίσις aspires to full communion with the divine person(s) in the manner of personhood, in the manner of existence-as-relation. Maximus' substantial difference from Aristotle is that, according to his writings, motion itself has an end and purpose (τέλος) beyond createdness: creation's returning motion towards its uncreated Creator (himself beyond motion and motionlessness) transcends the cycle of motion and is the end and purpose (τέλος) of motion itself, not only of beings-in-motion. Motion does not only lead beings towards their consummation, towards their end and purpose (τέλος), but motion *itself* has an end and purpose to be attained, namely the full communion of creation and Creator.[67]

As such, motion is a central aspect of Maximus the Confessor's cosmology, as it circumscribes the mode in which existence has been generated and exists. And the *end* and *purpose* of motion and beings-in-motion is a central aspect of the Church Father's ontology, as it discloses the meaning and true nature of beings and reality. The fact that the ontological integrity of being and beings is disclosed through their origin and cause but is consummated at their end and purpose frames the subject in question in a context of temporality, as the ontological integrity of being and beings seemingly resides in their *future*, not in their past or present. To articulate it more concisely, the atemporality of the fullness of repose for both being and beings is *to come*, integrating the element of eschatology into ontology itself.

Bibliography

Balthasar, Hans Urs von. *Cosmic Liturgy: The Universe According to Maximus the Confessor*. Translated by Brian E. Daley. A Communio Book. San Francisco: Ignatius Press, 2003.

Betsakos, Vasilios. *Στάσις ἀεικίνητος. Ἡ ἀνακαίνιση τῆς Ἀριστοτελικῆς κινήσεως στὴ θεολογία τοῦ Μαξίμου Ὁμολογητοῦ* [Ever-Moving Repose: The Renewal of Aristotelian Movement in the Theology of Maximus the Confessor]. Athens: Armos, 2006.

Blowers, Paul Marion. "Maximus the Confessor, Gregory of Nyssa, and the Concept of 'Perpetual Progress.'" *Vigiliae Christianae* 46 (1992) 151–71.

Bradshaw, David. "Time and Eternity in the Greek Fathers." *The Thomist* 70 (2006) 311–66.

Cvetković, Vladimir. "St Maximus on Πάθος and Κίνησις in Ambiguum 7." *Studia Patristica* 48 (2010) 95–104.

---

67. See ibid., 282–83.

Gersh, Stephen E. *Κίνησις Ἀκίνητος: A Study of Spiritual Motion in the Philosophy of Proclus.* Leiden: Brill, 1973.

Lampe, Geoffrey W. H., ed. *A Patristic Greek Lexicon.* 5 vols. Oxford: Oxford University Press, 1961–68.

Liddell, Henry G., et al. *A Greek-English Lexicon.* 9th ed. Oxford: Clarendon, 1968. Abbreviated as LSJ.

Loudovikos, Nikolaos. *A Eucharistic Ontology: Maximus the Confessor's Eschatological Ontology of Being as Dialogical Reciprocity.* Translated by Elizabeth Theokritoff. Brookline, MA: Holy Cross Orthodox Press, 2010.

Louth, Andrew. *Maximus the Confessor.* The Early Church Fathers. London: Routledge, 1996.

Maximus the Confessor. *Ambigua ad Iohannem.* Edited and translated by Nicholas P. Constas. In *Difficulties*, 1:62–450; 2:2–330. Abbreviated as *AI*.

———. *Ambigua ad Thomam.* Edited by Bart Janssens. CCSG 48:3–34. Abbreviated as *AT*.

———. *Ambigua to Thomas; Second Letter to Thomas.* Translated by Joshua Lollar. Corpus Christianorum in Translation 2. Turnhout: Brepols, 2009.

———. *Capita de caritate* [Four Centuries on Charity]. Edited by Aldo Ceresa-Gastaldo. In *CSC*, 48–238. Abbreviated as *CChar*.

———. *Capita theologica et oeconomica* [Gnostic Chapters]. Edited by François Combefis. PG90:1084A–173A. Abbreviated as *CGn*.

———. *De duabus unius Christi Dei nostri uoluntatibus (Theologica et polemica xvi)* [On the Two Wills of the One Christ Our God]. Edited by François Combefis. PG91:184C–212B. Abbreviated as *TP16*.

———. *Disputatio cum Pyrrho* [Dispute with Pyrrhus]. Edited by François Combefis. PG91:288A–353B. Abbreviated as *DP*.

———. *Epistula i* [Epistle 1, To the Eparch George on Sailing for Constantinople]. Edited by François Combefis. PG91:364A–92D. Abbreviated as *Ep1*.

———. *Mystagogia.* Edited by Raffaelle Cantarella. In *MAS*, 122–214. Abbreviated as *Myst*.

———. *On Difficulties in the Church Fathers: The Ambigua.* Edited and translated by Nicholas P. Constas. 2 vols. Dumbarton Oaks Medieval Library 28–29. Cambridge: Harvard University Press, 2014. Abbreviated as *Difficulties*.

———. *On the Cosmic Mystery of Jesus Christ: Selected Writings from St. Maximus the Confessor.* Translated by Paul Marion Blowers and Robert L. Wilken. St. Vladimir's Seminary Press Popular Patristics Series. Crestwood, NY: St. Vladimir's Seminary Press, 2003. Abbreviated as *CMofJCh*.

———. *Quaestiones ad Thalassium.* Edited by Carl Laga and Carlos Steel. CCSG 7:3–539; 22:3–325. Abbreviated as *QThal*.

———. *Quaestiones et dubia* [Questions and Doubts]. Edited by José H. Declerck. CCSG 10:3–170. Abbreviated as *QD*.

———. *Scholia in corpus Areopagiticum* [Scholia in Pseudo-Dionysius]. PG4:16A–184C. Abbreviated as *SchD*.

———. *Selected Writings.* Translated by George C. Berthold. Classics of Western Spirituality. New York: Paulist, 1985. Abbreviated as *SelWrts*.

———. *St. Maximos the Confessor's Questions and Doubts.* Translated by Despina D. Prassas. DeKalb: Northern Illinois University Press, 2010.

———. *Variae definitiones (Theologica et polemica xiv)* [Various Definitions]. Edited by François Combefis. PG91:149B–53B. Abbreviated as *TP14*.

Mitralexis, Sotiris. "Maximus' 'Logical' Ontology: An Introduction and Interpretative Approach to Maximus the Confessor's Notion of the Λόγοι." *Sobornost* 37 (2015) 65–82.

———. *Ever-Moving Repose: A Contemporary Reading of Maximus the Confessor's Theory of Time*. Veritas 24. Eugene, OR: Cascade, 2017.

Plass, Paul C. "Moving Rest in Maximus the Confessor." *Classica et mediaevalia* 35 (1984) 177–90.

———. "Transcendent Time and Eternity in Gregory of Nyssa." *Vigiliae Christianae* 34 (1980) 180–92.

———. "Transcendent Time in Maximus the Confessor." *The Thomist* 44 (1980) 259–77.

Sherwood, Polycarp. "Introduction." In Maximus the Confessor, *The Ascetic Life; The Four Centuries of Charity*, translated by Polycarp Sherwood, 3–102. Ancient Christian Writers 21. Westminster, MD: Newman, 1955.

Tollefsen, Torstein. "Causality and Movement in St. Maximus' *Ambiguum 7*." *Studia Patristica* 48 (2010) 85–93.

Yannaras, Christos. *The Freedom of Morality*. Translated by Elizabeth Briere. Crestwood, NY: St. Vladimir's Seminary Press, 1984.

PART II

Epistemology: Knowledge, Apophaticism, and Language

7

"A Greater and More Hidden Word": Maximos the Confessor and the Nature of Language

Maximos Constas

Maximos the Confessor never produced a systematic account of his thinking concerning the nature of language. While something like a philosophy of language can be reasonably derived from his writings, it is, as we might expect, closely connected to all the other elements of his thought. In particular, language for the Confessor is but one element in a continuous, unbroken whole encompassing the dynamics of motion, time, history, eschatology and divinization. If there is a theory of language to be found in the Confessor's writings, it is a decidedly Christian—and deeply christological—theory of language, built largely on the historical and eschatological vision of the New Testament.

It is therefore unsurprising that Maximos exhibits only minimal interest in late-antique debates about the philosophy of language.[1] However, he is quite fluent in the rules of grammar and predication, that is, in the semantic and epistemic conditions under which sentences operate and can be said to be true. For Maximos, language is rooted in logic, and there is no logic that is not an effect of ontology, and thus a kind of onto-logic. Beneath meaningful verbal expressions are laws of thought, which manifest the truth of beings, the Λόγος himself—"the Word who speaks silently through words"[2]—who

---

1. For example, whether or not words represent conventional mental constructions or concrete objects in the world; or to what extent the former are "images"; or whether speech and sound are superior to written letters, etc.; cf. Sorabji, "Philosophy of Language."

2. A phrase from Symeon the New Theologian, *Practical and Theological Chapters* 2.5.5–6: "τοῦ λόγου μόνου τοῦ ἐν τῇ φωνῇ ἀφώνως φθεγγομένου." All unattributed translations (including biblical passages) are mine.

is the foundation of all reason, logic, and language. If true propositions can be affirmed, it is because truth is not simply a conventional property of sentences and statements, but is above all a transcendental determination of being as such.

On questions of language, then, the Confessor keeps company, not with the philosophers of language, but with the grammarians and logicians, namely, the late-antique commentators on Aristotle's *Categories, On Interpretation,* and the *Prior Analytics*.[3] Possessing a virtuosic command of this tradition, Maximos produced variations on many of its themes, including his celebrated distinction between the "λόγος of being" and "mode of existence," which may very well be an ontologizing interpretation of Ammonios's grammatical distinction between "subjects" and their "modal adverbs."[4]

Gregory of Nyssa

These secular influences notwithstanding, it is clear that Maximos' understanding of language was profoundly shaped by the work of the Cappadocian Fathers, who in response to the linguistic claims of Eunomios had elaborated a sophisticated theory of language, which became firmly established within Christian discourse.[5] Maximos held the work of the two Gregories in high regard, and it will be instructive to compare Maximos' theory of language with the linguistic theory put forward by Gregory of Nyssa. Of all the Cappadocians, Nyssa produced the most sustained and sophisticated theory of language, which was a corollary of his ontology, epistemology, and metaphysics. It was also a theory that Maximos found himself in the greatest degree of tension with.

As is well known, Gregory of Nyssa endeavored to undermine the theology of Eunomios by promoting a radical and systematic division of the created and uncreated, a move that was without precedent in the Greek philosophical tradition.[6] Gregory's stark separation of God and the world

---

3. I.e., the first three works in the standard order of Aristotle's writings.

4. On which, see Barnes, "Ammonius and Adverbs." Maximos makes a similar move from the rules of predication to a grammar of divinization in *Amb.* 20.2–3; cf. Allen, "Participation and Predication in Plato's Middle Dialogues." All references to the *Ambigua* are from my edition and translation, *Difficulties*.

5. For recent overviews, see DelCogliano, *Basil of Caesarea's Anti-Eunomian Theory of Names*, 49–134; Radde-Gallwitz, *Basil of Caesarea, Gregory of Nyssa*, 96–112.

6. See, for example, Gregory of Nyssa, *Contra Eunomium* 1.1.295; *Catechetical Oration* 39. See also Mateo-Seco, "Creation"; Balthasar, *Presence and Thought*, 15–23.

had direct consequences, not simply for Christian cosmology and ontology, but also—and as Gregory had intended—for epistemology and language.

In a recent monograph on the Cappadocian theology of language, Scot Douglass signals some of these consequences in the title of his book, *Theology of the Gap*, which foregrounds the space or distance (διάστημα) between God and creation.[7] In keeping with this metaphor, Douglass pays special attention to Nyssa's extensive use of spatial imagery. He speaks of a general Cappadocian "exploitation of spatiality" (149), and describes Nyssa's theology in particular as a "poetics of spatiality" (84). He claims that Nyssa's exegesis of Scripture is "spatially-dependent" (233) and calls his spirituality a "mysticism of the gap" (236). Douglass additionally uses the Heideggerian phrase "topology of being" to characterize what he calls Nyssa's "spatially-dependent truth" (203).[8]

Douglass contends that, for Gregory, language is a symptom of the infinite gap between God and the world (62), and that language can never be anything more than a conventional, human construction; a flimsy, linguistic fig leaf concealing a "lack of presence" (71). Within Nyssa's spatially divided universe, the ultimate significance of language would seem to be its *failure* to signify, and theological language in particular is reduced to metaphors that "function architecturally" as so many "buttresses of sacred space," although in themselves they "are invariably negations" (165). Douglass sees Gregory as promoting what he calls a "positive nihilism," which left the Cappadocians with "nothing but interpretations," which could "never be grounded, and were constitutionally barred from *adiastemic* presence and essence" (196).[9]

Douglass describes Nyssa as rejecting any "state or condition of coming to rest," which he claims is "Platonic," and argues that the human person must "continue to exploit this distance in order to keep moving forward, to reconstitute himself perpetually, to continue to take the first step, which is his millionth, with no fatigue or despair that there are a billion more. The hope of eternity is the hope of eternal motion" (191). This infinite distance is of course the basis for Gregory's theology of "perpetual progress,"

7. Douglass, *Theology of the Gap*. Gregory's focus on the "gap" between God and creation was first highlighted by Balthasar, *Presence and Thought*, 27–35.

8. On which see Malpas, *Heidegger's Topology*. It seems to me that Heidegger's *Topologie des Seins* corresponds more closely to Maximos' notion of θέσις (i.e., place/placing) than to διάστημα, and suggests a potentially fruitful area for comparative study.

9. Douglass acknowledges, however, that such a reductive theory of language is only a partial view of the matter: "Such a stance, useful in refuting a rival's theology, cannot be the final word from the Cappadocians on the potential use of language . . . if they are to avoid a radical agnosticism and the absolute frustration of their deepest desires (i.e., to know God)." Douglass, *Theology of the Gap*, 87.

which is the fate of creatures caught within a condition of becoming, lacking any fixed point or permanence. The notion of ἐπέκτασις (cf. Phil 3:13, "ἐπεκτεινόμενος"), which is generally accepted as the signature element of Gregory's spirituality, insures that this distance will never be overcome, that the gap will never be crossed, so that, like Moses on Sinai, we shall perpetually advance toward the perpetually receding back parts of God (cf. Exod 33:23).

What is so obviously missing from Gregory's "theology of the gap" is a coherent and effective strategy for *bridging* the gap. On Douglass's reading, Nyssa established a division that he was unable to overcome, for by systematically emphasizing the difference between God and the world he paid comparatively little attention to their potential (albeit qualified) identity. Nyssa's totalizing doctrine of divine transcendence is not balanced by an equally robust doctrine of divine immanence, with rather withering consequences for human thought and language, which are denied ontological depth.

Nyssa's "theology of the gap" was of course conditioned by the polemical context in which he was writing, but it was also the result of an insufficiently developed Christology. Douglass puts it this way: "The Incarnation does little to bridge the gap, since it was an affirmation of distance and instability," inasmuch as the Λόγος "sets in motion an infinite discourse not grounded in stability," and indeed "sanctifies the instability of creation" (158).

Even more to the point is Nyssa's muted doctrine of divinization, which follows from his ontology, since any emphasis on human participation in divine life would have obscured the fundamental division between God and the world, which was central to his polemic.[10] What little Gregory says about divinization is not grounded in the kind of participatory cosmology articulated by Maximos, for whom creation exists because it shares in (μετέχειν) the life of the Λόγος. By grafting this participatory worldview, that is, the doctrine of the λόγοι, onto Christology, Maximos effectively integrated cosmology into the framework of the divine economy.[11] Ultimately, the

10. See Balás, "Deification," 212: "That Gregory, starting with his controversy with Eunomius, avoids the terminology of the deification of the human being . . . can be easily understood: he wanted to keep clear of anything that could have obscured the fundamental division between creatures and the Triune God." See Russell, *Doctrine of Deification*, 226: "He (Gregory of Nyssa), appeals to the doctrine of deification very rarely. Deification for the bishop of Nyssa refers primarily to the transformation of the flesh assumed by the Son at the Incarnation . . . and secondarily to man's participation in the divine perfections."

11. On this question, see the important monograph by Tollefsen, *The Christocentric Cosmology*.

Confessor's theology of the hypostatic union as a περιχώρησις of the created and the uncreated in the person of the incarnate Word provided him with the dialectic of identity and difference that is lacking in Gregory of Nyssa.[12] This more integral approach endowed language with expansive analogical possibilities, because between language and its foundation in the eternal Λόγος there was now a relationship of metaphysical causality. Among other things, this enabled Maximos to maintain that the incarnate Λόγος had embodied himself, not simply in the flesh or in creation more generally, but in the very letters and sounds of language itself.[13]

I am not suggesting that Gregory of Nyssa and Maximos the Confessor did not share common beliefs, ideas, and terminology. Instead, I am drawing attention to the basic principles from which each thinker begins and to which he gives characteristic emphasis. To be sure, one cannot expect to find in a fourth-century writer the same subtle synthesis of Christology and theoretical ontology that is found in the seventh-century writings of Maximos the Confessor. The theological developments of several centuries enabled the Confessor to build on the Christology of the Councils of Ephesus (431), Chalcedon (451), and Constantinople (553), as well as on the metaphysics of participation articulated by Proclus Diadochos and Dionysios the Areopagite, none of which was available to Gregory of Nyssa.

Gregory of Nyssa and Maximos the Confessor

Douglass may be overstating his case, or may have failed to grasp the whole of Gregory's theological vision, but his findings accord with the work of several other scholars. Paul Blowers, for example, in one of the few comparative studies of Maximos and Nyssa, reached essentially the same conclusions.[14] Blowers does not take up the question of language, be he directly addresses the ontological and metaphysical structures in which langauge is embedded. Blowers demonstrates the extent to which Maximos "reworked Gregory's theology" and "circumvented his proposal of an eternally positive mutability" (158). This was necessary, Blowers argues, because Gregory's theology ran the risk of "grounding the ontological stability of rational beings solely on their own, uncertain, moral movements" (158). In response to

---

12. For alternative interpretations, cf. Perl, "Methexis," who sees greater continuity between Nyssa and Maximos; and Boersma, "Overcoming Time and Space."

13. See *AI* 33.2: "Or one could say that the Λόγος 'becomes thick' in the sense that, for the sake of our thick minds, he consented to be both embodied and expressed through letters, syllables, and sounds."

14. Blowers, "Maximus the Confessor, Gregory of Nyssa."

Gregory's doctrine of "perpetual progress" and its corollary of perpetually deferred meaning, Maximos recovered the Origenist ideal that the aspirations of rational beings will "culminate in a real condition of rest, a once-for-all stabilization" (163).

Polycarp Sherwood and Lars Thunberg, comparing the different evaluations of διάστημα found in Nyssa and Maximos, had earlier reached more or less the same conclusions.[15] According to these scholars, Maximos obviously accepts the basic difference between creator and creation but approached the concept differently. Both scholars note, for example, that διάστημα for Maximos is intimately connected, not with space, but with motion, and that motion is central to the whole of his philosophical and theological system. Thunberg in particular emphasizes Maximos' strategies for overcoming distances and divisions, and argues that on certain levels of human and divine experience, such distances disappear altogether.[16] Because διάστασις exists in a relative relation to στάσις, "distance" is overcome in the dynamic of divinization, that is, in the communication of divine properties to human beings. While a basic, natural διάστημα in relation to God remains, human beings participate in the perichoretic, non-distanced character of the hypostatic union of distinguished but not separated natures, activities, and wills.

It seems clear, then, that Nyssa's emphasis on division and spatial distance ran contrary to the tendency of Maximos' theology, which was not about division but union, in particular the communion of difference and identity. This is perhaps most strongly evident in *AI* 41, where the famous five divisions (including that of created and uncreated) are overcome and united in the person of the incarnate Word. Maximos' focus on unity and identity made him less interested in a "poetics of space" and encouraged something more like a "poetics of time," encompassing the historical and metaphysical movement of creatures toward the creator. Gregory's ontology of a radical disjunction between God and creation, on the other hand, created a boundary that was impossible to traverse even with infinite effort. For Maximos, however, *within* the ultimate division between God and God's creation are multiple levels of being in eternal analogy to God,

---

15. Sherwood, in fact, had corrected von Balthasar on this point, charging that the latter had "minimized the difference between Gregory of Nyssa and Maximos." See Thunberg, *Microcosm and Mediator*, 58n64, citing Sherwood, *Earlier Ambigua*, 109.

16. Thunberg, *Microcosm and Mediator*, 58, citing Maximos, *Ep2* 396CD: "According to the principle of nature, we are all, as it were, one nature, and thus we are able to have one inclination and one will with God and with one another, not having any distance (διάστασις) from God or one another, whenever by the law of grace, through which by our inclination the law of nature is renewed, we choose one and the same thing."

insuring that each being is grounded in its proper location in the cosmic order, which is also its mode of participation. Moreover, the intentionality of the divine mind for creatures, the divine "wills" for creation (*AI* 7.24), are mirrored in the intentionality of human reason, both of which are drawn together through mutual yearning, so that "God and man are paradigms of each other" (*AI* 10.9), bound together in a relationship of real reciprocity.[17] Nyssa's muted doctrine of divinization, mentioned a moment ago, hardly compares to the far-reaching synthesis articulated by Maximos, for whom Tabor transcends Sinai, just as ἔκστασις surpasses ἐπέκτασις.[18]

Embedded within these different understandings of God and the world are different theories of language. Linguistic theories always already have ontological presuppositions, or at the very least, implications. In the context of his debate with Eunomios, Nyssa insisted on the conventional nature of language, which he believed was a human construction, a cultural artifact having no ontological relationship to signified objects or beings.[19] In a different context, and without this particular polemical constraint, Maximos is much closer to Dionysios, who wrote a treatise on "divine names" that are given by God in creation and that point back toward the Giver. In a way that is without parallel in Nyssa, language for Maximos both reveals

---

17. According to Maximos, the incarnate God and divinized man are caught up in a relationship of mutual causality, so that God's incarnation in the human virtues is the effect of a human cause. Man is God's image, yet God has accepted to make this image his own image, and thus by creating and giving identity to beings, and ultimately by becoming a human being, God simultaneously accepts to *receive* an identity. Through the Incarnation, God and man have the capacity, through love, to become each other. It should also be noted that the idea of a common, divine-human paradigm is already built into the model of the body-soul relationship as a paradigm of the union of divinity and humanity in Christ (cf. *AI* 7).

18. Which is to say that Gregory's notion of perpetual progress maintains the creature in its fixed state of natural being, allowing it to advance incrementally without any fundamental change to its existential structure, whereas the doctrine of "ecstasy" requires a fundamental "going outside of oneself," a passive assumption of the self by the greater reality of God, expressed most cogently in Maximos' remarks on Paul's ascent to the third heaven in *AI* 20.2–3.

19. It would be worth studying Maximos' use of ἐπίνοια, which is markedly different from the way Nyssa uses this word. Normally translated as "notion" or "concept" in the sense of an abstract, rational construct, Maximos uses the word to mean something more like a "concrete principle," and not a mere mental abstraction; cf. *AI* 31.9, 32.4, 62.2; and *QThal* 63.156–57, where Maximos, referring to the incarnate Word, uses the phrase "κατὰ τὴν ἐπίνοιαν τῆς ἀνθρωπότητος." In my translation of the *Ambigua*, I regret not translating these terms consistently, but in the second printing they will all be rendered as "principle." For a discussion of this term in the later Byzantine period, and with specific reference to Maximos the Confessor, see Demetracopoulos, "Palamas Transformed."

and conceals.[20] Epistemology and ontology are intertwined in concurrent descending and ascending movements of negation and affirmation through both perceptible and conceptual phenomena. If for Gregory, all language is equally inappropriate to name the being of God, Maximos (following Dionysios) is able to identify and distinguish levels of appropriateness, for language is part of the divine gift of creation and manifests the divine presence while simultaneously signaling its transcendence. Participation and analogy are integral to Maximos' understanding of language, guaranteeing a relation as much as the distance and difference that prevents the relation from collapsing into absolute identification.[21]

Language and Eschatology

It is well established that, for Maximos, eschatology and divinization are virtually identical, and together are constitutive of his overall thinking, and as such must also be constitutive of his thinking about language. The remainder of this paper will explore this hypothesis in a number of key texts.

At first glance, Maximos seems to present us with something similar to the traditional structuralist distinction between synchronic and diachronic aspects of language.[22] The synchronic approach understands language as a timeless system informed by fixed laws known as a "general grammar," through which the plenitude of meaning is always already present. The synchronic paradigm represents a kind of spatial logic, a field of signs in which the intelligible content of language is immediately available, like the simultaneous presence of forms on the surface of a painting.

The diachronic approach, on the other hand, views language (and its meaning) as a series of sequential speech-acts that follow one another in time, an evolving succession of signifiers whose meaning is available only in and through the history. Here the model is obviously linear, unfolding in a decidedly forward-moving direction.

Both of these approaches can be found in the writings of Maximos. My sense, however, is that, given the constitutive role of motion in Maximos' cosmology and anthropology, we need to pay special attention to the diachronic dimension, which is often embedded within seemingly synchronic frameworks.

---

20. See for example, *AT* 5.5, and *AI* 10.28–34.

21. Here I am indebted to the work of Jones, *A Genealogy of Marion's Philosophy of Religion*, ch. 2.

22. For what follows, see de Saussure, *Course in General Linguistics*, parts 2–3.

The Book of Creation

Here it will suffice to focus on the celebrated image of the "Book of Creation" in *AI* 10.31–35. In this passage, Maximos compares the world to a book, contending that the physical elements of creation function like words in a sentence, because the Word has "inscribed" or "imprinted" himself on the parchment of visible phenomena. To understand these words, readers have only to open their noetic eyes, look into the book, and begin reading. Somewhat unusually, the diachronic character of reading as a linear and sequential experience does not seem to apply to the book of creation, the inner meaning of which is synchronically present to the mind.

We might be tempted to see in this kind of spatial model, in which intelligible content is lurking somewhere just above or below the sensible surface, a vestige of Platonism. However, Maximos himself largely obviates such an interpretation by conflating the spatial metaphor of "above" with Paul's belief that we shall "meet the Lord in the air," that is, at a point in the future, in the dawning of the ἔσχατον (1 Thess 4:17 NIV).[23] The Confessor's eschatological vision is in fact far more pervasive than we might expect, and even the seemingly static model of the cosmic book can, I believe, be fairly understood in eschatological terms.

In the first place, it is helpful to recall that Maximos introduces the metaphor of the book in the course of "contemplating" the Transfiguration of Christ, an eschatological revelation *par excellence*.[24] In addition, there is an intriguing parallel to Maximos' metaphor in the work of the sixth-century writer, Kosmas Indicopleustes. In Kosmas's *Christian Topography*, which was heavily illustrated, Christ appears at the celestial summit of the universe, his features imprinted in the parchment-skin canopy of the firmament (figure 1).[25]

---

23. QThal 50.46–63.

24. Cf. Dionysios, *On the Divine Names* 1.4, 114.7–115.1: "Then (i.e., in the ἔσχατον), when we shall be incorruptible and immortal, and will have come at last to that Christlike and most blessed repose, then, as Scripture says, 'we will always be with the Lord' (1 Thes 4:17), through all-pure contemplations, with the visible manifestation of God covering us with glory, as the disciples in the most Divine Transfiguration (cf. Mt 17:1–8; Mk 9:2–8), and participating in his gift of spiritual light."

25. For a recent study of this manuscript, see Kominko, *The World of Kosmas*, 184–87; cf. Kessler, "Gazing at the Future."

Figure 1. The Universe, ninth-century illuminated edition of Kosmas Indicopleustes, *Christian Topography*, Vaticanus graecus 699, fol. 43r.

At first glance, this might appear to be yet another spatial construal of the relation of God to creation, with God above and the earth below. However, what appears to be synchronically "above" is in fact a reality that is decidedly "ahead," that is, coming to us diachronically from the future. This is because Kosmas's map of the universe is modeled directly on the plan of the Tabernacle, so that the scroll of the heavens is in fact the veil of the Holy of Holies. In a subsequent image, figure 2, we see a cross-section of the same model but this time in its lateral form. The upper portion represents the "Holy of Holies," which symbolizes the age to come; the lower portion represents the "Holy Place," a symbol of the present age. The effusive inscription at the top of the plan reads: "The second tabernacle, the holy of holies, the kingdom of the heavens, the future world, the second state, the place of the righteous."[26] The inscription at the bottom reads: "The present world, in which are angels and men, and the present state."[27]

---

26. "Ἡ δευτέρα σκηνή, τὰ ἅγια τῶν ἁγίων, ἡ βασιλεία τῶν οὐρανῶν, ὁ μέλλων κόσμος, ἡ δευτέρα κατάστασις, ὁ τόπος τῶν δικαίων."

27. "Ὁ κόσμος οὗτος, ἐν ᾧ εἰσιν νῦν ἄγγελοι καὶ ἄνθρωποι καὶ ἡ νῦν κατάστασις."

Figure 2. Plan of the Tabernacle (side view of the universe), Vaticanus graecus 699, fol. 108r.

A related image from the same manuscript depicts the Second Coming (figure 3). Christ appears in the Holy of Holies, sitting in judgment, his eschatological presence mediated through the veil of the heavens. Below him (or better, in front of him) are angels, human beings, and the souls of the dead rising from their graves.[28] The inscription on either side of Christ is taken from the Judgment Parable in Matthew 25:34: "Come, O blessed of my Father, inherit the kingdom that has been prepared for you."

---

28. These figures are identified with phrases from Phil 2:10: "in heaven and on earth and under the earth" (NRSV).

Figure 3. The Second Coming of Christ, Vaticanus graecus 699, fol. 89r.

Kosmas's map of the universe suggests that seemingly spatial and synchronous realities may in fact unfold on a linear, diachronic plane in a process of becoming that will be fully realized only in the ἔσχατον, with the advent of Christ. Man progresses to God by advancing through the veil of the temple of creation, and through the same membrane God progresses to man, imprinting himself, as it were, in the forms of the visible world.[29] Kosmas's image of Christ imprinted on the parchment skin of the heavens (cf. Ps 103:2; Rev 6:14) presents us with a striking parallel to Maximos' parchment-book of creation, which is the catalyst of his universe, its generative center, where the material and the immaterial—a present semblance and a future fulfillment—converge in a unity without confusion.

"A Greater and More Hidden Word"

However we choose to evaluate the eschatological overtones of the cosmic book, Maximos elsewhere aligns language directly with history and eschatology. Again, one example will have to suffice, namely, *AI* 21. In this eschatological *tour de force*, Maximos delineates the relationship between this age and the age to come, in such a way that Scripture, man, and the unfolding of the divine economy are united in the diachronic framework

---

29. For a detailed discussion of this theme, see Constas, "St. Symeon of Thessaloniki," 163–83.

of "shadow, image, and truth" (Hebr 10:1). This threefold framework is inspired by Hebrews 10:1: "The law has but a shadow of the good things to come, instead of the true image of the realities (πράγματα)," which is also cited by Kosmas (who retains the word πράγμα, which Maximos has replaced with ἀλήθεια).[30]

In *AI* 21, Maximos contends that the written words of both the Old Testament and the New Testament are an "elementary" or "elemental" exposition (στοιχείωσις), communicating a present grace while simultaneously (and iconically) pointing to a future one.[31] Whereas the future promise of the Old Testament is manifested in the New Testament, the promise of the New Testament will be fully realized only in the ἔσχατον, with the Second Coming of Christ. The words of the Old Testament point to the Word made flesh and are fulfilled in him. The words of the New Testament point to a future word, the fulness of the truth, which has not yet been revealed.

Maximos carries this idea further, and argues that, just as the words of the four Gospels are "elementary introductions" to the eschatological world, so too are the four virtues (prudence, courage, chastity, and justice) the "elements" of the spiritual world, all of which prepare us for and lead us to the future age, enabling us to receive the Word to come (*AI* 21.5–12). This idea of the elements is further applied to the powers of the soul and the bodily senses. When the senses discern the presence of the λόγοι in visible realities, they convey them to the mind, like words in a book, enabling the mind to "read" the Λόγος inscribed therein (*AI* 21.7). Together with the virtues, the synthesis that flows from this makes us receptive to the world of the age to come. The final synthesis of the virtues into love is the consummation of the movement from shadows to truth, which is deification, through which human beings become "living images of Christ and Christ himself" (*AI* 21.15).

The locus of this eschatological movement is the hypostatic union of the incarnate Word as flesh and spirit, humanity and divinity, for he himself is the cosmic word, sign, symbol, and sacramental mystery, and thus a "forerunner of himself" (*AI* 21.15–16), or as Maximos puts it in *AI* 10.77: "He became both a type and a symbol of himself," so that the diachronic structure of movement from present to future, from image to truth, and from history to what is beyond history, is marked out by the two advents of the Word, recapitulated in Christ, the great cosmic *signum*, both signifier

---

30. E.g., Kosmas Indicopleustes, *Christian Topography* 5.4, where the "image" corresponds to the Christian sacraments, such as baptism, the "reality" of which will be manifested in the resurrection of the dead.

31. Cf. Origen, *Commentary on John* 13.5.30: "I think that all of the Scriptures, even when perceived very accurately, are only very elementary rudiments of (στοιχεῖά τινα ἐλάχιστα) and very brief introductions to all knowledge."

and signified, who both inhabits our words and us forward to a "greater and more hidden word" (*AI* 21.16).

Bibliography

Allen, Reginald Edgar. "Participation and Predication in Plato's Middle Dialogues." *Philosophical Review* 69 (1960) 147–64.

Balás, David L. "Deification." In *The Brill Dictionary of Gregory of Nyssa*, edited by Lucas Francisco Mateo-Seco and Giulio Maspero, translated by Seth Cherney, 210–13. Leiden: Brill, 2010.

Balthasar, Hans Urs von. *Presence and Thought: Essay on the Religious Philosophy of Gregory of Nyssa*. Translated by Mark Sebanc. A Communio Book. San Francisco: Ignatius Press, 1995.

Barnes, Jonathan. "Ammonius and Adverbs." In "Aristotle and the Later Tradition," edited by Henry J. Blumenthal and Howard Robinson, supplement, *Oxford Studies in Ancient Philosophy* (1991) 145–63.

Blowers, Paul Marion. "Maximus the Confessor, Gregory of Nyssa, and the Concept of 'Perpetual Progress.'" *Vigiliae Christianae* 46 (1992) 151–71.

Boersma, Hans. "Overcoming Time and Space: Gregory of Nyssa's Anagogical Theology." *Journal of Early Christian Studies* 20 (2012) 575–612.

Constas, Nicholas. "St. Symeon of Thessaloniki and the Theology of the Icon Screen." In *Thresholds of the Sacred: Architectural, Art Historical, Liturgical, and Theological Perspectives on Religious Screens, East and West*, edited by Sharon Gerstel, 163–83. Washington, DC: Dumbarton Oaks Research Library and Collection, 2006.

DelCogliano, Mark. *Basil of Caesarea's Anti-Eunomian Theory of Names: Christian Theology and Late-Antique Philosophy in the Fourth-Century Trinitarian Controversy*. Supplements to Vigiliae Christianae 103. Leiden: Brill, 2010.

Demetracopoulos, John A. "Palamas Transformed: Palamite Interpretations of the Distinction between God's 'Essence' and 'Energies' in Late Byzantium." In *Greeks, Latins, and Intellectual History, 1204–1500*, edited by Martin Hinterberger and Chris Schabel, 263–372. Leuven: Peeters, 2011.

Douglass, Scot. *Theology of the Gap: Cappadocian Language Theory and the Trinitarian Controversy*. American University Studies 235. New York: P. Lang, 2005.

Jones, Tamsin. *A Genealogy of Marion's Philosophy of Religion: Apparent Darkness*. Bloomington: Indiana University Press, 2011.

Kessler, Herbert L. "Gazing at the Future: The Parousia Miniature in Vaticanus graecus 699." In *Byzantine East, Latin West: Art-Historical Studies in Honor of Kurt Weitzmann*, edited by Doula Mouriki-Charalambous et al., 365–76. Princeton: Princeton University Press.

Kominko, Maja. *The World of Kosmas: Illustrated Byzantine Codices of the Christian Topography*. Cambridge: Cambridge University Press, 2013.

Malpas, Jeff. *Heidegger's Topology: Being, Place, World*. Cambridge: MIT Press, 2006.

Mateo-Seco, Lucas Francisco. "Creation." In *The Brill Dictionary of Gregory of Nyssa*, edited by Lucas Francisco Mateo-Seco and Giulio Maspero, translated by Seth Cherney, 183–90. Leiden: Brill, 2010.

Maximus the Confessor. *Ambigua ad Iohannem*. Edited and translated by Nicholas P. Constas. In *Difficulties*, 1:62–450; 2:2–330. Abbreviated as *AI*.

——. *Ambigua ad Thomam*. Edited and translated by Nicholas P. Constas. In *Difficulties*, 1:2–58. Abbreviated as *AT*.

——. *Epistula ii* [Epistle 2, To John the Chamberlain]. Edited by François Combefis. PG91:392D–408C. Abbreviated as *Ep2*.

——. *On Difficulties in the Church Fathers: The Ambigua*. Edited and translated by Nicholas P. Constas. 2 vols. Dumbarton Oaks Medieval Library 28–29. Cambridge: Harvard University Press, 2014. Abbreviated as *Difficulties*.

——. *Quaestiones ad Thalassium*. Edited by Carl Laga and Carlos Steel. CCSG 7:3–539; 22:3–325. Abbreviated as *QThal*.

Perl, Eric David. "Methexis: Creation, Incarnation, Deification in Saint Maximus Confessor." PhD diss., Yale University, 1991.

Radde-Gallwitz, Andrew. *Basil of Caesarea, Gregory of Nyssa, and the Transformation of Divine Simplicity*. Oxford: Oxford University Press, 2009.

Russell, Norman. *The Doctrine of Deification in the Greek Patristic Tradition*. Oxford: Oxford University Press, 2004.

Saussure, Ferdinand de. *Course in General Linguistics*. Edited by Charles Bally and Albert Sechehaye in collaboration with Albert Riedlinger. Translated by Wade Baskin. Rev. ed. London: Fontana, 1974.

Sherwood, Polycarp. *The Earlier Ambigua of Saint Maximus the Confessor and His Refutation of Origenism*. Studia Anselmiana, philosophica theologica. Rome: "Orbis Catholicus"/Herder, 1955.

Sorabji, Richard. "Philosophy of Language." In *The Philosophy of the Commentators, 200–600 AD: A Sourcebook*, edited by Richard Sorabji, 3:205–49. Ithaca: Cornell University Press, 2005.

Symeon the New Theologian. *Practical and Theological Chapters* [Capita theologica]. Translated by Jean Darrouzès. In *Chapitres théologiques, gnostiques et pratiques*, 40–186. Sources chrétiennes 51. Paris: Cerf, 1957.

Thunberg, Lars. *Microcosm and Mediator: The Theological Anthropology of Maximus the Confessor*. 2nd ed. Chicago: Open Court, 1995.

Tollefsen, Torstein. *The Christocentric Cosmology of St. Maximus the Confessor*. Oxford Early Christian Studies. Oxford: Oxford University Press, 2008.

8

Both Mere Man and Naked God: The Incarnational Logic of Apophasis in St. Maximus the Confessor

Jordan Daniel Wood

Introduction

If, as Martin Heidegger alleged,[1] the god of the philosophers is but an acquisitive attempt to master (and so mask) Being's ontological difference from beings, what becomes of the claim to know and speak of God at all? Hence the "apophatic rage," which whirls in Heidegger's wake like a typhoon drawing upon the waters of Dionysian negative theology.[2] Yet it is surprising that St. Maximus, the great expositor of the Areopagite's thought for both East and West, hasn't received much scholarly attention on exactly this point. A comparative study of Dionysius and Maximus has been undertaken by few,[3] and only a few more have compared the specific theme of ἀπόφασις in the two thinkers.[4] Those who have are immediately

---

1. Heidegger, "The Onto-theo-logical Constitution of Metaphysics."

2. See the collection of essays, edited by Coakley and Stang, titled *Re-thinking Dionysius the Areopagite*. Especially see Coakley's "Introduction" for a brief resume of the contemporary "apophatic rage" (an epithet of Martin Laird, OSA) and Tamsin Jones' essay "Dionysius in Hans Urs von Balthasar and Jean-Luc Marion," on a particularly notable example of one such retrieval of Dionysius, that of Jean-Luc Marion.

3. Balthasar, *Cosmic Liturgy*, 115–27; Völker, "Einfluss," 331–50; Louth, *Maximus the Confessor*, 28–32.

4. Balthasar, *Cosmic Liturgy*, 81–96; Louth, *Maximus the Confessor*, 52–56; Thunberg, *Microcosm and Mediator*, 406–14; esp. de Andia, "Transfiguration et théologie

struck by the unique interlacement of apophaticism and Incarnation in Maximus' complex theology.[5] Before an exhaustive comparison of the two luminaries can occur, though, one needs to attend to the specific articulation of ἀπόφασις in each. Here I assay a contribution to this task as regards Maximus.

If Maximus betrays his originality in the way he binds speech about God to speech about the Incarnation of divine Speech, Christ the Incarnate Word, then one might rightly expect an idiosyncrasy in his Christology to effect an idiosyncrasy in his ἀπόφασις. This it does, I argue. Three decades ago, Pierre Piret noted an innovation in Maximus' articulation of traditional christological formulae, specifically in his oft-employed tripartite formula: the Person of Christ exists not only "out of two natures" (ἐκ δύο φύσεων) and "in two natures" (ἐν δύο φύσεσιν) (as much post-Chalcedonian Christology put it), but, adds Maximus, "*is* two natures" ("αἱ φυσεῖς ἐστιν ὁ Χριστός").[6] The peculiar emphasis on identity (Maximus' "is") is a semantic innovation that signals an epistemic innovation wrought by the Incarnation. Divine and human natures are not only incommensurably different while perichoretically unified, but ineffably *identical* in Christ. An identity of this order breaks upon new heights of divine transcendence. God is not merely transcendent, nor merely immanent, but is mysteriously the identity of both, and this renders him all the more transcendent. Put in terms of apophatic theology: Christ *is* the knowable and the unknowable, the affirmed and the negated, and it is precisely this "is" that at once manifests and conceals the proper ineffability of divine nature (for what conceivable being is, by nature, both?). Divine ineffability is thereby radicalized, relativized, and radicalized anew by the incarnational logic of Maximian ἀπόφασις.

I proceed in three moves. The initial section treats a rarity in Maximus' corpus—an extensive commentary on one of Dionysius's most important

---

négative," 293–328; and most recently Williams, Williams, *Denying Divinity*, ch. 5.

5. Ysabel de Andia notes how "le mystère du Christ" lies for Maximus "au centre ... de la théologie mystique, et plus précisément l'union hypostatique des deux natures" ("Transfiguration et théologie négative," 309). Williams thinks the *perichoretic* intertwining of apophatic and cataphatic speech in Maximus notes "how closely Maximus' visions of theological speech and of Christology were connected." See Williams, "Incarnational Apophasis," 633. McFarland resources Maximus to argue that "the more authentically apophatic one is, the more christocentric one will be (and vice versa)." See McFarland, "Developing an Apophatic Christocentrism," 200.

6. Piret, "Christologie et théologie trinitaire," 215–22. Though primarily concerned with Maximus' Epistles (esp. *Ep12* and *Ep15*) and *Opuscula*, Piret notes, "Un second signe de l'importance de cette formule est sa fréquence, et plus exactement sa permanence, dans l'ensemble de l'oeuvre de Maxime." See Piret, "Christologie et théologie trinitaire," 215.

epistles (*AT* 5). Maximus' fascinating interpretation yields the insight that the most truly innovative element of the divine Incarnation was that the "modes" of divine and human natures were innovated (not destroyed) *by being identical* in Christ. Hence the question arises concerning the prospective impact such Christology might have on ἀπόφασις, an impact already detectable in Maximus' peculiar reversal of the cataphatic-apophatic dialectic. The following two sections respond more directly. I first argue that Maximus' identification of absolute identity on the level of hypostasis nullifies any attempted reconciliation of the created and the uncreated on the level of natures. Thence Maximus' radical ἀπόφασις. Finally, I contend that the same hypostatic identity which underwrites and radicalizes natural difference also relativizes it; for though God's nature remains utterly unknown, *he* is known personally—hypostatically, as it were—through his human nature (objectively) and through faith (subjectively). Yet this very fact, that in Christ God is unknown and known, means that God is supremely known *as* unknown, supremely ineffable. That the unknowable is known, that Christ is the symbolized and the symbol, is at once the most fundamental justification for the apophatic-cataphatic dialectic as well as the indelible mark of its sheer ineptitude in knowing God.

Incarnation as Innovation of Divine Transcendence

Incarnation as Innovation

Perhaps many erred in their interpretation of Dionysius's talk of Christ's "theandric activity" because they read his letter backwards.[7] Or perhaps they only read the last few lines. Whichever, Maximus' exposition of Dionysius's *Fourth Letter* offers a corrective not simply by imposing an "orthodox" structure on it, but by reading it in order from start to finish.[8] Two aspects of the Incarnation were at the time incontrovertible: it instituted something new, and this newness was patently manifest in its union of divine and human natures. The *mode* of union (and so the character of innovation), however, was not always clear. Along this vein Maximus' explication of Dionysius sought to ward off any notion of composite "synthesis" as the character of the christological innovation (à la monophysitism, and espe-

---

7. Dionysius the Areopagite, *Epistle* 4 17-20: "by the fact of being God-made-man he accomplished something new in our midst—the activity of the God-man (ἀλλ' ἀνδρωθέντος θεοῦ, καινὴν τινὰ τὴν θεανδρικὴν ἐνέργειαν ἡμῖν πεπολιτευμένος)." Greek text according to CD 2, translation of Colm Luibhéid, in Pseudo-Dionysius the Areopagite, *Pseudo-Dionysius: The Complete Works*, 265.

8. Bellini, "Maxime interprète du Pseudo-Denys," 42.

cially monenergism).⁹ The "theandric activity" of the God-Man was not the activity of a monstrous hybrid, but of something else altogether.

Dionysius's letter begins with an inquiry about how Jesus was "in the entirety of his essence," truly man.¹⁰ After affirming, with Dionysius, the full humanity of Christ, Maximus' fundamental concern surges to fore: full man, but not "mere man," "for this would be to divide the union that transcends thought (τὴν ὑπὲρ ἔννοιαν ἕνωσιν)." Neither is Christ "naked God," since this would come to the same (*AT* 5.3). But "out of his infinite longing for human beings," says Maximus, "he has become truly and according to nature the very thing for which he longed," and so human nature was "united to him according to hypostasis (ἑνωθείσης αὐτῷ καθ' ὑπόστασιν)" (*AT* 5.4). In his very person (ὑπόστασις) Christ is both God and man *by nature* (*AT* 5.20, 24), and the contemplation of this identity elicits Maximus' first outburst of bewilderment at the newly revealed depths of divine transcendence, poignantly expressed in apophatic terms:

> His own Incarnation, which was granted a birth beyond being, was more incomprehensible than every mystery. As much as he became comprehensible through the fact of his birth, by so much more do we now know him to be incomprehensible precisely because of that birth (τοσοῦτον καταληπτὸς δι' αὐτὴν γεγονὼς ὅσῳ πλέον ἐγνώσθη δι' αὐτῆς ἀπληπτότερος) ... what could be a more compelling demonstration of the Divinity's transcendence of being? For it discloses its concealment by means of a manifestation, its ineffability through speech, and its transcendent unknowability through the mind, and, to say what is greatest of all, it shows itself beyond being by entering essentially into being. (*AT* 5.5)

An amalgam of natures, even if ghastly, would at least be understandable. But a real identity of natures which also preserves their absolute difference—this inspires wonder and reconfigures the horizon of divine transcendence. Maximus again evokes Dionysius, but from a different epistle: "'For he remains hidden even after his manifestation,' says the teacher, 'or, to speak more divinely, he remains hidden *in* his manifestation. For the mystery remains concealed by Jesus, and can be drawn out by no word or mind, for even when spoken of, it remains ineffable, and when conceived,

---

9. Uthemann, "Das anthropologische Modell," 229–32.

10. *AT* 5.1–2: "αὐτὸ κατ' οὐσίαν ὅλην ἀληθῶς ἄνθρωπος ὤν." Unless otherwise noted, the Greek and English, as well as the precise enumeration of the *Ambigua* (both to Thomas and to John) come from the edition of Nicholas Constas (referred to in this volume as *Difficulties*).

unknown."[11] That the incomprehensible is also comprehensible, the unknown, known, the concealed, manifested—this itself reveals just how opaque is the divine darkness, how impenetrable its nature.[12]

Incarnation as Identity of Opposites

It is only after observing Dionysius's doctrine of the full humanity and full divinity of Christ that Maximus takes up phrases like "became a human being in a manner beyond being" ("ὑπὲρ οὐσίαν οὐσιώθη"), "in a manner beyond man he works the things of a man" ("ὑπὲρ ἄνθρωπον ἐνήργει τὰ ἀνθρώπου"), and ultimately "a certain new theandric activity."[13] He is especially wont to juxtapose the first two (again respecting the order Dionysius's letter), and in this way expose the absurdity of a monenergist reading. Negatively, he argues that if one takes the superhuman element of Christ's works (the second phrase) to imply the erasure of genuine human activity, then one is likewise obliged to say that the superhuman element of Christ's becoming man (the first phrase) implies the annihilation of the human nature (*AT* 5.10–11). But Dionysius has already denied anything less than a human nature "in the entirety of its essence." He must then deny anything less than a full human activity.

Dionysius is admittedly ambiguous at this point. How can the natures remain unadulterated while also being "innovated" in their constitutive activities?[14] Maximus appropriates a well-known, crucial distinction between a nature's λόγος and its τρόπος.[15] "In both instances" Dionysius "shows the newness of the modes (τὴν καινότητα τῶν τρόπων) preserved in the permanence of their natural principles (τῶν φυσικῶν λόγων), without which no being remains what it is" (*AT* 5.9). A thing's λόγος, as Maximus makes clear in his doctrine of creation and in his discussion of miracles, is that "according to which" it is made, the eternally willed principle which alone grounds and defines it.[16] Should it be even slightly modified, it ceases to be at all,

---

11. *AT* 5.5, quoting Dionysius's *Epistle 3*.

12. So Constas' rendering of "Ἰησοῦ κέκρυπται" as a "dative of agent," though not syntactically necessary, is conceptually very precise.

13. *AT* 5.6–17 for the first two, 18–26 for the last.

14. In addition to Dionysius's "new theandric activity," Gregory Nazianzen had spoken of the "innovation of natures" wrought by the Incarnation (cf. *AT* 5.6, *AI* 41.1).

15. For the importance of this distinction see Sherwood, *Earlier Ambigua*, 165, and 55–66, for a survey of its development in pre-Maximus patristic tradition in the context of trinitarian reflection.

16. See e.g. *AI* 7.15–25, 22.1–2, 42.13–16. The literature on Maximus' doctrine of the λόγοι is vast, but see especially Balthasar, *Cosmic Liturgy*, 115–36, and Perl, "Methexis," ch. 5.

"since the nature in question no longer possesses inviolate the principle according to which it exists (τὸν καθ' ὅν ἐστι λόγον)." "Every innovation," then, "takes place in relation to the mode of whatever is being innovated." So, for instance, miracles do not destroy the fundamental nature of things but rather change the *way* those natures persist (*AI* 42.29).

So it is with *the* Miracle, the hypostatic union of divine and human natures in Christ. While the primordial principles of the natures remained inviolate, they were innovated in their modes, which are the arena of activity.[17] Maximus thus interprets Dionysius's "beyond being" and "beyond man" adverbially—as disclosing that the *how* of the two natures, not the *what*, constitutes the "newness" of the activity of the God-Man. The integrity of both natures are maintained, as required by Dionysius's earlier comments, as well as the integrity and newness of their respective activities, these playing out on the level of innovated modes: "we should admit the motion together with the nature, without which there is no nature, recognizing that the principle of being is one thing, and the mode of its existence is another, the one confirming nature, the other the dispensation of the Incarnation" (*AT* 5.11).

The innovation of the Incarnation plumbs deeper still. It is not just that, in Christ, divine and human natures are perfectly preserved while their energies are executed in a new way. The very content of this "new way" is unprecedented: Christ himself "performs the activities proper to each nature *as a single subject* (ἤγουν ἑνοειδῶς)." Maximus returns to the crux of the matter—the hypostatic identity of the two natures—for how can Christ *be* the unity of natures if the natures are deprived of their "constitutive elements" (i.e., activities) in this very unity? It is here that Maximus employs, for the only time in this *Ambiguum*, his tripartite christological formula: Christ exists "out of" (ἐξ ᾧ) and "in" (ἐν οἷς) and "is" (ἅπερ ἐστὶν) the two natures (*AT* 5.12). The innovative "is" signals the profound innovation of Incarnation, that the absolute identity of natures (and so activities) in Christ is what procures their perfect περιχώρησις:

> The conjunction of these (i.e. λόγοι of human and divine natures) was beyond what is possible, but he for whom nothing is impossible *became their true union* (ἀληθὴς γενόμενος ἕνωσις), and was the hypostasis in neither of them exclusively, in no way acting through one of the natures in separation from the

---

17. Τρόπος and ἐνέργεια are elsewhere linked: "(a nature's) mode is the order whereby it naturally acts and is acted upon (τρόπος δὲ ἡ ἐν τῷ ἐνεργεῖν καὶ ἐνεργεῖσθαι φυσικῶς τάξις ἐστιν), frequently alternating and changing" (*AI* 42.26); "when God innovated the nature of the things that were innovated, he accomplished this with respect to their mode of activity, not their principle of existence" (τὸν τρόπον τῆς ἐνεργείας, ἀλλ' οὐ περὶ τὸν λόγον τῆς ὑπάρξεως) (*AI* 42.29).

other, but in all that he did he confirmed the presence of the one through the other, *since he is truly both* (ἄμφω κατ' ἀλήθειαν ὤν).[18]

Only when one "recognizes" the "generation of opposites" does one glimpse the unfathomable mystery which generates them, the one Person (ὑπόστασις) of Christ.[19] This, ultimately, is where Maximus divines the truest innovation: "(Dionysius) called this energy 'new,' insofar as it is characteristic of a new mystery, the principle of which is the ineffable mode of natural coinherence."[20] The mode of the identity of modes, activities, and natures sounds a pitch on the interval of divine transcendence never heard before: Christ, in person, "is God and man at the same time" ("ὡς Θεὸς ὁμοῦ καὶ ἄνθρωπος ὤν," *AT* 5.26).

The logic of *Ambiguum* 5 matches Maximus' broader christological reflection, encapsulated in the threefold formula of Christ "out of," "in," and himself "is" two natures. Just as Maximus first affirmed the perduring *difference* of the whole natures against "synthetic" readings, then the perichoretic *reciprocity* of their mutual activities, and finally the superlative transcendence of the radical, ineffable *identity* according to hypostasis—so too the three elements of the formula correspond to three successively intensifying specifications about the Incarnate Word. Christ exists "out of" two natures—this signifies their different ontological origins and their "exteriority."[21] He exists "in" two natures—this indicates their περιχώρησις, their mutual "interiority."[22] Christ "is" two natures—this affirms the radical identity of both natures, that they are not merely inseparable but, ineffably, the exact same (ταυτότης).[23]

---

18. *AT* 5.17, my emphasis. Cf. also, e.g., *AT* 4.8; *AI* 36.2; *Ep15* 552C (cited in Perl, "Methexis," 191).

19. *AT* 5.14: "τῇ τῶν ἐναντίων γενέσει γνωριζομένην."

20. *AT* 5.21. The "mode" (τρόπος) here is not the technical τρόπος of the λόγος-τρόπος distinction, as if the real site of identity in Christ rests on the level of the perichoretic "modes" of the natures (a point usually left vague, e.g. Louth, *Maximus the Confessor*, 51). They are certainly "unified" (*AT* 5.11 and 17), as are the "activities" (*AT* 5.11 and 25), yet are not themselves the unifying principle: the "communication of attributes" between natures "shows enhypostatisation, but not (the) hypostasis, since the hypostasis was never divided (δείκνυσιν ἐνυπόστατον, ἀλλ' οὐχ ὑπόστασιν· ὅτι μὴ καθ' αὑτὸ διωρισμένως ὑπέστη)" (*Ep15* 558D, my translation).

21. Piret, "Christologie et théologie trinitaire," 219.

22. Ibid., 220.

23. Ibid. So *AT* 3.3, 4; *Ep15* 560AB. Though von Balthasar and Thunberg express doubts about translating ταυτότης as an unqualified "identity," Perl rightly flags the importance of retaining the radical sense of the term: "Maximus is not content to speak of hypostatic 'union' (ἕνωσις) in Christ, which could suggest a mere co-presence of two

One alteration of divine transcendence remains. Perl touched upon it when, after demonstrating that Maximus thinks "identity requires difference," he noted the inverse—difference itself depends on an even deeper identity. "The very meaning of enhypostasization is that the hypostasis which is Christ the Λόγος gives *being* to the human nature which he assumes."[24] Maximus says this very thing in an aside of *Ambiguum* 5: the human "essence" "has no existence in and of itself, but instead receives its being in the person of God the Word" (*AT* 5.11). The hypostatic identity of divine and human natures is the ground of the human difference itself: *because* its identity is also its very concrete existence (ὑπόστασις), its identity generates its difference.[25]

The Incarnation's innovation—its identification of two incommensurable natures—is likewise that of divine transcendence: God's utterly transcendent nature is most manifest in his ability to be(come) the identity of created and uncreated nature. He is not merely beyond knowability and unknowability (speech and silence, affirmation and negation, etc.). This very transcendence is what allows him to be both at once, and his being both at once is therefore the premiere index of this newly appreciable transcendence. *Since* he is both knowable and unknowable, *then* he is supremely unknowable—that is the logic of Incarnation. Or as Maximus insists with Dionysius: his divinity is concealed not just "after," but "*in* his manifestation" (*AT* 5.5).

Innovation of Dialectic

Maximus explicitly links the logic of Incarnation with the language of *apophasis*. In his hypostasis, Christ

> joined together the transcendent negation with the affirmation of our nature and its natural properties (συνῆψε τῇ καταφάσει τῆς φύσεως καὶ τῶν αὐτῆς φυσικῶν καθ' ὑπεροχὴν τὴν ἀπόφασιν), and so became man, having united his transcendent mode of existence with the principle of his human nature, so

---

natures 'in' a single hypostasis, but rather insists on the hypostatic and personal *identity* (ταυτότης) of the two natures ... True union demands not a mere juxtaposition or joining of two things; rather, in a union there must actually be *one* of something, one same thing which each of the terms united is." See Balthasar, *Cosmic Liturgy*, 234–35; Thunberg, *Microcosm and Mediator*, 36; Perl, "Methexis," 190–91.

24. Perl, "Methexis," 202–3.

25. So there is not only a "coinherence (συμφυία)" (*AT* 5.21) and "conjunction (σύνοδος)" (*AT* 5.13), but a positive "generation (γένεσις)" (*AT* 5.14) of opposites in the hypostatic union.

that the ongoing existence of that nature might be confirmed by the newness of the mode(s) of existence, not suffering any change at the level of its inner principle, and thereby make known his power that is beyond infinity, recognized through the generation of opposites.[26]

The three familiar affirmations are evident, but their subjective order begins at the end of the passage. First, one recognizes the presence of true opposites in one man (immediately before this text, one hypostasis) and thus the resplendent divine power "beyond infinity" which effects such unity.[27] Hence the objective, ontological order: (1) the "transcendent negation" (divine nature) becomes (2) the "affirmation" (human nature) without change in either (λόγος-τρόπος distinction), and so (3) manifests (γνωριζομένην) the God "above infinity."[28]

This explains Maximus' inversion of the Dionysian cataphatic-apophatic order. In an oft-discussed contemplation, Maximus interprets the "dramatic events" on the Mount of Transfiguration as "the two general modes of theology," and places "complete denial" (διὰ ... παντελοῦς ἀποφάσεως) before "positive affirmations" (διὰ καταφάσεως μεγαλοπρεπῶς, AI 10.76). As in *Ambiguum* 5, it is the recognition of the identity of full humanity and full divinity in one hypostasis that unleashes the true heights of divine transcendence, retrospectively recalibrating every sort of predication of God. Theological speech is now keyed to these ineffable heights, for the unapproachable approached and became approachable. Hence Maximus' emphasis on divine initiative in the events of Tabor: though the disciples had not yet "cast off carnal life," they "were raised," their sense perception supplanted "by the activity of the Spirit," and "they beheld him transfigured," He who was "unapproachable by reason of the light of his face" (*AI* 10.28). The objective manifestation of divine brilliance induces a subjective corollary in the onlookers in the form of absolute negation: "by means of the theological negation that extols him as being beyond all human comprehension, they were raised up cognitively to the *glory of the only-begotten Son of the Father*" (*AI* 10.29, citing John 1:14). On the "mountain of his manifestation," the apophatic-cataphatic dialectic is cast in a new "Light," the very Light revealing the true depths of divine obscurity. To begin from this obscurity is to behold how he is concealed *in* his manifestation.[29]

26. *AT* 5.14 (trans. Constas, slightly modified).
27. Hence the dative of means: "τῇ τῶν ἐναντίων γενέσει" (*AT*, ibid.).
28. Cf. also *AI* 15.9.
29. So also de Andia on *AI* 71: "Quant aux 'surabondance divine,' c'est le mystère de la divine incarnation. Dans la théologie mystique de Maxime, la suréminence est l'Incarnation. C'est à partir d'elle que le jeu des négations et des privations peut se faire

Radicalized *Apophasis*

Maximus' is a "rigid apophatic theology."[30] Created and uncreated natures are flatly irreconcilable. Every conception of God fails extravagantly. If God is known through creation, the divine essence remains absolutely unknown. Two affirmations—that God is beyond relation and that God's nature is thus properly ineffable—carry the force of negations stultifying every notion of apprehending the divine.

God beyond Relation: Irreconcilable Opposites

As transcendent Cause of all things (e.g. *AI* 10.76, 5.2), God is not naturally related to anything, but "transcends relatedness (ἄσχετον)" (*AI* 10.98; cf. 10.58).

> God is one, without beginning, incomprehensible, possessing in his totality the full power of being, fully excluding the notion of "when" and "how" (τὴν, πότε καὶ πῶς εἶναι παντάπασιν ἀπωθούμενος ἔννοιαν) in that he is inaccessible to all and not discernible by any being on the basis of any natural representation.[31]

If God were by nature related to anything other than Godself, he would not be what he is without that other term. It would condition, limit, him. Neither a relation of "comparison" (συγκριτικῆς) nor of "differentiation"

---

et l'on comprend pourquoi l'ordre entre les négations et les affirmations est descendant." de Andia, "Transfiguration et théologie négative," 324. However, this insight is then relegated to the perichoretic "jeu" of affirmation and negation (humanity and divinity) rather than keyed to its outstripping on the level of hypostatic identity as well. Ibid., 326. McFarland notes that the order of theological modes "follows the logic of the biblical narrative," but misses that this is also the logic of the Incarnation itself. See McFarland, "Developing an Apophatic Christocentrism," 210.

30. Thunberg, *Microcosm and Mediator*, 406.

31. *CGn* 1.1, 1084A. Trans. Berthold, *SelWrts*, slightly modified. See also *CGn* 1.6–7. All translations outside *The Ambigua* are from *SelWrts*, unless noted differently. De Andia finds a stark difference between Dionysius and Maximus in that the former bases the distinction of theological speeches on the dual implications of God as Cause (so related and yet prior to all things), while the latter emphasizes the coinherence of the two modes by virtue of "une référence, la parole." See de Andia, "Transfiguration et théologie négative," 309–10. It would be better to say, as this text implies, that the difference between the two is not absolute but developmental: Maximus too knows the distinction issuing from God as Cause but circumscribes this relation of *natures* within the more comprehensive mystery of their identity in *hypostasis* (argued below). He incorporates Dionysius' key insight while thinking it in a uniquely christological manner.

(διακριτικῆς) pertains (*AI* 9.2; *CGn* 1.8). One cannot place God *with* or *apart* from anything so as to define him. But this is *the* characteristic of created things: "no being," says Maximus, "is completely free from the condition of general relation to what is Itself totally unconditioned," for to be created is to be acted upon, to be preceded, to be related to (*AI* 41.10). It is to be found already in a "when" and a "where," related to and mutually conditioned by the manifold network of creaturely beings.[32] No wonder, then, that created and uncreated natures "never come together with each other" (*CGn* 1.6).

Of course, the perennial problem of any apophatic theology persists here. All of the above amounts to an affirmation of the denial of affirmation and denial, of dialectic. To affirm that God is beyond all relation is to negate predication itself—or at least predication on the same level of being. That is how Maximus begins to cope with this dilemma. In another creative appropriation of Dionysian thought, Maximus distends the mutually-implicating dialectic across various hierarchical levels of being, so that an affirmation about God on one plane is simultaneously a negation about him on a higher plane (and the reverse), since knowledge on the former is (properly) nothing compared to knowledge on the latter. "For every nature of rational beings," Maximus avers,

> is initiated into and imitates the cognitive states, propositions, and affirmations of the order and essence above it, and it does this by way of privation, that is, through the apophatic negations (ἀφαιρετικαῖς ἀποφάσεσι) of what is proper to itself.[33]

Every negation is a higher affirmation, and every affirmation both negates (what is lower) and is negated (by what is higher).

Far from being a regrettable obstruction, the ineluctable circularity of dialectic becomes the very animus of the mind's vertical movement towards the God beyond all movement, as evidenced in Paul's rapture to the "third heaven." Here Paul finds himself "beyond every relation to being." Dialectic finally opens upon an absolute negation:

> there follows the immediate negation of knowledge concerning God, a negation beyond any positive affirmation by absolutely any being, since there is no longer any boundary or limit that could define or frame the negation.[34]

---

32. *AI* 41.10, 10.91–3. Cf. Constas' note on "when" and "where" as "qualities of relation." See *Difficulties*, 489–90n66. Cf. also von Balthasar, *Cosmic Liturgy*, 87.

33. *AI* 20.5. The Incarnation itself is depicted in such terms: *AI* 71.3.

34. *AI* 20.5–6. Oddly, Williams sees in Maximus "no discussion, in the manner of Dionysius, of the 'way up through negations.'" See Williams, *Denying Divinity*, 105. *AI* 20 is absent from his treatment of "Ascent" in Maximus. See ibid., 104–7.

Having traversed the ontological ladder through dialectic, dialectic stalls. The specter of epistemic and linguistic dearth reasserts itself without reserve, for even the highest echelon of created being is still created, still relational, still powerless to match even the most pure apophatic illumination with an adequate affirmation of that unapproachable Light.[35]

God's transcendence of relation does not just jeopardize the adequacy of any correspondence, positive or negative, between a concept and God. Concepts themselves are relational, and so inept from the outset. Specifically, a concept or "thought" (νόησις) is the natural synthesis of what thinks (ὁ νοῶν) and what is thought (ὁ νοούμενος), subject and object, and so is "an intermediary relationship" of extremes ("Μέση γάρ ἐστι τινῶν ἀκροτήτων σχέσις").[36] Thoughts, then, have to do with two mutually related terms. But since they stand in *natural* relation to one another, they need each other to be what they are (thinker and thing thought). But then God cannot be either reciprocally-conditioned term, for "he would be limited."

> Thus there remains only the rejoinder that God can neither conceive nor be conceived but is beyond conception and being conceived. To conceive and to be conceived pertain by nature to those things which are after him.[37]

One should rather not speak at all.[38]

Things after God: Unknowability of Divine Nature

Divine nature cannot be known (*AI* 10.9). Even from his varied activity in creation one knows only *that* God exists (τὸ μόνον εἶναι), but never *what* he is (τὸ τί εἶναι).[39] This knowledge of sheer existence is unqualified and in no way speaks to any conceivable aspect of his nature.[40] In *AI* 17, Maximus

35. See also the Prologue to the *Mystagogy* for an identical ordering of dialectical ascent. I therefore cannot follow von Balthasar and others who claim that there is "in Maximus' ontology, no absolute affirmation or negation." See von Balthasar, *Cosmic Liturgy*, 90–1; de Andia, "Transfiguration et théologie négative," 326; McFarland, "Developing an Apophatic Christocentrism," 211.

36. *CGn* 1.82, 1116B. See also *AI* 17.9.

37. *CGn* 2.2, 1125C (trans. Berthold, *SelWrts*, slightly modified).

38. *CGn* 1.83: "It is precarious to attempt to speak the ineffable in verbal discourse."

39. *AI* 15.2; also 10.99, 34.2. See too Thunberg, *Microcosm and Mediator*, 412; de Andia, "Transfiguration et théologie négative," 301–3.

40. *AI* 10.92, my emphasis: "Thus when we say the Divine 'exists' (τὸ θεῖον 'εἶναι' λέγοντες), we do not say it exists in a certain way. And for this reason we say of God that he 'is' and 'was' in *a simple, infinite, and absolute sense* (ἁπλῶς καὶ ἀορίστως καὶ ἀπολελυμένως). For the Divine is beyond closure in language or thought, which is why

takes up Gregory's anti-Eunomian polemic first by asserting that "precise comprehension (ἀκριβὴς κατάληψις) even of the most infinitesimal creatures is beyond the reach of our rational activity" (*AI* 17.2). This, since every predication is of qualities more general than the subject itself. That is, the characteristics predicated of any subject are generic activities apprehended as common attributes, and so not the particular subject.[41] The apophatic character of every creature is further exacerbated when their λόγοι are considered, the intensely singular, eternally-willed principles of beings.[42]

Hence an argument *a fortiori*: if created being is properly apophatic, so much more is uncreated (*AI* 17.12), especially since

> the alpha-privatives or negations that are contemplated around something are not the thing itself (around which they are contemplated), otherwise they would assuredly be among the items signifying what this thing is, as being that very same thing, and not signifying what the thing is not. (*AI* 16.2)

Thus ensues a "linguistic shell game."[43] The assemblage of affirmations "around God" as Cause, which are themselves not God and are negated, show "only by analogy that (the) Creator exists" (*AI* 34.2). But even analogical knowledge is provisional, for right thinking from sensibles and intelligibles to God issues in complete unknowing: the mind "simply casts itself forward to be united with God, without thinking any way whatsoever, or reasoning about God . . . For infinity is around God, but it is not God himself, for he incomparably transcends even this" (*AI* 15.8–9).

Difference in Identity

Maximus never even slightly relinquishes "the infinite distance and difference between the uncreated and the created" (*AI* 7.12). Yet his refusal of epistemic respite in the smallest inkling of the divine nature does not

---

when we say the Divine 'exists,' we do not predicate of it the category of being (καθ' ὃ οὔτε κατηγοροῦντες αὐτοῦ τὸ 'εἶναι' λέγομεν αὐτὸ εἶναι), for though being is derived from God, God himself is not 'being' as such." McFarland remarks that for Maximus divine "attributes" are not "properties," but "events." See McFarland, "Developing an Apophatic Christocentrism," 210.

41. *AI* 17.4–6—an argument derived from Aristotelian metaphysics and the roots of Porphyry's tree (Constas, *Difficulties*, 496–97nn8–9).

42. *AI* 17.7–10 (cf. 20.3). All the more so if, as McFarland contends, the λόγοι are only truly intelligible in the revelatory radiance of the Λόγος Incarnate. See McFarland, "Developing an Apophatic Christocentrism," 205–8; e.g., *CChar* 1.95.

43. von Balthasar, *Cosmic Liturgy*, 88.

contradict but confirms the radical knowability of God in the hypostatic identity. For, as was observed, the innovation of divine transcendence wrought in the Incarnation issued in the realization that identity enables and indeed generates difference itself. Just as Maximus belied any "synthesis of natures" in Christ such that identity qualifies difference,[44] so does he tenaciously defend the borders of the incommensurability of natures, of "the unknowable" and the known.[45] Their identity is of a different order.[46]

Relativized *Apophasis*

Maximus juxtaposes two seemingly contradictory Scriptures, Paul's knowing "in part" and John's "we have seen his glory."

> And why did St. Paul say that he knew in part the knowledge of the divine Word? For he is known only to a certain extent through his activities. The knowledge of himself in his essence and personhood remains inaccessible to all angels and men alike and he can in no way be known by anyone.

What would otherwise be the platitudes of an unalloyed apophatic zeal are straightaway tempered by the singularity of the Incarnation:

---

44. *AT* 5.20: "for there is no kind of intermediate nature in Christ that could be the positive remainder after the negation of two extremes." See also *DP* 348A6–7.

45. *Myst* prol., 664BC: "He has in fact a simple existence, unknowable and inaccessible to all and altogether beyond understanding which transcends all affirmation and negation (καὶ πάσης καταφάσεώς τε καὶ ἀποφάσεως οὖσαν ἐπέκεινα)."

46. Here I depart from von Balthasar, who narrates Maximus' apophatic theology as a "dialectic of analogy" which corrects a mere "dialectic of transcendence," see von Balthasar, *Cosmic Liturgy*, 81–91. His tendency is to stress identity in ever-greater difference to the point of missing the absolute difference grounded in absolute (hypostatic) identity, against the better instincts evident in his comments on Maximus' christological synthesis. See ibid., 90–91, 122, 249–50. Thunberg's preoccupation with περιχώρησις yields a more flagrant faux pas, that hypostatic identity is in some sense *grounded* in difference. So Maximus makes his "most important contribution" to neo-Chalcedonian Christology "not only by emphasizing the continuing difference between the two natures as well as the unity of the hypostasis, but above all by making the one aspect directly related to and dependent on the other. The union of the two natures *is based on* (my emphasis) a certain *polarity* between them in virtue of the very fact that they are human and divine." See Thunberg, *Microcosm and Mediator*, 31. This may be true of *perichoretic* "unity," but certainly not of the hypostatic identity. The causal priority of the hypostasis is built into the innovative element of Maximus' christological formula since, unlike in the Trinity where one can say that the three hypostases are the nature and the nature is the three hypostases (*CGn* 2.1), one never says that the two natures *are* the one hypostasis, but only the reverse. As Bellini remarks, "l'hypostase divine du Fils demeure le principe premier." See Bellini, "Maxime interprète du Pseudo-Denys," 221.

> But St. John, initiated as perfectly as humanly possible into the meaning of the Word's incarnation, claims he has seen the glory of the Word *as flesh* ... For it was not as God by essence, consubstantial to God the Father, that the only-begotten Son gave this grace, but as having *in the incarnation become man by nature*, and consubstantial to us, that he bestows grace on us who have need of it.[47]

That Christ's hypostasis, his Person, is human, procures human knowledge of the unknowable God in two ways: by the objective manifestation of God through human nature, and by the subjective "initiation" of the believer through grace into a knowing beyond mere knowing, faith.

Knowability of God in the Divine Hypostasis

Because Christ was visible "as flesh," he was known. Being "the true hypostases of true natures united in an ineffable union," Christ was "visible to the eyes and known by the intellect, as God by nature and man by nature" (*AT* 4.8). The divine Christ is so thoroughly flesh that his divinity is susceptible to misrecognition:

> Our mind does not in this first encounter hold converse with the naked Word, but with the Word made flesh, certainly in a variety of languages; though he is the Word by nature he is flesh to the sight, so that many think they see flesh and not the *Word even if he is truly the Word* (εἰ κατὰ ἀλήθειάν ἐστι Λόγος).[48]

His fleshly appearance is only the beginning of an ascent toward perception of and participation in his divinity, but it is him no less. His flesh reveals not a part, but the whole of him. "As God, he was the motivating principle of his own humanity," says Maximus, "and as man he was the revelatory principle of his own divinity (τῆς οἰκείας ἐκφαντικὸς ὑπῆρχε θεότητος)."[49] He is known through his humanity, for humanity, a created nature, is knowable.

---

47. *CGn* 2.76, 1160CD, my emphasis. Cf. 1 Cor 13:9 and John 1:14 (and *AI* 10.29).
48. *CGn* 2.60, 1152A, my emphasis.
49. *AT* 5.18. See too *AT* 5.12.

Faith

The logic of hypostatic identity may explain certain of Maximus' statements on faith which otherwise seem to contradict radical ἀπόφασις regarding divine nature. He says, for instance, that although the name "Monad" itself—which puts God beyond any relation and so "absolutely inaccessible" to "all language"—is no real signification of the Godhead, nevertheless "based on our faith in the Godhead, we furnish ourselves with a *definition* of it (ἀλλ' ἑαυτοῖς ὅρον τῆς εἰς αὐτὴν πίστεως παρέχομεν), which is accessible to us and within our reach."[50] Again, God is "beyond infinity" and "cannot be known in any way whatsoever by any beings"—"except through faith" (*AI* 10.99).

How can such extravagantly *cataphatic* affirmations about the knowledge of God cohere with the superlatively *apophatic* negations of the same surveyed above? The answer lies, I think, in the object of faith. For Maximus, the object is not only the bare heights divine transcendence, "naked God," but the Word-made-flesh. "Both of these," he meditates, "are hard to understand and to prove in any definite way. It is better to say that they are completely inaccessible if they are searched after apart from faith" (*CGn* 2.36, 1141C). And who "can grasp the manner in which God becomes flesh and yet remains God? Or how, remaining true God, he is true man?" Answer: "Faith alone can grasp these things."[51]

The Incarnation is also faith's subjective structure. In the most apophatic of Maximus' *Chapters on Theology* faith is called "a true knowledge" (γνῶσις ἀληθὴς), "clearer than any demonstration" ("πάσης ἀποδείξεως βασιμώτερον"), of the indemonstrable. This because "it is the *hypostasis* (ὑπόστασις) of realities which are beyond intelligence and reason."[52] What is the significance of Maximus' enigmatic use of the scriptural term hypostasis for faith (Heb 11:1)? There it is the "substance" or "assurance" of eschatological rewards, while here—though one must tread cautiously with too neat a distinction—the ground of epistemic apprehension of things "beyond." Does this subjective hypostasis ground in the same manner as that of Christ's objective hypostasis? Is it too an ineffable identity which subjectively unites opposites—known and unknown? One text supports the affirmative, though the term "faith" is there absent:

> For God is not an object of knowledge or predication, so that he might be intellectually grasped by the soul according to a certain condition, but rather (is grasped) according to *simple union*

---

50. *AI* 10.97, my emphasis.
51. *AT* 5.21; the same in ibid. 5.16.
52. *CGn* 1.9, 1085CD, my emphasis.

as unconditioned and beyond all thought (κατά τινα σχέσιν ἡ ψυχὴ τὴν αὐτοῦ δύνηται νόησιν ἔχειν, ἀλλὰ κατὰ τὴν ἁπλῆν ὡς ἄσχετον καὶ ὑπὲρ νόησιν ἕνωσιν), on the basis of a certain unutterable and indefinable principle, which is known only to the One who grants this ineffable grace to the worthy.[53]

God, unknowable by nature, is known because of an ineffable union (ἕνωσιν)[54] given by grace; not unlike the grace, presumably, of which John spoke regarding the "grace and truth" exuded from the Word incarnate. "Faith supremely knows the supremely unknowable in a supremely unknowable way (ὁ διὰ πίστεως ἀληθοῦς τὸν ὑπεράγνωστον ὑπεραγνώστως ὑπερεγνωκώς)."[55] Faith stands as subjective counterpart to the hypostatic union in Christ: it *is* both "knowing" and "unknowing" God, and, being both at once, is the properly mysterious identity of the two ("in a supremely unknowable way").[56]

Christ, the Symbol and the Symbolized

Maximus discerned a deep continuity between objective and subjective hypostatic identities, which rent the heavens and exposed new notions of divine transcendence. What is radically "new" in the hypostatic union is God's self-manifestation as not merely beyond representation, but as personally and really represented. "He is a symbol of himself," says Maximus (*AI* 10.77). That is, the hypostatic identity surpasses the order of symbol and referent, *for God is both the symbol and the symbolized.*

---

53. *AI* 15.9, slightly modified, my emphasis.
54. Von Balthasar too marvels at the term. See von Balthasar, *Cosmic Liturgy*, 93.
55. *CChar* 3.99, trans. Berthold, *SelWrts*, slightly modified.
56. Williams glosses this text: "It would appear that faith, as the apprehension of that which is beyond intelligence and reason, is to some extent synonymous with unknowing." See Williams, *Denying Divinity*, 109. But faith is also synonymous with "knowing," for it "knows." I take issue with Cooper's general narration of knowing God in Maximus. Here negative theology (God's unknowability) is like a precursor to the "knowledge" of faith, which affirms God in praise: "It is the paradoxical reciprocity between denial of God's knowability on the one hand, and affirmation of his knowability through faith on the other that Maximus commends as the basic structure of divine revelation," see Cooper, "Structural Dynamics of Rvelation," 168–69. But what is paradoxical about a failure of one mode of knowledge and the resulting need of another mode, i.e., faith? The true paradox is that faith does not arrive as the subjective savior of failed cognition but as the mysteriously given capacity to know the unknowable as both knowable and unknowable at the same time. For Maximus, faith assumes, not abandons, "true knowledge" of the true Mystery.

This finally reconfigures the character (not just the order) of the apophatic-cataphatic dialectic: one affirms and negates not just because God transcends every relation, but because he *is* both poles of the dialectic at once. The familiar Maximian binaries—the "visible" and "hidden" Word (*CGn* 1.97), the "thick" and the "thin" Word (*CGn* 2.37), the "fleshy" and "spiritual" Word (*CGn* 2.39), etc.—are circumscribed and vitalized by the identity of the Word with each term. Hence for Maximus failure to deploy the dialectic is indeed irreverent idolatry,[57] but, what is more, deicide:

> Let us, then, make manifest what is hidden by means of an apophatic negation—leaving aside every capacity to picture the truth by means of figures and signs, being lifted up in silence by the power of the Spirit from written words and visible things to the Word himself—or let us conceal what has been manifested by giving it positive names and attributes. Otherwise we, like Greeks will be murderers of the Word. (*AI* 10.32)

Elsewhere he adds that avoidance of deicide must occur "by faith" (*CGn* 1.71).

"And what greater paradox could there be?" (*AI* 42.6). We return full circle to the innovation of transcendence wrought by the Incarnation. Paradox is the right word, for the hypostatic identity means: God, the utterly unknown, is known *as* unknowable in an unknowable way—all of which reveals his nature to be that much more unknowable. The apophatic-cataphatic dialectic is simultaneously justified and outstripped, for its suitability to God renders it all the more unsuitable.[58] The identical validity of affirmation and negation culminates in a truly absolute negation that in no way negates the dialectic—*ad infinitum*.[59]

---

57. Positive affirmations of the divinity are irreverent (*AI* 10.76), while blithe affirmations of sensibles characterizes idolatry (*CGn* 2.12).

58. This calls for a reassessment of one of de Andia's major conclusions: "Dieu n'est pas au-delà de la négation, chez Maxime, et le statut de la négation est différent: il ne fait pas de distinction entre l'ἀπόφασις (relative negation) et l'ἀφαίρεσις (absolute negation), ce qui me semble être la différence fondamentale entre la théologie négative de Denys et celle de Maxime." See de Andia, "Transfiguration et théologie négative," 326. If there is an absolute negation which arises precisely *because* God (in Christ) is able to be affirmed *and* negated, then perhaps the difference between Dionysius and Maximus is one of development rather than contradiction, in tandem with Maximus' development of Chalcedonian christological formulations (as discussed earlier).

59. Williams' notion of "apophatic nondualism" often approaches this realization: "(Maximus) does not resolve dualisms, either by means of syntheses or by the victory of one of the poles of the dualism over the other; rather he gathers both poles into a unity by affirming (or denying) them both, while insisting on the preservation of the very characteristics which engender their opposition." See Williams, *Denying Divinity*,

Conclusion

Maximus' idiosyncratic christological formulation has a counterpart in his apophatic articulation. The order and character of the apophatic-cataphatic dialectic are suffused with a distinctly incarnational logic. The logic runs:

(1) According to hypostasis, Christ *is* human and divine by nature.
  (1a) He *is* human by nature, so he must be sensed, known, affirmed, spoken of, symbolized, etc.
  (1b) He *is* divine by nature, so he must be unperceived, unknown, negated, honored in silence, beyond symbolization, etc.
(2) Yet the very identity of incommensurable natures in Christ is the sign and revelation *par excellence* of divinity's unspeakable transcendence.

We negate because Christ is divine by nature (1). We affirm because Christ is human by nature (1). We negate both negation and affirmation *because* Christ is both by nature, and yet this negation only further validates dialectic itself—a proper paradox utterly improper to anything "after God" (2).

Bibliography

Andia, Ysabel de. "Transfiguration et théologie négative chez Maxime le Confesseur et Denys l'Aréopagite." In *Denys l'Aréopagite et sa postérité en Orient et en Occident: Actes du Colloque International; Paris, 21–24 septembre 1994*, edited by Ysabel de Andia, 291–326. Collection des Études augustiniennes. Série Antiquité 151. Paris: Institut d'Études Augustiniennes, 1997.

Balthasar, Hans Urs von. *Cosmic Liturgy: The Universe According to Maximus the Confessor*. Translated by Brian E. Daley. A Communio Book. San Francisco: Ignatius Press, 2003.

Bellini, Enzo. "Maxime interprète du Pseudo-Denys l'Aréopagite: Analyse de l'*Ambiguum ad Thomam 5*." In *Maximus Confessor: Actes du Symposium sur Maxime le Confesseur, Fribourg, 2–5 septembre 1980*, edited by Felix Heinzer and Christoph Schönborn, 37–49. Fribourg: Éditions Universitaires, 1982.

113–14. So ἀπόφασις represents a kind of hypostatic union of positive and negative theology, grounded in the incarnate union." See Williams, "Incarnational Apophasis," 635. But this crucial insight tends to degenerate into a pure affirmation of both poles of the dialectic, which together *constitute* the unity of natures: "these two separate theologies undergo a kind of περιχώρησις in which each takes on the characteristics of the other, and they *achieve* a kind of 'hypostatic union' in their complementarity and affinity as applied to the divine." See Williams, *Denying Divinity*, 115 (my emphasis). Yet they do not unify themselves in their complementary difference; rather they are hypostatically unified *so that* they might remain irreconcilably different.

Coakley, Sarah. "Introduction: Re-thinking Dionysius the Areopagite." In *Re-thinking Dionysius the Areopagite*, edited by Sarah Coakley and Charles M. Stang, 1–9. Directions in Modern Theology. Malden, MA: Wiley-Blackwell, 2009.

Coakley, Sarah, and Charles M. Stang. *Re-thinking Dionysius the Areopagite*. Directions in Modern Theology. Malden, MA: Wiley-Blackwell, 2009.

Cooper, Adam G. "Maximus the Confessor on the Structural Dynamics of Revelation." *Vigiliae Christianae* 55 (2001) 161–86.

Heidegger, Martin. "The Onto-theo-logical Constitution of Metaphysics." In *Identity and Difference*, translated by Joan Stambaugh, 42–74. New York: Harper & Row, 1969.

Jones, Tamsin. "Dionysius in Hans Urs von Balthasar and Jean-Luc Marion." In *Re-thinking Dionysius the Areopagite*, edited by Sarah Coakley and Charles M. Stang, 213–24. Directions in Modern Theology. Malden, MA: Wiley-Blackwell, 2009.

Louth, Andrew. *Maximus the Confessor*. The Early Church Fathers. London: Routledge, 1996.

Maximus the Confessor. *Ambigua ad Iohannem*. Edited and translated by Nicholas P. Constas. In *Difficulties*, 1:62–450; 2:2–330. Abbreviated as *AI*.

———. *Ambigua ad Thomam*. Edited and translated by Nicholas P. Constas. In *Difficulties*, 1:2–58. Abbreviated as *AT*.

———. *Capita de caritate* [Four Centuries on Charity]. Edited by Aldo Ceresa-Gastaldo. In *CSC*, 48–238. Abbreviated as *CChar*.

———. *Capita theologica et oeconomica* [Gnostic Chapters]. Edited by François Combefis. PG90:1084A–173A. Abbreviated as *CGn*.

———. *Disputatio cum Pyrrho* [Dispute with Pyrrhus]. Edited by François Combefis. PG91:288A–353B. Abbreviated as *DP*.

———. *Epistula xii* [Epistle 12, To John the Chamberlain]. Edited by François Combefis. PG91:460A–509B. Abbreviated as *Ep12*.

———. *Epistula xv* [Epistle 15, To Cosmas the Deacon, of Alexandria]. Edited by François Combefis. PG91:544D–76D. Abbreviated as *Ep15*.

———. *Mystagogia*. Edited by François Combefis. PG91:657C–717D. Abbreviated as *Myst*.

———. *On Difficulties in the Church Fathers: The Ambigua*. Edited and translated by Nicholas P. Constas. 2 vols. Dumbarton Oaks Medieval Library 28–29. Cambridge: Harvard University Press, 2014. Abbreviated as *Difficulties*.

———. *Selected Writings*. Translated by George C. Berthold. Classics of Western Spirituality. New York: Paulist, 1985. Abbreviated as *SelWrts*.

McFarland, Ian A. "Developing an Apophatic Christocentrism: Lessons from Maximus the Confessor." *Theology Today* 60 (2003) 200–214.

Perl, Eric David. "Methexis: Creation, Incarnation, Deification in Saint Maximus Confessor." PhD diss., Yale University, 1991.

Piret, Pierre. "Christologie et théologie trinitaire chez Maxime le Confesseur, d'après sa formule des natures 'desquelles, en lesquelles et lesquelles est le Christ.'" In *Maximus Confessor: Actes du Symposium sur Maxime le Confesseur, Fribourg, 2–5 septembre 1980*, edited by Felix Heinzer and Christoph Schönborn, 215–22. Fribourg: Éditions Universitaires, 1982.

Pseudo-Dionysius the Areopagite. *Corpus Dionysiacum II: Pseudo-Dionysius Areopagita, De coelesti hierarchia; De ecclesiastica hierarchia; De mystica theologia;*

Epistulae. Edited by Günter Heil and Adolf Martin Ritter. Patristische Texte und Studien 36. Berlin: de Gruyter, 1991. Abbreviated as CD 2.

———. *Pseudo-Dionysius: The Complete Works*. Translated by Colm Luibhéid in collaboration with Paul Rorem. Classics of Western Spirituality. New York: Paulist, 1987.

Sherwood, Polycarp. *The Earlier Ambigua of Saint Maximus the Confessor and His Refutation of Origenism*. Studia Anselmiana, philosophica theologica. Rome: "Orbis Catholicus"/Herder, 1955.

Thunberg, Lars. *Microcosm and Mediator: The Theological Anthropology of Maximus the Confessor*. 2nd ed. Chicago: Open Court, 1995.

Uthemann, Karl-Heinz. "Das anthropologische Modell des hypostatischen Union bei Maximus Confessor: Zur innerchalkedonischen Transformation eines Paradigmas." In *Maximus Confessor: Actes du Symposium sur Maxime le Confesseur, Fribourg, 2–5 septembre 1980*, edited by Felix Heinzer and Christoph Schönborn, 223–33. Fribourg: Éditions Universitaires, 1982.

Völker, Walther. "Der Einfluss des Pseudo-Dionysius Areopagita auf Maximus Confessor." In *Studien zum Neuen Testament und zur Patristik: Erich Klostermann zum 90. Geburtstag dargebracht*, edited by Gerhard Delling, 331–50. Berlin: Akademia-Verlag, 1962.

Williams, Janet Patricia. *Denying Divinity: Apophasis in the Patristic Christian and Soto Zen Buddhist Traditions*. Oxford: Oxford University Press, 2000.

———. "The Incarnational Apophasis of Maximus the Confessor." *Studia Patristica* 37 (2001) 631–35.

9

Roots of Scientific Objectivity in the *Quaestiones ad Thalassium*

Michael Harrington

In his book-length essay on what it means to be European, Rémi Brague notes that, as a child, he was "fascinated by the knick-knacks on sale along the coast or in the mountains in which one drowned in translucent plastic, according to the case, a sea horse or an edelweiss."[1] The solid plastic prevents anyone from unmediated contact with the object, but it is transparent and supports the object on all sides, and so it also presents the object to the observer. Brague calls this model of receiving foreign objects "inclusion," and when applied not to seahorses but to texts and cultures, he takes it to be distinctively European. For example, when the medieval scholars of western Europe receive an ancient Greek text by storing it in a library, making copies of it, and writing commentaries on it, they are preserving the foreignness of the text while at the same time making it more accessible to its potential readers. Though Brague does not identify this model of reception as objective, we will find that its adoption is necessary to what we now call "scientific objectivity," and that it applies as much to natural objects as to texts and cultures. That is, the child who looks at a seahorse encased in plastic is adopting the perspective that also governs the work of the marine biologist. To get a better sense of why this is the case, we may look at one of the more vocal early proponents of natural contemplation, the seventh-century Byzantine monk Maximus the Confessor.

Brague may find this last statement surprising, as he resists including Byzantium within the bounds of the European tradition. According to Brague, the Byzantine and Islamic traditions do not employ the model

---

1. Brague, *Eccentric Culture*, 106.

of inclusion, but what he calls the model of digestion. In the model of inclusion "the foreign body is maintained in its otherness," while in the model of digestion "the object is assimilated to such a point that it loses its independence."[2] For instance, when the Muslim scholars of medieval Persia receive an ancient Greek text by paraphrasing it—that is, by making it speak the language of their own culture—and then discarding the original text, they assimilate the text to the point that it no longer exists except as part of their contemporary culture.[3] In the Byzantine tradition, Brague sees assimilation not through the translation of an ancient Greek text into a different language, but through the assumption that the original text uses the same Greek as a medieval Byzantine.[4] When the words of the ancient text are given the meanings of Byzantine Greek, that text loses its independence even though it has not been paraphrased and then discarded. The original text may be preserved in a library, but it is nonetheless assimilated, so long as it is understood to speak the language of a Byzantine Greek.

How do the models of inclusion and digestion function when what is received is a natural object rather than a text or a culture? The model of digestion cannot yield objective knowledge, since it cannot separate the one who receives from the thing that is received. Knowledge is objective when it allows its object to remain an object—that is, something that is thrown down or lying (*iactum*) apart (*ob-*) from the observer. Receivers who digest the things they receive, on the other hand, either identify these things with themselves or become identified with the things. For instance, because I see the sun as the size of my thumbnail, I may say that the sun itself must be that size, identifying it only by its relation to myself. Of course, my senses cannot help but establish a relationship to their objects, which results in a kind of digestion of them, but I can use my intellect to reestablish the model of inclusion. I can recognize that the relationship I establish to the sun through my senses does not grant me access to the sun as it is in itself. This compensatory activity of intellect first appears in the Presocratic philosophers, but it is most clearly described by Plato, who notes that when the sense of sight sees a stick partially submerged in water as broken, the intellect can compensate for it to understand that the stick is in fact not broken (*Resp.* 602c).

Maximus the Confessor explores this tension between the intellect and the senses in a series of questions from the *Quaestiones ad Thalassium*, beginning with the fifty-eighth and extending through the sixty-first. The

---

2. Brague, *Eccentric Culture*, 107.

3. Ibid., 96–98, 104–6. As these pages make clear, Brague sees the same model at work in the Syriac Christian tradition.

4. Ibid., 98–99.

fifty-eighth question is prompted by a passage from the scriptural first letter of Peter, which reads: "for a little while now, you must be pained by that in which you rejoice, in many trials."[5] The question that Maximus takes up in response to this passage is: how can someone who is pained in many trials be able to rejoice in what pains him? The answer, which Maximus revisits over the course of the next few questions, is that we can experience pleasure in one faculty at the same time as we experience pain in another. The senses, for instance, can experience pain while the intellect experiences pleasure, and vice versa. In fact, one or the other of these situations must always be the case. The intellect and the senses can never share their pleasures or pains, because their activities are incompatible with each other. This is the case, as Maximus puts it, "because of the extreme difference and otherness of their objects."[6] The objects of the intellect are "intelligible and bodiless substances, whose substances it naturally receives," while the objects of the senses are "sensible and bodily natures."

This is not to say that the intellect and the senses can function independently of one another. Maximus follows the Aristotelian tradition of holding that human beings cannot contemplate intelligible objects directly, but only through the mediation of sensible objects.[7] He says this quite plainly in question fifty-eight: "it is not possible for the intellect to cross over to the intelligibles that are of its kind without the contemplation of the sensibles that have been projected as mediators." The sun's visible appearance, for instance, must be contemplated in however erroneous a way before the sun itself can be understood. The appearance mediates between the intellect and its object. Since only the senses can contemplate the appearance, the intellect's own contemplation "cannot at all come about without sensation, which is set together with it, but is of the same kind according to nature as the sensibles." Though no knowledge at all can come about without the senses, their use poses a risk for the intellect. "It is reasonable," Maximus says, that the intellect "relate itself to the appearances of the visible things that strike it, supposing the sensation set together with it to be its natural activity." That is, it is reasonable that the intellect identify itself with the senses, treating their relation to the visible appearance as yielding knowledge of the thing itself, with the result that the intellect sees its own activity as a relation to the appearance.

Although it is reasonable for the intellect to make this mistake, Maximus thinks that it is nonetheless possible to avoid it. "If the intellect cuts off

---

5. 1 Peter 1:6, cited at *QThal* 58, 592CD. All translations from Greek texts are my own.

6. Ibid. 58, 596D4–7. The following quotes are from *QThal* 58 as well.

7. See Harrington, "Creation and Natural Contemplation," 197.

the appearance as soon as sensation is struck by visible things," he says, "it will contemplate the spiritual λόγοι purified of the shapes that exist in them." As soon as the senses have served their purpose of mediating between the intellect and its proper object, they can and should be left behind. Maximus does not think that the intellect and the senses can each simultaneously contemplate their own proper objects. Even though the intellect can feel pleasure that is simultaneous with the pain felt by the senses, the soul can only contemplate one thing at a time. When the intellect contemplates the λόγοι, "it will bring about the pleasure of the soul," but it will cause the senses pain by preventing them from contemplating their proper object. This is the answer to question fifty-eight: "how can someone who is pained in many trials be able to rejoice in what pains him?" It is the senses that feel the pain, while the intellect rejoices.

When Maximus notes that "it is reasonable" for the intellect to make the mistake of identifying itself with the senses, he is laying the ground to consider intellectual contemplation not as something that comes readily to the soul, but as requiring a preparatory exercise or ἄσκησις.[8] The sixty-first question will explain historically how human beings came to require this exercise. In the fifty-eighth question, it is simply clear that the soul must train itself not to identify with the appearances that present themselves to the senses, but to move its contemplation immediately beyond them to their λόγοι. The contemplation of the λόγοι here does not involve the intellect transcending itself in an ecstatic union with the divine, since it is contemplating what is "of its kind," but such contemplation does nonetheless have a transformative effect on the soul. The soul becomes virtuous, by escaping the domination of the senses even when it knows that they will cause it pain. This virtue—which closely resembles the Hellenistic ἀπάθεια or freedom from the passions—belongs to the soul in the present, and must be kept separate from the hope of future union with the divine. Maximus identifies hope as the source of the pleasure taken by the soul in contemplation, when the rejoicing soul "is gladdened by the hope of goods to come" (QThal 58, 597C6). That is, it is not the fact that contemplation is the intellect's natural activity that makes it pleasurable, as it would be for someone like Aristotle. Instead, the λόγοι bring pleasure to the soul because they point to something other than themselves, the future experience of God without the accompanying pain of the senses. The λόγοι themselves may be contemplated objectively by the soul, since the soul is not tempted by pleasure to identify itself with them.

---

8. See Lollar, *To See into the Life of Things*, 229–34, for how dispassion is required for contemplation.

How do the λόγοι point to something other than themselves, such that the soul that contemplates them "is gladdened by the hope of goods to come"? Much has been written on the subject of the λόγοι, but it is worth reviewing one way that they can signify something other than themselves.[9] When discussing the contemplation of the λόγοι in the *Liber Ambiguorum*, Maximus refers to one mode of this contemplation as proving the existence of God. "When we seek the cause of beings," he says, "we are taught through the substance of these beings that the cause exists, without undertaking to know what it is in its substance."[10] When I contemplate the λόγος of a particular rose, for instance, I see that its substance is not simply that of an individual, but can be subsumed under the species of rose, and under the genus of plant. Maximus understands the subsumption of individual under species, and species under genus, as a kind of movement. If the λόγος of the particular rose is moved, "then it is not without a principle. If it is not without a principle, then clearly it is not ungenerated, but . . . receives its being and movement from the only one that is ungenerated and unmoved" (*AI* 10, 1177D–1180A). To contemplate the substance of a being is not to be united with God, but it gives the soul hope that such union is possible by supplying the knowledge that God exists.

Does such a form of contemplation have anything in common with contemporary scientific objectivity? Not every contemporary analysis of scientific objectivity uses language that is easily compared with that of Maximus. The work of Pierre Hadot, however, does meet Maximus halfway, as it were. Hadot is interested in both scientific objectivity and the spiritual exercises by which the soul renders itself virtuous. Since Hadot's discussion of spiritual exercises is rooted in the philosophers of the Hellenistic period and Late Antiquity, his terminology is not jarring when used to interrogate the work of Maximus. In *The Veil of Isis: An Essay on the History of the Idea of Nature*, Hadot suggests that even the contemporary scientist requires a certain kind of spiritual exercise. Science, he says, demands something of us, "that we not choose any other end than knowledge, and that we seek knowledge for itself, without any other utilitarian consideration."[11] Because science requires the setting aside of all other ends than knowledge itself, Hadot says that "scientific research is a 'spiritual exercise' to the highest degree." It presupposes, he says, "an 'ascetics of the mind,' or an effort at transcending

---

9. On the contemplation of the λόγοι, see Thunberg, *Microcosm and Mediator*, 343–55; Lollar, *To See into the Life of Things*, 240–46.

10. *AI* 10, 1133C2–4. For a more thorough treatment of the five modes of natural contemplation, see Harrington, "Creation and Natural Contemplation," 197–207; Lollar, *To See into the Life of Things*, 235–40.

11. Hadot, *Veil of Isis*, 186.

oneself and mastering the passions." He borrows the phrase "ascetics of the mind" from the Nobel-prize winning biologist Jacques Monod. The process of becoming objective requires that one transcend oneself by correcting for the errors of one's own perspective, as happens when one no longer identifies with the content of one's sensations. It also requires that one master the passions, overcoming our propensity to pursue the pleasure of sensation and avoid the pain of its absence.

Such an approach turns scientific research into a pleasurable pastime. It is pleasurable, Hadot says, "because it is akin to the game that consists of solving puzzles."[12] It is a pastime because it is an end in itself, being placed in the service of no higher goal or activity. Hadot finds that this approach to knowledge as a pleasurable pastime does not belong to the Hellenistic period so much as to Greek Antiquity, as exemplified by Plato's *Timaeus*. Without going into any detail on the method adopted in the *Timaeus*, we may note that the protagonist of the dialogue, Timaeus, says that "someone who examines likely reasonings concerning generation will obtain a guiltless pleasure" (*Tim.* 59c–d). In Hadot's reading, we gain pleasure from contemplating things in the realm of generation because we do not have to commit ourselves to our reasoning concerning them. Timaeus says that our reasoning is only "likely" and not "true," and also that we take it up "for the sake of a respite." A "likely" course of reasoning does not have to be taken seriously, and so is a fit subject for a period of relaxation. As Hadot notes, the narrative of the *Timaeus* is itself set during a festival. He also notes that the contemplation of the realm of generation is said by Timaeus to require the overcoming the passions, and so the dialogue itself may be considered as a kind of spiritual exercise.[13]

Though Hadot's Platonist and Monod's modern scientist both practice the contemplation of nature as a spiritual exercise, they differ from the Hellenistic philosopher. For the scientist, "it is scientific research that is an end in itself," while "elevation of consciousness and pleasure in knowing come along as an extra."[14] In other words, one must transcend oneself and master the passions in order to do scientific research objectively, but these practices are simply the means to that end. The Hellenistic philosophers reverse the causal sequence: "their respective physics were placed in the service of a way of life." That is, they practiced objectivity as an exercise so that they could achieve the end of living well. Hadot notes that the contemporary scientist may also regard objectivity as a means, to "a transformation of the material

12. Ibid., 182. For the degree to which natural contemplation may considered a game in Maximus, see Lollar, *Life of Things*, 35–40.

13. Hadot, *Veil of Isis*, 183, referring to *Tim.* 90d.

14. Ibid., 187.

conditions of human life" and so to a different kind of living well.¹⁵ That is, scientific objectivity may become a means to serve humanity by finding cures to illnesses, introducing labor saving devices, and so on. Hadot warns that "in all periods, and since antiquity, the 'service of mankind' has been in danger of meaning the service of individual or collective egoisms. Modern science is more and more in danger of being closely linked to industrial technology, the demands of corporations, and the will to power and profit."¹⁶ This critique of modern science is often employed as a general critique of modernity, but Hadot recognizes that this particular feature of modern science is a problem "in all periods." The conquering of the passions in Hellenistic philosophy, for instance, could and was put in the service of the later Roman Empire, one of Hadot's "collective egoisms." Monod's objectivity, which is an end rather than a means, avoids this problem, but it also divorces scientific research from the end of the scientist's own life.

Maximus does not follow any of these paths precisely. Like Monod, Maximus says that one masters the passions and abandons identification with the senses as a means to contemplating the λόγοι. Unlike Monod, Maximus understands this contemplation of the λόγοι as a means to a further end: the union with God that is to come. The pleasure taken in contemplation is not "an extra," as Hadot puts it, deriving from the intellect engaging in a pastime or in its natural activity, but comes from the intellect's anticipation of an experience signified by the λόγοι. This experience constitutes a different kind of intellectual contemplation, one that is not objective, since it involves the identification of the soul with what it contemplates. As Maximus will put it in the *Ambigua*, "if one intellects, then one loves completely what has been intellected. If one loves, then one suffers completely an ecstasy toward it in so far as it is loved" (*AI* 1073C11–13). Those who suffer this ecstasy "come to be entirely within the entirety of what is loved and entirely circumscribed by it" (*AI* 1073C16–17). That is, the soul no longer defines or circumscribes itself, but is defined or circumscribed by the thing that it contemplates. Even if it remains a different substance from its object, it only understands itself through and as that object.

The sixtieth of the *Quaestiones ad Thalassium* distinguishes the intellect's ordinary contemplation of the λόγοι from this ecstatic experience. It refers to them as two forms of insight or γνῶσις. "The first," Maximus says, "is relational, set in reason alone and its intellections. It does not possess the activity of sensing through experience that into which it has insight. In our present life we are governed by it" (*QThal* 60, 621C11–14). That is, our present life is governed by a form of insight deprived of sensation and

15. Ibid., 188.
16. Ibid., 188–89.

experience. Maximus calls this insight "relational" because it is relative to reason or intellect, and does not break down the soul's boundaries to put it in direct contact with the thing into which it has insight. Where the earlier discussion of question fifty-eight emphasized that this contemplation is pleasurable, since it provides the soul with the hope of future goods, here Maximus emphasizes the distance between this insight and its object. It does not "possess the activity of sensing through experience that into which it has insight." The sensation in question here is not the sensation of bodily appearances discussed in question fifty-eight, since it does not connect the soul to appearances but to God. The two forms of sensation nonetheless have in common a lack of objectivity, since they do not maintain a distance between the observer and the observed. The insight that occurs in reason maintains its distance precisely because it is "in" something other than what it knows. That is, it takes place "in reason alone and its intellections," a point so important to Maximus that he makes it twice in the same passage (*QThal* 60, 621C11–12; 621D5–6.)

The sensation of appearances and the sensation of God also have in common their incompatibility with the contemplation of the λόγοι in the intellect. Just as sensual pleasure cannot be felt at the same time as intellectual pleasure, so also the intellect's internal activity cannot occur simultaneously with its sensation of God. According to Maximus, "the wise say that it is impossible for reasoning concerning God to subsist together with the experience of God, or for intellection concerning God to subsist together with the sensation of God" (*QThal* 60, 624A). While Maximus is sometimes concerned to differentiate reasoning from intellection, here he is only interested in the activity they share. Reasoning, he says, is "an analogy drawn from beings concerning God," while intellection is "the simple and unitary insight drawn from beings and concerning God." Reasoning is not simple and unitary like intellection, but they both contemplate God through the medium of created beings. Their incompatibility with sensation and experience does not only come into play when God is the object. Maximus says more generally that "experience of a particular matter puts a stop to reasoning concerning it, and sensation of a particular matter works the idleness of intellection concerning it." If I am smelling a rose, I cannot at the same time be thinking about how it belongs to the genus of plants or how its substance proves the existence of God. If I begin to think about these things, I will cease to experience the rose.

The contemplation of the λόγοι in the intellect occupies a unique position between the sensation of appearances and the sensation of God. In the sensation of appearances, the soul treats the appearances as an extension of itself. In the sensation of God, the soul treats itself as an extension of God.

During the contemplation of the λόγοι in the intellect, the substance of the thing contemplated remains separate from the soul, as though "drowned in translucent plastic" like the knick-knacks seen by Rémi Brague at the seashore. So long as the intellect contemplates the λόγοι in this way, it occupies a remarkable place outside sensation or experience, and recognizably similar to that of the modern scientist. The fact that Maximus identifies λόγοι does not by itself locate him in the European tradition, since there are Eastern analogues to the λόγοι. There are thinkers outside the European tradition who not only understand themselves to be living in an orderly world, but who have a precise terminology with which to describe it.[17] Maximus sets himself squarely in the European tradition because of his thoroughgoing sense of the difference between the contemplation of the λόγοι in the intellect on the one hand, and the sensation of appearances or God on the other. Though he regards the contemplation of the λόγοι in the intellect as a means to ecstatic union with God, he clears a space for the independent use of intellect that will later become the space of modern science.

Bibliography

Brague, Rémi. *Eccentric Culture: A Theory of Western Civilization*. Translated by Samuel Lester. South Bend, IN: St. Augustine's Press, 2002.

———. *Europe, la voie romaine*. 2nd rev. ed. Idées. Paris: Critérion, 1992.

Hadot, Pierre. *The Veil of Isis: An Essay on the History of the Idea of Nature*. Translated by Michael Chase. Cambridge: Harvard University Press, 2006.

Harrington, Michael. "Creation and Natural Contemplation in Maximus the Confessor's *Ambiguum* 10:19." In *Divine Creation in Ancient, Medieval, and Early Modern Thought: Essays Presented to the Reverend Dr. Robert D. Crouse*, edited by Michael Treschow, Willemien Otten, and Walter Hannam, 191–212. Leiden: Brill, 2007. doi:10.1163/ej.9789004156197.i-460.53.

Lollar, Joshua. *To See Into the Life of Things: The Contemplation of Nature in Maximus the Confessor and His Predecessors*. Turnhout: Brepols, 2013.

Maximus the Confessor. *Ambigua ad Iohannem*. Edited by Franz Oehler. PG91:1061–417C. Abbreviated as *AI*.

———. *Quaestiones ad Thalassium*. Edited by François Combefis. PG90:244–785B. Abbreviated as *QThal*.

Rosker, Jana. *Traditional Chinese Philosophy and the Paradigm of Structure (Li)*. Newcastle Upon Tyne: Cambridge Scholars, 2012.

Thunberg, Lars. *Microcosm and Mediator: The Theological Anthropology of Maximus the Confessor*. Acta Seminarii Neotestamentici Upsaliensis 25. Lund: Gleerup, 1965.

---

17. See, for instance, Rosker, *Traditional Chinese Philosophy*, 147–48, for an account of the Chinese equivalent of λόγος.

10

The Theo-Phenomenology of Negation in Maximus the Confessor between Negative Theology and Apophaticism

Natalie Depraz

Introduction

When one broaches the philosophical issue of negation in the context of theological studies, one is led straightforward to the central question of "negative theology," which is in turn often equated with apophaticism.

In this contribution I would like to show how Maximus the Confessor, *as a philosopher*, remarkably helps distinguishing between negative theology and apophaticism. He makes this possible thanks to his distinction between the essence (οὐσία) of God and God's energies/operations/activities (ἐνέργειαι).[1] Indeed for Maximus the essence of God is absolutely *un*knowable because of its *im*participable character, whereas it is participable to the human being through its energies. I will investigate here the specific philosophical character of such a "θεωρία of essence and energies," which is so peculiar to the so-called "Eastern" Orthodox θεωρία and was hardly noticed, dealt with, and taken into account by Western theologians and *a fortiori* philosophers. I will show how it brings about a conception of negation

---

1. The Greek theological term ἐνέργεια was translated into English/French either as "energies," or "operations," or again as "activities." I will not go into the discussion of the more or less relevance of these different choices, which is not crucial here for the sake of my argumentation. For reasons of simplicity and early usage, I will in the following keep the translation with "energy."

that allows to identify a *third* way beyond the classical formal philosophical duality between relative and absolute negation. The former corresponds to a lack considered as a lesser being and exemplarily understood as *privatio* by Descartes and post-Cartesian philosophers like Leibniz. The latter ends up as nothingness seen as a radical irreducible negation of being in the way it is unfolded in Schopenhauer and later on in Sartre and Heidegger.

But why is such a philosophical distinction between essence and energies so important in order to figure "another" concept of negation? Because it provides a "form" for the experiential distinction suggested by Gregory of Nyssa between mystical and symbolical theology and it "dialectizes" the remanent duality between affirmative and negative theology to be found in Dionysius the Aeropagite. Maximus thus appears as a true "western" philosopher able to formalize and to dialectize emerging experiential distinctions and abstract dualities. But at the same time he inherits the precious Eastern stance, which never sets aside the crucial necessity to embody and experientialize distinctions, dogmas, and theories. In short, such a θεωρία of essence and energies helps understand why a philosophy, to be genuine,[2] needs to anchor its conceptual intellectual formalization in its experiential dynamics. It is also here that Maximus operates as a true phenomenologist: thanks to his conception of negation which, as we will see, appears in his distinction between essence and energies, he contributes to identify the true philosophical, that is, experiential, distinction between "negative theology" as limited to an intellectual understanding, and apophaticism, as opened to an experiential guiding.

My steps in this contribution will be the following: first I will present Maximus' understanding of negation through his distinction between essence and energies and situate it in contrast with Western philosophical conceptions of negation. Secondly, I will use such a distinction in order to situate Maximus' view with regard to Gregory of Nyssa and Dionysius the Aeropagite, and thus unfold his philosophical contribution to a clarified distinction between negative theology and apophaticism. Finally, I will show how and why Maximus' philosophical view might fit better into Husserl's experiential eidetic phenomenology than into Heidegger's radical ontology and how it specifically reverberates on his distinction between negative theology and apophaticism.

---

2. And here we have to get rid of still partial distinctions between Western or Eastern properties.

The Maximian Approach of Negation

Major Western Philosophical Conceptions of Negation

In the Western philosophical classical tradition, we find multifarious ways of identifying negation at the experiential-ontological level and at the language-logical level.

Plato in his *Sophist* defines negation as a "non-being" (τὸ μὴ ὄν), which *is* in a certain sense (τὸ μὴ ὄν εἶναι, 237a3–4), thus paving the way for the *possibility of knowing* what is not. In contrast to Plato and prior to him, Parmenides had radically rejected any access to what is *not*: "being is, non-being is not." With Plato on the contrary, non-being becomes something "other than" being: thus it is a *mode* of being, therefore being "relative" to it.[3]

Such a possible knowledge of nothingness will be the main option with regard to negation in the history of philosophy: Descartes in his *Metaphysical Meditations* (1641) defines negation as a *privatio* of being, that is, as a "lesser" being, Kant in his turn with his mathematician background will be interested in promoting the graduation of negations in the general scale of different growths, Hegel finally puts to the fore the genuine move and work of negativity in experience, ending up in an achieved identifying synthesis. In short, each of these philosophers beyond their important differences claim negation is relative to being, experience, and identity and it is thus, knowable.[4]

Contrary to such a "metaphysical" relativization of negation for the sake for its knowability, contemporary thinkers tracing back from Schopenhauer and Nietzsche to Heidegger, Sartre, Levinas, Blanchot, Bataille, or Derrida all underlined the radicality of negation. So negation quite obviously ends up in amounting to its irreducibility, its *uncatchupbility*—to cite Levinas: "irrécupérabilité." Such a radical negation will be given various names according to the authors and contexts, either ontological (nothingness, void, nullity), or existential ones (absence, death), or again an ethical one (radical alterity). But beyond these various names and forms, the observation is the same: negation cannot be assimilated to a knowledge, it can only be experienced as an event that is incomprehensible, that remains a rupture and in the end a non-sense in the radical meaning of the word.

Western philosophy as a whole offers two contrasted meanings of negation, a relative one and an absolute one, which are completely

---

3. Cordero, "Une conséquence inattendue de l'assimilation du non-être à l'autre dans le *Sophiste*."

4. For more details see, for example, Elissalde, *La négation*.

heterogeneous one to the other and give way either to a logic understanding or to an existential one.

The Maximian Distinction between Essence and Energies as an Entry into His Early Renewed Conception of Negation

Quite remarkably in the Eastern Orthodox philosophical context as a contrast, the approach of negation is primarily linked to the relationship between humanity and divinity, and the ontological and logical levels, which are central to Western philosophy, are put at the service of this primal theological level.

In such a general epistemological framework *lato sensu* and as far as negation is concerned, Maximus the Confessor, like other philosophers–theologians like Gregory of Nyssa and Dionysius the Aeropagite, thus broaches the issue of negation in the light of the relationship between negative theology and apophaticism. But his unique philosophical thrust leads him to provide a new conceptual distinction, that is, the one between the essence (οὐσία) of God and its energies (ἐνέργεια). Whereas the οὐσία of God is absolutely *un*knowable insofar as—as I mentioned above—the human beings as finite creatures are not able to share anything of it, he appears to let himself be part of the human being through the specific force and activity of his energies. Surprisingly enough, such a differential relationship remained quasi unnoticed in the West, while it offers a unique articulation of the relationship between man and God and provides a true key into the distinction between negative theology and apophaticism.

At first sight though, the distinction between essence and energies gives way to two meanings of negation, one is relative, linked to the allowed participation of the human being to God through his energies, the other is absolute: the whole imparticipation of the essence of God to anything else than himself. So with these two negations (relative/absolute), it may appear Maximus comes to the same conclusion as Western philosophers, and it could be interpreted in such a way by narrow-minded rationalist philosophers.

But on the contrary: by relying on the Platonic θεωρία of the community (κοινωνία) of generic unchangeable forms–ideas (εἴδη/ἰδέαι), exemplarily presented in the *Sophist*, the relationship between God and the human beings becomes an *experiential* circulation. Furthermore, tracing back from Plato's endeavoring in the *Timaeus* to think, even in the form of the myth of the Demiurge, the mixing of intelligible forms and sensory matters and even the participation of the latter to the forms, Maximus is able to recast into his own theology the Platonic late view and open up the antinomic understanding of an operative double-directed dynamics of moving-growing human beings towards God, and of providing a unbridged space for God as a move of withdrawal and of ultimate passivity.

In that respect, negation as whole participation is not relative (as opposed to absolute), but it is the experiential dynamics as such of the growth of humanity. Reciprocally, negation as "imparticipation" (unknowability, non-communicability) is not absolute on the part of God (as opposed to relative), but it is the offering of a dynamic space for him to withdraw. In short, contrary to the metaphysical dual distinction between relative and absolute negation carried on by the Western philosophical tradition (and which would end up in parting God and man along a mere dichotomy), the Eastern dynamics of negation at work in the relationship between essence and energies provides a common space of mutual growth for man towards God, and for God withdrawing and thus offering a space for man.

Thus, the inter-face common ground of energies, uncreated and created, is the core of the dynamics: whereas the divine essence is transcendent, that is, beyond man's experience and comprehension, thus suggesting an ineffable distinction between the essence and energies within the uncreated God, the divine energies of God in their turn are forces proper to him, inseparable from God's essence, in which he manifests, communicates and gives himself to us.[5] Thus "uncreated energies" form a kind of "mobile bridge" (if such an image is allowed) between the essence of God as operating a move of active withdrawal and the energies of the human beings as benefiting from the divine forces directed towards them and thus supporting their growth towards God.[6]

It therefore furnishes us with a distinction that is antinomic in its core, which is in turn a remarkable key to clarify the distinction between negative theology and apophaticism as a new way of relating the one to the other.

---

5. Lossky, *Mystical Theology*, 70.

6. About the *theology* of divine essence, uncreated energies and human created energies, see *TP1* 33BC, where Maximus stresses the fact that the created energies are in the end the τέλος of the motion of divine essence; see also *TP7* 85A, where Maximus considers energy as the true common ground between the human being and God, ultimately bringing to the fore the person of Christ as the mediating figure containing in himself both created and uncreated energies.

The Specificity of the Maximian Distinction between Negative Theology and Apophaticism

These two expressions are commonly, even by great interpreters of Maximus, mistaken for one another.[7] In this second step, I would like to dismantle such an equivalence that is often taken for granted and show how the discrepancy between the two lies on and involves a contrasted meaning of negation.

As a first definition, negative theology names God by using negative adjectives: God is said to be invisible, unsayable, inexpressible (ἄ-φθεγκτος, ἄφραστος), indescribable, incomprehensible, unfathomable, in short, unknowable, according to a series of adjectival negations of any possible predication about God. Now, the word apophaticism derives from the Greek ἀπόφασις which can be broken down into ἀπό and φημί and refers to the verb ἀπόφημι, which means literally "to say no," "to negate": "to deny." From the use of etymology and grammar alone, you cannot really distinguish the two expressions: "apophaticism" amounts to a denial of God's being.

The meaning of apophaticism however, beyond grammar and etymology, is far from being reducible to the impossibility of naming God otherwise than with negative nouns. It refers profoundly to a move of withdrawal from the process of saying and of opening towards a dynamic experiential space of silent relation to the divine presence. From one meaning (negative naming) to the other (withdrawal and silent relation), negation radically changes and opens up an unexpected horizon of experience, which is quite different from the philosophical alternative between relative and absolute negations sketched above.

Gregory and Dionysius' Steps

Having in mind this first distinction between negative theology and apophaticism, I would like to situate Maximus' contribution with regard to two other main theologians-philosophers who lived before him, had direct or indirect links with him and equally brought a specific but also major view about negative theology and apophaticism. While doing so, my idea is to bring to light Maximus' specificity and to more precisely situate him in the history of apophaticism.

Gregory of Nyssa (331?–395) lived in the fourth century, Dionysius the Areopagite, whose life is full of legends (is he Paul's first century disciple

---

7. See for example Larchet, *La divinisation de l'homme*, 497n21. On negative theology according to Maximus, see Völker, "Einfluss."

on the Aeropagite mount, did he carry his head all the way to Saint Denis' Cathedral?) may have lived in the fourth or fifth century, while Maximus le Confessor (580–662) worked during the seventh century. All three were extremely influential as eminent representatives of the climax of what is usually called "mystical theology," or the theology of the mysteries.

For the sake of brevity, I will set aside the question of Maximus' influences, namely Plato's theory of the participation of ideas, or a discussion on John Scotus Eriugena, who translated Maximus into Latin as early as the ninth century. I will only synthetically examine how each of them features negative theology and how they deal with the distinction with and relation to apophaticism.

Gregory in his *Commentary on the Song of Songs* as well as in his *Life of Moses* makes a distinction between three ways leading to spiritual life. His way of writing is less conceptual than metaphorical, and he therefore suggests three biblical images: the Burning Bush, the Pillar of Fire, and Darkness. The last two images refer to the distinction between symbolic theology and mystical theology. The Pillar of Fire reveals the invisible *through* the visible, whereas Darkness makes us directly enter into the "night of the spirit." So the symbolic theology is to "extinguish" sensory organs and to transcend them. It is concerned with positive divine attributes, which are the analogical *concepts* we, as creatures, may ascribe to God: wisdom, power, charity. Such divine names are genuine; I indeed learn something about God by using them, but they do not reach his essence (οὐσία), which is beyond all knowledge, and as such unknowable. Only mystical theology, which involves a "night of the spirit," will be able to reach the divine essence. To echo Gregory, negative names are used *because they designate what God is not*. One cannot know divine nature itself, and those negative names do not aim at such knowledge, but rather at furthering our inquiry itself.[8]

From these two crucial stages of a spiritual life, requiring the practice of ἄσκησις and the development of contemplation, accounted for by Gregory thanks to images that embody his account, Dionysius will draw systematic expositions: whereas his *On the Divine Names* deals with symbolic knowledge, which builds concepts about God borrowed from the visible world, his *Mystical Theology* refers to the experience of Darkness, that is the negation of all things, the entry into the un-knowing ("l'inconnaissance" in French). Whereas the first book is a voluminous treatise, the second is a slim work, comprised of five short chapters. In the third middle chapter,

---

8. Among many examples, see Gregory of Nyssa's *Contra Eunomium* 2.1.582.1–583.1.

Dionysius sums up the results of the treatise and enters into "what is beyond the knowable":

> And in the book of the *Divine Names* I have considered the meaning as concerning God of the titles Good, Existent, Life, Wisdom, Power and of the other titles which the understanding frames, and in my Symbolic Divinity I have considered what are the metaphorical titles drawn from the world of sense and applied to the nature of God; what are the mental or material images we form of God or the functions and instruments of activity we attribute to Him; what are the places where He dwells and the robes He is adorned with; what is meant by God's anger, grief, and indignation, or the divine inebriation and wrath; what is meant by God's oath and His malediction, by His slumber and awaking, and all the other inspired imagery of allegoric symbolism. And I doubt not that you have also observed how far more copious are the last terms than the first for the doctrines of God's Nature and the exposition of His Names could not but be briefer than the Symbolic Divinity. For the more that we soar upwards the more our language becomes restricted to the compass of purely intellectual conceptions, even as in the present instance plunging into the Darkness which is above the intellect we shall find ourselves reduced not merely to brevity of speech but even to absolute dumbness both of speech and thought.⁹

Dionysius thus builds an analogy between the two experiential Gregorian ways, the symbolic and the mystical, and the two formal levels of "assertion" (κατάφασις) and "negation" (ἀπόφασις). It is the very title of this third chapter—"What are the affirmative expressions respecting God, and what are the negative"—where he details the relationship between the two as follows:

> Because, when affirming, the existence of that which transcends all affirmation, we were obliged to start from that which is most akin to It, and then to make the affirmation on which the rest depended; but when pursuing the negative method, to reach that which is beyond all negation, we must start by applying our negations to those qualities which differ most from the ultimate goal. Surely it is truer to affirm that God is life and goodness than that He is air or stone, and truer to deny that drunkenness or fury can be attributed to Him than to deny that we may apply to Him the categories of human thought.¹⁰

9. Pseudo-Dionysius, *Mystical Theology*, 197–98.
10. Ibid., 198–99.

Thus, the knowledge and existence of God is understood by both Gregory of Nyssa and Dionysius the Areopagite in two different modes: inside and outside the essence. They acknowledge two methods of understanding and experiencing God. The first one is a knowledge by intellectual and rational approximation, a cataphatic knowledge. It describes God within the rational realm of the created world and provides a critical language for manifestations of God through his names and energies. The second one is a knowledge by means of direct experience, which goes beyond sense perceptions in an apophatic way of towards union with God. This is the core of the antinomy of God considered at the same time as knowable (κατάφασις) and as unknowable (ἀπόφασις).[11]

Maximus' Contribution to the Clarification of the Distinction between Negative Theology and Apophaticism

Two centuries later, Maximus will also describe the process through which you reach God in accordance with the negation of all that he is not, thus following an inner concrete ἄσκησις made of gradual dispossessions or barenesses: the mystic gradually divests God of each of his names and ends up experiencing his radical unknowability. The νοῦς stops any movement, any inner thought. In an emphatic style, less metaphorical than Gregory but more concrete than Dionysius, Maximus writes,

> The νοῦς that has reached the innermost of the Mystical theology is a man whose λόγος of faith is grasped by the intellect within the unknowing, in mystagogies which are beyond all demonstration..., above which nothing pertaining to the realm of beings has any place, nor sensation, nor reason, nor νοῦς nor intellection, nor knowledge, nor known, nor intellected, nor named, nor sentient, nor felt...[12]

Like his predecessors, he claims the essence of God is unknowable, but he will formalize the distinction between symbolical/mystical (Gregory) or assertion/negation (Dionysius) by bringing into the framework the novel-unknown relationship between the essence of God and his energies, both uncreated and created: while God as essence is non-participable to man, through his energies he becomes. Maximus thus allows a dynamic move of mutual though asymmetric participation between man and God, where

---

11. Steenberg, "Epinoia & Ennoia."
12. Maximus the Confessor, QThal 25, PG90, 332C, CCSG 7, 25:54–61. Translation from the French by Yves Millou.

there was nothing but a dual separation of two levels, either as symbolic/mystical or as assertion/negation.

What is such a dynamic participative move made of? (*a*) There is a circulation of energies between man and God: the non-participable sphere of God's operation therefore is not a static separation, but it generates a dynamic move of withdrawal which opens up man's rising and increasing move toward God; (*b*) such a θεωρία emerges as an experiential dynamic before it results in a theoretical formalization, and the practical embodiment of such an experience of the divine presence in his very withdrawal is what guides intellectual understanding, never the contrary.

However, such a first investigation reveals a double-sided opposition, where the negative way is in the end always seen in link with the assertive one, as opposed to it but finally situated on the same level. It is therefore necessary to let a new and deeper dimension emerge that frees itself from the logic framework alone, either oppositive or dialectic, and allows to open up to a more radical way into apophaticism: the latter indeed operates as the "double unseen bottom" of the negative way itself, but if we keep approaching it from a discursive logical λόγο,Σ unavoidably it may never appear as such.

In order to "reveal" such a double unseen apophatic bottom, Gregory resorts to images and Dionysius appeals to an extreme soberness and poverty in his way of writing, which ends up in its disappearance: what he names here ἀπόφασις is a rhetoric image but also in fact the experience of a growing scarcity ending up in silence. Before silence, in the quite short fourth and fifth chapters of *Mystical Theology*, Dionysius makes use of a language of "double negation," where one quality-property *as well as* its very negation are rejected:

> [God does not] belong to the category of non-existence or to that of existence; nor do existent beings know It as it actually is, nor does It know them as they actually are; nor can the reason attain to It to name It or to know It; nor is it darkness, nor is It light, or error, or truth; nor can any affirmation or negation apply to it; for while applying affirmations or negations to those orders of being that come next to It, we apply not unto It either affirmation or negation, inasmuch as It transcends all affirmation by being the perfect and unique Cause of all things, and transcends all negation by the pre-eminence of Its simple and absolute nature-free from every limitation and beyond them all.[13]

---

13. Pseudo-Dionysius, *Mystical Theology*, 200–201.

Here even non-existence, even darkness are inadequate: it is no use denying anything, apophaticism is a radical process where negative naming is also refused.

In contrast with Gregory's poetic images and Dionysius' mystical double-negative radicalism, Maximus turns out to be a genuine philosopher: through his dynamic formalization of the relationship between essence and energies, he unveils a complex antinomic conceptualization in order to carry on articulating the negative and the positive ways, while asserting their irreducibility.

Maximus, a Husserlian Phenomenologist of Embodied Energies?

Maximian Essence-Energies and Husserlian
Invariant-Eidetic Variations

At this stage of our inquiry, it might be interesting finally to recast Maximus' philosophical thrust into apophaticism while drawing contemporary philosophical resources that help us shed a renewed light on the essence-energies conceptual-experiential challenge. What is the purpose of such a comparison? One first interest of it is to extend the understanding of such dynamics beyond its endogen νοῦς formulation while showing how contemporary concepts and methods may resonate with and provide it with a renewed meaning. Another complementary mirror benefit is to enrich some of our Western categories with another way of thinking and articulating experience, which help freeing the former from its conceptualizing tendency while opening it up other modes of thinking.

In that respect, we cannot but notice the striking analogy between essence and energies in Maximus on the one hand and εἶδος and kinesthetic lived experiences in Husserlian phenomenology on the other hand. Indeed, the eidetic variation lies in a double concurrent move: on the one hand, every sensory fact takes part in the emergence of the invariant essence as an empirical specific leading thread. For example, I differentiate between each red color inherent in the objects I meet while glancing around my dining room: the dark red of the armchairs, the fiery red of the curtains, the clear red of my pencil, etc. It does not take me long to notice the recurrent red-identity of these different red objects, thus extracting what remains invariant—the essence—beyond the variability of these various objects, on the other hand, the essence (here of red) is irreducible to every given red object, as a reality a priori existing in my mind before any empirical meeting. The eidetic variation as a phenomenological method is the experiential dynamic of both simultaneous moves from the sensory realm and from the spirit of man, the circularity of their mutual participative meeting giving way to an embodied though a priori εἶδος. It remarkably echoes the Maximian experiential dynamics between the essence of God and Its energies directed towards man: on the side of the essence, the irreducibility of the Husserlian εἶδος-invariant to sensory facts resonates with his negation-withdrawal from any human created finite participation, whereas his energies-operations allowing man's participation for his rising-increasing towards God echoes the taking part of sensory facts through their variation in the welcoming εἶδος. What is remarkable here is the surprise we have to find a common third term: *uncreated energies as divine forces* proceeding from the divine essence welcoming-supporting the human energies-activities, *processual variation as operating as a structure* from the very εἶδος and highly receptive to the multiplicity of the given sensory facts.

So my broader hypothesis—on the basis of such a first methodological convergence—would be to read Maximus' apophaticism with phenomenological Husserlian glasses and thus open up a complementary phenomenological interpretation of apophaticism to the one already unfolded thanks to a Nietzschean–Heideggerian projector.[14]

Dionysius as Marion's and Yannaras' Phenomenological Heideggerian Common Ground[15]

I refer here to both Christos Yannaras' and Jean-Luc Marion's key reference to Dionysius as a unique matrix of their reinterpretation of apophaticism with a phenomenological approach. Both claim to unfold a phenomenological *theologia* meant to be properly experiential and to dismantle the historical conceptual ontotheological metaphysical building. Both, therefore, rely on Nietzsche's and Heidegger's radical destruction of metaphysical scheme.

Both in Jean-Luc Marion's *The Idol and Distance* (first published in 1977) and in *God Without Being* (1982) and in Christos Yannaras' *On the Absence and Unknowability of God: Heidegger and the Areopagite* (1966–1967), we find at work a remarkable common, though not concerted, insight about the convergence between the Dionysian conception of apophaticism and the Heideggerian critics of theology as ontotheology: God is not a concept, a Causa sui. Both take their inspiration in Nietzsche, and Marion, implicitly

---

14. Such a hypothesis is only suggested here. It is beyond the scope of our present inquiry and will require another step in a coming contribution.

15. A systematic account on this comparison is provided in Depraz, "Apophaticism and Phenomenology."

following Yannaras, acknowledges that, if such a God is dead, the only true living God is the one in front of Whom you can dance and kneel, that is, the one you may meet directly in a lived bodily experience.[16]

Marion keeps articulating apophaticism with a negative theology opposed to a cataphatic one. On the contrary, Yannaras more radically claims a "radical apophaticism" ultimately ends up in silent experiencing and frees itself from any remaining logically articulated negative theology. However, they both commonly refer to Heidegger's radical ontology of nothingness. The latter indeed appears to welcome Dionysius' radical unknowing of God, far better at least than Maximus' care for driving God's unknowable essence toward man through the dynamics of the mutual move of uncreated and created energies.

In less dramatic existentialist accents, Maximus shows quite well how God's essence embodies through his own energies-operations and on the basis of his withdrawal. While so doing, he remarkably welcomes man as highly embodying himself while letting him rise towards him.

Husserl's eidetic variation in turn confirms the experiential phenomenological scope of such a double dynamic move of man rising towards God and of God withdrawing to let man come to him.

Bibliography

Cordero, Nestor-Luis. "Une conséquence inattendue de l'assimilation du non-être à l'autre dans le *Sophiste*." In *Plato's Sophist: Proceedings of the Seventh Symposium Platonicum Pragense*, edited by Aleš Havlíček and Filip Karfík, 188–99. Prague: Oikoumene, 2011.

Elissalde, Yvan. *La négation*. La philothèque. Levallois-Perret: Bréal, 2014.

Gregory of Nyssa. *Commentary on the Song of Songs*. Translated by Casimir McCambley. Archbishop Iakovos Library of Ecclesiastical and Historical Sources 12. Brookline, MA: Hellenic College Press, 1987.

Larchet, Jean-Claude. *La divinisation de l'homme selon saint Maxime le Confesseur*. Cogitatio fidei 194. Paris: Cerf, 1996.

Lossky, Vladimir. *The Mystical Theology of the Eastern Church*. Translated by Members of the Fellowship of St. Alban and St. Sergius. London: James Clarke, 1957.

Marion, Jean-Luc. *God without Being*. Translated by Thomas Carlson. Chicago: University of Chicago Press, 2012.

———. *The Idol and Distance: Five Studies*. Translated by Thomas A. Carlson. New York: Fordham University Press, 2001.

Maximus the Confessor. *Ad Marinum presbyterum (Theologica et polemica 1)* [To Marinus the Very Pious Priest]. Edited by François Combefis. PG91:9A–37D. Abbreviated as *TP1*.

16. Yannaras, *Absence and Unknowability of God*, 73–110; Marion, "The Crossing of Being," in *God without Being*, 53–107.

———. *Quaestiones ad Thalassium*. Edited by Carl Laga and Carlos Steel. CCSG 7:3–539; 22:3–325. Abbreviated as *QThal*.
———. *Tomus dogmaticus ad Marinum diaconum (Theologica et polemica vii)* [Dogmatic Tome Sent to Marinus Deacon in Cyprus]. Edited by François Combefis. PG91:69B–89C. Abbreviated as *TP7*.
Pseudo-Dionysius the Areopagite. *Œuvres complètes du Pseudo-Denys l'Aréopagite*. Edited and translated by Maurice de Gandillac. Bibliothèque philosophique. Paris: Aubier, 1943.
———. *On the Divine Names and the Mystical Theology*. Translated by Clarence Edwin Rolt. Translations of Christian Literature, series 1: Greek Texts 1. London: SPCK, 1920.
Völker, Walther. "Der Einfluss des Pseudo-Dionysius Areopagita auf Maximus Confessor." In *Studien zum Neuen Testament und zur Patristik: Erich Klostermann zum 90. Geburtstag dargebracht*, edited by Gerhard Delling, 331–50. Berlin: Akademia-Verlag, 1962.
Yannaras, Christos. *On the Absence and Unknowability of God: Heidegger and the Areopagite*. Edited by Andrew Louth. Translated by Haralambos Ventis. London: T. & T. Clark, 2005.

PART III

Anthropology: Human Nature, Ethics, and the Will

11

St. Maximos' Distinction between λόγος and τρόπος and the Ontology of the Person

Andrew Louth

St. Maximos' doctrine of the λόγοι of creation, together with the related topic of the distinction between λόγος and τρόπος has been the subject of many discussions over the last half-century or so. In this paper, I shall draw on these reflections and add some of my own; it is a well-worn topic and I doubt if I have anything dramatic to add to the accumulated wisdom of scholarship, but it perhaps worth reminding ourselves of the historical development of such reflection, and Maximos' own contribution.

A λόγος, in this context, means something like "principle," or "meaning." According to Maximos everything that exists has its λόγος which determines its nature; he speaks of λόγος τῆς οὐσίας or λόγος τῆς φύσεως. It means something like "definition," a meaning λόγος had for Plato. It is a central notion in many aspects of his thought. In relation to the Johannine notion of creation through the Λόγος, he develops an understanding of the λόγοι of creation, according to which all the λόγοι participate in the Λόγος of God—"the One Λόγος is many λόγοι, and the many λόγοι are One," as he asserts several times in *Ambiguum* 7—so that all the λόγοι preexist in God: the being and purpose of everything that exists exists as paradigm, predetermination, or will in God, in this context citing several times Dionysios' *Divine Names* 5.8. One can also speak of λόγος τῆς οὐσίας in relation to God, though here it cannot mean definition, as God is beyond definition, indeed beyond any kind of determination.

The origin of the word τρόπος in relation to λόγος goes back to Trinitarian theology and to the terminology made popular, if not invented, by the Cappadocian Fathers who, in conjunction between their distinction with οὐσία and ὑπόστασις, spoke of λόγος τῆς οὐσίας and τρόπος τῆς ὑπάρξεως—principle of being and mode of existence: the three Persons had a single λόγος τῆς οὐσίας, but each had his own τρόπος τῆς ὑπάρξεως. Mode of existence is, then, the equivalent of ἰδιότης, particularity, distinguishing feature; the term, mode of existence, seems to refer primarily to source or origination; it might be rendered mode of coming-to-be, used in relation to the Godhead analogically. This seems to be a settled result of modern scholarship, found in Prestige's now rather old *God in Patristic Thought*,[1] as well as in more recent discussions, such as those of Brian Daley.[2] When the language of nature and hypostasis was extended to Christology—a move given synodical authority by Chalcedon—the distinction between λόγος and τρόπος followed, and was used in later Patristic discussion of their understanding of the union of divine and human in Christ.

Maximos' developed doctrine of the λόγοι of creation opens the door to the use of τρόπος in this context, too, and it is a door through which Maximos treads. This is true, even though it seems to be the case that Maximos makes no particular use of the distinction between οὐσία and ὑπόστασις outside Trinitarian theology and Christology; his use of ὑπόστασις is that of most late antique Christian thinkers: ὑπόστασις simply refers to the particular case of a being defined by an essence—a particular man, or a particular horse, the use we find in the *Dialectica* of John Damascene, a theologian greatly influenced by the Confessor. The case is, I think, different with the distinction between λόγος and τρόπος, where Maximos exploits this distinction to bring out his understanding of what is involved in the creation and re-creation of the human, and therefore his understanding of what we might well call his "ontology of the Person."

It is best, I think, to approach Maximos' understanding of the ontology of the Personal, by following in this own thought the movement of the pair λόγος/τρόπος from Trinitarian theology, through Christology, to his understanding of the human.

In his *Mystagogia*, Maximos speaks of

> One God, one being, three hypostases, tri-hypostatic monad of being, consubstantial triad of hypostases, monad in triad and triad in monad, not one and another, nor one beside another, nor one through another, nor one in another, nor one from another, but the same in itself and according to itself, the same on its own and by itself both monad and triad, possessing union uncomposed and unconfused, and distinction undivided and

---

1. Prestige, *God in Patristic Thought*, 245–49.
2. Daley, "Nature and 'Mode of Union'"; Sherwood, *Earlier Ambigua*, 155–66.

inseparable, monad according to the λόγος of its essence and being but not by composition or combination or any kind of confusion, triad according to the λόγος of how it exists and subsists, but not by division or change or any kind of separation—for the monad is not divided into hypostases nor does it exist by relationship nor is it beheld in them, nor are the hypostases combined to form the monad nor do they bring it to fulfilment by contraction—but it is the same by itself, thought of in one way or another—for the triad of hypostases is the monad unconfused in being and the same by a single λόγος, while the holy monad is a triad in its hypostases and by the mode of existence—we are to think in both ways according to one and the other account, as we have said, the Godhead understood wholly as one and single, undivided and unconfused, simple, undiminished, and undeviating, existing wholly as monad in accordance with its being and wholly as triad shining identically in the hypostases as one ray of threefold light in a single form. (*Myst* 23, 840–63)

The characteristic language of Chalcedon has been transposed into a Trinitarian vein, and the distinction between the divine substance manifest in its λόγος τῆς οὐσίας, and the persons, or hypostases, distinguished by their τρόπος τῆς ὑπάρξεως, expressed by Maximos with care (and occasional paradox, thus underlining the limitations of human reason). Another shorter example of Maximos' sense of the divine unity manifest in being, while the trinity of persons is expressed in existence, can be found in *Ambiguum* 1, where he affirms that "(t)he Triad is truly a Monad, for such it is (ἐστίν); and the Monad is truly a Triad, for as such it subsists (ὑφέστηκεν), since there is one Godhead, being monadically and subsisting triadically." What this makes clear is the consistent and deliberate use of different verbs to describe being and existence.

With Christology, the use of these terms serves rather a different purpose. A good example of his concern can be found in *Ambiguum* 42, where he says,

And what greater paradox could there be than that, whereas he is God by nature and deemed it fitting to become man by nature, he did not alter the natural definitions of either one of the natures by the other, but being wholly God he became and remained wholly man? For being God did not hinder him from becoming man, nor did becoming man diminish his being God, and thus he remained wholly one and the same in both, truly existing naturally in both, being neither divided by the unadulterated integrity of the essential differences of the two natures, nor confused by the fact that the two natures came to exist in an absolutely single and unique hypostasis, and so he neither changed nature nor underwent a transformation into something he was not. (*AI* 42.6 = PG91, 1320BC; trans. Constas, *Difficulties*, 2:131–33).

Here the key point is the integrity of the natures, defined by their λόγοι. This is for Maximos an absolute principle. The λόγοι of creation are inviolable. God's endeavour in Christ to "renew the natures," as St. Gregory the Theologian had put it in one of his homilies, cannot mean the alteration of the natures defined by the λόγοι, even their improvement. Indeed, Maximos believes that because the λόγοι of creation exist in God, they are inviolable; even in the fallen world, the destructive effects of the fall do not reach to the λόγοι of creation—the fall is a matter of the distortion, hideous though it is, of the modes of existence, the τρόποι τῆς ὑπάρξεως. This seems to mean that the fall only affects rational creatures, as it is only the possession of a rational will that makes it possible for λόγος and τρόπος to get out of alignment. But this is to get ahead of ourselves.

There is another christological passage worth recalling here: the interpretation of the Transfiguration found in Question 191 of the *Quaestiones et dubia*. There we read:

> By the face (πρόσωπον) of the Word, which shone like the sun, we are to understand the characteristic hiddenness of his being. (*QD* 191.47–8)

and he goes on to expound the meaning of the Lord's body and garments which were radiantly white:

> By the body of the Word we are to understand the substance of the virtues, such as goodness, meekness, and the like; by the garments, we are to understand the words of Scripture and the work of creation that comes forth from and takes its being from God, which are seen as white by those who have put aside the thickness that attaches to the word of Scripture and behold by the contemplation of the spirit the radiant beauty of its concepts, and by removing the deceitful of the senses behold radiantly the sensible creation, understanding by analogy its creator from its vast beauty. (*QD* 191.53–63)

We find much the same interpretation of the Transfiguration in *Ambiguum* 10, with this significant addition: the overwhelming radiance of the face of Christ is called apophatic theology, while the radiance found in

Scripture and creation is called cataphatic theology. This suggests a personal encounter with the Word—for πρόσωπον means both face and person—which is beyond concepts, which are not rejected, but found at a lower level in the body and raiment of the transfigured Christ. I think we should note this.

Let us now pass on to consider the use of λόγος and τρόπος in Maximos' reflection on the nature of man: his creation, fall, and restoration or renewal. What we have seen so far—the consistent distinction of λόγος and τρόπος, whereby λόγος defines being, and τρόπος existence, and the notion of the inviolability of the λόγοι of creation—suggests an understanding of the human (and indeed of all rational creation) whereby the λόγος of being is given and determined by God, and this can be shaped by the mode of existence, the way of existing, the how of existing, which, in free rational creatures, is not determined. Who we are, as persons, is a matter both of our λόγος of essence and of our τρόπος of existing. I suggested something like this in my book on Maximos (and others have suggested a more determinedly existentialist version of this, to the point of suggesting that Maximos opposes essence and existence, locating the image of God at the level of existence). There I said,

> Maximus sometimes, as we have seen, expresses this distinction of levels by distinguishing between existence (ὕπαρξις) or subsisting (ὑφιστάναι), from which the noun, (ὑπόστασις) and being (οὐσία, or εἶναι): persons exist, natures are. Whatever we share with others, we are: it belongs to our nature. But what it is to be a person is not some thing, some quality, that we do *not* share with others—as if there were an irreducible somewhat within each one of us that makes us the unique persons we are. What is unique about each one of us is what we have made of the nature that we have (or are): our own unique mode of existence, which is a matter of our experience in the past, our hopes for the future, the way we live out the nature that we have.[3]

I don't suggest that this is altogether untrue—I am not making a retraction—but my reading of Maximos over the last nearly twenty years since I wrote that has made me realize that Maximos never quite puts it like that.

There seem to me two principal contexts in which Maximos uses the distinction λόγος/τρόπος in relation to the human condition. An example of the first can be found in a passage a little before the one already quoted from *Ambiguum* 42, in which Maximos affirms the inviolability of the λόγοι

---

3. Louth, *Maximus the Confessor*, 59.

of creation. There he says, in relation to the notion of the "three births" of mankind,

> [Y]ou must seek to understand what is the causal principle (ὁ κατ' αἰτίαν λόγος) that preceded the creation of man, which alas remains inseparably within its own proper state of permanence, and what is the mode of his Birth (ὁ τῆς γεννήσεως τρόπος) as a corrective dispensation directed to human sin, a mode which aims to reform the one corrected and restore him completely to the principle of his creation (πρὸς τὸν λόγον τῆς αὐτοῦ γενέσεως). By understanding these things, you will see clearly how God, in becoming man, became perfect in both, wisely restoring the mode of dispensation to the true principle of creation. (AI 42.5 = PG91, 1317D–1320A; trans. Constas, *Difficulties*, 2:129)

Here λόγος is associated with creation, and τρόπος with the οἰκονομία: λόγος corresponds to God's plan for the created order, τρόπος with the divine economy, in particular the Incarnation. We find the same idea expressed in *Ambiguum* 5, where Maximos talks of "recognizing that the principle of being is one thing, and the mode of its existence is another" ("ἕτερος μὲν ὁ τοῦ εἶναι λόγος ἐστίν, ἕτερος δὲ ὁ τοῦ πῶς εἶναι τρόπος," AT 5.117–8), the one confirming nature, the other the οἰκονομία." Τρόπος, then, in contrast to λόγος is less concerned with what we make of our λόγος of being, and more to do with how God, in the Incarnation, renews the natures.

We get a step closer to the idea of mine outlined above in several places where Maximos brings together his triad of being–well-being–eternal-being with the distinction λόγος/τρόπος. For instance in *Ambiguum* 10, he states,

> From their exact understanding of beings, the saints learned that there exist three general modes (καθολικοὺς τρόπους) accessible to human beings, modes by which God created all things, for he endowed us with substance and existence so that we might have being, well-being, and eternal-being. The two extremes (i.e., being and eternal-being) belong solely to God, who is their author, but the intermediate mode depends on our inclination and motion, and through it the extremes are properly said to be what they are, for if the middle term were absent, their designation would be meaningless, for the good (i.e., well-being) would not be present in their midst, and thus the saints realized that apart from their eternal movement toward God, there was no other way for them to possess and preserve the truth of the extremes, which is assured only when well-being is

mixed in the middle of them. (*AI* 10.12 = PG91, 1116AB; trans. Constas, *Difficulties* 1:167–69)

Being and eternal-being are determined by God; they are inscribed in the λόγοι of creation. Well-being (or ill-being) are up to us; they are not determined by the λόγος of creation but depend on our "inclination and motion" ("τῆς ἡμετέρας ... γνώμης τε καὶ κινήσεως"). It is, however, only well-being that will link up being and eternal-being; ill-being leads to the destruction of our natural powers. This presumably allows for different kinds of well-being: rational beings are free, not determined, but that freedom is only truly exercised in the fulfillment of eternal well-being.

A little later on in *Ambiguum* 42, Maximos returns to the distinction between λόγος and τρόπος in connexion with the renewal of natures, καινοτομία, the subject of the previous *Ambiguum*, no. 41. He says,

> Every innovation, generally speaking, takes place in relation to the mode of whatever is being innovated, not in relation to its principle of nature, because when a principle is innovated it effectively results in the destruction of nature, since the nature in question no longer possesses inviolate the principle according to which it exists. When, however, the mode is innovated—so that the principle of nature is preserved inviolate—it manifests a wondrous power, for it displays nature being acted on and acting outside the limits of its own laws. (*AI* 42.26 = PG91, 1341D; Constas, *Difficulties* 2:173)

Maximos goes on to give various examples such as the translation of Enoch and Elijah, the birth of Isaac to the aged Abraham and Sarah, the burning bush, and so on, leading up to the Incarnation:

> Together with and after all these mysteries, he brought about the utterly and truly new mystery of his Incarnation for our sake (on account of which and through which all the other mysteries occur), and thus he innovated nature with respect to its mode, not to its principle, assuming flesh through the medium of a rational soul, being ineffably conceived without seed, and being truly born perfect man without corruption, possessing a rational soul together with his body from the very moment of his ineffable conception. (*AI* 42.29 = PG91, 1344D–1345A; Constas, *Difficulties*, 2:177–9)

It seems to me that when Maximos is thinking of τρόπος, he is less concerned with the way the distinction of λόγος and τρόπος enables him to think what is meant by being a person, and much more concerned with reconciling God's act of re-creation in the Incarnation with his act of creation: re-creation, though radical, does not mean abolition of corrupted nature and literal re-*creation*, but rather with a fundamental renewal of natures at the level of their mode of existence. We need to cooperate with God's act of renewal, and this involves ascetic struggle, acquisition of the virtues (or, more precisely, making manifest virtue that is natural, cf. *DP* 309B), contemplation of the λόγοι of creation, and the rediscovery of the image of God in which we were created, but Maximos is most deeply concerned with understanding how God's act of renewal preserves the λόγοι of creation inviolable.

So, what is my conclusion? I think it is possible to find an inchoate understanding of what it is to be personal in the use Maximos makes of the λόγος/τρόπος distinction, and it is a notion of the person that includes both an element of the given—the image of God in which we were created which belongs to the λόγος of creation—and also an element that we make for ourselves, so that it is not just a matter of *being* a person, but of *becoming* a person, though one cannot become a person without being one. We have to realize, however, that, so far as Maximos is concerned, this is not what he is primarily interested in, and to the extent that we see persons created in freedom, we are probably finding in Maximos ideas that he would have found surprising, for even the exercise of the mode of existence that leads to well-being is much more assimilation of something achieved in the Incarnation, than something of our own.

Bibliography

Daley, Brian E. "Nature and 'Mode of Union': Late Patristic Models for the Personal Unity of Christ." In *The Incarnation: An Interdisciplinary Symposium on the Incarnation of the Son of God*, edited by Stephen T. Davis, Daniel Kendall, and Gerald O'Collins, 164–96. Oxford: Oxford University Press, 2002.

Louth, Andrew. *Maximus the Confessor*. The Early Church Fathers. London: Routledge, 1996.

Maximus the Confessor. *Ambigua ad Iohannem*. Edited and translated by Nicholas P. Constas. In *Difficulties*, 1:62–450; 2:2–330. Abbreviated as *AI*.

———. *Ambigua ad Thomam*. Edited by Bart Janssens. CCSG 48:3–34. Abbreviated as *AT*.

———. *Disputatio cum Pyrrho* [Dispute with Pyrrhus]. Edited by François Combefis. PG91:288A–353B. Abbreviated as *DP*.

———. *Mystagogia*. Edited by Christian Boudignon. CCSG 69:3–74. Abbreviated as *Myst*.

———. *On Difficulties in the Church Fathers: The Ambigua*. Edited and translated by Nicholas P. Constas. 2 vols. Dumbarton Oaks Medieval Library 28–29. Cambridge: Harvard University Press, 2014. Abbreviated as *Difficulties*.

———. *Quaestiones et dubia* [Questions and Doubts]. Edited by José H. Declerck. CCSG 10:3–170. Abbreviated as *QD*.

Prestige, George Léonard. *God in Patristic Thought*. London: SPCK, 1936.

Sherwood, Polycarp. *The Earlier Ambigua of Saint Maximus the Confessor and His Refutation of Origenism*. Studia Anselmiana, philosophica theologica. Rome: "Orbis Catholicus"/Herder, 1955.

12

The Conceptual Apparatus of Maximus the Confessor and Contemporary Anthropology

Georgi Kapriev

Delimiting the Thematic Field

Today there is a progressively growing scholarly interest in Byzantine philosophy. It is important to realize that this interest is directed not so much to the concepts having some analogy within the framework of Western thought, but rather towards those of its features which could be considered as a source of its particularity, originality and creativity. Interestingly, one can find this interest not only within the disciplines of philosophy and theology, but also in other disciplines such as, for example, sociology[1] and psychology.[2] It should not be difficult to realize that St. Maximus the Confessor is always at the center; he is the thinker to whom are dedicated most of the studies, significantly more than all other Byzantine philosophers taken together. In addition, it should be pointed out that this is not just a historical interest.

In this paper, I will focus my attention on the conceptual apparatus of Maximus the Confessor[3] which includes a set of fundamental concepts

---

1. Cf. e.g., Kapriev and Ivan, "Actor-Network Theory"; Tchalakov, "The Amateur's Action"; Kapriev, "The Byzantine Trace"; Tanev, "Actor-Network vs. Activity Theory."

2. Cf. e.g. Loudovikos, Ψυχανάλυση καὶ ὀρθόδοξη θεολογία; Tympas, *Carl Jung and Maximus the Confessor*.

3. The notion of conceptual apparatus was developed by Kazimierz Ajdukiewicz in the mid-1930s, within a standpoint of radical conventionalism. According to him, the picture of the world one has developed is not coming directly from the data of experience, but depends on the specific conceptual apparatus chosen.

which are highly relevant in Triadology and Christology. These concepts are becoming however increasingly relevant in anthropology. I will freely admit that my reflections on this topic were inspired by the anthropological themes which became central in the ongoing critical theological and philosophical[4] discussion of the theology of the Metropolitan of Pergamon John Zizioulas. This discussion has involved many contemporary thinkers[5] and has touched upon both some of the key themes in Orthodox theology and the philosophical positions providing their grounding.

In addition to the ongoing critical discussions in contemporary Orthodox theology I will also refer to the ongoing transformation/renewal of some of the contemporary sociological and philosophical concepts and, in particular, some of the concepts associated with the theories of Bruno Latour and his followers. While Orthodox theological discussions focus predominantly on Orthodox Patristics[6] and its specific conceptual apparatus, socio-philosophical studies are rather interested in acquiring some additional conceptual resources in a way that could enable the explanation of some specific phenomena that were not able to be explained within the

---

4. I am not hesitating to qualify the debate as theological/philosophical since in the Byzantine Orthodox tradition (from Gregory the Theologian through Maximus the Confessor, Photius of Constantinople, Symeon the New Theologian, Gregory Palamas, to Georgios Scholarius) speculative theology is considered as (the highest) part of the first philosophy or at least as being at the same epistemological level. It is not by accident that some of the scholars involved in the debate are directly speaking about the need of a proper philosophical approach in their argumentation and referring to the teaching of St. Maximus on being as one of the best such approaches.

5. The number of scholars involved in this discussion has grown to such extent that it is hard to provide an exhaustive list of references. From the Bulgarian authors I would only mention Stoyan Tanev and his doctoral thesis "The Theology of the Divine Energies in 20th Century Orthodox Thought" (in Bulgarian), defended in 2012 in the Faculty of Theology at Sofia University "St Kliment Ohridski," and published as a monograph *Ti, Koyto si navsyakǎde*, with its part dedicated to the theology of the metropolitan John Zizioulas, 106–148. From the literature in English and French I should mention at least the following works: Zizioulas, *Being as Communion*; Zizioulas, *The One and the Many*; Zizioulas, *Lectures in Christian Dogmatics*; Zizioulas, *Communion and Otherness*; Larchet, *Personne et nature*; Loudovikos, "Person instead of Grace"; Loudovikos, *Eucharistic Ontology*; Loudovikos, "Eikon and Mimesis"; Perishich, "Person and Essence"; Torrance, "Personhood and Patristics"; Turcescu, "'Person' versus 'Individual'"; Turcescu, *Gregory of Nyssa and the Concept of Divine Persons*.

6. I do really hope that limiting the debate to the authority of the Church Fathers from St. Basil the Great to St. John of Damascus would not be interpreted as a silent acceptance of the Western idea of Patristics, i.e., the temporal period between the fourth and the eighth century. In the Orthodox tradition the understanding of Patristics does not refer to any specific historical period of time, but to the unity of the thought of the Orthodox Church Fathers across the centuries.

context of their existing conceptual apparatus. It goes without saying that in both cases the conceptual precision is critically important.

The present text deals with several actively discussed groups of terms. The analysis will focus on two specific conceptual levels: the first one is the level of the natural and the hypostatic; the second one is the level of the universal and the particular. My reflections are drawn from a broader philosophical perspective and intentionally do not engage with the specific details of debate that was mentioned above. This is why the discussion will stay away from any personal, be it positive or negative, references to specific authors who have contributed to the interpretation of the concepts of interest.

The Primacy of the Existential and the Personal

Anyone possessing some historico-philosophical competences would agree that the idea of the personal is one of the most fundamental Christian contributions (if not the most fundamental one) to philosophy;[7] that the Christian way of doing philosophy deviates from the essentialist thinking of Ancient Greek philosophy for which the essence is the highest category and moves to the adoption of a personalistic thinking;[8] that in this way of philosophizing the most important unit of analysis is not the essence, the substance or being in itself, but its actuality, its activities and movements and therefore its existence; that in such way of philosophizing the personal and the existential have the highest priority. However, "a priority of the personal and of the existential" does not mean that what is natural and essential (what is related to the essence and nature of things) is left out of the philosophical investigation. The primacy of the hypostasis does not exclude at all the essence either from the existential sphere of being neither from the teaching on being. The essence should not and cannot be "marginalized" and especially within the structural context of the hypostasis. This is a point that receives a particularly strong emphasis by Maximus the Confessor (who is persistently used as a referee in the ongoing debates) in a definition which, to my great surprise, is rarely used or not used at all in the discussions.

Immediately after providing a definition of hypostasis and πρόσωπον he introduces the concept of ἐνούσιον: "Ἐνούσιον is that which is understood not only as having in itself the sum of the properties (τῶν ἰδιωμάτων ἄθροισμα) through which a thing is recognized as different from every other thing, but also as actually possessing what is universal for the nature to

---

7. Florovsky, "Resurrection of Life," 19.
8. Kasper, *Jesus der Christus*, 212.

which it belongs (τὸ κοινὸν τῆς πραγματικῶς κεκτημένον)" (*TP14* 152A). It is important to point out that it is not only the universal (i.e., the species) which is enhypostasized (it is actually πραγματικῶς-present in the corresponding individuals, *TP14* 149B) but also the hypostasis itself is immanent in the essence (ἐνούσιον). The essence is enhypostasized to the same degree as the hypostasis is en-essentialized. Ignoring the essence in its constitutive completeness which definitively includes the universal, automatically discredits the hypostasis.

One could say therefore that the above mentioned "priority of the existential and the personal" is above all a priority of the observation and of the attention. The first and most genuine Christian question is asking for the salvation of every specific man, the particular person. The horizon of each reflection is within the realm of the soteriological. It is in this and only in this sense that one can speak of "personalism" and "existentialism" in Christian philosophy.[9] The hypostasis is the primary theme, it is the subject which is the source of all philosophy, but not the only one. It is its first, but neither absolute nor sole foundation.

Nature and Essence

St. Maximus defines the term "nature" as that which is common (species, εἶδος) for all individual beings in which this nature *is*, and which *are* through it. Essence means a natural presence in being which is expressed through the various hypostases as carriers of the corresponding nature (cf. *TP26* 276AB). Maximus traditionally identifies "essence" with "nature." His definition is as follows: "Essence and nature mean the same thing. Both concepts are general and universal, because they are always predicated through the different hypostases and never with respect to a particular single person" (cf. *TP14* 149BC). The essence is predicated and manifested through and in all things by nature. "For that which is commonly and generically predicated of certain things constitutes the definition of their essence, the privation of which brings about the destruction of their nature, since no beings remain what they are when they are deprived of their natural, constituent elements."[10] The natural properties do not undergo any change, reduction or

---

9. It should be pointed out that in modern Western philosophy the concepts "essentialism," "personalism" and "existentialism" have very specific meanings. In this sense the Orthodox philosophical thinkers cannot be qualified neither as "essentialists" nor as "personalists" or "existentialists."

10. *AT* 2, 1037CD (trans. Constas, in *Difficulties*, 1:15.

amplification at any circumstances, even in the cases when multiple natures co-inhere in a composite hypostasis (*TP14* 149D).

The essence is manifested in individuals according to their existence, so it is always something enhypostasized (ἐνυπόστατον), which cannot be known in itself (καθ' αὐτὸ), even though its actuality should not be seen as a mental product or accident, but as actually existing species (εἶδος πραγματικῶς).[11] The terms "Essence" and "Nature" acquire their central place in Christian thought through their inherent relationship to the term hypostasis, with which they are in constant communication and interdependence. One cannot think of hypostasis without nature, but nature does not coincide with its hypostasis: the two concepts are mutually exclusive.[12] Moreover, the distinction drawn by Leontius of Byzantium is fully valid for St. Maximus. It emphasizes that the overall concept is the nature of the species ("φύσις ἐν τῷ εἴδει θεωρουμένη"), which however exists and can be seen only as a nature of a particular being ("φύσις ἐν τῷ ἀτόμῳ θεωρουμένη"), as "an indivisible particular nature." This nature has an actual being which is not in the form of some preexisting autonomous independence, but only as subsisting in a hypostasis.[13] The nature does not existentially precede the individual beings, which are its carriers. The aim of this distinction does not consist in focusing on the logical abstraction, but on the actual existence by insisting that any particular hypostasis is not identical with the rest of the hypostases of the same species. It is "similar" to them since it carries the characteristics of the particular hypostasis alone.[14]

11. Cf. *TP14* 149C–153A; *TP16* 205AB.

12. *TP23a*, 264A; *Ep15* 549C. Maximus incorporates in his definitions what has been achieved before him and further develops it. Although the concepts of essence and hypostasis were used by Origen and Athanasius of Alexandria, their ultimate definitions came from the Cappadocian Fathers. In the text of a letter that has become known as *Letter 38*, Basil the Great introduces "nature" as a name referring to the universal nature and not to a specific being. The universality of the nature equally covers all things which are named in the same way. These πράγματα that are characterized by one single definition of the essence/οὐσία (which is also referred to as nature), are consubstantial (ὁμοούσιοι). The essence/nature is the foundation of the thing that it is referred to and points to its definition as a genus; see Basil of Cesaraea, *Epistle 38*, 2–3. In other words, the Cappadocian Fathers assign the term "essence" to the so called second essence (δευτέρα οὐσία) in Aristotle; see *Categories* 5, 2a11–19; *Topica* 2, 115b8–10. They do not put into question the existential reality of the universal nature. However, according to them, it does not exist in finite beings except in the individuals possessing it (this however does not have the same validity in the simple Divine nature).

13. Such position may lead to ignoring the concept of an "individual essence" (μερικὴ οὐσία), which since the times of the Cappadocians to John Philoponus had usually been positioned in the same class of concepts as "individual," ὑπόστασις and πρόσωπον.

14. John of Damascus makes a special emphasis on this particular point: *De*

It is well known that there is a resistance of many modern theoreticians against the concept of essence. I believe that such resistance is the result of a kind of terminological inertia which tends to reduce the essence to a logico-epistemological *abstractum*. Driven by the nausea from the absurdity of such kind of being, J.-P. Sartre, for example, uses the terms "essence" and "nature" as referring to the actual "image" or "figure" of the Self. He is however also fully aware that by means of his or her potential capacities every human being is a human and not "moss, mould or cauliflower." This is why he is forced to accept the existence of a conditional human universality ("une universalité humaine de condition"). He prefers to speak of "human condition" ("condition de l'homme") instead of "human nature." This is "the ensemble of the *a priori* boundaries drawing the fundamental human situation in the universe" ("l'ensemble des limites a priori qui esquissent sa situation fondamentale dans l'univers)." These boundaries are neither objective either subjective, but have both objective and subjective aspects. The existential human project aims their redrawing and rearrangement, overcoming or adapting to them.[15] One should also add the drawing of these boundaries does not delimit an empty space, but the actual potentialities of the human, which are actualized through their personal activities. Interestingly, the Byzantine understanding of "essence" and "nature" could be even described in a very similar way.

If one follows the line of thought of the Cappadocians and Maximus, one should say, using the words of John of Damascus, that the "essence" is predicated only with respect to self-subsisting beings.[16] The nature is the common λόγος of the being of things having the same essence as well as the

---

haeresibus, 83addit. 23–79. Cf. *Expositio de fide orthodoxa* 55 (3.11): "The nature is may either be taken purely theoretically, since it is not self-subsistent; or it may be taken as what is common to persons of the same species and connects them, in which case it is said to be a nature taken specifically; or the same, with accident added, may be considered wholly in one person, in which case it is said to be a nature taken individually, which is the same as taken specifically." Translation by Frederic H. Chase, in John of Damascus, *Writings*, 289.

15. Sartre, *L'existentialisme est un humanisme*.
16. Cf. *Dialectica* 4; 10; 39.

beginning of their movement and rest.¹⁷ The particular on the other hand is called individual, ὑπόστασις, πρόσωπον.¹⁸

ἄτομον, ὑπόστασις, πρόσωπον

ἄτομον

The interpretation of the term "individual" illustrates to the greatest extent the terminological irresponsibility which is manifested in the course of the contemporary debates. The irresponsibility is an expression of the inability to make a difference between two specific classes of conceptual levels or orders: the first one makes a distinction between the universal and the particular; the second one distinguishes between the natural and the hypostatic. When one makes the distinction between the universal and the particular, the term individual should be included in the class of the particular together with such terms as hypostasis and πρόσωπον. The terms individual, ὑπόστασις, πρόσωπον and individual/separate essence denote the same thing when considered within the horizon of their distinction from the universal, i.e., the εἶδος.

St. Maximus defines the term hypostatic difference (ὑποστατικὴ διαφορά) by pointing out that the division by number of different things having the same essence is expressed in the multiplicity of the individuals (*TP14* 152B). He considers the term ἄτομον as a category of the essence

---

17. These and similar definitions appear to be the basis for the following reflection of Photius of Constantinople: The synonyms "man," "human nature," the "species man" are logical concepts (λογικὰ ὀνόματα) which cannot be predicated with respect to something actual and self-existing, but only with respect to the thing which is said to possess what is meant by them. Humanity (ἡ ἀνθρωπότης) and Divinity (ἡ θεότης) however are the names of things that are not logical, but natural (φυσικῶν πραγμάτων ὀνόματα), things that are being according to their nature. By "man" we refer to the inner nature of the hypostasis, by "humanity" we refer to the same nature, but not as inherently existing in the hypostasis but in itself, in its activity in a way that is abstracted from existing matter (*Amphilochiae*, 27.5–15, 27.105–112, 27.150–5, 75.42–52, 230.17–42). The "Divinity" and the "humanity" refer to Divine and human nature, respectively, in terms of their proper activity.

18. Cf. *Dialectica* 5; 10; 30; 41. In this text John of Damascus points out that "individual" is the same as ὑπόστασις or "person" as far as it refers to someone who is well defined and belonging to a given nature. As far as the terms could be conceptualized as referring to the numerically singular within the context of the general, they could be used as meaning the same thing. This however does not mean that they are synonymous (and not only in the context of the Trinity) when considered against the natural and the hypostatic orders. "Individual" is a term that is rather associated with the natural order than with the hypostatic properties—cf. *Dialectica* 5; 11; 50.

resulting from the distinction between genus and species, in other words, as a category which belongs to the natural order and not the hypostatic one.[19]

The Latin *individuum* and the Greek ἄτομον both mean the same thing: "indivisible." They both name the smallest particular which carries a common nature which cannot undergo any further destruction or reduction since it will result in a loss of the characteristics of the common nature. Every individual-atom is the single separate carrier and representative of its nature. It is the carrier of the commonly valid and commonly possessed properties, characteristics and potencies. Individual/atom is a term belonging to the natural order. Through the term "individual" every separate being is recognized namely in its non-uniqueness, in its similarity to all other atoms of the same type. By definition it is not associated with uniqueness, but on the contrary.[20]

The difference between "individual" and hypostasis cannot be expressed, however, by means of dialectic criteria such as "closedness-openness" or "egotism-love." There is no any good reason to claim that the atom/individual is by definition non-relational or that it carries any negative connotations, such as, for example, some of the connotations used in anthropology referring to the isolation of human being from other human beings, or from any other creature in general. Furthermore it is equally impossible for the individual to be thought of as a hypostasis that has failed to become or manifest itself as a person, as far as the two concepts belong to the two different conceptual orders that are irreducible to each other. It is even less appropriate to consider the individual and, respectively, individuality, as some kind of "breakdown," "collapse" or annihilation of the hypostasis. It should be also pointed out that the "individual" is not just a biological, social or some other type phenomenon: it is a single particular being from the point of view of its natural valence which is commonly valid for its genus. An individual cannot seek to become a hypostasis or to be established as a hypostasis because, by definition, it reflects aspects of what is universal and commonly valid within the singular and the particular, whose uniqueness is expressed by the term hypostasis.

---

19. TP16 201D–204A, 205BC. Larchet, *La divinisation de l'homme*, 146.

20. This fact appears to be most relevant in contemporary physics and chemistry. Physicists and chemists are both fully aware that each and every atom has its particular uniqueness, but it is not this particular uniqueness which defines its atomic identity. What is most relevant for the particularity of a specific atom is its association with all other atoms belonging to the corresponding chemical element which is defined by the number of its electrons and protons.

ὑπόστασις and πρόσωπον

The defects of the discussions of the scholars involved in the current debates using the term hypostasis are most sharply manifested in the failure to take into account the historical shaping of the definitions. In essence, the correct insistence on the homogeneity of tradition often turns into its self-confident interpretation as ahistorical and indifferent towards the course of intellectual history. Meanwhile, it is exactly the account of the historical semantic accumulations which makes it possible to withhold the homogeneity of the tradition. Maximus the Confessor is the one who manages to recapitulate the continuous previous work on the concept of hypostasis and offer a set of definitions that is still completely valid today.

The first attempt to define the concept in the Christian tradition is the work of the Cappadocians, and it almost exclusively from the point of view of Triadology. Ὑπόστασις represents the universal in a particular subject, which however is based on its own proper characteristics ("ἐν τῷ τινὶ πράγματι διὰ τῶν ἐπιφαινομένων ἰδιωμάτων"). Ὑπόστασις is characterized by what distinguishes it from the general and the universal: by its own inherent, unreplaceable and unique properties ("διὰ τῶν οἰκείων γνωρισμάτων").[21]

The Cappadocian concept of hypostasis emerged within the triadological problematics and showed some deficits in the course of the later christological controversies. In addition, there was the not fully established terminology and the difference in the conceptual apparatuses corresponding to the realms of theology and Divine economy (which was finally overcome by Maximus); but not only that. The automatic application of the Cappadocian definition of hypostasis which emphasizes the specific characteristics leads to an excessive asymmetry between the two natures in Christ, as far as his human nature does not have its own hypostasis. Leontius of Byzantium is the thinker, who was able to overcome the tension between the definition of hypostasis through the focus on the uniqueness of its characteristics and through the focus on its self-subsistence.[22] The extension of the definition

---

21. Basil of Caesaraea, *Epistle 38*, 3.8–25. This is why when a ὑπόστασις/person is assigned definitive properties coming from biological, social, religious, familial, or other associations, there is a typical case of a replacement of concepts. Such cases concern the individual characteristics, i.e., characteristics providing additional specifications for the individual, which is positioned in some class of commonality, i.e., of un-uniqueness. Even though such classes have a limited degree of commonality, the characteristics defined by them are also individual and not hypostatic.

22. Without denying or undermining the properties providing the uniqueness of the hypostasis, he emphasizes the productive relevance of the being-for-itself (τὸ καθ' ἑαυτὸ εἶναι) and existing-for-itself (καθ' ἑαυτὸ ὑπάρχειν); see Leontius of Byzantium, *Contra Nestorianos et Eutychianos* 1, PG86a, 1280A; *Epilyseis*, PG86b, 1917D.

points out a specific constitutional aspect of the hypostasis, which by staying within the horizon of the hypostatic, stands above the enhypostasized nature or natures, without trying to derive them from within this same hypostatic horizon. The emphasis on this specific constitutional aspect helps in the emergence of two unsubordinated conceptual levels: the natural and the hypostatic. The term ἐνυπόστατον introduced by Leontius plays a key role in emphasizing this distinction.

When defining the term ὑπόστασις Maximus refers simultaneously to the two definitions that were formed in the tradition before him, considering hypostasis and "person" as equivalent. His starting point is that hypostasis and person mean the same thing." They both exist separately and with distinctive properties ("μερικόν τε καὶ ἴδιον") with regard to their inner content ("ὡς ἐφ ἑαυτῶν τὴν περιγραφήν"), which cannot be predicated in terms of the nature of the multitude of things (TP14 152A). Therefore, the distinctive feature of the hypostasis is that it not only differs by number from the other hypostases of the same species, but is also treated in every respect as self-existent (TP14 152D).

According to another broader definition, hypostasis is defined as something that exists separately and by itself ("it is of itself"), and at the same time it is an essence together with particular or unique properties which makes it different from the hypostases which are of the same species not only in terms of number (Ep15 557D). The particular and unique properties ("τοῖς χαρακτηριστικοῖς ἰδιώμασι," TP26 276B; TP23a 261 B, 264A) make an individual of a specifically given species different, already as a hypostasis, from other individuals of the same species. Ὑπόστασις signifies the unrepeatably separate (καθ' ἕκαστον), the uniquely particular (ἰδικόν).[23]

An hypostasis outlines and describes the universal and the indescribable (in other words, the unique) as proper of a particular thing ("Ὑπόστασίς ἐστιν, ἡ τὸ κοινόν τε καὶ ἀπερίγραπτον ἐν τῷ τινι ἰδίως παριστῶσα καὶ περιγράφουσα," TP23c 265D1–3). Nature itself is rather the appropriation of a hypostasis, as a nature has its existence only as enhypostasized (ἐνυπόστατον). Here one can speak of mutual immanence where the enhypostasized is actually implementing the existential; it manifests what has been en-existentialized, while the ὑπόστασις acquires the possibility to actualize the natural energy (TP16 205AB; TP23a; TP23b; TP23c).

The identification of hypostasis with "person" is the result of a long historical process[24] culminating in Maximus' conceptual framework. One

23. Cf. Petrov, *Maksim Ispovednik*, 17.

24. The process started with their opposition by Basil the Great, continued with the reconciling formulas of Gregory the Theologian and passed through the conjunction in the dogmatic formula of Chalcedon.

can see that in a "scandalously" plain way in one of his definitions where he points out that the essence and nature can never be defined through a single person (*TP14* 149B). The general sense of the definition, however, suggests the use of hypostasis.

It should be pointed out however that the close connection between the concepts should not erase the distinction that is based on the fact that while it is only rational beings (God, angels, man) that could have a πρόσωπον or person, the hypostasis is associated with every single thing or being that is self-subsisting, has a nature and unique properties. In his specific analyzes Maximus has obviously taken into account that particular difference. This is why John Damascene, who was following the course of Maximus' thought, has used the terms interchangeably, but has also pointed out the incomplete correspondence between the two terms. The focus of the term ὑπόστασις is on the individual self-determined existence, while "person" rather refers to the specific actions associated with the personal properties in terms of their relational aspects with respect to others.[25] It is therefore possible for a person to represent or act instead of others, while it is impossible to think of hypostases in the same way.[26] In this sense, "person" means the ability of a hypostasis to un-spontaneously enter into relationships and relate to the other hypostases which are involved in those relations.

Problems Associated with the Terms Hypostasis and Person

The different scope of the terms ὑπόστασις and person does not seem to create serious problems in their use. The problems however happen (and specifically in in the contemporary debate) under the pressure of a dialectical move which is ultimately based on the above mentioned difference between them.

There is certain paradox: if, while remaining faithful to the tradition, we can argue that each hypostasis radiates the energy which is inherent in the enhypostasized nature (or natures),[27] then any self-existent being

---

25. As is the case of a Prefect who is ruling in the name of the Emperor representing him in person.

26. Cf. *Dialectica* 30; 43; *De haeresibus*, 83 addit. 104–11.

27. Here I do not intend to neglect at all the fundamental place of the teaching on the distinction between essence and energies in the Eastern Christian Tradition. Today one can hear opinions according to which the teaching was a competitive ideology developed by Gregory Palamas and his followers and, therefore, having only a situational historical value. On the contrary, I can point out at least three recent books demonstrating that the teaching was constituted and articulated in the period between Athanasius of Alexandria and John of Damascus: Bradshaw, *Aristotle East and West*,

should be in a continuous state of active relational exchange with other hypostases. In other words, it should be dialogical in its existence by necessity, becoming part of a "dialogical network" of relations including the relations with the Divine. In contrast, every man as a rational being is preordained with the duty to be dialogical: a rational man should be in communion and relational as part of its constitutional characteristics, to establish himself as freedom and love—two properties which he or she, obviously, may or may not possess in moments of selfishness, self-closing, isolation. There is therefore a certain discontinuity in the communion and relationality that could be assigned to the human person.

Every rational reflection is by definition a procedural termination of the spontaneous action. Each movement of the human mind or consciousness "discredits" the action and introduces an alternative. It was Aristotle who was one of the first to observe that the reasonable and sensory soul is "in a sense, everything that is" as far as it consciously perceives and reflects on all knowable phenomena.[28] Only a rational being can relate in a reflective way and consciously "take the place of" and be "instead or on behalf of" something or someone else. A person/πρόσωπον is not only relational (it is not just in relation), but it is truly dialogical in the real sense of the word. This statement could be expressed in the language of the teaching on the Divine and human energies in order to emphasize that a person un-spontaneously redirects, modulates, concentrates or disperses the personally radiated energies. As we shall see, a person has all the necessary mechanisms to do that. This is the special way for a particular human being "to take the relay" (in the language of Bruno Latour and actor-network theory). A person controls and regulates its own relations, and this is exactly the basis for the nuanced fine distinction between "person" and ὑπόστασις.[29]

I would like to emphasize here that, despite of this nuance, the Byzantine authors continued to use those terms synonymously. This is obvious in the first cited definition of Maximus where he declared that essence and nature were never defined trough a single πρόσωπον. In this statement the identification of the two terms have been done automatically.

153–220; Kapriev, *Philosophie in Byzanz*, 21–149; Larchet, *La théologie des énergies divines*. In the last chapter of his book Larchet indicates thirty fundamental positions of the teaching on the Divine energies which were relevant already in the eighth century, see ibid., 455–60.

28. Cf. Aristotle, *De anima* 3.8, 431a20–23.

29. I would like to emphasize here that, despite of this nuance, Byzantine authors continued to use those terms synonymously. This is obvious in the first cited definition of Maximus, where he declared that essence and nature were never defined through a single πρόσωπον. In this statement the identification of the two terms has been done automatically.

The above reflections lead to an unpleasant message about one of the central concepts in the contemporary debates. According to some authoritative participants in the debates, the relations are constitutive of or constitute the ὑπόστασις/person. The person is seen only as σχέσις, which results in a relational theory of the ὑπόστασις/person which is extended into a relational ontology: a "personal ontology of relations." Of course there are such theories and some of them have been developed with a solid internal consistency. The most popular among them is the Marxist anthropology which can be aphoristically summarized in the famous thesis of Marx: "But human nature is not an *abstractum* which is internally available to each individual. In its reality/actuality it is the ensemble of social relations."[30] Right after this statement Marx rejects the notion of nature as just a "genus," as an internal, mute universality which naturally links the different individuals.[31]

The procedure illustrated above is quite exemplary: first the essence is reduced to its logical-cognitive *abstractum* ("οὐσία ἐν τῷ εἴδει θεωρουμένη," respectively "καθόλου θεωρουμένη"), which is subsequently postulated as the core of the nature/essence: it must be universal and indifferent, but "really" present in each individual. As an alternative to this absurd construction of being Marx offers the "ensemble" of social relations in their entirety. This "real" universal core becomes a very specific, personally existing structure through the specific situational network of relationships which ultimately forms the person. Within the scope of this horizon there is neither a need to reject the existence of the nature (Marx does not), nor to problematize the ontological integrity of the individual being. In this situation, the statement that "any existing being has an essence" protects the logical legitimacy (especially in anthropology) of the theory. It requires however the additional agreement that such "essence" is the "ensemble" of external relations forming the individual being. If we expand to the extreme the scope of the predicate "social" we can see that Marx provides a model for any relational anthropology.

Whatever the merits of such relational anthropology, we have to note that it comes in sharp contrast to the authoritative Christian thought. For example, in His second commandment, the Lord Jesus Christ said, "love your neighbor as yourself (ὡς σεαυτόν)" (Mark 12:31 NRSV). There should be therefore a foundational self (αὐτός) as the source or factor forming the relations (including the relations to our neighbor or the intimately close

---

30. Marx, *Thesen über Feuerbach*, 6: "Aber das menschliche Wesen ist kein dem einzelnen Individuum inwohnendes Abstraktum. In seiner Wirklichkeit ist es das ensemble der gesellschaftlichen Verhältnisse."

31. Ibid.: "[N]ur als 'Gattung,' als innere, stumme, die vielen Individuen *natürlich* verbindende Allgemeinheit."

ones) and making them possible. A relationship-σχέσις cannot be primary in terms of being even though the relationality of a hypostasis towards other hypostases is an essential element of their existence. It is unquestionable that every human hypostasis in its self-activity and its specific existential presence is relational: it is a person. The directional relationality is fundamental to its existence. By definition, however, it does not have its existence from the relation or the relations.[32] In terms of both its being and its existence it is before everything a πρᾶγμα αὐθύπαρκτον.[33]

It is not by accident that the Byzantine authorities emphasize the self-existence of unique hypostasis, but this emphasis should be understood within the context of its en-essentialized status, as well as within the context of the actuality of the concretely enhypostasized essence or nature. This is the perspective providing the basis for the articulation of the distinction between "λόγος or principle of nature—τρόπος or mode of existence."

λόγος/Principle of Nature and τρόπος/Mode of Existence: Definition

The conceptual dyad: principle of nature (or being—λόγος τῆς οὐσίας or λόγος τοῦ εἶναι) and mode of existence (τρόπος τῆς ὑπάρξεως or τοῦ πῶς εἶναι τρόπος), emerged as part of the argumentation practice of the Byzantine thinkers as early as the fourth century and was appropriated by the monastic circles from the fifth to the seventh century. It was used exclusively in the Trinitarian context. Leontius of Byzantium introduced it within the context of the christological debates. Its use in for the theological reflection on being is due to Maximus the Confessor. The general perspective of the dyad is the distinction between "what something is" (τί ἐστίν) and the how of its being (the how-being) (πῶς ἐστίν).

According to Maximus the λόγος of nature (or existence, AT 5, 1052B; Myst 23, 701A) is the constitutive definition of nature. It is immutable, unchangeable and corresponds to the law of nature. The unchangeable λόγος is part of the divine law (νόμος) for any nature that exists and was created

32. This is exactly what provides the basis for the examination of the inner existential constitution of the being of each ὑπόστασις (both human and non-human) which defines its ability to enter into existential interactions. It is this existential constitution which allows for such examination and constitutes it as possible. It does not allow ignoring the inner structural order and the potential of the ὑποστάσεις or considering them as "formidable castles now in ruins," "black boxes," etc.

33. Cf. the interpretation of the concept by Michael Psellos in his treatise "Εἰς τὸ οὐσία πρᾶγμα αὐθύπαρκτον," i.e., *Opusculum 7* (in *Michaelis Pselli Philosophica minora*, ed. John M, Duffy, 22–28).

according to this law (*AI* 31, 1280A). The λόγος is the carrier of its definition or normative constitution. Any hypothetical alteration or renewal of the λόγος would lead to the destruction of the specific kind of nature. Without any doubt that this λόγος/law carries also the natural necessity: it sets all the properties and characteristics of the self that are constitutive of it and without which it would not be itself. In the case of a reasonable nature such necessary characteristics are the mind, the rationality/intellect and the free will which implements the freedom. The necessity mentioned above is not the necessity which could be seen as an imposed obedience and which constraints and counteracts the personal freedom.

The mode/τρόπος of existence is the order of natural action. It carries the variation, modification or innovation (even in quite large amplitudes) within the context of the explicit immutability of the λόγος (*AI* 42, 1341D). While the λόγος establishes being, the τρόπος establishes the specific presence of this being (*AT* 5, 1052B). Every self-existing thing does not simply have being, but how-being (τὸ πῶς εἶναι), which is the first kind of restriction (εἶδος περιγραφῆς) on the predefined in the λόγος being of the essence (*AI* 10, 1180B). The exact words of St. Maximus are: "The very being of beings itself does not exist simply or without qualities, but in a particular way, which constitutes its first form of delimitation—as well as a powerful demonstration that there is a beginning of beings and of their coming to be."[34] The possession of a λόγος of nature and τρόπος of existence is a necessary condition for the existence of every particular being—its existence is impossible without them (*AI* 42, 1341D).

Problematizing the Contemporary Debate

A key moment of the contemporary debate is the different answer to the question whether the field of applicability of the term τρόπος of existence is the nature/essence or hypostasis. Whether it is natural or personal? Whether the distinction between τί ἐστὶν and πῶς ἐστὶν is identical with the distinction "nature"—hypostasis? And whether it is acceptable to construct an opposition between the following two conceptual links: first, the link "essence/nature-necessity-law" which is characteristic of the λόγος of nature and; second, the link "hypostasis/person-relation-freedom-love-grace" which is characteristic of the τρόπος τῆς ὑπάρξεως and directly associated with the hypostasis? Here a mere quoting of the authoritative texts of modern researchers cannot solve the problem.[35] Since the focus is on the hu-

---

34. *AI* 10, 1180B (trans. Constas, *Difficulties*, 1:291–93).

35. Some scholars associate the "mode of existence" directly and uniquely to the

man hypostasis, the criterion cannot be the application of the terms in the Trinitarian dogma, because the case of the Holy Trinity is too special to be applied in the anthropological domain.

As early as the second half of the fourth century the Cappadocian fathers have made quite explicit clarifications with respect to the formulation of the Divine divisibility in terms of hypostasis and the Divine unity in terms of essence or nature emphasizing the simplicity of the nature and the lack of discontinuity and intervals in the Divine being. Maximus the Confessor speaks of Divinity as an exception to the general mode of operation of the dyad Λόγος–τρόπος. Since the Divine nature is not divided, distributed or simply represented in Divine persons, but exists fully to each one of them, the Divine hypostases coincide with the modes of existence of the divine essence (cf. AI 67, 1400D–1401A). In the case of the Divinity, the distinction Λόγος–τρόπος helps the clear articulation of the fact that the three hypostases of the Trinity are nothing else but the Divine nature and the way of divine existence in the three hypostases does not violate the simplicity and the actuality of the nature. The existence of the hypostases with their properties and their relations is the very existence of God is not. This does not weaken and or relativize the proper being of nature and its principle.[36] The Trinitarian context cannot be the model explaining anthropological one.

Unfortunately, the compromise based on the teaching on the λόγοι does not give an answer to the above question either. Some of the participants in the debate suggest a specific type of λόγος that could be interpreted as relational reality which is ontologically and permanently related to the way of being seen as a personal realization of the dialogue inherent in the λόγος. The human personal λόγος is understood as a personal divine proposal or invitation awaiting a response. This dialogue is seen as representing

---

hypostatic order referring to the works of Polycarp Sherwood, Hans Urs von Balthasar, Christoph von Schönborn, Alain Rioux and J.-M. Garrigues. I have enough reasons to claim that in most of them this position is ideologically founded in order to serve catholic theologians in their debates with the "Neo-Palamites" in the 60s and the 70s of the twentieth century, aiming at discrediting the teaching on the natural energies.

36. This is in line with the reflections of John of Damascus. The three Divine hypostases are not just similar but of the same essence. The unity of the Divinity is not constituted by the hypostases; it is in three hypostases and is three hypostases each one of which has the perfect completeness of the Divine essence and existence. The hypostases differ between each other only in terms of their unique hypostatic properties. In the case of the Divinity, the hypostatic properties coincide with their existence and express the mode of existence (τρόπος τῆς ὑπάρξεως) of the single nature which is proper for each of the hypostases. There are two kinds of properties: natural, which constitute the difference of different species, and hypostatic, which make the difference between specific hypostases; see *Expositio de fide orthodoxa* 1.13, 58–61.

the personal natural status of the communion with God. In addition, the λόγοι of the things are directly seen as Divine energies.

One must admit that this is a very sympathetic version. It however does not help in formulating the necessary answers. This is because the λόγος of every being which actually defines its ontological constitution and ultimate purpose (QThal 64, 709B) as well as defines the individual thing as an individual (AI 7, 1077C), by protecting its inner constitution, is actually a complex set of multiple and heterogeneous divine words–λόγοι that form the complete determination of its being. Every particular being is consistent with a multiple number of λόγοι: the λόγος identifying its essence; the λόγος that situates it in a specific genus and species; the λόγος, defining its various but concrete and unique properties; the λόγος corresponding to its coming into being and existence defining its existential certainty, etc.[37] There is no one singular λόγος, which corresponds to each individual, but a multiplicity of λόγοι carrying both the universality and the particularity, synthesizing the coherence of the λόγος which is proper of a particular being incorporating all the aspects of its being and existence.

Indeed, all creatures are "part" of God, exactly through and in the λόγοι which are not some type of processions from the Divine nature, but Divine thoughts and wishes flowing from his Wisdom and will, defined as powers and even as the power of God. In addition, the λόγοι are not directly identical with neither the essential nor the creative energies of God in themselves—rather they could be contemplated in them, as well as in all created things (AI 22, 1257AB). As far as the λόγοι are not a substantial mediator between God and the creatures, but rather a dynamic reality, conveying actions which are subsequently crystallizing in the creatures, all created beings, being dependent on God, all have their relative self-autonomy: they are and exist on their own being determined in their being by their own essences, powers, energies, etc. The λόγοι are not identical with God's essence, but they are not identical either with the things themselves in the created world, with nothing in them, including their nature or hypostasis (AI 7, 1081AB).

One can see that the complex mediated "dialogue" that happens by and in the λόγοι of things cannot be really refer the one which is the subject of debate. In addition, the "λόγος of nature" is only one among those λόγοι. One can also see that the sympathetic theory discussed above does not provide an answer to the question whether the "τρόπος of existence" refers to the nature or to the hypostasis.

---

37. QThal 2, 272A; 60, 625A; Ep12 485D; AI 7, 1081A; 42, 1328AB; 1329BC.

The Solution That Can Be Found in St. Maximus the Confessor

If one reads Maximus the Confessor without too much ideological loading one can see that he is sufficiently clear. The "τρόπος of existence" is the form of the various manifestations of nature; it is the way in which the essence exists, acts and functions. The term "existence" does not refer only to the hypostasis. The hypostatic mode is not equivalent to that of existence itself (ὕπαρξις, ὑπάρχειν) which considered by Maximus to be originally to the natural order (*AI* 42, 1329A; 1341D; 1344D). Τρόπος τῆς ὑπάρξεως is the way the nature actually exists. It refers to the nature in its specific reality.

In what it concerns human nature Maximus distinguishes between two classes of ways of existence that are in a specific correspondence with each other. They refer directly to the nature and allow to be analogically attributed to any formal-material being. On the one hand he talks about the ways of existence of the human nature in history: before the Fall, after the Fall, after the Incarnation of the Word, and after the Judgment. On the other hand, he outlines three universal ways of the existence of nature: being–well-being/evil-being–eternal-well-being/eternal-evil-being. The transition from λόγος to τρόπος is the transfer of the essential order to the existential order. It is a completely different issue that every τρόπος of existence of the nature is realized in hypostases, as far as there no un-hypostatic essence or nature. The hypostasis "recapitulates" the τρόπος of existence as far as the nature is known only as the content of a hypostasis.

Precisely in order to prevent the identification of "τρόπος of existence" with hypostasis and make a clear distinction between nature and hypostasis, Maximus talks about hypostatic being in terms of both the "λόγος of hypostasis" and the "τρόπος of existence of hypostasis" both comparing and contrasting them to the τρόπος and the λόγος of the essence (*AI* 36, 1289C; *Ep*12 493D). Here λόγος τῆς ὑποστάσεως refers to the inner constitution of a particular hypostasis: the enhypostatization of its nature, the implementation of the hypostasis in a corresponding τρόπος of existence of the nature, the framework of its proper conditions of being, the structure of its unique properties.[38] The τρόπος τῆς ὑποστάσεως refers to the way a person uses its

---

38. As it appears Photius of Constantinople uses this concept and applies it to Trinitarian theology. He does not leave any room for doubting the relevance of the λόγος of nature which ensures the consubstantiality of the hypostases. At the same time, by pointing to the Divine monarchy, he emphasizes that the Father is the cause for the being of the Son and of the Holy Spirit according to the λόγος of his hypostasis, in which λόγος there is no place for any other hypostasis. The proceeding of the Holy Spirit from the Father is not just coming out into existence, but causation in terms of essence and nature. The Father however is the cause of the other two ὑποστάσεις not according to the λόγος of nature, but according to the λόγος of ὑπόστασις ("λόγος

natural abilities or qualities in guiding and using its own will (*DP* 294A)—what distinguishes it from other human beings in their common way of natural existence. The τρόπος τῆς ὑποστάσεως may vary in the historical time of the particular person, without violating its general hypostatic constitution. This is the unique and specific "how" of the organization of the natural and all other activities carried out by the particular hypostasis.

In this context, Maximus points out very instructively: "Everyone acts (ἐνεργεῖ) fundamentally as something, in other words as a person. As someone, for example Paul or Peter, he forms (a specific) mode of action (τὸν τῆς ἐνεργείας τρόπον), for example by reduction or amplification, forming himself through the specific mode of action according to his internal volitional attitude (κατὰ γνώμην). It follows that the differences in the persons with respect to the mode of action is recognized by their activities (πρᾶξις), while the identity of the natural action follows from the λόγος of nature."[39] The natural energy is the same in all individuals. Its unity and uniqueness actualizes the presence of the nature in every individual. It is carries the form of the species. This form is actualized however hypostatically through the complex set of attitudes and characteristics which are uniquely inherent in each person.

The difference between the two λόγοι (natural and hypostatic) and their corresponding mode of existence does not imply, however, some contrapositioning. On the contrary: as it can be seen, the natural finds its unique articulation through the hypostatic. Maximus the Confessor explained the reason and the mechanism for the implementation of this articulation by the concept of ἕξις.

The thorough reference to the gnomic will (γνώμη) in the course of the contemporary debate persistently misses the fact that it is only a special case of ἕξις. It is a very important case, indeed, as far as it refers to the personal articulation namely of the will (systematically seen by Maximus and the entire tradition after him as inherent in the nature, as its force; δύναμις). The doctrine of the ἕξεις positions the problematics of being in a strongly personal perspective.

The word ἕξις has three main meanings that are in close connection with the content of the philosophical concept. It means "possession" in opposition to στέρησις (deprivation, withdrawal), which allows translating it as "the property of having inherent character or inherence" and, respectively, "property." The word could also mean a "stable state, a particular

---

τῆς ὑποστάσεως") and, more specifically, according to his own ὑπόστασις ("λόγος τῆς πατρικῆς ὑποστάσεως"). Cf. Photius, *De spiritu sancti mystagogiae* 15—16.

39. *TP10* 137A.

order or position" and in this sense stands in opposition to σχέσις (relation). In addition, ἕξις could also mean "personal capacity, respectively, possibility of appropriation" which is achieved based on experience. Although all three meanings have a place in the way the concept was used by Maximus, his understanding of ἕξις should be interpreted mostly as "stable internal personal state."

In any case, for Maximus the term is antithetical to the concept of θέσις (laying, setting or positioning) which belongs to the class of concepts used with respect to nature. In accordance with the λόγος of being, all beings are part of an order (τάξις), specifying their overall positioning (θέσις) and relations (σχέσις) to others. The "overall positioning" expresses the natural normativity which is ultimately set by God through the creative act and which is authoritative for the natural powers and energies in their unqualified condition.[40]

For Aristotle, ἕξις is a sub-concept of "quality": it denotes the accidental form which characterizes every being through stable and durable properties. In this sense Aristotle differentiates the concept from the term διάθεσις which refers to transitionary and unstable properties. There are both acquired and innate ἕξεις. In the second case, Aristotle opposes ἕξις of "deprivation" (στέρησις), giving the example of vision and blindness (*Cat.* 8, 8b25–9a13; 10, 12a–12b): the presence or absence of such property does not violate the essential determination of a particular being. In Aristotle (as well as in Maximus) ἕξις is neither something anti-natural nor something which is necessarily natural; it is the suitability for the actualization of a given predisposition.

In Maximus the concept ἕξις stands in permanent connection with ἐνεργεία and it is continuously applied in the context of the triad "being-well-being/evil-being–eternal-well/evil-being." Maximus defines ἕξις as a "constitutive characteristic" (συστατικὴ ἰδιότης) for the activity of the hypostasis (*DP* 352A). Mutatis mutandis the concept of ἕξις corresponds to *Gestimmtsein, Stimmung* and *Befindlichkeit* in Heidegger. Heidegger interprets the *Befindlichkeit* as a constitutive element of the *In-Sein*.[41] The ἕξεις are best understood as subject-carrying mediators. Their basis of their conceptual content can be described relatively easily at the level of the volitional problematics.

In explaining the transition to the personalization of the volitional, or in other words, the transition from θέλησις (will) as a natural force βούλησις or ποιὰ θέλησις, to a "qualified will," which is already formed personally,

---

40. Cf. *AI* 7, 1073BC; 10, 1176C; 15, 1217A; 65, 1392AB.
41. Heidegger, *Sein und Zeit*, 11.

Maximus notes that γνώμη refers to προαίρεσις, which is a specific volitional decision, in the same manner as ἕξις refers to ἐνέργεια. Both γνώμη and ἕξις are defined as "ὄρεξις ἐνδιάθετος" (inner striving or predisposition, *TP1* 17C). They are the factors carrying self-determination where ἕξις is associated directly with actual implementation process (προχείρησις, *DP* 324D–325A) in the course of time. Maximus connects γνώμη with the way of life (τρόπος ζωῆς, *DP* 308B). In this way it is emphasized that γνώμη (the same as ἕξις) stands in relation not with the λόγος of nature, but with τρόπος χρήσεως, the way of use of the natural powers within the specific way of life.

The crucially important link between ἕξις with the natural powers and energies should be explained again by analogy with γνώμη. The γνώμη is instantiated between the will, which is a natural power, and the volitional action or decision. In the same way the ἕξεις are considered as intermediaries between the natural forces/powers and energies. They are the intermediary between intention and realization, between theory and practice, between the internal and the external in human life. In this way they, existing at the level of the potential, define the personal determination of the natural energies.

The ἕξεις shape the unique and very concrete determination of being in the τρόποι of its dynamics. Thus, they are defined as a fundamental demonstration of human freedom. Both the powers and the energies are indeed natural, but they are specified personally; they are hypostatically defined and directed through the "filter" of ἕξεις. They are the factor personalizing the natural: a personalizing factor. In this way we can finally explain by the fact of unequal intensity, focus and specificity of the natural energies radiated by different people or by the same person at different moments of his or her personal history. Through the personification of the natural energies a specific person becomes responsible for the constitution of his or her personal being.

Some Lessons Learned That Are of Relevance for the Contemporary Debate

It should be noted that some of the conceptual formulations given in the course of today's discussion, diminishes the anthropological concept formulated by the Orthodox tradition and especially Maximus the Confessor.

First, one should note the elimination of historicity. The opposition between natural and hypostatic aspects of being (or between nature and hypostasis) and linking the term "τρόπος of existence" to the hypostasis alone inevitably leads to the loss of the universal historical horizon. The natural loses its historicity which forces the inner hypostatic changes to become the only valid and relevant factor which, however, appears to operate beyond and despite all the macro-historical processes.

On the other hand, Maximus assigns a crucial importance to the universally historical. He does not think at all history as some autonomous and therefore defective movement in time of all contingent beings after the Fall—a movement that is incompatible with the eternity of Divinity and the immutability of the principles of being. History is not the space-time of corruption and fallibility, neither an impairment that should be completely overcome and eliminated. On the contrary, it binds unequivocally the finite and the infinite, the eternal and the transient, namely in the field of history, which has its beginning and purpose, its meaning and its dynamic paradigm in the Λόγος of all λόγοι. History is not the "completely other" to λόγοι of being, considered as an abstract meta-physical basis, and standing beyond any movement, time and matter. From this particular perspective history should be defined as "metaphysics" to the extent that this foundational basis is and acts in it in the same way as the Λόγος acts in it.[42] "History" and "metaphysics" are not in correspondence or co-existing. They are one and the same. In this specific horizon the τρόπος of existence of every created nature not only does not exclude, but even suggests the emergence of new, previously undetectable historical forms of its existence. It should be noticed that Maximus used the term "novelty," "innovation" and "renewal" (καινοτομία) with respect to the mode of existence of nature in a neutral and technical sense. In addition, he emphasizes that the saving work of Christ is not just a renewal of the way of hypostatic existence of the assumed human nature, but a renewal of human nature in general, and with it—the nature of all creatures (cf. AI 42, 1309A–1313D).

A "novelty" or "innovation" in terms of human nature is the way of existence after the Fall.[43] There is another innovation, however, which is the one of the way of existence of human nature after hypostatic union of Christ, which allows the potential of human nature to be fully actualized

42. It is not by accident that Maximus speaks about three types of incarnation. The Word is being "en-fleshed" (παχύνεσθαι ὁ Λόγος) in three different forms of his coming down to us (συγκατάβασις) to the level of created humanity. First, the Λόγος is incarnated in the λόγοι of all being (λόγοι τῶν ὄντων). Second, he is incarnated in the λόγοι–words of Scripture. Third, the Λόγος abides in flesh (παρουσία ἔνσαρκος). This is what provides the basis for the three aspects of the Divine economy: Creation, Revelation and Salvation—AI 33, 1285C–1288A.

43. Here one could refer to the reflections of Photius of Constantinople with respect to the organic link between nature and grace without losing sight of the un-self-sufficiency of the human nature; see Homiliae, 9.91.27—93.17; Amphilochiae 64.58–64, 167.13–49.

within both, the soteriological and the eschatological perspectives. Deification is to be achieved in the course of the historical and metaphysical process and presupposes salvation as its first level—the "recovery" of the status of human nature which is the starting point towards the super-natural τρόπος of deification (AI 31, 1273B; QThal 61, 632A). This "recovery" of nature, however, is realized as a renewal. Yet at the level of salvation, human nature is assigned a status higher than the original. This became possible because both salvation and deification are linked to the Incarnation and are unthinkable without it (QThal 22, 321A; 63, 684A). It gives a new τρόπος of existence, which is super-natural and seemingly paradoxical, because it is according to the Divine principles. Christ is both a model and a program for the existence of a Christian ("τύπος καὶ πρόγραμμα," AI 42, 1333BC).

The negative interpretation of human nature, the rejection of its ability for eternal being and the postulation of two contrary opposed aspects of being (natural and hypostatic) leads to the reduction of the existential integrity and the being of the very hypostasis, specifically within a completely soteriological perspective.

It is essential to see that the emergence of a new mode of existence of nature while preserving its λόγος is the perspective in which Maximus discusses the difference between the deification of the Old Testament saints and of the followers of Christ who are worthy of it. He stresses that the deification of the righteous from the time before the Incarnation does not differ fundamentally from the deification happening afterwards. In both cases it is based on God's grace. The essential difference is that before Jesus Christ the grace was given to the chosen ones for their special mission. Grace has, so to speak, a functional nature, related to the specific vocation of the respective chosen one. Here the Communion with the Divinity becomes possible only through a strictly personally directed, "particular" theophany (AI 10, 1137B; 1144A; 1164C).

After the historic saving work of Christ, however, the deification has become possible in principle for anyone baptized following Christ. Maximus carefully emphasizes that in the historical time of the "old Israel" God did not renew the τρόπος of existence, but the τρόποι of action (τρόπος τῆς ἐνεργείας) of the nature of the ones that were renewed. With the Incarnation, however, God renewed the τρόπος of existence of human nature (without, of course, changing its λόγος; AI 10, 1164C; 42, 1344D–1345A). The Λόγος remained unchanged through all the historical statuses of nature.[44] The new

---

44. The renewal of the nature cannot be valid only in the case of the hypostasis of Christ as far as the mode of existence does not coincide with the mode of hypostatic action which, in addition in the case of Christ is not human, but theanthropic. See the analysis of the "new theandric energy" of Christ in AT 5, 1056B–1057D; DP

mode of existence of human nature, endowed by Christ, enables a higher value of the specific historical human hypostasis and uncovers unexpected horizons for each man, which is in principle possible for all humanity.[45] The denial of this position diminishes not only human nature, namely, but also the human hypostasis and the importance of its free actions.

Conclusion

The aim of this paper was to demonstrate that the terminology available especially after Maximus the Confessor, is perfectly sufficient, very dense and subtle enough to address the majority of the problematic topics that were raised in contemporary debates. The conceptual system is able to do that without any need for an update, rejection or correction of its essential dimensions. It allows additional interpretations including new interpretations of the concepts, but not their radical reformatting. This is exactly what makes it so productive when a modern debate decides to use the treasury of its conceptual resources.

—Translated from Bulgarian by Stoyan Tanev

Bibliography

Bradshaw, David Houston. *Aristotle East and West: Metaphysics and the Division of Christendom*. Cambridge: Cambridge University Press, 2004.

Florovsky, George. "The Resurrection of Life." *Bulletin of the Harvard University Divinity School* 49 (1952) 19–26.

Heidegger, Martin. *Sein und Zeit*. 11th ed. Tübingen: Max Niemeyer, 1967. Reprinted in unchaged form since 1967 in sequentially numbered editions.

John of Damascus. *Writings*. Translated by Frederic H. Chase. Fathers of the Church: A New Translation 37. Washington, DC: Catholic University of America Press, 1958.

Kapriev, Georgi. "The Byzantine Trace." In *Le sujet de l'acteur: An Anthropological Outlook on Actor-Network Theory*, edited by Georgi Kapriev, Martin Roussel, and Ivan Tchalakov, 25–64. Paderborn: W. Fink, 2014.

———. *Philosophie in Byzanz*. Würzburg: Königshausen und Neumann, 2005.

Kapriev, Georgi, and Tchalakov Ivan. "Actor-Network Theory and Byzantine Interpretation of Aristotle's Theory of Action: Three Points of Possible Dialogue." *Yearbook of the Institute for Advanced Studies on Science, Technology and Society* 57 (2009) 207–38.

Kasper, Walter. *Jesus der Christus*. 10th ed. Mainz: Matthias Grünewald, 1986.

345C–348A; *TP8* 101A–104A; *TP9* 120A.

45. This does not neglect the grace that is personally given. The discussion of this point, however, would go beyond the scope of this text.

Larchet, Jean-Claude. *La divinisation de l'homme selon saint Maxime le Confesseur.* Cogitatio fidei 194. Paris: Cerf, 1996.

———. *La théologie des énergies divines: Des origines à saint Jean Damascène.* Paris: Cerf, 2010.

———. *Personne et nature: La Trinité—le Christ—l'homme; contributions aux dialogues interorthodoxe et interchrétien contemporains.* Théologies. Paris: Cerf, 2011.

Loudovikos, Nikolaos. *A Eucharistic Ontology: Maximus the Confessor's Eschatological Ontology of Being as Dialogical Reciprocity.* Translated by Elizabeth Theokritoff. Brookline, MA: Holy Cross Orthodox Press, 2010.

———. "*Eikon* and *Mimesis*: Eucharistic Ecclesiology and the Ecclesial Ontology of Dialogical Reciprocity." *International Journal for the Study of the Christian Church* 11.2-3 (2011) 123–36. doi:10.1080/1474225X.2011.571411.

———. "Person Instead of Grace and Dictated Otherness: John Zizioulas' Final Theological Position." *The Heythrop Journal* 52 (2009) 684–99. doi:10.1111/j.1468-2265.2009.00547.x.

———. Ψυχανάλυση καὶ ὀρθόδοξη θεολογία. Περὶ ἐπιθυμίας, καθολικότητας καὶ ἐσχατολογίας [Psychoanalysis and Orthodox Theology: On Desire, Catholicity and Eschatology]. Athens: Armos, 2006.

Marx, Karl. *Thesen über Feuerbach*. In Karl Marx and Friedrich Engels, *Werke*, 3:5–7. Berlin: Dietz, 1959.

Maximus the Confessor. *Ad Catholicos per Siciliam constitutos (Theologica et polemica ix)* [To the Christ-Loving Fathers, Superiors, Monks, Dwelling Here in Sicily and to the Orthodox People]. Edited by François Combefis. PG91:112C–32D. Abbreviated as *TP9*.

———. *Ad Marinum Cypri presbyterum (Theologica et polemica x)* [Copy of a Letter Sent to Sir Marinus, Priest of Cyprus]. Edited by François Combefis. PG91:133A–7C. Abbreviated as *TP10*.

———. *Ad Marinum presbyterum (Theologica et polemica i)* [To Marinus the Very Pious Priest]. Edited by François Combefis. PG91:9A–37D. Abbreviated as *TP1*.

———. *Ambigua ad Iohannem*. Edited by Franz Oehler. PG91:1061–417C. Abbreviated as *AI*.

———. *Ambigua ad Thomam*. Edited by Franz Oehler. PG91:1032A–60D. Abbreviated as *AT*.

———. *De duabus unius Christi Dei nostri uoluntatibus (Theologica et polemica xvi)* [On the Two Wills of the One Christ Our God]. Edited by François Combefis. PG91:184C–212B. Abbreviated as *TP16*.

———. *Disputatio cum Pyrrho* [Dispute with Pyrrhus]. Edited by François Combefis. PG91:288A–353B. Abbreviated as *DP*.

———. *Epistula xii* [Epistle 12, To John the Chamberlain]. Edited by François Combefis. PG91:460A–509B. Abbreviated as *Ep12*.

———. *Epistula xv* [Epistle 15, To Cosmas the Deacon, of Alexandria]. Edited by François Combefis. PG91:544D–76D. Abbreviated as *Ep15*.

———. *Exemplum epistulae ad episcopum Nicandrum de duabus in Christo operationibus (Theologica et polemica viii)* [Copy of an Epistle Addressed to the most Sacred Bishop, Sir Nikander by Saint Maximus, on Two Operations in Christ]. Edited by François Combefis. PG91: 89C–112C. Abbreviated as *TP8*.

———. *Mystagogia*. Edited by François Combefis. PG91:657C–717D. Abbreviated as *Myst*.

———. *On Difficulties in the Church Fathers: The Ambigua*. Edited and translated by Nicholas P. Constas. 2 vols. Dumbarton Oaks Medieval Library 28–29. Cambridge: Harvard University Press, 2014. Abbreviated as *Difficulties*.

———. *Quaestiones ad Thalassium*. Edited by François Combefis. PG90:244–785B. Abbreviated as *QThal*.

———. *Variae definitiones (Theologica et polemica xiv)* [Various Definitions]. Edited by François Combefis. PG91:149B–53B. Abbreviated as *TP14*.

Maximus the Confessor and Anonymous. *Ex quaestionibus a Theodoro monacho illi propositis (olim Theologica et polemica xxvi)* [From the Things Asked Him by the Monk Theodore]. Edited by François Combefis. PG91:276A–80B. Abbreviated as *TP26*.

Michael Psellus. *Michaelis Pselli Philosophica minora*. Vol. 1, *Opuscula logica, physica, allegorica, alia*. Edited by John M. Duffy. Bibiotheca scriptorum Graecorum et Romanorum Teubneriana. Leipzig: Teubner, 1992.

Perishich, Vladimir. "Person and Essence in the Theology of St. Gregory Palamas." *Philotheos* 1 (2001) 131–36.

Petrov, Valeriy V. *Maksim Ispovednik: Ontologiya i metod v vizantiyskoy folosofii VII v.* [Maximus the Confessor: Ontology and Method in Byzantine Philosophy in the 7th Century]. Moscow: Russian Academy of Sciences, Institute of Philosophy, 2007.

Pseudo-Maximus the Confessor. *Capita de substantia seu essentia et natura, deque hypostasi et persona (olim Theologica et polemica XXIIIa)* [Chapters on Ousia and Nature, Hypostasis and Person]. Edited by François Combefis. PG91:260D–4C. Abbreviated as *TP23a*.

———. *De substantia seu essentia et natura et hypostasi (olim Theologica et polemica xxiii c)* [Of Ousia and Nature and Hypostasis]. Edited by François Combefis. PG91:265C5–8A. Abbreviated as *TP23c*.

———. *Eulogii Alexandrini capita vii (olim Theologica et polemica xxiii b)* [Seven Chapters of Eulogius of Alexandria on the Two Natures of Our Lord and Savior Jesus Christ]. Edited by François Combefis. PG91:264D–5C4. Abbreviated as *TP23b*.

Sartre, Jean-Paul. *L'existentialisme est un humanisme*. Collection Pensées. Paris: Nagel, 1946.

Tanev, Stoyan. "Actor-Network vs. Activity Theory: Dealing with the Changing Nature of the Asymmetry in Human-Technology Inter-actions." In *Le sujet de l'acteur: An Anthropological Outlook on Actor-Network Theory*, edited by Georgi Kapriev, Martin Roussel, and Ivan Tchalakov, 65–86. Paderborn: W. Fink, 2014.

———. *Ti, Koyto si navsyakăde i vsichko izpălvash. Săshtnost i energiya v pravoslavnoto bogoslovie i văv fizikata* [You, Who Art Everywhere Present and Fillest All Things: Essence and Energy in Orthodox Theology and Physics]. Sofia: Universitetsko izdatelstvo "Sv. Kliment Ohridski," 2013.

Tchalakov, Ivan. "The Amateur's Action: On the Limits of Actor-Network Account about Resistance and Endurance in Scientific Research." In *Le sujet de l'acteur: An Anthropological Outlook on Actor-Network Theory*, edited by Georgi Kapriev, Martin Roussel, and Ivan Tchalakov, 133–43. Paderborn: W. Fink, 2014.

Torrance, Alexis. "Personhood and Patristics in Orthodox Theology: Reassessing the Debate." *The Heythrop Journal* 52 (2011) 700–707. doi:10.1111/j.1468-2265.2010.00669.x.

Turcescu, Lucian. *Gregory of Nyssa and the Concept of Divine Persons*. American Academy of Religion Academy Series. Oxford: Oxford University Press, 2005.

———. "'Person' versus 'Individual,' and Other Modern Misreadings of Gregory of Nyssa." *Modern Theology* 18 (2002) 527–39. doi:10.1111/1468-0025.00202.

Tympas, Grigorios Chrysostom. *Carl Jung and Maximus the Confessor on Psychic Development: The Dynamics between the Psychological and the Spiritual*. London: Routledge, 2014.

Zizioulas, Jean. *Lectures in Christian Dogmatics*. Edited by Douglas H. Knight. London: T. & T. Clark, 2008.

———. *The One and the Many: Studies on God, Man, the Church, and the World Today*. Edited by Gregory Edwards. Contemporary Christian Thought Series 6. Alhambra, CA: Sebastian Press, 2010.

Zizioulas, John. *Being as Communion: Studies in Personhood and the Church*. Contemporary Greek Theologians 4. Crestwood, NY: St. Vladimir's Seminary Press, 1985.

———. *Communion and Otherness: Further Studies in Personhood and the Church*. Edited by Paul McPartlan. London: T. & T. Clark, 2006.

13

The Face of the Soul, the Face of God: Maximus the Confessor and πρόσωπον[1]

Marcin Podbielski

Putting Together a Picture, Reconstructing a Theory

While many words have been written about Maximus the Confessor's view of human nature and persons, none of the seriously respected studies have been informed by a complete investigation of his vocabulary. In my opinion, it is precisely this omission that makes those studies prone to the serious error warned against by Jean-Claude Larchet, when he says that "it is not methodologically correct to wish to pronounce judgments on ancient usage [of terms] on the basis of present usage."[2]

It must be admitted that studying a Patristic author like Maximus, who wrote either polemical texts or biblical commentaries, and whose conceptions are rarely developed into any form of systematic exposition, presents

---

1. The paper presents some results of the research project Reconstructing Early Byzantine Metaphysics, financed by Poland's National Science Center (grant UMO-2012/05/B/HS1/03305). It was first published in *Forum Philosophicum* 19 (2014) 107–44. The version offered to readers of the volume is almost identical to that in the journal. There are, however, the following differences: (1) with the publication by Marek Jankowiak and Phil Booth of "A New Date-List," Sherwood's numbering has been replaced by theirs; (2) some notes have been modified in order to take into account claims made in their article; and (3) a number of minor errors have been corrected, with some editorial remarks not needed in a volume devoted exclusively to Maximus being removed. As a result, the note numbering in this paper does not match that in the journal version.

2. "[I]l n'est pas méthodologiquement correct de vouloir juger de l'usage ancien à partir de l'usage actuel." Larchet, "Hypostase, personne et individu," 44.

many challenges. Contemporary investigations into Maximus' thought seem to be modeled on the approach of classical works, like Hans Urs von Balthasar's *Cosmic Liturgy* and Lars Thunberg's *Microcosm and Mediator*. Those scholars sought to propose synthetic pictures of Maximus' views by organizing his remarks, set forth in various works, into a logically cogent order. Their method was possibly a necessity in studies that aimed at reawakening interest in this theologically important and inspiring author. Nevertheless, in later investigations, their method should have been completed by a truly analytical approach, so that the reconstruction of Maximus' views would then itself crown a detailed and comprehensive analysis of his texts, performed from philological, philosophical and theological angles. Yet the scholars who try to explain what being a person, a hypostasis, an individual, or having a nature, means in Maximus—or, at least, the major scholars whose work I have been able to consult—give their inquiries the structure of global and consistent pictures, created out of a patchwork of quotes and references.[3] The internal consistency of those pictures and references to various works is probably considered to constitute a guarantee of the methodological correctness of the interpretations they are proposing of personhood in Maximus. One might even argue that this is the appropriate method for studying an author like him, as it is impossible to grasp his views clearly without building a whole out of the many sets of ideas he tossed around in his work.

It can be admitted that assembling a consistent picture on the basis of a multiplicity of remarks appears similar to putting pieces of jigsaw puzzle next to one another. In a given puzzle, however, there is a pre-ordained place for every such piece. In a synthetic doctrinal picture, shown in a short paper or a chapter, there is (*a*) no possibility to take all elements into consideration; (*b*) no guarantee that the elements actually fit together in the manner in which they are being organized, as this would require logical and doctrinal analysis of the arguments in which they figure; (*c*) no guarantee that those elements constitute parts of such a postulated picture at all, especially if the person who created them never bothered with establishing such a picture himself; and (*d*) no guarantee that the consistency of the theoretical image created in this way does not stem from a superimposed idea. The building blocks of ideas, like physical building blocks, do not have to fit one

---

3. Zizioulas, "Person and Nature"; Skliris, "'Hypostasis,' 'Person,' 'Individual,' 'Mode'"; Tollefsen, "St Maximus' Concept"; Thunberg, *Microcosm and Mediator*, 47–48, 106–7; Törönen, *Union and Distinction*, 52–59, also 86–91; Bathrellos, *Byzantine Christ*, 101–107; Tollefsen, *Christocentric Cosmology*, 128–29; Madden, "Composite Hypostasis," 187–89; Larchet, *La divinisation de l'homme*, 131–34; Garrigues, "La personne composée du Christ," 189–204.

to another, and those which do can be arranged according to almost any plan or preconception whatsoever.

Precisely for this reason, we may suspect that someone who finds personhood defined in Maximus as a self-determining reality is superimposing a modern view of personhood on him. What appears closely linked to a modern view of personhood is, especially, the insistence that Maximus refrains from referring the term person to non-intelligent beings, and that he asserts the ontological primacy of persons in respect of nature, or that, when speaking about the Divine grace which elevates human beings above nature, he suggests that this consists, actually, in liberating persons from nature.[4]

In this paper, I wish to approach the issue of personhood in Maximus in a manner in line with the methodological principles of classical studies, which do not allow one to proceed immediately to a more or less summary overview. Quite obviously, though, I can only propose to perform one single task out of the many in fact required before any synthetic image could be offered by way of conclusion. This will be the task of comprehensively analyzing the usage of the term "πρόσωπον" in the Maximian corpus. I view it as an initial, but also unavoidable, stage within any comprehensive inquiry into the issue of personhood.

Patristic Investigation and the Methodology of Classical Studies

The proposal of conducting an analysis of occurrences of a word and its cognates, as an initial task forming part of an extended investigation into personhood in Maximus, stems from accepting a notion which is, ostensibly, obvious and hardly questioned at all: that patrological inquiries should apply the contemporary methodology of classical studies in all its integrity. Let me point, below, to some components of this methodology, and explain how they apply to investigations of the problem of personhood in Maximus.

(1) Correct Textual Basis

Practically all major ancient Greek authors can be read nowadays in modern editions, which take into consideration all known manuscripts and recent textual findings. This will, hopefully, also be the case with Maximus, once the new complete edition of his works has been produced by the classical and Byzantine scholars from the Catholic University of Leuven and their

---

4. Cf. e.g. Zizioulas, "Person and Nature," Kindle locs. 1852, 2005, 54, 246 and note 72, loc. 247.

collaborators.⁵ At the moment, Peter Van Deun, Basile Markesinis, and Bram Roosen are working on new editions of the so called minor works of Maximus—his opuscula and epistles. Some of their proposals and new editions are already accessible in their papers. Bram Roosen's unpublished thesis ("EfR") allows one to glimpse future volumes of Maximus' Opera. It is already clear that certain opuscula and letters considered important for Maximus' view of personhood must be rejected, as without a doubt they do not represent his views. The list shown below contains only those works in which instances of "πρόσωπον" or related vocabulary can be found. Roosen's important editorial decisions, pertinent to the issue of personhood, are discussed in the next section.

1. The text usually referred to as *Theologica et polemica 23*
2. The first part of *Theologica et polemica 26*
3. *Loci Communes* (CPG 7718)
4. *Diversa capita ad theologiam et oeconomiam spectantia deque virtute et vitio (xxvi–d)* (CPG 7715)
5. *Scholia in Ecclesiasten* (CPG 7711/05)

In my search I will be labeling as dubious the two important texts—both of which have been attributed by many (though not all) distinguished scholars to Maximus:

6. The passages ascribed by Beate Suchla (CD 4/1), Paul Rorem, and John C. Lamoreaux (RL) to Maximus within the *Scholia in Corpus Aeropagiticum*
7. *Capita gnostica* [The Moscow Gnostic Century] (CPG 7707/11)

In line with the tradition originating from the Combefis edition, I retain within the Maximian corpus some of the texts relating events from his life and adducing his purported utterances. These are *Relatio Motionis*, *Disputatio Bizyae*, and also *Disputatio cum Pyrrho*. This inclusion must be done, however, with caution. As Jacques Noret shows, there are reasons for treating the last work as having been written well after the events it depicts, and possibly in order to make a statement in the theological politics of that era. In turn, as Noret holds, other reports regarding Maximus's discussions

---

5. I mean here former and current scholars from KU Leuven Michel Van Esbroeck, Geerard Maurits, Noret Jacques, Constant De Vocht, Carl Laga, Carlos G Steel, Gysens Steven, Bart Janssens, Peter Van Deun, Basile Markesinis, Bram Roosen, and also José H. Declerck from Gent and Christian Boudignon from Université d'Aix-Marseille.

and speeches can be accepted with rather less scepticism.⁶ For those reasons, I classify all works of this kind as a separate group of "relata." While I do not engage in chronological considerations, I do wish to make it easier for readers to draw conclusions of that kind. Thus, abbreviations of titles of Maximus' works are accompanied by their chronological numbering.⁷

(2) Comprehensive Lexical Inquiry

Modern classical scholarship does not rely any more on thesauri, either of Greek literature as a whole or those devoted to particular major authors. They used to be necessary for establishing the meaning of key terms in philosophy and theology—terms that also had a plethora of everyday meanings, preserved from antiquity until the present day. Now, in the era of digital classical scholarship, those thesauri can easily be replaced by computerized searches of texts. This development is even more important for Maximus, whose works were never indexed completely on paper. New editions of Maximus' works are in the process of being successively included into the Thesaurus Linguae Graecae database, while works that can be consulted in the Combefis edition only have been digitalized in a separate project.⁸ There are no obstacles anymore for Maximian scholars that would prevent them from supporting their claims about Maximus' terminology through comprehensive studies of his word usage.

As I believe, undertaking this is particularly important in the case of the issue of personhood. The very word usually rendered as "person," "τὸ πρόσωπον," has never lost, in Greek, its original meaning of "face," while acquiring, according to the dictionary of Dimitrios Dimitrakou,⁹ altogether

6. See Noret, "La rédaction de la Disputatio cum Pyrrho." Cf. Sherwood, *Annotated Date-List*, 53. Cf. also Bram Roosen's article "On the Recent Edition of the *Disputatio Bizyae*."

7. Thus, an abbreviation may be followed by the brackets "[ ]," with a number placed between the latter, corresponding to one of the chronological numbers attributed to the majority of extant texts by Marek Jankowiak and Phil Booth in "A New Date-List." These replace those proposed by Polycarp Sherwood in his *Annotated Date-List*.

8. This work has been performed as a task of the EU Regional Development Project Interreg IIIA "Δρόμοι τῆς πίστης – ψηφιακή Πατρολογία," at the Aegean University, Department of Cultural Technology and Communication, in 2006. All materials produced in the project can be freely used, provided their source is pointed to. It is a pity that those materials are no longer available at the former official site of the project (http://patrologia.ct.aegean.gr). Cf. the short pieces of information at http://www.i-m-patron.gr/i-m-patron-old.gr/news1/news_2007/dromoi_pistis.html. Some of them may be found at http://www.myriobiblos.gr/texts/greek/maximos/index.htm. Still, all unofficially published materials produced by the project remain in the public domain.

9. Dimitrakou, *Μέγα λεξικὸν*, s.v. "πρόσωπον."

twelve other related meanings. Its technical theological meaning is only the last of these. All those meanings are interconnected. Besides, the word has great metaphorical potential due to its frequent usage in the Septuagint. The Septuagint regularly re-literalizes the Hebrew verb "תונפל" (meaning "to turn, to face") as "πρόσωπον," and "ינפמ" (meaning "from, in favor of," or, in the Bible, also "because of, due to, as expression of") as "ἀπὸ προσώπου" or "from the face." For all those reasons, focusing *a priori* only on theological contexts should be considered an error. The scale of the error it may actually engender is something that will only emerge in the final part of this paper.

In this text, I will offer a detailed study of the vocabulary of "πρόσωπον" in Maximus. Unlike the recently published article of Jean-Claude Larchet,[10] it scrutinizes all kinds of instances and is based on a study of the complete Maximian corpus. It uses the methods of classical philology, in that it proceeds by grouping and comparing instances. The study covers 373 instances, distributed unevenly among 46 of the 169 works and opuscula: 242 in authentic works, 15 in dubia, 40 in spuria, 76 in relata. Metaphorical usages are set apart and their meaning is analyzed with all the attention they deserve. The philological approach is completed by preliminary textual analysis, which allows one to pass from the study of word usage to definitions of the concepts expressed in the terminology. While final theoretical conclusions cannot be reached in this way, several building blocks that contribute to our picture of personhood in Maximus are reconstructible using this approach.

(3) Comparative Theoretical Inquiry and Synthetic Reconstruction

This kind of analysis is usually followed, in classical studies, by a comparative study, which itself involves various kinds of analysis. Terms used in various contexts should be set one against another, and possible conclusions evaluated comparatively. Analyses of logical consistency, external influences, and internal development, are performed at this stage of the investigation. Concepts are viewed at this juncture as functioning within arguments and claims.

A synthetic reconstruction of the views of an author normally follows on from all those earlier stages. At this point, arguments and claims are viewed as a whole. This stage of investigation is concerned with the theory of the author being scrutinized. While logically different from the inquiries of the preceding stage, the sort of analysis that examines a theory as a whole can also be intertwined with detailed comparative analysis. This is because

---

10. Larchet, "Hypostase, personne et individu."

any theory must be recovered from the texts being studied rather than being imposed on them.

Most obviously, it is impossible to contain the theoretical part of the examination of personhood in Maximus in one short paper. Thanks to the lexical analyses presented below, however, it is possible to rule out the idea that Maximus held views somehow similar to modern forms of personalism. I can already assure the reader that the analyses I wish to offer here are, somewhat surprisingly, by no means dull and technical. They point to some groups of usages overlooked by all of the authors who have studied the issue, and which shed much light on their strictly anthropological discussions. It turns out that preliminary conclusion based on a comprehensive analysis can overturn a complex and consistent, still purely synthetic, picture.

"Person" in the Ontology of Christology and Trinitology

Not only is it the case that none of the studies of the issue of personhood in Maximus are based on a complete scrutiny of the vocabulary relating to "πρόσωπον"; none of the respected studies tries to look beyond the contexts of christological and trinitological discussions. Thus it is that those discussions and theoretical considerations of the concepts used therein have become the place to go for those seeking a definition of "person" in Maximus. Various authors deliberate as to whether the meaning of "πρόσωπον" differs from that of "ὑπόστασις" or "ἄτομον"—and, if so, in what respects it differs and what conception of persons it conveys. Even the most comprehensive study, while very balanced in the conclusions it draws from those contexts, does not look into most loci of Maximus' work.[11]

I am not going to engage in this kind of discussion of the meaning of "person," even if I could bring into those debates a complete survey of the usage of "πρόσωπον" in the contexts in question. My reluctance has a very simple reason: the way in which the word was used in those contexts is rooted in a figure of speech that becomes canonical through its prominent place in the Chalcedon statement, but which actually dates from much earlier. The relevant passage of the Chalcedon, whose content and letter were staunchly defended by Maximus, is not long:

> Following thus the Holy Fathers, we also all affirm univocally in our teaching one and the same Lord of us, Jesus Christ, who is the same perfect in divinity and in humanity, . . . one and the same only-begotten Christ, known as being unconfused,

---

11. I mean here the aforementioned paper of Jean-Claude Larchet, "Hypostase, personne et individu."

unchangeable, undivided, inseparable in two natures—as the difference of the natures is by no means destroyed because of the union, but rather the peculiarity of each of the natures is preserved and concurs into one person and one hypostasis—[we affirm the Christ] who is neither split nor divided into two persons, but is the one and the same only-begotten Son of God, the Word, Lord Jesus Christ.[12]

This formulation, rooted in the doctrines of Cyril of Alexandria but encountered very frequently since Gregory of Nyssa,[13] places the terms "ὑπόστασις" and πρόσωπον in a hendiadys. In a classical hendiadys, the two terms brought together create a new meaning and receive a new reference. It is not exactly the case here. Rather, the two terms are used in this way in order to point to the fact that their extension (if one can use this term in respect of the Trinity) is identical. The emphasis brought about by their usage in the hendiadys points to the fact that the two terms are, in a way, imperfect in their applicability to the mystery of the Trinity, and should not be separated. This in turn means that while their referents are identical, their import is somewhat different.

This interpretation of the Chalcedon statement's hendiadys—obvious if one considers the rhetorical customs of Ancient Greek, but possibly less incontrovertible in the case of a Patristic text—is, in fact, confirmed by one of the first texts in which the two terms show up together. In his *Panarion*, Epiphanius of Salamis quotes a letter from George of Laodicea. George, after having summarized the orthodox doctrine of the Persons in the Trinity (73.14.3 = III.286.22–27), explains that "the easterners say 'hypostases' as an acknowledgment of the subsistent, real individualities of the persons."[14] In other words, he points to the fact that the doctrinal emphasis of "ὑπόστασις" is different from that of "πρόσωπον," which is treated in his synopsis as a standard label for the members of the Trinity, pointing as he does to their differing in respect of their properties.

An important Maximian definition would seem to confirm this kind of reading. It contains a double hendiadys, and allows for a difference in

---

12. *ACO* 2.1.2.129.23–5, 129.30—130.2. All translations whose author is not mentioned are mine.

13. See e.g. *Ad Graecos ex communibus notionibus* 3,1.31.18, 33.4; *Contra Eunomium* 1.1.228.2, 229.6, 503.6; *Epistulae*, 24.7.7.

14. Epiphanius of Salamis, *Panarion* 73.16.1 = III.288.21–22, "ὑποστάσεις οἱ ἀνατολικοὶ λέγουσιν, ἵνα τὰς ἰδιότητας τῶν προσώπων ὑφεστώσας καὶ ὑπαρχούσας γνωρίσωσιν." The translation used here is that of Frank Williams, in Epiphanius of Salamis, *The Panarion*. Cf. also an almost identical expression in 73.16.2 = III.288.28–30.

the meanings of the terms. It also situates the two concepts in a theoretical framework:

> Hypostasis and person are the same, for both [are identifiable with] particular and the proper, as far as it concerns their description [περιγραφή], but they do not possess their own predication, in the manner of natures, referable to the multiplicity [of things]. (*TP14* [17.2] 152A1-4)

Firstly, the definition affirms that the two words have the same reference. This is clear, since the two, used in a generic manner, are attributed the features conveyed by the terms "particular" and "the proper," but their meaning is not identified with the meaning of those terms. Furthermore, they are explained through their place in predication. As they are not predicable of multiple objects and cannot point, in this way, to any kind of nature, the two terms are shown to function in a manner similar to that of proper names. This means that both "ὑπόστασις" and "πρόσωπον" are characterized here as metalinguistic terms, referable to all kinds of names of individuals, by virtue of emphasizing the fact of particularity and the uniqueness of an individual. Yet, it does not seem that particularity and uniqueness describe either "ὑπόστασις" or "πρόσωπον" separately. Rather, they are used as a common περιγραφή—i.e., description—of one and the same type of reality with two names and, possibly, two different meanings.

While Maximus is well aware that some things can differ either conceptually or actually,[15] and that, because of that, one ought to be able also to distinguish between conceptual and merely verbal differences between two co-extensive terms, he does not bother, at least in this definition, to distinguish between the meanings of "ὑπόστασις" and "πρόσωπον." If this were his practice in the rest of his work, then it would make sense to explain the meaning of each of them separately, in order to go back to the hendiadys. If the definition reflects the typical way in which the terms are used by Maximus, the next step would not be analyzing their theological hendiadys, but, instead, placing them within the context of Maximus' logical remarks

---

15. Such a distinction may be found in a later text of Maximus, *Two Difficulties of the Byzantine Deacon Theodore Rhetor and Synodikarios of Paul Archbishop of Constantinople* [45] (*TP19* 221D8-224A1). One encounters there a passage devoted to the issue of whether the wills of Christ are known merely "in conceptual division, without verifiable evidence," "ἐν τῇ κατ' ἐπίνοιαν διαιρέσει, ψιλῶς," and the Incarnation is "viewed in the mode of separation [i.e., abstraction] and of imagination," "κατὰ διαίρεσιν . . . λαμβανομένη καὶ φαντασίαν," or those wills are known "properly and as realities," "κυρίως καὶ πραγματικῶς γνωρισθήσονται," and, as a result, the Incarnation is considered as something φυσικόν, i.e., present in nature. See also *Ep12* [48] 468C14-D2. Cf. also *TP16* [65] 189A1-10.

and his views of how the terms are predicated. The concluding remark in the definition adduced above can be viewed, actually, as a simplified reference to Porphyry's *Isagoge*, where the only reality not predicated of other things is individual, ἄτομον, while the proper, ἴδιον, can be predicated of both genus and individual.[16]

Naturally, such a course of action can be taken only if Maximian usage of "πρόσωπον" in christological and trinitological contexts is related, in actuality, to the Chalcedonian hendiadys. If it is so, tracing down other, non-theological contexts of "πρόσωπον" will make even more sense. Thus, in this study, I will limit myself to verifying the patterns of Maximus' deployment of the terminology of persons in just those contexts.

It can be said that those patterns do conform broadly to the one established by the Chalcedonian statement. My claim requires, however, some qualifications. Firstly, it is so, providing we accept the textual findings of Bram Roosen. Secondly, there are some peculiarities and significant exceptions to the pattern of hendiadys.

A very frequently adduced definition, which differentiates between "πρόσωπον" and "ὑπόστασις" and relates them to each other, can be found in a text re-edited and athetized by Bram Roosen, *Capita de substantia*, formerly referred to as the first part of *Theologica et polemica 23*, i.e., *Capita de substantia seu essentia et natura, deque hypostasi et persona*.[17]

> Ὅτι ἡ μὲν ὑπόστασις(,) πρόσωπον ἀφορίζει τοῖς χαρακτηριστικοῖς ἰδιώμασι.[18]

> [He says] that a hypostasis determines a person through characteristic properties.

There can be no doubt that this passage is a quote from a statement of Leontius of Byzantium. The text shown above differs from a phrase in Leontius' *Contra Nestorianos et Eutychianos* merely by the fact that its author replaced "καὶ" by "ὅτι," making it clear in this way that his phrase is a kind of quotation. However, the complete passage from Leontius, on which the notes that constitute *CSu* are based, is much more easy to read. The author of the *CSu* cuts into pieces the following Leontian sentences, among others, in an effort to turn them into a set of ostensibly definitional claims:

---

16. Cf. Porphyry, *Isagoge* 4,1.2.17–18, 4,1.3.1–3.
17. Rejection explained in "EfR," 694–708. Cf. also 715–16, 825–29.
18. *TP23a* 261A13–14 = *CSu* γ′[δ′] 1–2, comma in "⟨⟩"-type angle-braces added by Roosen.

(a) Οὐ ταὐτὸν, ὦ οὗτοι, ὑπόστασις καὶ ἐνυπόστατον, ὥσπερ ἕτερον οὐσία καὶ ἐνούσιον. | (b) Ἡ μὲν γὰρ ὑπόστασις τὸν τίνα δηλοῖ, | (c) τὸ δὲ ἐνυπόστατον τὴν οὐσίαν· | (d) καὶ ἡ μὲν ὑπόστασις πρόσωπον ἀφορίζει τοῖς χαρακτηριστικοῖς ἰδιώμασι, τὸ δέ γε ἐνυπόστατον τὸ μὴ εἶναι αὐτὸ συμβεβηκὸς δηλοῖ, ⟨ὃ ἐν ἑτέρῳ ἔχει τὸ εἶναι, καὶ οὐκ ἐν ἑαυτῷ θεωρεῖται| ⟨— τοιαῦται δὲ πᾶσαι αἱ ποιότητες, αἵ τε οὐσιώδεις καὶ ἐπουσιώδεις καλούμεναι, ὧν οὐδετέρα ἐστὶν οὐσία, ⟩ | (e) ⟨τουτέστι πρᾶγμα ὑφεστὼς⟩ | (f)— ⟨ἀλλ' ἀεὶ περὶ τὴν οὐσίαν θεωρεῖται,⟩ (g) ὡς χρῶμα ἐν σώματι καὶ ὡς ἐπιστήμη ἐν ψυχῇ. (*CNE* Daley 8.20–28 = PG86a, 1277C13–D6)

In the text adduced above, the author focuses on distinguishing between "hypostasis" and "the in-hypostatic." The first term refers to "the someone," i.e., to human beings, whom we, but not the author, call "persons." "The someone," defining hypostasis, is not identical with "πρόσωπον." Being "πρόσωπον" appears to be a consequence of the fact that every human is a hypostasis, as it is thanks to her or his hypostasis that a "person" is determined by characteristic properties. It seems, thus, that those characteristic properties, while being ontologically linked with the hypostasis or the substance, also shape a functional reality called the "person." The "in-hypostatic," in turn, refers to the substance as something which is not an accident in a hypostasis. Substance is different from hypostasis, but is also a "subsistent thing"—i.e., something that has the kind of being proper to a hypostasis. It seems, thus, that the two terms point to two sides of a reality that is an irresolvable and organic composition of being "substance" and "hypostasis"—to its independent existence and to its possession of a "substance" in the sense of a set of defining, non-accidental properties. This substance-and-hypostasis is thus an independent, complete thing, not just a collection of properties. The latter is a feature of persons, which turns out to be a kind of functional expression of the hypostasis itself.

Such an interpretation is very difficult to reach on the basis of the version of the text contained in the Maximian corpus. In the quote above, vertical bars point to the places in which Leontius' argument was cut into phrases and dispersed over *CSu*.[19] The "⟨⟩"-type angle braces show the text which has been significantly altered by the author of *CSu*. The first alteration can

19. The text of each part of the quote can be found in the following lines of *CSu*: (a) β' [γ'] 1–2 (*TP23a* 261A13–4); (b) α'[β'] 2 (A1–2); (c) absent; (d) altered with possible change of subject in first angle bracket, altered without changing sense in second bracket, γ'[δ'] 2–5 (A12–B5); (e) δ'[ε'] 2 (A8–9), altered as "ἢ πρᾶγμα ὑφεστὼς καθ'ἑαυτὸ," (f) altered as "ἀλλ'ἀεὶ περὶ τὴν οὐσίαν καὶ τὴν ὑπόστασιν θεωροῦνται," referred to "ἐνυπόστατον ἢ ἐνούσιόν" instead of qualities, in δ'[ε'] 6–7 (C1–3); (g) practically unaltered, δ'[ε'] 3 (B10–11).

even change the subject of the phrase. As a result, various interpretations of the ostensibly Maximian passage have been offered, aimed most frequently at demonstrating his personalism along lines similar to the modern view of a person as "someone"—i.e., a unique human being. A conclusion of this sort could, however, only be derived from the distorted text. *CSu*, even if drafted by Maximus, neither presents his authentic thought nor makes any consistent interpretation possible. Therefore, I do not consider it necessary to introduce considerations of "the work formerly known as *Theologica et polemica 23*" into debates about the Maximian understanding of persons.

The next text affected by the findings of Bram Roosen is the one formerly known as *Theologica et Polemica 26, Ex quaestionibus a Theodoro monacho illi propositis*.[20] The definition of hypostasis in this work is adduced by almost every scholar dealing with the issue of personhood in Maximus, as it appears to identify hypostasis with a particular human "being personally distinguished from other people":

> Ὑπόστασις δέ ἐστιν, κατὰ μὲν φιλοσόφους, οὐσία μετὰ ἰδιωμάτων· κατὰ δὲ τοὺς Πατέρας, ὅ καθ' ἕκαστον ἄνθρωπος, προσωπικῶς τῶν ἄλλων ἀνθρώπων ἀφοριζόμενος. (*TP26* 276A1–B3)

This may be read as suggesting that, according to the Fathers, hypostasis is the metaphysical principle of specifically human personhood. However, the text, as corrected by Roosen on the basis of a wider range of manuscripts, is somewhat different:

> Ὑπόστασίς ἐστι, κατὰ μέν φιλοσόφους, οὐσία μετὰ ἰδιωμάτων, κατὰ δὲ τοὺς πατέρας, καθ'ἕκαστον ἄνθρωπον προσωπικῶς τῶν ἄλλων ἀνθρώπων ἀφοριζόμενον. (*QThGFr2* 11–13)

The definition "according to the Fathers" in the corrected version only completes the definition "according to philosophers." While the philosophers say that hypostasis is substance with properties, the Fathers add that this hypostasis is something that distinguishes personally a particular human being from other humans. The meaning of "προσωπικῶς" is not explained. The text clearly states, though, that being "personally distinguished" is a result of being a hypostasis. This definition, then, allows for the extensional synonymy of "person" with "hypostasis," as in the Chalcedonian hendiadys. Yet it also suggests that the term "personal" has, by itself, a different meaning from "hypostatic," as personal determination in a human is caused by, but not identical to, hypostasis.

20. Cf. "EfR," 753–77, 733–40.

As a matter of fact, the Chalcedonian hendiadys shows up frequently in the texts and establishes an indubitable extensional identity between the two terms. The exceptions to this pattern point, in turn, to a different sense of person. The latter, however, cannot be discovered on the basis of exclusively scrutinizing the Trinitarian and christological contexts. This is because "person" as such is not defined in the indubitably authentic Maximian works.

There are, altogether, thirty instances of the hendiadys of person and hypostasis in the Maximian corpus analyzed for the purposes of this paper: twenty-eight in authentic, and two in spurious passages.[21] There are a few texts in which the hendiadys is particularly frequent: *TP14*, with three instances, including the one adduced above, *Ep12* with four instances, and *Ep15* with thirteen instances. The minority of cases follow the Chalcedonian pattern exactly,[22] while the majority, dominated by the twelve cases in *Ep15*, move "ὑπόστασις" to the front position.[23] This is consistent with the broad Maximian tendency to give priority to the language of hypostasis in these contexts. In a quick search, 549 instances of ὑπόστασις-language showed up in the Maximian corpus, including instances in the titles added by the scribes. All of them are used in the context of Trinitology, of Christology, or of theoretical contexts that serve to explain theological concepts. There are, in turn, 150 instances, including 112 authentic Maximian usages, of person-language in those contexts.[24]

The pattern established by the hendiadys also seems to inform the contexts in which "πρόσωπον" and its cognates are used as stylistic replacements of "ὑπόστασις." There are, altogether, thirty instances belonging to this type in the authentic works of Maximus (forty-one altogether in the corpus, including eight occurrences in spurious passages and three in the relata). The work in which the greatest number of cases of this type can be found is also the one with the most instances of hendiadys: *Ep15*. Throughout the

---

21. *CSu* α′2, in the inauthentic part of the text, drawn from *Ef22|CSu*, 70.11; *QTh-GFr2*, 2, 17, in the text not contained in *TP26*, corresponding broadly to *Ef20|QThGFr*, but in a line not known to Epifanovich, reversed hendiadys.

22. Eleven cases in authentic works: *TP13(b)* [16] 145C2; *TP14* [17.2] 149C3, 152C15; *TP16* [65] 192C1; *TP19* [45] 221C8, an imperfect instance; *TP21* [83] 249C12; *TP24* [70] 59 (PG91, 269C14); *Ep12* [48] 469D5, D10, 492C3; *Ep15* [36] 553D3.

23. *TP1* [44] 37B12; *TP2* [61.1] 40C7; *TP14* [17.2] 152A1; *QThGFr2* [75.1] 9 (PG91, 276A14); *Ep12* [48] 468D3; *Ep15* [36] 545A4, 549B6, B12, B13, C8, C13, D2, D10, 552A5, A8, C3, C12.

24. There are also twenty-seven such instances in "relations," twelve cases in spurious works, and one occurrence in a passage of dubious authenticity (*SchD* 212B5, RL 212.2, Suchla, CD 4/1, 212.18).

entire Epistle, the stress is laid on hypostasis. There are many more instances of "ὑπόστασις" there than of "πρόσωπον": 119 usages of "ὑπόστασις" (occurrences in the titles added by the scribes and in the scholia having been excluded) versus 22 instances, and 8 cognates, of "πρόσωπον."[25] Maximus regularly inverts the Chalcedonian hendiadys in *Ep15*. Through those cases of inverted hendiadys he reminds the reader that he is speaking about one and the same thing: the very same person or hypostasis that the Fathers, whom he adduces *in extenso* in the first section of the Epistle (545A1–49A9), spoke of. By doing this, he turns "πρόσωπον" in *Ep15* into a mere stylistic equivalent of "ὑπόστασις." There is no other text with so many cases of "πρόσωπον" used in place of hypostasis-language. In *TP3* and *TP13*, there are just four such usages in each work.[26] More emblematic is the language of *Ep13* 〚15〛, where a single instance of "πρόσωπον" (517D14) stands in the company of thirty-seven christological usages of "ὑπόστασις" (including third-person usages in section titles).[27]

A different pattern, less frequent, consist in using the language of "πρόσωπον" rather than that of "ὑπόστασις" when speaking about Sabelians or Nestorians. This is related to the fact that Gregory of Nazianzus and Basil the Great "preferred the word 'hypostasis' [to the word "πρόσωπον"], because of the links that the word 'prosôpon' still had in their era with the Sabelian modalism, and because of the risk of confusion that using it could have entailed for some readers."[28] Accordingly, thirty-five instances of "πρόσωπον" in the corpus express the heretical claims, while "ὑπόστασις" is either absent from the context or appears in juxtaposed orthodox assertions. It must be admitted that the majority of such cases occur in *DP* 〚—〛, a work composed in order to defend Maximus from charges of heresy.

25. Other occurrences of "πρόσωπον" in *Ep15* 〚36〛 are: 545B3, B8, 549B14, C2, 552A6, 553B11, 557A3, 560A12, 568C6. There are also instances of "προσωπικός" in 552B10, C7, 553B13, D5, 556B6, D11, 557A1, 565D7.

26. *TP3* 〚61.2〛 49A1, 53C9, 56B5; *TP13* 〚16〛 145B8, B10, B12, C2.

27. Other authentic usages: *AT* 〚38〛 1.13 (however, this is a special case, based on a quote in *EpTh*, 1.16, which will be discussed below); *TP5* 〚67〛 64C11; *TP15* 〚69〛 173B15 (used to express an orthodox claim, yet in the context of speaking about heretics using "πρόσωπον," as discussed below); *TP16* 〚65〛 200D8. Usages in relata, discussed below in more detail: *DP* 〚—〛 289D10, 340B7, B9. Usages in spuria: *SchD* 212A5 (RL 209.11, Suchla, CD 4/1, 209.5); *CDiv* 1329D1; *CSu* α'. 3, α'. 5, α'.9, α'.10, α'.12, γ' [δ'] 1–2 (PG91, 261A13).

28. "Il faut cependant noter que chez Grégoire de Nazianze et plus encore chez Basile l'usage du mot *prosôpon* reste rare (il est symptomatique que Maxime cite le nom de Basile, mais aucun texte de lui contenant le mot même) et que ces deux Pères lui préféraient le mot *hypostasis*, en raison de liens que le mot *prosôpon* avait encore à leur époque avec le modalisme sabellien et des risques de confusion que son usage pouvait comporter pour certains lecteurs." Larchet, "Hypostase, personne et individu," 42.

In *DP* there are, altogether, twenty-one instances of "πρόσωπον" being employed in christological contexts. There are also twenty cases of "ὑπόστασις," whose only purpose is to discuss issues pertaining to Christology. Most frequently, when the disputants speak about Nestorius, they adopt his language, as Maximus does in 336D5–337A13. When he opposes the heretics in this passage through an orthodox claim, he goes back for a moment to the language of "ὑπόστασις." Yet the heretical conclusion, shown as such by Maximus, mentions "person."[29] In some such cases it is Pyrrhus who avails himself of person-invoking language. In one utterance attributed by the composer of the dialogue to Pyrrhus, a premise that the speaker adopts, and which leads to a conclusion denounced by Maximus as heretical, refers to human beings by means of "πρόσωπον."[30]

This custom of reserving the language of persons especially for Nestorians, Sabellians, and Severians is followed by Maximus himself in many of his works, especially in *TP25* and *TP15*.[31] In *TP2* [61.1], however, Maximus refers to the views of Severus through a hendiadys of "ὑπόστασις" and "πρόσωπον" (40C7). The custom is reflected also in the usage of the term "προσωπικός." The Nestorian "personal difference" is mentioned in *Ep12* [48] 493C8, when Maximus speaks about the errors of Nestorius, Apolinarius and Eutyches, who did not know the natural difference in Christ, or in *TP3* [61.2] 56C5, where it is linked with Nestorians and Severians, and opposed to hypostatical union.[32] In *TP19*, the discussions of "hypostatical or personal wills" aim to show that adopting this idea and accepting "personal otherness," as the Severians and Apollinarians seem to do, would lead to "cutting Christ into persons."[33] Yet "personal difference" also appears in a short outline of orthodox views in *TP7* [41] (73C4, C6).

---

29. Usages: 336D5, D7, D7, 337A2, A9, A10.

30. These are occurrences in 292A3, A6. Other similar instances in *DP*: 289D10 (with "ὑπόστασις" one line before, in a conclusion from Sabellius), 305A14, B2, B3, 313C1, 336A5 (Pyrrhus speaks), B3, D1 (Pyrrhus speaks), 337A14, B4, B5, B7, B11, D2, 340B7, B9. The last two instances belong to the larger context of 340A13–B12, where "ὑπόστασις" is used for orthodox statements.

31. All similar instances: *PN* [7] 424; *QThal* [4] sch. 1, 62.3, to 62.43; *TP20* [42] 232A14; *TP24* [70] 45 (PG91, 269B6); *TP25* [62] 273A14, B3, B6, B8, B8 (second instance in the same line); *TP2* [61.1] 45B2, B5; *TP15* [69] 173B6 (quote from Nestorius), 180A12, 184B9; *DB* [—] 287 (PG90, 148C15), 487 (PG90, 156C1). There is also an instance of "μονοπρόσωπος" in this work in 173B15, after the quote from Nestorius. In this place, the heretical doctrine of Paul of Persia is discussed. Very closely, hypostasis "ὑπόστασις" is used in expressions of orthodox doctrine. Cf. also "μονοπρόσωπος," "πολυπρόσωπος" and "ἀπειροπρόσωπος" in *TP3* [61.2] 53B9, C3, C12, C14.

32. See also *Ep12* 484A10.

33. *TP19* [45], "προσωπικός": 225A8, A9, A13, C3; "πρόσωπον" 225C3.

In almost all of the passages mentioned up to now, Maximus makes his usage of "πρόσωπον" dependent on an external factor. Either he tries to emphasize that any reference to a person in a context relates, as a matter of fact, to a hypostasis, or he makes the person, or a "personal" feature, a part of the statement he is rejecting. While the term is accepted in the language of his Christology and in auxiliary theoretical considerations, it is adopted with caution.

There are, however, a few passages devoted to christological issues in which "πρόσωπον" seems to be used as the proper and primary term. One of them is the passage of *TP16* 201C1–204A5. Not only is "πρόσωπον" identified there with "ἄτομον" in a hendiadys (201C4–5), but also the limits of this identification are pointed out.

The passage apparently identifies the "person and individual" with a human being, or at least the reality of the compound being of two natures, as it begins with the claim that there is no difference between existence (ὕπαρξις) and natural activity (φυσικὴ ἐνέργεια) in substance and nature, but there is such a difference in "person and individual." It is so because there are many natures and many natural activities in a person. Such a person/individual resembles the Patristic human uniting the two natures of the body and the soul, and the Patristic Christ unifying in himself the human and the Divine natures. Maximus emphasizes this inner difference in the person, who is composed of "other and other," establishes (παριστᾷ) "the other and other" of her or his natural activity, and even "knows himself" by performing those activities:

καὶ διαφόρους τε γὰρ φύσεις, τὰς ἐξ ὧν συνέστηκεν, καθορῶμεν,
καὶ τὰς φυσικὰς κινήσεις, αἷς ἐνεργοῦν κατὰ φύσιν γνωρίζεται,
τὴν οἰκείαν πιστούμενος ὕπαρξιν. (C6–9)

Such an individual is not enclosed (περικλείεται) in one natural activity, and because of that, neither is it enclosed in one nature (D1–3). Therefore, as Maximus seems to conclude, the number of its natures equals the number of its substantial movements (D4–6).

In this context, the concept of "person/individual" seems referable to the reality we now call "a person"—a self-conscious being recognizable by her or his actions. Only the idea that this kind of individual is also the individual of logic may seem strange. Actually, Maximus rejects this linkage of logical and human individuality a few lines later, where Christ is concerned. Christ cannot be called "individual" because He does not belong to a division from the most general genus to the most specific species—a division which would inscribe Him into His own "procession." Because of that, as

Cyrillus says and Maximus appears to re-affirm, the name of Christ has no power of definition (D7-204A3).

I will return later to the Neoplatonic term "procession" used in this context. Let me only remark here that, for the first time in the scrutinized material, the choice of the vocabulary of persons in a broad christological context is made on Maximus' own terms. Here, what matters is what he wants to say, as opposed to emphasizing what he wants to avoid saying. Furthermore, the reason why the term "πρόσωπον" is used both for a human individual and for Christ here seems to be the fact that it describes a composite, active, and self-cognizant being.

There are a few more instances of this kind. Almost none of them, however, occurs in a passage that is so rich in content and so clear about intentions. The only exception is the text of *TP10* 136C10–137B1. This text offers a marginal critical remark on the work of Theodore of Faras, who may be identified with Theodore Rhaïthu. Maximus criticizes him for providing the authors of the *Ekthesis* with an unorthodoxly worded, and even inconclusive, formulation on which they then built their theses. His mistake consists in "introducing hypostatical actualization," or "activity," (136D3) and "giving to the person as person an actualization which characterizes, or marks distinctively, their nature" (D8-10). What he should have attributed to persons was "the quality, and a precise qualification, of the mode in which [acts] flow according to nature" (136C10-137A1, "ἐκβάσεως" is verbalized in translation).

The term "πρόσωπον" ostensibly acquires a metaphysical meaning— that of modality. This meaning, however, must be regarded in both an epistemological and an ethical light, as the following lines of the passage declare:

> [B]y this [flow] the difference between those who act and the things that are done, whether they are according to nature or against nature, is recognized. For, chiefly as something, and not as someone, everyone of us is actualized: i.e., as a human, and as someone, like Peter or Paul, [everyone] shapes the *mode of actuality* (τῆς ἐνεργείας σχηματίζει τρόπον), which may happen to [occur] through setting or relaxing (ἐνδόσει τυχὸν ἢ ἐπιδόσει) [the tenor of the soul, the latter] being molded so or otherwise depending on his judgment. Because of that, it is in the [determination of the] mode that the differentiation of persons in respect of their actions is known. For neither is someone more nor someone else less actualized or rational, but we equally possess reason and its actuality [in the sense of "faculty"], arising according to nature. More and less, and in this way and in another way, someone is just or unjust, by the virtue of one following

more what is according to nature and the other abstaining from this [course of action]. (137A1–B1)

The text speaks quite clearly about how differentiation between persons arises. The key word of the text is "τρόπος," understood both as a modality and in the later sense of "temper." Maximus claims that there are two levels of actualization of potentialities that are rooted in human nature: we have faculties, at the level of our humanity, and we happen to have specific kinds of action, at the level of being a "someone." The latter is described through the pair of words "ἔνδοσις" and "ἐπίδοσις." Emmanuel Ponsoye remarks that those words correspond in Maximus to the ethical terms "θύμος" and "ἐπιθυμία," "anger" and "desire."[34] They appear to be being used here, though, along the lines of Stoic ethics, very broadly conceived. "Ἔνδοσις," in one of its principal meanings, refers to the action of "striking the key-note."[35] I assume that "setting a proper tone" (ἔνδοσις) and "relaxing that tone" (ἐπίδοσις) is is the proper meaning of the text. According to the Stoic understanding of ἐπιθυμία, it consists in irrational stretching, in being "ὄρεξις" in its literal meaning. In turn, virtue is a good disposition of the soul.[36] As "ἔνδοσις" does not show up in any other place within the Maximian corpus, while "ἐπίδοσις" can actually refer to desire in his works (eg. *Ep1* [36] 365B15), one may conclude that Maximus is speaking here, as a matter of fact, about the modality/temper of virtue, as opposed to that of desires. The choice of a language dependent on an interpretation of Stoic ethics allows him to view particular actions as building up our characters through modifying, "impressing," yet not altering, the substance of what we are. That view, which is both anthropological and ethical, is expressed in the final lines of the passage.

As a result, personhood turns out in this passage to be (1) an ethical reality, (2) rooted in our choices and our evaluation of those choices, (3) also, however, modifying our substance—our "what we are" into "who we are"—and (4) thus making it possible to discern one human from another.

It seems that some elements of this view of persons in *TP10* can be recognized in some other passages. In the hendiadys of *TP16* 192C1, "πρόσωπον" precedes "ὑπόστασις" and is rhetorically emphasized. Maximus speaks there about the gnomic will as the definitional feature of the person.

---

34. Maximus the Confessor, *Lettres*, 184n2. The note refers to his translation of the terms as "tension" and "relaxation."

35. LSJ, s.v. ἔνδοσις, meaning 1. Cf. also Dimitrakou, *Μέγα λεξικὸν*, s.v. ἔνδοσις, meaning 2.

36. Cf. Long and Sedley, *The Hellenistic Philosophers*, sections 60J, 1B(9), 5B in each volume.

The very same idea is mentioned in a rhetorically similar manner in *TP3* [[61.2]], when Maximus paraphrases and criticizes the arguments of Severus (53C9). More importantly, it seems to inform the definition of hypostasis in *QThGFr2* 11–13, adduced above. Hypostasis, according to this definition, distinguishes a particular human from other humans "προσωπικῶς"—i.e., "personally." Apparently the personal features, while rooted in the hypostasis, cannot be identified with being a hypostasis.

Across the entirety of these passages, "person" turns out to be something we call "character"—i.e., a particular set of features that emerges in human life through those of our decisions that make us good or evil, and thanks to which we differ from other people and can be characterized as such. If "πρόσωπον" can be defined in this way, it is an extensional synonym of "ὑπόστασις." However, being such a person is only a manifestation of being a hypostasis. If this is the sense that Maximus associates with the very word "πρόσωπον," his avoidance of this word in christological contexts and his emphasis on "ὑπόστασις" can be better explained. The term is both necessary, when the manifestation of being a hypostasis is at issue, and potentially misleading, given that manifestation can be confused with being.

It must be emphasized, however, that this solution to the problem of "πρόσωπον" in christological contexts is, in many respects, imperfect. It is so because it is not clear whether being such a person can be identified with being an individual, and what the relation is between a hypostasis and an individual. The second part of the passage on persons and individuals in *TP16*, in 201D7–204A10, presents ἄτομον in the manner in which it is discussed in Porphyry's *Isagoge*—i.e., as the lowest and undefinable object of predication (4,1.2—3.20). This view of individuality is consistent with the picture of hypostasis in *Ep15*,[37] and with the definition of "hypostasis and person" in *TP14*. Yet, in the passage of *TP16* scrutinized above, and in the lines which follow it (up to 204D6), the person of Christ is not only presented as different from an individual, due to its not belonging to a genus and species and not possessing a definition, but also identified with the compound hypostasis of Christ. Besides, the process through which an individual is defined—in a manner consistent with Porphyrian logic—is referred to as "πρόοδος," a metaphysical term borrowed from Plotinus and Porphyry that is usually rendered in modern scholarship as "procession" and never used by Porphyry in his own logic.[38] The term describes the generation of lower genera

37. See my forthcoming paper "The Mirror of Hypostasis."

38. Plotinus, *Enneades* 3.6[26].17.7; 4.2[4].1.44; 4.8[6].5.33, 6.5; 5.2[11].1.27; 5.5[32].3.9; 6.3[44].12.14, 22.7, 22.47; 6.6[34].11.26. Porphyry, *Sententiae* 24.1, 31.19; *In Platonis Timaeum* 2.70.8; *Historia philosophiae*, fr. 18.11. The term is frequent, however, in Proclus. 864 instances show up in TLG lemma search.

from higher intellectual principles, and cannot, because of that, be applied to the philosophy of individuals. Its usage by Maximus echoes the language of Gregory of Nazianzus (*De Filio*, *Or.* 29.2), which Maximus quotes in *EpTh* ⟦39⟧ 1.16. Gregory speaks there, in broadly similar terms, about the procession of persons in the Divine Monad. Maximus adopts this language in *EpTh* 1.25, 1.37 and in *AT* 1.13. However, in the *Ambigua ad Thomam* he switches over almost immediately to speaking about hypostases. All of this means that an explanation of the sense of "πρόσωπον" in Maximus' christological and Trinitarian discussions will not itself resolve the problem of what the reality actually is that is being named by this word "person" or "character," and whether it should be construed in line with Neoplatonic metaphysics and logic. Furthermore, as there are very few contexts in those discussions where the meaning of "πρόσωπον" is clearly affirmed, one has no option but to relate this specific usage of the language of persons to other more frequently occurring applications of that same language.

"πρόσωπον" and "Face"

The Primary Sense of "πρόσωπον"

It should be remembered that christological and Trinitarian contexts of the language of persons, as well as such theoretical considerations as clarify the meanings of terms used in those contexts, represent only one of the tertiary functions of the word "πρόσωπον." Its basic meaning, "face," does not occur frequently in Maximus' authentic works, and most instances of that kind belong to a text that Maximus himself only adduces. There are altogether forty-five more or less literal instances of "πρόσωπον" in the scrutinized corpus. Nineteen of them belong to indubitably authentic Maximian works, two may be found in dubious passages,[39] four in relations,[40] and nineteen in spurious works.[41]

39. The two instances in *Ef11¦GnCn* ⟦—⟧ 46.32, 51.1; quoted from Jugd 6:1 (6:2) and 16:1 (16:3).

40. *DP* ⟦—⟧ 288B4, 353A6; *DB* ⟦—⟧ 652 (PG90, 164B2), 723 (165C11); used in the meaning of "face" in narrations and/or in utterances of other speakers than Maximus. In the second instance in *DP*, "by face" may be understood also as "personally": Pyrrhus wants to visit the sepulchers of the Apostles and become worth of viewing the most holy Pope "by face," and giving him a book about the absurdities they discussed.

41. These are the following instances: (1) "face" *tout court*, (a) used by the author, *SchE* 7.64; *CDiv* 1360C12; (b) quoted, *SchE* 7.20, 7.210, 7.211; *LC* 740C1, 756A7, 917D3, 925C5, 945A13, 996C14, 997A5; (c) adopted, *SchE* 7.30; *CDiv* 1197C3 (from 2 Cor 3:12); (2) literalized Hebrew meaning of "facing," quoted, *SchE* 8.2, 8.133; (3) literalized Hebrew meaning of "surface," quoted, ibid. 10.31; (4) nominalized Hebrew

Maximus himself, unlike the authors of spurious texts, in most cases does not seem to have been misled by the re-literalized and nominalized instances of "πρόσωπον" that occur frequently in the Septuagint. When he uses the word literally, he usually means a face: either the face of the brother (*CChar* [2] 3.89.1, 4.34.2), or that of an enemy (*Ep12* [48] 461A7), or the faces of friends, seen in imagination (*Ep22* [53] 605C9), or—apparently also imagined—the benign face of God (*Ep1* [49] 381C10), at which the imagined angels do not look, turning their faces down (381C8). The physical and visible face of Moses (*AI* [3] 10.15.2 = PG91, 5.1117C5)—or, for that matter, that of Christ (10.28.5 = 17.1125A8, 10.29.1 = 1125D6)—may be marked by the light of grace. This light cannot be looked at, because this physically visible light exceeds, in actuality, the domain of the physical. As Moses becomes the type, or impression of a deiform type, so this light becomes the basis of the metaphorical meaning of "face," important for the Maximian view of the human person.

More frequently, however, Maximus quotes passages in which "πρόσωπον" is used in the literal meaning of "face," sometimes before asking and answering the question of the metaphorical value of the adduced text.[42] In many such cases, it is not even clear whether, in some Scriptural passage or other he is quoting or paraphrasing, "πρόσωπον" has any literal significance at all. I have therefore not included those 10 instances in authentic works, or the single instance in a dubious one, in the count of literal usages of "πρόσωπον."[43] In three instances, two of which belong to a quote, "face," used with a preposition, conveys the idea of personal presence. In the text he writes himself as a commentary to Gen 3:24 (*QD* [5] 158.16), the fiery sword is also a metaphor for the power of discerning the costs of wrongdoings. As it stands before our faces, it also examines our conscience.[44] The way leading from a literal to a secondary or tertiary usage of "πρόσωπον" is short.

---

verb "turn," quoted, *SchD* 133C7 (RL133.2); (5) with a possible metaphorical value of "characteristics," *LC* 913B4, B6.

42. Maximus asks such a question in respects of instances in *QThal* [4] 54.3, 54.8, 54.47; and does not ask in quotes in *QD* [5] 70.1, 92.17, 191.4; and in *QThal* 65.34 (adopted language rather than a quote).

43. Authentic instances, all in *QThal* [4]: 5.5, 5.8, 9.32, 9.33, 10.94, 10.95, 54.62, 55.52, 65.4, 65.277. The dubious instance comes from *SchD* 36C6 (RL 36.2).

44. Similar instances in quotes: *Ep1* [49] 372C9, 381A13.

Secondary Usages of "πρόσωπον"

Under the heading of "secondary usages," I am grouping many kinds of different instances that present a kind of natural extension of the primary meaning of "πρόσωπον." I am discerning altogether eighty-eight instances of this kind, fifty-four of them in authentic texts, nine in relata, three in dubious works, and twenty-one in spurious ones.

It must be admitted that in some cases my grouping could be open to being questioned. This is the case, especially, with instances in which the literal meaning of "face" seems to have been superimposed with the metaphor of human "character." Such instances are only two, and the two are rooted in the usage of the Septuagint (*QThal* [4] 50.7, 50.147). Still, even those two instances share the basic feature of all "secondary" instances: a metaphorical sense of "face" is fixed in them.

This metaphorical power of "πρόσωπον" is something Maximus is well aware of, and also ready to use in contexts in which this power is given a well-defined reference. In a scholion to *QThal*, authored most probably by Maximus himself, we find the following statement:

> As the face is the characteristic [component] in a particular, so spiritual cognition characterizes expressively the divine. The one who searches for it searches for the face of God. (*QThal* sch. 65.21.98–101 to 65.277)

The metaphorical power of "πρόσωπον" resides in the face's capacity to express what is hidden in humans.

While this statement justifies an important metaphorical usage, discussed in the next section, this usage becomes almost fixed, in the later part of *QThal* 65, as a secondary sense of "πρόσωπον." The "face of the Lord" stops being explained there, and appears to adopt the meaning of "manifestation of God in knowledge."[45] Most of the secondary meanings of "πρόσωπον" are, however, taken over by Maximus from current usage. Certainly we should count as such the 18 instances where he cites or paraphrases the language of Scripture, and in which "πρόσωπον" completely loses the meaning of "face," and instead means "surface"[46] or, together with a preposition—like

---

45. 65.283; sch. 21, 65.98 and 65.100, to 65.277; 65.286; 65.287.
46. Five instances in authentic works: *AI* [3] 42.6.34 = PG91, 1321A4; *QThal* [4] 62.6, 62.128; *Ep43* [22] 641A5 = *Ep24* [22] 612B8. Two instances in dubia: *SchD*112B11 (RL 112.7), 112B13 (RL 112.7). Three instances in spurious works: *SchE* 1.53 (the author speaks himself), 11.1; *SchD* 336C9 (RL 336.4, Suchla, CD 4/1, 336.36).

in Hebrew, which was translated extremely literally in the Septuagint—"to" or "from."[47]

Among secondary uses of "person," probably the best known is its employment to convey the concept of a "representative." However, in all four instances in his corpus that are both authentic and not just either quotes or paraphrases, the meaning of "representative" is conveyed by the expression "ἐκ προσώπου." It is worth emphasizing that Maximus uses this expression to emphasize in whose name the Scripture speaks: according to Maximus, in Ps 60:11 (59:13) the prophet asks for salvation in the name of the entire fallen human nature (*Ps59* [6] 322); in Deut 32:22 Moses speaks in the name of God (*LA* [1] 473 [*MAS* 27.6]); the passage from Hos 12:11, which Maximus adduces, is uttered in the name of God (*Ep2* [25] 401B10), and this is how the Scripture speaks in Lev 26:27–28 (*QThal* [4] 44.30).[48] It is possible that the idea of calling humans "persons" stems from this usage, combined with the Trinitarian application of the word "πρόσωπον." As the human writers of Scriptures speak "from the face of" the Lord, or as distressed humans turn towards God, the word "face" starts to refer to the person represented by the speaker. There is nothing strange, therefore, in Theodosius' trying to explain in *DB* [—] 424 (PG90, 153B13) why the Synod did not "anathemize personally"—i.e., did not mention particulars in its anathema.

The sense of being "someone's representative" should not be confused, therefore, with that of "mask"—not, at least in the era in which Maximus was writing. The word which Maximus uses for "mask," and to which he grants the metaphorical meaning of deception, is "προσωπεῖον."[49]

The old sense of an actor's facial mask, identified with a character of a drama, is reflected, though, in the approach to people presented in the Scripture. Since Maximus is most interested in the symbolic meaning of the Bible, those characters turn out to also be "figures"—types of a different

---

47. 13 instances in authentic works: *LA* [1] 492 (*MAS* 27.26), 499 (27.33), 790 (37.78), 816 (38.2), 898 (40.48); *CChar* [2] 2.22.4; *Ps59* [6] 118, 132; *QD* [5] 80.27, 147.3; *AI* [3] 10.67.3 = 311a.1161B7; 41.9.3 = 1309C14; *QThal* [4] 49.3. There is also one instance in relata, *DP* [—] 312B12, and there are five instances in spuria: *SchE* 3.80, 10.15; *LC* 732C3, 865D6, 964A11. Cf. also "ἀντιπρόσωπος" quoted in ibid. 929B5 from Basil's *Enarratio in prophetam Isaiam* 3.120.14.

48. There is also one instance in authentic *Ep18* [46] 584D3, placed by the scribes in the title. There are also six cases in relata, none of them referring to the Bible: 2 in *DP* [—] 328C2, 329A8, where Maximus speaks himself; four in *DB* [—] 17 (PG90, 137A8), 19 (137A11), 590 (161A5), 744 (168A7), all in the narration of the dialogue. Only in a spurious passages of *SchD* 48A4 and A9 (RL 45.4) the expression is referred to the Scripture speaking "in the name of the Lord."

49. *QD* [5] 32.7, 54.3; *TP9* [68] 129C6. Cf. also the spurious instances in *LC* 789A7, A12, A13, A13, 896A9, all in quotes attributed to John Chrysostomus.

reality. In a lengthy passage of *AI* [[3]] 37.5-6 (PG91, 1293A13-1296A5), Maximus sets outs the principles for symbolic interpretation of the Scripture. As he says there, the scriptures possess a single spiritual significance, but this may be amplified in ten modes. These are place, time, genus, person, and social position (or employment), which are reduced, by the three modes of practical, natural, and theological philosophy, and, subsequently, by the modes of presence and future, into Logos, who embraces all of them.[50]

Ezekias, whom we can imitate in his role in the sacred history, is treated as such a character in the Scriptures in *QThal* [[4]] 51.216, as is Jonas in scholion 31 (64.116) to line 710 of *QThal* 64. Maximus may even have wondered whether he should explain allegorically the words of blamable characters (*QThal* 38.6). In some cases, he just offers his exegesis.[51] In other cases, he emphasizes features of characters when speaking about such biblical "persons." Thus, the spiritual meaning of the characters of the perjurer and the thief in Zechariah 5:4 may be explained as different "τρόποι τῶν ἐνεργειῶν" (*QThal* 62.275)—modalities or variants of the diabolic deceitful activities (instances in 62.268, 274, 306).[52]

Such a confusion of a person and her or his character results in assigning the name of "πρόσωπον" to important characters in real life (*AI* [[3]] 7.29.14 = 1089C15; *Ep44* [[50]] 648C4),[53] and, moreover, to any person we might perceive: the latter meaning appears when Maximus discusses visions occurring in solitude. It is phrased as "μὴ παρόντος προσώπου" (*AI* 19.3.8 = 1236A2) and "ἀπροσώπως" (19.3.3=1233D5). That extension of the literary term obviously predates Maximus and is reflected, as a matter of fact, in passages of the New Testament of the sort that he might be expected to have commented on, such as Rom 2:11, which contains the word "προσωποληψία," meaning "wrongful respect of persons," and which is discussed in *QThal* 27.156.[54]

This development of the idea of an actor into that of a symbolical character in the Bible on the one hand, and that of an active character in life on the other, does not destroy the primary metaphorical power which "πρόσωπον" possesses as "face." Moses, who "carries sometimes the person of God and Father, and sometimes that of our nature," "τοῦ θεοῦ καὶ πατρὸς

50. Instances of "πρόσωπον" in 37.5.5 (1293B3), 5.11(B9), 6.20 (D10). There is also a similar passage in *QThal* [[4]] 64.11-15, with an instance of "πρόσωπον" at 64.12.

51. *QD* [[5]] 33.1, 33.3, 35.26, 54.3, 172.1, 172.4; *AI* [[3]] 50.4.21 = 1369C4. Similar instance in dubia, *SchD* 181A13 (RL 181.4); in spuria, *SchD* 85C4 (RL 85.6); *CGn* [[8]] 1336 C2.

52. Cf. also spurious *SchD* 181A13 (RL 181.4); *LC* 964A2.

53. Cf. also *DP* [[—]] 352C11.

54. Cf. also *LC* 788C5, as well as 861B6, quoting Acts 10:34, "προσωπολήπτης."

πρόσωπον ἐπέχει, ποτὲ δὲ τῆς ἡμετέρας φύσεως" (*QD* ⟦5⟧ 1.11) is not only a symbol, but also an actual representative and a physical expression of both human and divine natures—in his words, in his actions, and sometimes, even, as Maximus says in other places, in the aspect of his face. When we see God "in a mirror and dimly" (1 Cor 13:12), then, in actuality, the disposition of virtues within our soul turns into a synthetic "face of God" within us. It is not a symbol, but a kind of remote similitude to God (*QThal* 46.6–8). It is an ethical similarity, showing outside what He is like inside. This idea, in which "face" means, apparently, "expression" and "resemblance," grows in Maximus into the complex metaphor of the face of the soul and the face of God.

The Metaphor of the Face

The word "πρόσωπον" occurs in a number of metaphorical contexts in Maximus, yet the metaphor of the face of God, which is also the face of Christ, the face of the soul of the saints, and their persona, being reflected in their physical faces, plays a central role in Maximus' metaphorical usage of the vocabulary of persons. This metaphor even seems, in some places, to be connected with the meaning of "person" that emerges from the anthropological considerations that constitute the backdrop to Maximus' christological discussions.

It must be emphasized that the idea of the "face of the soul," or "the face of God within us," as it is developed in various Maximian works, shows a peculiar Maximian approach to the question of human personality as it assimilates to God. It does not appear in the works considered spurious by at least some authors, yet it permeates all truly Maximian exegesis. A brief summarizing of the relevant statistics may be helpful in understanding the role of this metaphor within the Maximian approach to the issue of personhood.

There are altogether seventy-six metaphorical usages of "πρόσωπον" in the corpus scrutinized for the purposes of this work. Forty-five of these can be found in the indubitably Maximian works, eight in passages that may be considered dubious. The spurious passages can be divided into three groups. In the first group, one should include all eight instances in *SchE*, in which the Bible, speaking about "the face of God," seems to be read as speaking in a metaphor, yet the metaphor is either left in a quote without any explanation[55] or explained, very broadly, as some complete future knowledge of

---

55. *SchE* 2.246, 2.249—Eccl 2:26; 5.2—Eccl 5:1; 5.29—Eccl 5:6 (5:5); 7.177—Eccl 7:26; 8.62, 8.64—Eccl 7:26.

archetypes.[56] In the second group we should count the eight instances of the Maximian metaphor of the face of the soul in *CDiv*, which are adopted from his other works, even though it is difficult, without very detailed analysis, to refer them to particular passages in Maximus. It is distinctive of all those passages that the aspect of scriptural exegesis is neglected by their author.[57] Within the last group, it is possible enumerate the metaphorical instances in those passages of *SchD* that have been attributed by Paul Rorem and John C. Lamoreaux to John of Scythopolis. Among those metaphorical usages, one is a broad explanation of the concept of "the face of God" (189A14), one can be considered a literal usage within a symbol, which is the uncovered face of a bishop (153B11) and the four that occur in the two passages not ascribed by Beate Suchla to John of Scythopolis explain, very broadly, "face of the glorified people" as their intellectual vision.[58]

In turn, the seven out of eight instances in the passages of *SchD* usually attributed to Maximus explore the idea of the many faces of Seraphim, explaining it consistently as their cognitive powers.[59] By contrast, in most indubitably Maximian passages in which a metaphor of face can be found, virtue or vice are also at stake. At least, that is so when the meaning he attributes to an instance of "πρόσωπον" is clear. Sometimes, a quote or biblical paraphrase seems to require a metaphorical or figurative reading, but this meaning must be guessed by the reader.[60] In all other cases, there is an ethical element. All but six are linked with the metaphor of the face of the soul.

56. 8.30, in ref. to 1 Cor 13:12 (two instances).

57. Other instances, ordered by the metaphor and its meaning: "face of the intellect," as it knows the heights of truth, 1272D4; "face of the soul," referred to people born in spirit, 1341C2; to the purified souls, informed by impressed knowledge, 1356A6, 1356B9; "face of Christ" as exemplar of virtues, 1360C8, C9, D1, 1373A5.

58. Two instances in 345D8 (RL 345.3, Suchla, CD 4/1, 345.50), two in 413D11 (RL 413.3, Suchla, CD 4/1, 413.55), quoting 1 Cor 13:12.

59. The exception is "πρόσωπον" in 197C3 (RL 197.4, Suchla, CD 4/1, 197.31), referring to the face of God, whose metaphorical meaning is not explained. The instances in which the words refer to the many faces of Seraphim are: 81B3 (RL 81.3), "πολυπρόσωπος," not explained, in ref. to Ezek 9:5 and 1:10; 89C14 (RL 89.4), "πρόσωπον," about angels "approaching God," in ref to Ps 22(23):6; 100C1 (RL 100.10), "πρόσωπον," also C5 (RL 100.10), "πολυπρόσωπος," and C11 (RL 100.13), "πρόσωπον," explained as "cognitive powers of the Serafim"; 156C14 (156.19), "πρόσωπον," and D1, "πρόσωπον," also "cognitive powers of the Serafim."

60. Instances with "face of God": *LA* [1] 828 (*MAS* 38.15), quoted from Isa 64:6; 858 (40.8), quoted from Ps 95:2 (94:2); 866 (40.15), quoted from Isa 59:2; *Ps59* [6] 94; in ref. to Ps 60:1 (59:3); *QD* [5] 184.3, paraphrasing Jonah 1:3; *AI* [3] 7.8.9 = 1073A5, quoted from Ps 42:2 (43:3); *Ef30¦EpB* [51] 85.3, author's own wording. Instances with "human face": *QD* [5] 187.23, paraphrasing Joel 2:20; *QThal* [4] 65.763, quoted from Luke 2:31.

Four out of six instances mentioned above occur in *Ps59* [6] 136–146.⁶¹ There Maximus explains the expression "πρὸς τὸ φυγεῖν ἀπὸ προσώπου τόξου" from Ps 60:4 (59:6). These days the line is translated as "to rally out of bowshot" (NRSV), or, more frequently, "to be displayed because of the truth" (NASB), in line with the traditional and Talmudic meaning of the Hebrew verb "קשט." The Septuagint offers, as it usually does, an extremely literal translation of the verse. It renders as "from the face" the Hebrew expression "מפני," whose secondary and most frequent meaning is "from" or "due to," and associates it with the literal meaning of identically pronounced "קשת," i.e., with "τόξον," "bow," rather than with the idea of truth as direct as a bow shot, which "קשט" conveys here. In this way, the Hebrew "because of truth" becomes the Greek "the face of the bow," and is explained by Maximus as an "appearance of the bodies that awakens sensitivity" and leads to a "demoniacal passion."

In most of the remaining 29 instances, matters revolve around virtues rather than vices. Those instances are inspired by, and sometimes explain, such biblical passages as 1 Cor 13:12, where Paul speaks about seeing God "face to face," or 2 Cor 3:18:

> But we all, with unveiled face (ἀνακεκαλυμμένῳ προσώπῳ), beholding as in a mirror the glory of the Lord, are being transformed into the same image from glory to glory, just as from the Lord, the Spirit. (NASB)

According to those lines, viewing the glory of God also alters who we are. This is the core idea which Maximus incorporates into his vision of assimilation to God and translates, in his metaphorical exegesis, into the terms of his soteriology and aretology, doing so as he proceeds to explain the meaning of Scriptural references to the human face, the face of God, the face of Christ, the faces of glorified people, the face of the soul, the face of intellect—but also, by opposition, the face of laws, the face of pleasure, and the face of Darius. This meaning is best summarized in the final lines of chapter 7 of the *Mystagogy*, where the vision Paul speaks about in 2 Cor 3:18 is explained as "the treasures of knowledge" (cf. Col 2:3) written by grace in the Spirit—on the tablet of the human heart. The ethical and intellectual aspects of this vision of the blessed are, for Maximus, inseparable (*Myst* [9] 597 [*MAS* 7.61]).⁶²

This kind of interpretation can also be found in *QD* [5], *TP1* [44], *TP7* [41], and *AI* [3], but it is most conspicuously present in *QThal* [4],

---

61. Instances of "πρόσωπον" in lines 137, 139, 143, 145.

62. Only in *TP7* 73A4 (2 instances), is viewing God "face to face" from 1 Cor 13:12 not linked explicitly with ethical transformation.

in fourteen instances[63]—where, moreover, it is also propounded by means of a theoretically complex hermeneutics. It is on *QThal* that my exposition below is based, albeit with references, when appropriate, to other Maximian works.

The most meticulous formulation of the idea of the "face of the soul" may be found in *QThal* 54.49–56, in the commentary to 1 Esd 4:58–60. The narrative about Zorobabel leaving the court of Darius and turning his face to heaven in the direction of Jerusalem receives a complex exegesis, in which the face of Zorobabel becomes the ethical face of the human intellect: i.e., something we might call a "persona." This persona, however, does not exist in everyone. In Maximus' approach, almost no one would have such a "πρόσωπον." This ethical face of the human intellect exists only in those who display in themselves the ethical persona of God.

In order to sketch a complete picture of how such a persona emerges in a human being we must start reading the text of *QThal* 54 a little bit earlier, from line 24. Maximus claims there that Zorobabel symbolizes human philosophical intellect, which is lifted above the dispersion of its powers in the senses through the works of justice (cf. 24–28). In this manner, it is "at rest" (ἀνάπαυσις), having created all kinds of peace and connected the soul's practical part to that which is, by nature, good, and the theoretical part to the truth which is truth by its nature (29–32). Such an intellect is not disturbed: neither in the practical component of the soul, nor in the theoretical one, because it is clad in God himself, the only good and true reality, which is above all essence and intellection (34–39). This intellect recognizes where its grace comes from and turns its face to heaven (40–49). Zorobabel's face, turned to the heavens, symbolizes the inner disposition of such an intellect.

Maximus explains, subsequently, that "person" in 1 Esd 4:58 stands for a specific disposition, of an intellectual kind, of the hidden place in the soul. This place holds the paradigmatic impressions of all of the virtues (49–51). We turn it towards heaven, i.e., towards the heights of intellection (52), while remaining in front of Jerusalem, i.e., in the state of impassibility (ἀπάθεια), which has the character of a disposition (51–53). An intellect, in this disposition of impassibility, looks for an abode "in heaven" (2 Cor 5:2) and "in the city of those inscribed" (Heb 12:23) in heaven (53–56).

The "hidden place of the soul" is not mentioned any more—neither in *QThal*, nor any other text of Maximus—even though the biblical phrase "τὸ κρυπτὸν τῆς καρδίας" shows up a dozen times in his works. As it emerges from the lines that follow the definitional passage, this "hidden place" can

---

63. *QD*: 6; *TP1*: 1, *TP7*: 2; *AI*: 5; *QThal*: 14. To the latter can be added 5 cases of the "fixed" metaphor of "manifestation of God in knowledge," mentioned in note 434.

hardly be identified with the highest part of the soul—the intellect—contemplating God. The "persona" or "face" of the intellect is only a precondition for this kind of contemplation. Maximus says that being lifted up to the height of contemplation and cognition in the state of impassibility is the only possible mode of praising God. This "non-hostile and peaceful constitution" (56–58) serves as a re-definition of the persona of the intellect—or rather, as we read here, of the soul. Impassibility is the "persona," or "face," of the disposition in which our soul finds itself, and which amounts to a composition of multiple and different virtues. They assume the modalities of "χαρακτῆρες," impressions or engravings, which means that the virtues are impressed in us from without. The latter can only be read, in this context, as referring to the intellect's being impressed by the eternal types of the virtues.

This reading is clearly confirmed by a passage in QD 99.1–23. Maximus quotes and interprets the text of Gregory of Nazianzus' Or. 40 (412.6–14). Gregory speaks about the "Sodomian" punitive fire which is prepared for the devil and his angels, and which never ends. This fire burns before the face of God. Maximus sees in this fire divine energies, like goodness, love of men, gentleness and others alike—characteristics of the "face of God." They work as fire, because they illuminate those who are close to God as his family, while they burn those who are of an opposed disposition and alienate their similarity to God.[64] The face of human intellect meets the face of God.

God is not the only power that has a "face" that influences human actions. Both the devil and laws may also have a kind of invisible face. The face of the devil, found by Maximus in the "face of shame" with which the vanquished Sennacherib returns to Assyria (2 Chr 32:20–21), is the "smooth appearance of pleasure," through which the devil rules the souls that prefer sensible enjoyment of sensible things (QThal 50.178, 50.182). However, the expression may refer to no more than evil human actions (QD 187.29). The "face of Darius," in turn, is discussed in QThal 55 as the figure of natural law. Zorobabel, symbolizing the theoretical intellect, turns away his face from the face of Darius (QThal 55.48–69, instance of "πρόσωπον" in 55).

The idea that Maximus is presenting in all these passages amounts to saying that our actions are informed by what our intellect contemplates. Our virtues come from outside, from their eternal paradigms, from the Divine energies, that we both contemplate and express in our actions. This is our inner persona, which, as a matter of fact, is the persona of God in virtuous people. Yet, in those who live without God's grace, it is the persona of natural laws, or even that of the Devil, both of these being powers that lead us to condemnation and consumption by the eternal fire.

64. Instances of "πρόσωπον" at 99.4 (quote), 99.17, 99.19.

The idea of "the face of the intellect" is simplified in other passages of *QThal* 54,[65] and never reappears in precisely this formulation in other Maximian texts. It is discussed in its external expression as "the face of virtues," and the faces of the people who are glorified, "the face of the soul," and as "the face of Christ."

In *QThal* 65.659, olive oil is identified with a face filled with cheerfulness. It is explained as an external expression, "χαρακτηριστικόν," of the brilliance in the intellect, which stays "in line with the impassibility of spiritual grace."[66] In scholion 7 (63.30) to *QThal* 63.350 it is called the "face of the soul" and attributed a perceptible nature. It is the visible external expression (χαρακτήρ) of God having been born in the virtues of saints, which can be seen in the alteration of their modes of life (τρόποι). Above, a number of similar usages, of a more straightforward nature, were counted as literal instances. Such a confusion of literal and metaphorical senses is possible, because

> [o]ur face is the life, which expresses, like the external appearance, what kinds of people we are in respect of the internal man. (QD 70.3)

Yet, as our life expresses the inner man, so it expresses, or is the face of, the Divine Logos, who is the true nature of this life (*TP1* 9A16). The "face of Christ" symbolizes the good exemplar of virtue for all believing nations (*QThal* 65.769, commenting on Luke 2:31), but also is the expression of the truth of the eternal λόγοι of being that reside in Him (65.776).[67] Christ is expressed in us, because he is present from within, through the action of Divine energies, which are His eternal λόγοι. Yet He himself, when seen in the Transfiguration scene (Matt 17:1–2; Mark 9:2–3; Luke 9:28–29), with a shining face, symbolizes "the external noetic expression of

---

65. In question 54, we encounter an instance in which "πρόσωπον," quoted in the Septuagint's version of Lam 4:20, seems to be understood as "the face of the intellect," thanks to a slight alteration of the standard Greek text of the Scripture (*QThal* 54.223). In q. 55, the same passage from the 1st book of Esdras is read as referring to a cognitive disposition of the theoretical intellect "in line" or "in accordance" with virtue (55.74). In scholion 1 to 65.33, an intellect, purified through the virtues, gains in this way knowledge of the λόγοι of virtues. This divinely impressed cognition of the virtues is its "face" (sch. 1, 65.1–4, "πρόσωπον" in line 4). See also sch. 3, 54.17, to 54.40; 55.74. Cf. also usages in *QThal* epist. 402, 420, 423: with the "covered face" of 2 Cor 3:18, we view sensible things through sensuous perception, as appearances and a source of passions. The uncovered face of discursive cognition can see the glory of God. A similar instance can be found in *AI* 10.52.12 = 22a.1148D9, where it is referred to the viewing powers of reason in Moses, who typifies a soul going up to God.

66. *QThal* sch. 41, 65.229–234, to 65.659, "πρόσωπον" in line 231.

67. Cf. also *AI* 10.59.28 = 27.1156B5.

His hidden essence, whose depths it is impossible to gaze into by means of argument-based explanation" (QD 191.47). His shining face is the symbol of His unperceivable secrecy, as He transgresses all potency and activity of the intellect (AI 10.64.2 = 31a.1160B13). What He is himself is hidden from us. We see only an external expression. The "persona" is not who he is.

Conclusion

The issue of person and personhood cannot be separated from Maximian usage of the language of "πρόσωπον." This language, in turn, is deeply permeated by the primary sense of the word "πρόσωπον"—that of the face. It is the face that expresses who we are, through our actions. Yet, this external expression is never identical with the inner man. The few cases in which "πρόσωπον" is referred by Maximus to a human being as the proper term, and not a stylistic replacement, or a heretical expression, emphasize the fact that we create an "external persona" through our actions. We are recognized through this persona, but, as a matter of fact, are something more. The issue of whether the proper Maximian term for expressing the conception of the metaphysical principle of individual human being is ὑπόστασις goes beyond the limits of this study. Yet the metaphor of the face, which points to the ethical "persona" both of the human being and of Christ, makes it clear that no metaphysical principle of individuality such as Maximus might speak of leads to any kind of modern idea of person and individuality.

This is so because, in Maximus, the truly ethical persona we build and display is not something we create ourselves. Our decisions, even if they shape our persona, do not stem from our powers. We are a part of the universe, whose nature was created by God, yet also need to be raised up by God after the Fall. Our decisions can have their roots, therefore, in three different powers, and none of them is ourselves. We can either let God act in us and raise us from our fallen state, or turn to the powers of nature and its law, or to the power of the devil. Each of them only impresses our intellect and our behavior, but never appears contained within the limits of our being. God, especially, while granting us an impression of His eternal λόγοι and energies, remains transcendent. What is created in us, thanks to meeting Him in the persona of his energies, is a "face of the intellect," a reflection of the perfect order. The latter becomes expressed in our life, in our actions, even in our face. Thus, we have an inner persona and an external one. Yet both are, as a matter of fact, an expression of the persona of Christ, of His image, which He creates first in our cognition, then in our actions.

As a result, the more we are such a persona, the less we are ourselves. We may remain the individuals that logic speaks about, but we are not persons in the sense of self-relying actors. Such may seem to be those who try to decide themselves, using their gnomic will, what is good and bad. Yet our true persona, the true expression of our virtues, can be rooted only in the grace that impresses in us a complete picture of the entire logically connected system of virtues. The more we have this kind of persona, the less we decide for ourselves. Intellection of complete eternal truth replaces the partial and relative γνώμη on which our will used to rely. We cannot look for self-expression or self-realization, because we express and realize Him. Through this persona—His persona in us and the only one Maximus deems worth writing about—we are more similar to Christ than to ourselves, and we are less persons and more an image of God.

Bibliography

Anonymous. *Capita de substantia et hypostasi, una cum excerptis e Ps. Clementis Alexandrini De prouidentia et Maximi Confessoris Epistula 13 in appendicibus i et ii (olim Theologica et polemica xxiii a)*. [Chapters on Ousia and Nature, Hypostasis and Person]. In "EfR," 711–13. Abbreviated as *CSu*.

———. *Scholia in Ecclesiasten*. Edited by Santo Lucà. CCSG 11:3–87. Abbreviated as *SchE*.

Bathrellos, Demetrios. *The Byzantine Christ: Person, Nature, and Will in the Christology of Saint Maximus the Confessor*. Oxford Early Christian Studies. Oxford: Oxford University Press, 2004.

Dimitrakou, Dimitrios. Μέγα λεξικὸν ὅλης τῆς ἑλληνικῆς γλώσσης. Athens: Ekdosis Domi, 1964.

Epiphanius of Salamis. *Panarion*. Edited by Karl Holl. In *Ancoratus und Panarion*, 1:153–464; 2:5–523; 3:2–6. Die Griechischen christlichen Schriftsteller der ersten drei Jahrhunderte 25, 31, 37. Leipzig: Hinrichs, 1915–31. Abbreviated as *Panarion*.

———. *The Panarion of Epiphanius of Salamis, Books II and III, De Fide*. Translated by Frank Williams. 2nd rev. ed. Nag Hammadi and Manichaean Studies 79. Leiden: Brill, 2013.

Garrigues, Jean-Miguel. "La personne composée du Christ d'après saint Maxime le Confesseur." *Revue thomiste* 74 (1974) 181–204.

Jankowiak, Marek, and Phil Booth. "A New Date-List of the Works of Maximus the Confessor." In *OHMC*, edited by Pauline Allen and Bronwen Neil, 19–83. doi:10.1093/oxfordhb/9780199673834.013.2.

John of Scythopolis and Maximus the Confessor (passim). *Corpus Dionysiacum IV/1: Ioannis Scythopolitani prologus et scholia in Dionysii Areopagitae librum De divinis nominibus cum additamentis interpretum aliorum*. Edited by Beate Regina Suchla. Patristische Texte und Studien 62. Berlin: de Gruyter, 2011. Abbreviated as CD 4/1.

Larchet, Jean-Claude. "Hypostase, personne et individu selon saint Maxime le Confesseur." *Revue d'histoire ecclésiastique* 109 (2014) 35–63. doi:10.1484/j.rhe.1.103884.

———. *La divinisation de l'homme selon saint Maxime le Confesseur*. Cogitatio fidei 194. Paris: Cerf, 1996.

Leontius of Byzantium. *Libri tres contra Nestorianos et Eutychianos*. Edited by Brian E. Daley. In Brian E. Daley, "Leontius of Byzantium: A Critical Edition of His Works, with Prolegomena," 1–76. DPhil diss., Oxford University, 1978. Abbreviated as *CNE*.

Liddell, Henry G., et al. *A Greek-English Lexicon*. 9th ed. Oxford: Clarendon, 1968. Abbreviated as LSJ.

Long, Anthony A., and David N. Sedley. *The Hellenistic Philosophers*. 2 vols. Cambridge: Cambridge University Press, 1988.

Madden, Nicholas. "Composite Hypostasis in Maximus Confessor." *Studia Patristica* 27 (1993) 175–97.

Maximus the Confessor. *Ad Catholicos per Siciliam constitutos (Theologica et polemica ix)* [To the Christ-Loving Fathers, Superiors, Monks, Dwelling Here in Sicily and to the Orthodox People]. Edited by François Combefis. PG91:112C–32D. Abbreviated as *TP9*.

———. *Ad eundem ex tractatu de operationibus et uoluntatibus (Theologica et polemica ii)* [To Marinus the Very Pious Priest, Chapter 50 from the Treatise on Operations and Wills]. Edited by François Combefis. PG91:40A–5B. Abbreviated as *TP2*.

———. *Ad Marinum Cypri presbyterum (Theologica et polemica x)* [Copy of a Letter Sent to Sir Marinus, Priest of Cyprus]. Edited by François Combefis. PG91:133A–7C. Abbreviated as *TP10*.

———. *Ad Marinum presbyterum (Theologica et polemica i)* [To Marinus the Very Pious Priest]. Edited by François Combefis. PG91:9A–37D. Abbreviated as *TP1*.

———. *Ad Stephanum presbyterum et hegumenum* [Epistle B, To Stephen, Priest and Superior]. Edited by Sergey L. Epifanovich. In *Ef*, 84–85. Abbreviated as *Ef30¦EpB*.

———. *Aduersus eos qui dicunt dicendum unam Christi operationem (Theologica et polemica v)* [Responses to Arguments of the Monenergetists]. Edited by François Combefis. PG91:64A–5A. Abbreviated as *TP5*.

———. *Ambigua ad Iohannem*. Edited and translated by Nicholas P. Constas. In *Difficulties*, 1:62–450; 2:2–330. Abbreviated as *AI*.

———. *Ambigua ad Thomam*. Edited by Bart Janssens. CCSG 48:3–34. Abbreviated as *AT*.

———. *Capita de caritate* [Four Centuries on Charity]. Edited by Aldo Ceresa-Gastaldo. In *CSC*, 48–238. Abbreviated as *CChar*.

———. *Capita theologica et oeconomica* [Gnostic Chapters]. Edited by François Combefis. PG90:1084A–173A. Abbreviated as *CGn*.

———. *Capita x de duplici uoluntate Domini (Theologica et polemica xxv)* [Ten Chapters on the Two Wills of Our Lord and God and Saviour Jesus Christ]. Edited by François Combefis. PG91:269D–73D. Abbreviated as *TP25*.

———. *De duabus Christi dei nostri uoluntatibus (Theologica et polemica xxiv)*. [That it is Impossible to Say One Will of Christ]. Edited by Bram Roosen. In "EfR," 731–32. Abbreviated as *TP24*.

———. *De duabus Christi naturis (Theologica et polemica xiii)* [On the Two Natures in Christ]. Edited by François Combefis. PG91:145A–9A. Abbreviated as *TP13*.

———. *De duabus unius Christi Dei nostri uoluntatibus (Theologica et polemica xvi)* [On the Two Wills of the One Christ Our God]. Edited by François Combefis. PG91:184C–212B. Abbreviated as *TP16*.

———. *De qualitate, proprietate et differentia, seu distinctione, ad Theodorum presbyterum in Mazario (Theologica et polemica xxi)* [On Quality, the Proper and Difference, to Theodore Priest in Mazaria]. Edited by François Combefis. PG91:245D–57A. Abbreviated as *TP21*.

———. *Disputatio cum Pyrrho* [Dispute with Pyrrhus]. Edited by François Combefis. PG91:288A–353B. Abbreviated as *DP*.

———. *E quaestionibus a Theodoro monacho illi propositis*. Edited by Sergey L. Epifanovich. In *Ef*, 67–68. Abbreviated as *Ef20¦QThGFr*.

———. *Epistula i* [Epistle 1, To the Eparch George on Sailing for Constantinople]. Edited by François Combefis. PG91:364A–92D. Abbreviated as *Ep1*.

———. *Epistula ii* [Epistle 2, To John the Chamberlain]. Edited by François Combefis. PG91:392D–408C. Abbreviated as *Ep2*.

———. *Epistula secunda ad Thomam* [Second Letter to Thomas]. Edited by Bart Janssens. CCSG 48:37–49. Abbreviated as *EpTh*.

———. *Epistula xii* [Epistle 12, To John the Chamberlain]. Edited by François Combefis. PG91:460A–509B. Abbreviated as *Ep12*.

———. *Epistula xiii* [Epistle 13, To Peter the Illustrious]. Edited by François Combefis. PG91:509B–33A. Abbreviated as *Ep13*.

———. *Epistula xliii* [Epistle 43, To John the Chamberlain]. Edited by François Combefis. PG91:637B–41C. Abbreviated as *Ep43*.

———. *Epistula xliv* [Epistle 44, Letter of Recommendation to John the Chamberlain]. Edited by François Combefis. PG91:641C–8C. Abbreviated as *Ep44*.

———. *Epistula xv* [Epistle 15, To Cosmas the Deacon, of Alexandria]. Edited by François Combefis. PG91:544D–76D. Abbreviated as *Ep15*.

———. *Epistula xviii* [Epistle 18, Written in the Name of George, the Praiseworthy Eparch of Africa to Nuns Apostate from the Catholic Church at Alexandria]. Edited by François Combefis. PG91:584D–9B. Abbreviated as *Ep18*.

———. *Epistula xxii* [Epistle 22, To Auxentius]. Edited by François Combefis. PG91:605B–C. Abbreviated as *Ep22*.

———. *Epistula xxiv* [Epistle 24, To Constantine Sacellarius]. Edited by François Combefis. PG91:608B–13A. Abbreviated as *Ep24*.

———. *Ex eodem tractatu caput 51, quod Patres qui duas in Christo uoluntates dixerunt, naturales leges significarunt, non uoluntates ex sententia (Theologica et polemica iii)* [To Marinus the Very Pious Priest, Chapter 51 from the Same Treatise]. Edited by François Combefis. PG91:45B–56D. Abbreviated as *TP3*.

———. *Expositio in Psalmum lix* [On Psalm 59]. Edited by Peter Van Deun. CCSG 23:3–22. Abbreviated as *Ps59*.

———. *Fragmenta duo e Quaestionibus a Theodosio Gangrensi Maximo Confessori propositis*. Edited by Bram Roosen. In "EfR," 743–44. Abbreviated as *QThGFr2*.

———. *Lettres*. Translated by Emmanuel Ponsoye. Edited by Jean-Claude Larchet and Emmanuel Ponsoye. Paris: Cerf, 1998.

———. *Liber asceticus* [On the Ascetical Life]. Edited by Peter Van Deun and Steven Gysens. CCSG 40:4–123. Abbreviated as *LA*.

———. *Mystagogia*. Edited by Christian Boudignon. CCSG 69:3–74. Abbreviated as *Myst*.

———. *Orationis dominicae expositio* [On the *Our Father*]. Edited by Peter Van Deun. CCSG 23:27–73. Abbreviated as *PN*.

———. *Quaestiones ad Thalassium*. Edited by Carl Laga and Carlos Steel. CCSG 7:3–539; 22:3–325. Abbreviated as *QThal*.

———. *Quaestiones et dubia* [Questions and Doubts]. Edited by José H. Declerck. CCSG 10:3–170. Abbreviated as *QD*.

———. *Spiritualis tomus ac dogmaticus . . . ad sanctissimum Dorensem episcopum Stephanum (Theologica et polemica xv)* [Spiritual and Dogmatic Tome . . . Addressed to Stephen the Most Holy Bishop of Dora]. Edited by François Combefis. PG91:153B–84C. Abbreviated as *TP15*.

———. *Theodori Byzantini, [monothelitae], quaestiones cum Maximi solutionibus (Theologica et polemica xix)* [Two Difficulties of the Byzantine Deacon Theodore, Rhetor and Synodikarios of Paul Archbishop of Constantinople]. Edited by François Combefis. PG91:216B–28A. Abbreviated as *TP19*.

———. *Tomus dogmaticus ad Marinum diaconum (Theologica et polemica vii)* [Dogmatic Tome Sent to Marinus Deacon in Cyprus]. Edited by François Combefis. PG91:69B–89C. Abbreviated as *TP7*.

———. *Tomus dogmaticus ad Marinum presbyterum (Theologica et polemica xx)* [Dogmatic Tome to the Priest Marinus]. Edited by François Combefis. PG91:228A–45D. Abbreviated as *TP20*.

———. *Variae definitiones (Theologica et polemica xiv)* [Various Definitions]. Edited by François Combefis. PG91:149B–53B. Abbreviated as *TP14*.

Maximus the Confessor (testimony). *Disputatio Bizyae* [The Dispute at Bizya]. Edited by Pauline Allen and Bronwen Neil. CCSG 39:73–151. Abbreviated as *DB*.

Maximus the Confessor and Anonymous. *Ex quaestionibus a Theodoro monacho illi propositis (olim Theologica et polemica xxvi)* [From the Things Asked Him by the Monk Theodore]. Edited by François Combefis. PG91:276A–80B. Abbreviated as *TP26*.

Noret, Jacques. "La rédaction de la Disputatio cum Pyrrho (CPG 7698) de saint Maxime le Confesseur serait-elle postérieure à 655?" *Analecta Bollandiana* 117.3–4 (1999) 291–96.

Podbielski, Marcin. "The Mirror of Hypostasis: An Attempt at a Philosophical Commentary on Maximus." Manuscript, 2015.

Pseudo-Maximus the Confessor. *Capita de substantia et hypostasi*. Edited by Sergey L. Epifanovich. In *Ef*, 70–71. Abbreviated as *Ef22¦CSu*.

———. *Capita de substantia seu essentia et natura, deque hypostasi et persona (olim Theologica et polemica XXIIIa)* [Chapters on Ousia and Nature, Hypostasis and Person]. Edited by François Combefis. PG91:260D–4C. Abbreviated as *TP23a*.

———. *Capita gnostica* [The Moscow Gnostic Century]. Edited by Sergey L. Epifanovich. In *Ef*, 33–56. Abbreviated as *Ef11¦GnCn*.

———. *Diuersa capita ad theologiam et oeconomiam spectantia deque uirtute et uitio (xxvi-d)*. Edited by François Combefis. PG90:1188A9–392A. Abbreviated as *CDiv*.

———. *Loci communes* [Sententiae]. Edited by François Combefis. PG91:722A–1018C. Abbreviated as *LC*.

Pseudo-Maximus the Confessor [John of Scythopolis et al.]. *Scholia in corpus Areopagiticum* [Scholia in Pseudo-Dionysius]. PG4:16A–184C. Abbreviated as *SchD*.

Roosen, Bram. "Epifanovitch Revisited: (Pseudo-) *Maximi Confessoris Opuscula varia*; a Critical Edition with Extensive Notes on Manuscript Tradition and Authenticity." PhD diss., Katholieke Universiteit Leuven, 2001. Abbreviated as "EfR".

———. "On the Recent Edition of the *Disputatio Bizyae*: With an Analysis of Chapter 24 *De providentia* of the *Florilegium Achridense* and an *index manuscriptorum* in Appendix." *Jahrbuch der Österreichischen Byzantinistik* 51 (2001) 113–31.

Rorem, Paul, and John C. Lamoreaux. *John of Scythopolis and the Dionysian Corpus: Annotating the Areopagite*. Oxford: Clarendon, 1998. Abbreviated as RL.

Sherwood, Polycarp. *An Annotated Date-List of the Works of Maximus the Confessor*. Studia Anselmiana, philosophica theologica 30. Rome: "Orbis Catholicus"/Herder, 1952.

Skliris, Dionysios. "'Hypostasis,' 'Person,' 'Individual,' 'Mode': A Comparison between the Terms That Denote Concrete Being in St Maximus' Theology." In *KPC*, 437–50.

Thunberg, Lars. *Microcosm and Mediator: The Theological Anthropology of Maximus the Confessor*. 2nd ed. Chicago: Open Court, 1995.

Tollefsen, Torstein. *The Christocentric Cosmology of St. Maximus the Confessor*. Oxford Early Christian Studies. Oxford: Oxford University Press, 2008.

———. "St Maximus' Concept of a Human Hypostasis." In *KPC*, 115–28.

Törönen, Melchisedec. *Union and Distinction in the Thought of St. Maximus the Confessor*. Oxford Early Christian Studies. Oxford: Oxford University Press, 2007.

Zizioulas, John. "Person and Nature in the Theology of St Maximus the Confessor." In *KPC*, 85–114.

14

The Philosophical Basis of Maximus' Concept of Sexes: The Reasons and Purposes of the Distinction between Man and Woman

Karolina Kochańczyk-Bonińska

Introduction

Sexual differentiation is connected to various crucial elements of Maximus' thought. On the one hand, it is strongly connected to such theological problems as the original sin and eschatological vision, and on the other with Maximus' understanding of human nature and the idea of man as a microcosm, which are philosophical ideas and a part of his vision of the world. In my paper, I would like to focus only on the metaphysical elements underlying sexual distinction and the original state of human nature. Then, I will show the inevitable consequences of such assumptions in eschatological future. Finally, I will try to clarify some incoherencies in Maximus' thought and the possible reasons and solutions of such situation.

The Origin of the Division

Maximus claims that "the creation of our forefather Adam took place in a hidden, secret manner."[1] The original state is being described by Maximus in various places and has been already the subject of numerous studies.[2] In

---

1. *AI* 42.10 = PG91, 1324D (trans. Constas, in *Difficulties*, 2:141).
2. Thunberg, *Microcosm and Mediator*, 152–53.

this paper, I will focus on the most important elements. But what should be strongly stressed at the beginning is that if, according to the Confessor, the fall was supposed to be somehow nearly simultaneous with the creation (*QThal* 61, 628A), the original state should be treated as the idealistic vision or model, as the ultimate aim rather than the important starting point.

Before the transgression, Adam was sinless in his creation (γένεσις, *AI* 42.4 = PG91, 1317A). In *Difficulty* 45 Maximus develops his theory of different kinds of bodies which human beings were supposed to have before the fall (*AI* 45.3 = PG91, 1353AB). The Confessor underlines that Adam experienced harmony in his corporality. According to Adam Cooper—and I agree completely with this interpretation—Maximus rejects the connection between the punishment of sin and corporeal creation of a human being.[3] The first Adam was innocent, although he was corporeal (*AI* 45.3). "Consistent with this temperament, the first man was naked, not because he was fleshless or bodiless, but because he did not possess the temperament which 'thickens the flesh and makes it mortal and obtuse' (Gregory the Theologian, *Or.* 45 8 = PG36, 633A)."[4]

For Maximus, following Gregory of Nyssa, the nature of human beings took on sexual difference as an addition to God's original plan in the light of human sin.[5] In the cosmic order from the very beginning the human being has its mediating value as humans stand on the border and between animals and angels,[6] between purely corporeal beings and those purely spiritual.

"When (the first man) had sinned while transgressing the commandment, he was condemned to an engendering through passion and sin. Because of this, natural genesis became a law in the passible element of sin (ἐν τῷ παθητῷ τῆς ἁμαρτίας)."[7] A similar topic could be found in *Difficulty* 45. It is not the sexual differentiation itself which is a consequence of the fall, as it has already been underlined, but the sexual procreation which becomes an instrument of transmission of the consequences of sin, which is now inscribed into the human mode of existence. According to Maximus, as it has been extensively presented, nature, or—using terminology specific for Maximus in this context—the λόγος of nature (λόγος φύσεως), the uncreated λόγοι of beings are unalterable.[8] And what is particularly important, as we can read in *Difficulty* 41, the λόγος does not include sex distinction:

3. Cooper, *Body in St Maximus the Confessor*, 80.
4. *AI* 45.3.14–17 (trans. Constas, in *Difficulties*, 2:195).
5. Partridge, "Transfiguring Sexual Difference," 17.
6. Ibid., 23.
7. *QThal* 21, 312B–13B. See Larchet, "Ancestral Guilt," 30.
8. *AI* 42.15 = PG91, 1329 BC; Mitralexis, "Ever-Moving Repose," 118.

"This sexual differentiation clearly depends in no way on the primordial reason (λόγος) behind the divine purpose concerning human generation."[9] The Confessor points out that after Adam's sin the human mode (τρόπος) of existence changes. This change is underlined by Maximus with different terms that describe the creation of the first human being and the beginning of other people's life after sin. Adam's transgression changed the intended mode of generation.[10] The distinction between man and woman, male and female is not than a function of the λόγος of human beings, but is connected with mode (τρόπος).

"The Sacrament of Sin"

After Adam's fall, the mode of transmitting human nature changed from purely spiritual into a sexual one,[11] or—using the Confessor's language— into a beastly one (*AI* 10.21 = PG91, 1121B). This motif had been already present in patristic legacy and Maximus continued and developed Gregory of Nyssa's hypotheses. He presents the sexual mode of engendering as the best way to transmit mortality and other consequences of Adam's fall.[12] The consequences of first man's fall, even those that are not sinful themselves, are transmitted onto their offspring. Because of Adam's fall human beings were condemned to be born through pleasure and corruption. We should definitely underline the connection between the ancestral sin, pleasure and possibility (*QThal* 61, 626D–645C). There are many studies about the origin of this problem. But I would like to let Maximus speak for himself.

> The choice of Adam's natural reason, being at first corrupted, corrupted with itself nature which has abandoned the grace of impassibility (τῆς ἀπαθείας τὴν χάριν). The first sin, which is blameful, is the fall from good to the evil of choice; the second, caused by the first one, is the change, which is blameless, from incorruptibility to corruption. These two sins took place, with the ancestor, by the transgression of the divine commandment. One is blameful, the other not. That of choice willingly puts

---

9. *AI* 41.3 = PG91, 1305C (trans. Louth, in *Maximus the Confessor*, 155).

10. This is discussed in *QThal* 61, 626D–645C; cf. Partridge, "Transfiguring Sexual Difference," 152.

11. *AI* 31.3 = PG91, 1276C; 41.7 = 1309A; 42.1–3 = 1316–17A.

12. This is discussed in *AI* 31.3 = PG91, 1276C; 42.1–4 = 1316B–17C; *QThal* 61, 628AC; 632D.

good apart; that of nature unwillingly leaves immortality, because of this choice.[13]

Sexual differentiation (and engendering) has for Maximus a specific link to sin; while it is not evil, nor sinful in and of itself, as von Balthasar argued, it is a kind of "the sacrament of sin," indeed an outward and visible sign of it.[14] The Confessor does not condemn either the body that was part of Adam's construction from the beginning, or the sexual mode of engendering which was imprinted into the human mode of existence later, after the fall. In *Difficulty* 42 he states clearly,

> For if marriage is evil, then it is obvious that the natural law of creation is also evil. And if natural law of creation (κατὰ φύσιν γενέσεως) is evil, it is equally obvious that the One who created nature, and gave it this law, should just fall under indictment. (*AI* 42.24 = PG91, 1340B; *Difficulties*, 2:167–8)

Sexuality is understood as a kind of a function that appeared in human nature just after Adam's fall. This function is necessary to transmit the nature which was changed as a result of the first sin.

Difficulty 42: Genesis (γένεσις) and Engendering (γέννησις)

Creation (γένεσις) is understood as the first formation of a human being; formation by which Adam received a perfect human nature directly from God.[15] "[A]nd [he had] no need of the natural intercourse of marriage. In this way he showed, I think, that there was perhaps another way, foreknown by God, for human beings to increase, if the first human being kept the commandment and not cast himself down to animal state."[16] In *De opificio hominis*, Gregory suggests that it was the angelic mode of procreation.[17] But he does not precisely specify how he understands this spiritual mode. It is not the subject that would particularly interest Maximus either.

So, γένεσις is used to describe the creation of innocent Adam and Incarnation of Christ. All people that were born after the fall receive the corrupted mode of existence connected with sensual pleasure. Engendering (γέννησις) is connected with this corrupted mode of existence and is similar

---

13. *QThal* 42, 405C; Larchet, "Ancestral Guilt," 34.
14. Balthasar, *Cosmic Liturgy*, 199; Partridge, "Transfiguring Sexual Difference," 148.
15. Cooper, *Body in St Maximus the Confessor*, 216.
16. *AI* 41.7 = PG91, 1309A (trans. Louth, in *Maximus the Confessor*, 157).
17. Gregory of Nyssa, *De opificio hominis* 17, 189–92.

those of the beasts. In *Difficulty* 42, the Confessor underlines that Jesus bridged the gulf between γένεσις and γέννησις. Christ-new Adam started his existence as a human being without procreation. Maximus explains that

> In becoming flesh, the Savior did not in any way assume sinful passion or corruption into himself, but he accepted their consequences, and so made birth the salvation of creaturely origin, and paradoxically renewed the incorruptibility of creation by means of the passibility made possible by his birth. At the same time he made creaturely origin preservative of birth, sanctifying the possibility of birth by sinless of creation, so that he might completely restore the integrity of creaturely origin, which holds nature together, by its divinely perfect inner principle. (*AI* 42.4 = PG91, 1317BC; *Difficulties*, 2:127)

Difficulty 41

According to Maximus sexual differentiation serves remedial purposes as a result of original Adam's fall, and is then subject to radical transfiguration in the wake of Christ's recapitulation of creation.[18] In *Difficulty* 41, which is absolutely crucial for our subject, Maximus describes five fundamental divisions that destroy the harmony of the cosmos. He writes about the division between (*a*) male and female; (*b*) paradise and inhabited world; (*c*) earth and heaven; (*d*) sensual and intelligible; (*e*) created and uncreated. It was presented in Partridge's dissertation that "male and female, alone of all creation, do not explicitly unfold out of the previous layer, the 'inhabited world.'"[19] This unique role that the humans have in the cosmic schema is presented here. Human beings constitute not only the last of the five layers but also the glue that holds the universe together.[20] "Human beings are found on both sides of each division: they belong in paradise but inhabit the inhabited world."[21] In order to understand the Confessor's concept of sex differentiation, we should remember that he sees human nature as a bond (σύνδεσμος) of creation.[22] Directly after describing the union with God that humans enable the cosmos to achieve, Maximus continues:

18. Partridge, "Transfiguring Sexual Difference," 146–47.
19. Ibid., 133.
20. Ibid.
21. Louth, *Maximus the Confessor*, 73.
22. Partridge, "Transfiguring Sexual Difference," 3.

> For this reason the human person was introduced last among the beings, as a kind of natural bond mediating between the extremes of the whole through the associated parts, and leading into one in itself the things set apart from each other according to nature by a great distance, in order that, gathering everything in union with God as cause, beginning first with its own division, next, advancing through the middle parts by sequence and order, it reaches the end of the high ascent which has emerged through all things according to the oneness, to God, in whom there is no division.[23]

Cosmic reconciliation starts with mediation between the male and the female.[24]

> In order to bring about the union of everything with God as its cause, the human person begins first of all with its own division, and then, ascending through the intermediate steps by order and rank, it reaches the end of its high ascent, which passes through all things in search of unity, to God, in whom there is no division. It accomplishes this by shaking off every natural property of sexual differentiation into male and female by the most dispassionate relationship to divine virtue. This sexual differentiation clearly depends in no way on the primordial reason behind the divine purpose concerning generation. Thus it is shown to be and become simply a human person in accordance with the divine purpose, no longer divided by being called male or female. It is no longer separated as it now is into parts, and it achieves this through the perfect knowledge,[25] as I said, of its λόγος, in accordance with which it is.[26]

This simple humanity that shook off every natural property of sexual differentiation into male and female is not by now a new concept in the Confessor's thought, but returning to beginnings: "wholly transfigured according to him and bearing his saving and completely unadulterated image, which does not take part in any of the marks of destruction in any mode."[27]

---

23. *AI.* 41.3.1–10 = PG91, 1305BC (trans. Louth, in *Maximus the Confessor*, 155, with revisions).

24. Thunberg, *Microcosm and Mediator*, 396.

25. Claudio Moreschini suggests that we should correct "γνῶσιν" that has not been introduced here and put there the term "ἕνωσιν." See Maximus the Confessor, *Ambigua: problemi metafisici e teologici*, 698n9.

26. *AI* 41.3.5–19 = PG91, 1305BD (trans. Louth, in *Maximus the Confessor*, 155, with revisions).

27. Maximus the Confessor, *AI.* 41.9 = PG91, 1312A; translation based on Andrew

According to Maximus, people and their mode of existence will be renewed through Incarnation. Human beings will exist in full accordance with their λόγοι. The Confessor proves that this restoration concerns especially the mode of existence and does not change anything in the λόγοι of nature as they have not been changed after the fall.

There are many questions and ambiguities that occur when we read those crucial texts. There are also different hypotheses. What we know for certain about the Confessor's ideas are the following assumptions:

- In eschatological future human beings will exist according to their λόγοι
- Sexual differentiation depends in no way on the primordial reason (λόγος)
- Human beings have their unique role as a bond (σύνδεσμος) of creation
- In fact, what humans are called upon to do as the first step of their unifying role is to "shake" this difference "out of (their) nature."[28]
- And what has not been yet underlined strongly enough, and what seems to be one of crucial points of Maximus' thought is the identity of bodies (*AI* 7.42–3 = PG91, 1101BC).

> For after the death of body, the soul is not called "soul" in an unqualified way, but the soul of man, indeed the soul of particular human being, for even after the body, it possesses, as its own form, the whole human being, which is predicated of it by virtue of its relation as a part to the whole. The same holds in the case of the body, which is corruptible by nature, but has a particular relation on account of its origin. For the body, after its separation from the soul, is not simply called "body," even though it will decompose and be dissolved into elements from which it was constituted, but the body of man, indeed of a particular man. For like the soul it possesses the form of the whole human being predicated of it, by virtue of its relation as a part to the whole. (*AI* 7.42 = PG91, 1101B; *Difficulties*, 1:139–41)

The relation between body and soul is so strong that they can be separated only in thought (*AI* 7.43 = PG91, 1101C).

One of the most important questions is whether humans that will exist neither male nor female could be considered to remain fully human.[29] If this

---

Louth's in *Maximus the Confessor*, 158.

28. Partridge, "Transfiguring Sexual Difference," 135.

29. Ibid., 173.

λόγος does not include male and female with its reproductive possibilities, how can we say for certain exactly what does or does not change in human bodies?[30] It is much more coherent to confirm—as some contemporary scholars tend to do—that the Confessor did not envision any morphological change in embodied sexual characteristics in this lifetime.[31] Adam Cooper, for instance, has argued that "the reconciliation or union between male and female does not require the abolition of physical distinction but is primarily a matter of knowledge and will."[32] Partridge claims that he does not believe that it is possible to say exactly how much of human embodiment, and indeed of human morphology, is subject to change, and how much of such change takes place gradually over the course of a lifetime as opposed to being delayed until the ἔσχατον.[33] Of course, Maximus leaves such questions "ambiguous" and every hypothesis is permitted. But we cannot neglect the fact that Maximus promotes the idea that the division between sexes will eventually vanish.

> Thus God-made-man has done away with the difference and division of nature into male and female, which human nature in no way needed for generation, as some hold, and without which it would perhaps have been possible. There was no necessity for these things to have lasted forever. "For in Christ Jesus," says the divine Apostle, "there is neither male nor female" (Gal 3:28).[34]

And in the same *Difficulty* 41:

> First he united us in himself by removing the difference between male and female, and instead of men and women, in whom above all this manner of division is beheld, he showed us properly and truly to be *simply human beings*, thoroughly transfigured in accordance with him, and bearing his intact and completely unadulterated image, touched by no trace at all of corruption.[35]

Here Maximus comes to the conclusion which was the starting point for Gregory of Nyssa who began his protology with this important

---

30. Ibid., 221.
31. Ibid., 119.
32. Cooper, *Body in St Maximus the Confessor*, 222.
33. Partridge, "Transfiguring Sexual Difference," 211.
34. *AI* 41.7 = PG91, 1309AB (trans. Louth, in *Maximus the Confessor*, 157).
35. *AI* 41.9 = PG91, 1309D–12A (trans. Louth, in *Maximus the Confessor*, 160, my emphasis).

question—how divided the nature can be in the image of God; God in whom there is no division or distinction between male and female.

Therefore, we have to face tremendous ambiguity in Maximus' thought. Many a time and straightforwardly enough, the Confessor underlines that there will exist only simple human beings without sex traces. But with the same determination he proclaims the identity of the human body. What are the reasonable solutions? How should we interpret this state? I cannot agree with the suggestions that it is only a linguistic difference and Maximus claims that only the division will be dismissed but there will still be some kind of a distinction between man and woman. The entire *Difficulty* 41 should have been aborted in order to make this theory convincing. Another, much more reliable theory should also be mentioned. It is based on the fact that not all of the functions of the mode of existence (τρόπος) will disappear in the eschatological future; so, despite the fact that there is no division between the sexes in the λόγοι of beings, this division can still remain in the mode of existence.[36] In other words, if sexual identity is connected with the mode of existence, it may remain even though it was not envisioned in the λόγος of being.

Still, I believe that we cannot ignore all inconsistencies that occur in the Confessor's thought. The attempts to weaken those ambiguities would at the same time weaken two constitutive elements of Maximus' system. One of them is the affirmation of human corporeality and identity that was presented in the polemic with Origenism. The other is the understanding of man as a microcosm and a mediator, where overcoming of all divisions is the necessary step to establish a perfect union with God. The Incarnation and, later, the transfiguration of Christ realized the reconciliation, understood as the return to the original state desired and present in the Λόγος, possible. Maximus stresses that this reconciliation must start with removing the distinction between man and woman. This is not connected with a negation of sexuality as such, but with an abandonment of the function related to the mode of existence which represents life after the fall. What kind of body will this simple human being have? This is a most obscure case. What we know for certain is that the human being will still be corporeal and will rise from the dead in its own transformed body.

We clearly notice that Maximus had a problem with the identity of bodies in eschatological life. If we are supposed to rise from the dead in our own transformed bodies, how can we abandon our gender? Maximus leaves this question unanswered. Like other Christian Neoplatonic philosophers, he had a great problem with maintaining consistency between his

36. I am very grateful to Dionysios Skliris for suggesting this theory to me.

philosophical system and the Christian faith in the resurrection of bodies. The most spectacular sign of the inconsistency between those two orders, the order of biblical faith and the philosophical order, can be seen when St. Paul proclaims Christ's resurrection before the entire council of the Areopagus (Acts 17:19–32).

I am quite convinced that we should respect what Maximus wrote, even though it seems to be (or really is) lacking in cohesion at certain points. It was extremely important for the Confessor to proclaim the resurrection of our own transformed bodies. But it was equally important to present his vision of eschatological future without any divisions, where simple human beings are not only a sign of the renewed and uncorrupted mode of being, but also reveal God's image and a perfect union with him.

Bibliography

Balthasar, Hans Urs von. *Cosmic Liturgy: The Universe According to Maximus the Confessor*. Translated by Brian E. Daley. A Communio Book. San Francisco: Ignatius Press, 2003.

Cooper, Adam G. *The Body in St Maximus the Confessor: Holy Flesh, Wholly Deified*. Oxford Early Christian Studies. Oxford: Oxford University Press, 2005.

Larchet, Jean-Claude. "Ancestral Guilt according to St. Maximus the Confessor: A Bridge between Eastern and Western Conceptions." *Sobornost* 20 (1998) 26–48.

Louth, Andrew. *Maximus the Confessor*. Early Church Fathers. London: Routledge, 1996.

Maximus the Confessor. *Ambigua ad Iohannem*. Edited and translated by Nicholas P. Constas. In *Difficulties*, 1:62–450; 2:2–330. Abbreviated as *AI*.

———. *Ambigua: problemi metafisici e teologici su testi di Gregorio di Nazianzo e Dionigi Areopagita*. Edited and translated by Claudio Moreschini. Il pensiero occidentale. Milano: Bompiani, 2003.

———. *On Difficulties in the Church Fathers: The Ambigua*. Edited and translated by Nicholas P. Constas. 2 vols. Dumbarton Oaks Medieval Library 28–29. Cambridge: Harvard University Press, 2014. Abbreviated as *Difficulties*.

———. *Quaestiones ad Thalassium*. Edited by François Combefis. PG90:244–785B. Abbreviated as *QThal*.

Mitralexis, Sotiris. "Ever-Moving Repose: The Notion of Time in Maximus the Confessor's Philosophy through the Perspective of a Relational Ontology." PhD diss., Freie Universität Berlin, 2014.

Partridge, Cameron Elliot. "Transfiguring Sexual Difference in Maximus the Confessor." ThD thesis, Harvard Divinity School, 2008.

Thunberg, Lars. *Microcosm and Mediator: The Theological Anthropology of Maximus the Confessor*. 2nd ed. Chicago: Open Court, 1995.

PART IV

Maximus in Dialogue: From Antiquity to Contemporary Thought

15

Analogical Ecstasis: Maximus the Confessor, Plotinus, Heidegger, and Lacan

Nicholas Loudovikos

The concept of ἔκστασις forms one of the points around which Western thought constantly gravitates. Western philosophical thought can possibly be referred to as *a thought of/on* ἔκστασις, in the sense that ecstasis constitutes the manifest or hidden core of transcendental meaning or reference, forming the very ontological identity of beings. As Charles Taylor has pertinently shown, this transcendental referentiality has been doubted in modern times, thus inaugurating an *age of secularization*. Nevertheless, as modern psychoanalysis clearly demonstrates and as we will see in the final section of this paper, ecstatic reference and outlet form an essential part of human ψυχή.

Maximus the Confessor's Analogical Ecstasis

In what sense is ecstasis analogical for Maximus? He writes the following:

> Thus the divine, which is altogether unmoved in its essence and nature, being infinite, boundless and limitless, is said to be in motion, like some innate intelligent principle in the essences of things, when by his Providence he moves each thing that exists according to the λόγος whereby it naturally moves. (*AI* 23, 1260B)

This immobility of God's uncreated nature does not conflict with his personal, willed, and loving relationship with created things, which is a relationship not of essence but of an ecstatic λόγος/will/energy. The primary contributor to this subject is the Areopagite, who goes on to call this dynamism on God's part a movement "outside himself," an "ek-static, superessential power." According to the Areopagite, this ἔκ-στασις on the part of God enables him to be called not only "longed for and beloved" but also "intense longing and love":

> To tell the truth, we should be so bold as to say even this: he who is the cause of all, in his beautiful and benevolent longing (ἔρως) for all, is carried outside himself in his providential wills for all creatures through the superabundance of his loving goodness, being, as it were, beguiled by goodness, love, and intense longing. And from his place of being above all things and removed from all, he comes to be in all according to an ἐκ-στατικὴ superessential power inseparable from himself.[1]

Maximus begins by adopting this Areopagitic position in, perhaps, the most substantive text he has given us on the topic:

> As intense longing (ἔρως) and love (ἀγάπη), the Divine is in motion, while as the longed for and beloved he draws to himself everything that is receptive to (his) intense longing and love. To put it more clearly: he is in motion in that he creates a relationship of innate ἔρως and love in those receptive to these (emotions), while he causes motion inasmuch as he attracts by nature the desire of entities that move towards him. And again: he moves others and is in motion in that he thirsts to be thirsted for, and longs intensely to be longed for, and loves to be loved. (*AI* 11, 1206C)

This loving movement of God as an ecstatic offering of himself to creation is one that, as a second step, "draws upwards," seeking a reciprocal relationship of ἔρως and ἀγάπη with "those receptive to these (emotions)." It is a movement of divine desire, which also aspires to move humanity's desire towards the Desired. As Maximus says, adding his own contribution to the Areopagitic text, it constitutes an expression of God's ecstatic love, which becomes real for humanity through the imitation of his desire to be loved and to be the object of thirst. So, according to the Confessor, the Divine moves ecstatically within rational beings and, at the same time, moves beings through their inner principles. It is this initial ecstatic and loving movement/energy of God's that then stimulates, in reciprocity, the loving ek-stasis/syn-ergy of rational beings towards him. He "draws them to himself and moves them to spiritual erotic union, and he produces movement

---

1. Dionysius the Areopagite, *De diuinis nominibus* 4.13, 712AB.

in that he moves every one (of his creations) through its own λόγος to return to him" (*SchD* 265D). λόγος is an analogy of participation for Maximus, offered by God to each of his creatures. Maximus again follows the Areopagite here, but he does so in his own way.[2] In this sense, λόγος is God's analogical, divine way to ecstatically offer himself in different ways and on different levels/ranks/orders to creation, as a constantly different proposal/invitation to participate; as such, it causes the ecstatic elevation of beings according to their own analogy, i.e., capacity for participation. This is what the Areopagite calls *synergy*: "every kind of hierarchical order is elevated toward divine synergy according to its own analogy."[3]

Thus, we see that there is a certain analogical reciprocity of ek-static love between man and God. Divine λόγοι represent God's analogical, energetic, erotic ecstasis towards man. At the same time, the λόγοι/energies enable man's response, causing a rational being to also become analogically/syn-ergetically ek-static in that it responds to God's love of being loved by wholly attaching itself "to God alone in an ἔκ-στασις of intense longing" (*CGn* 1.39, 1097C). In principle, this involves a transformation of man's natural incensive power and desire. Desire is changed by the contemplative intellect into "the unmingled pleasure of divine ἔρως and immaculate beguilement," and the natural incensive power is transformed "into spiritual ardor, fervent perpetual motion, and sober madness" (*QThal* 55, 548CD). This sober madness or ἔκ-στασις is a condition experienced by the whole being; it is by no means an exclusively intellectual construct. It is ἔρως. Here is the most characteristic passage:

> If an intelligent being moves intellectually in the way appropriate to it, then it certainly also has an intellectual perception. If it perceives intellectually, then it certainly experiences intense longing for what it perceives. If it experiences longing, then it certainly undergoes ἔκστασις towards its beloved object. And if it undergoes (this), it is obvious that it presses on eagerly. If it presses on eagerly, it certainly increases the intensity of its motion. And if it increases the intensity of its motion, it does not cease until it is wholly contained in the totality of the object of its love, being entirely embraced by it. (*AI* 9, 1073CD)

This movement of the intellect leads to ἔρως, which in turn causes a complete, existential ἔκ-στασις towards the object of its ardor. The experience of ἔκ-στασις causes the movement to be urgent and unrelenting until

---

2. Dionysius the Areopagite, *De coelesti hierarchia* 3.2, 165A; 12.1-2, 292B-3A; *De diuinis nominibus* 4.5, 700D-701A; 5.8, 824C.

3. Dionysius the Areopagite, *De coelesti hierarchia* 2.3, 168A.

lover and beloved finally embrace. Analogical ἔκ-στασις is the vehicle of reciprocal ἔρως. As Maximus affirms, it is the erotic dynamism of the totality of a rational being, its reciprocal, analogical movement towards God's analogically ecstatic love, an analogical ecstatic syn-ergy or syn-energy, which ultimately leads a being to take on the quality of his beloved. In this way, man shows that he no longer wants to know himself only, but rather wishes to be known by the beloved in whom he is then contained, "circumscribed," as air is contained within light or the iron within the fire. After all, it is God Himself Who first desires to be known, not merely as God but also as the "son of Man." This means that the utmost manifestation of God's reciprocal analogical ἔκστασις is Christ himself, since he represents the ontological consummation of this dialogical/analogical ecstatic syn-energy out of mutual love between God and man.

Thus, the image conforms unto its prototype through this analogical, mutual, dialogical, and synergetic ἔκστασις unto the One who first expressed love for the creature. As ἔκστασις, it has nowhere else to go, nor can it move anywhere else or, rather, it would not even desire to be directed elsewhere since it has already been deified, becoming unique and eternal in Christ. In the end, there is "only one energy (operating) through all things, that of God and those who are worthy of God—or rather, that of God alone, since in accordance with his goodness he has wholly interpenetrated all those who are worthy" (*AI* 7, 1076C). Analogical ἔκστασις, thus, leads to a perfect syn-energy, to God's ecstatic analogical love, which offers participation through Christ in the infinite, divine, delightful, and incomprehensible knowledge of things and of his wonders in exchange for man's ecstatic analogical response (*AI* 7, 1077AB). Hence, this analogically ek-static love both 'draws' and 'unites' those, whether human or divine, who are motivated by it and reach final perfection in it. This mutual attraction and unification, when it is achieved by men in Christ, iconizes the Trinitarian unity of God; it is empirical knowledge of the unity-in-communion of the Holy Trinity (*AI* 10, 1193C–1196C). Analogical ἔκστασις facilitates knowledge-through-participation of the dialogical mode of existence of entities, of their truly ecstatic/dialogical existence in the image of the Trinity.

In the past, I have used four different terms in four different books of mine in order to describe analogical ecstasis. The first is *dialogical reciprocity*,[4] which refers to the analogical ecstasis between man and God, where ecstasis is realized as a non-passive dialogue on the part of man through the divine λόγοι as divine ontological proposals, on the one hand, and human-created λόγοι-responses, on the other; this is a dialogical reciprocity in which the

---

4. Loudovikos, *Eucharistic Ontology*, especially in 211–46.

final *mode of being* of things is discussed between man and God. The second term is the *inter-hypostatic syn-energy*,[5] which describes the way in which analogical ecstasis occurs in general between rational beings, as a mutual, step-by-step hypostatic activation of their natural energies. The third term is *intra-inter-co-being*,[6] which describes analogical ecstasis as an internal event within man, an expression that is formed in dialogue with modern depth psychology. The fourth and final term is the *will to consubstantiality*,[7] which describes the way this spiritual feat can be conceived in anthropological terms. We shall have the opportunity to briefly discuss these terms at the end of this paper.

Plotinus' Non-analogical Ecstasis

In *Ennead* 3.9.3.7–17, we read the following:

> The partial soul [i.e., the individual], then, is illuminated when it goes towards that which is before it—for then it meets reality—but when it goes towards what comes after it, it goes toward non-existence. But it does this, when it goes towards itself, for, wishing to be directed towards itself it makes an image of itself, the non-existent, as if walking on emptiness and becoming more indefinite; and the indefinite image of this is every way dark: for it is altogether without reason and unintelligent and stands far removed from reality. Up to the time between it is in its own world, but when it looks at the image again, as it were directing its attention to it a second time, it forms it and goes to it rejoicing.[8]

According to this passage, the individual soul is somehow seduced by its own image and led toward non-existence, remaining without reason, unintelligent and indefinite. Reality and ontological consistency is indicative of participation for Plotinus, since, as we read in 5.1.1, what makes the soul fade into oblivion is "the will to belong to itself."

Another danger for the soul is its mingling with the body. Again, in Plotinus' words:

> For, as there are two reasons why the soul's fellowship with body is displeasing, that body becomes a hindrance to thought and

---

5. Loudovikos, Ὀρθοδοξία καὶ ἐκσυγχρονισμός.
6. Loudovikos, Ψυχανάλυση καὶ ὀρθόδοξη θεολογία.
7. Loudovikos, Κλειστὴ πνευματικότητα, especially ch. 2:1.
8. Translation by Arthur H. Armstrong, in Plotinus, *Enneads*, 3:411–3.

> that it fills the soul with pleasures, desires, and griefs, neither of these things could happen to a soul which has not sunk into the interior of its body, . . . since the body belongs to it, and is of such a kind as to want nothing and be defective in nothing, such that the soul will not be filled with desires or fears; for it will never have any frightening expectations concerning a body of this type, nor does any involvement make it turn to what is below and take it away from the better, blessed vision.[9]

So the soul must cleanse itself, though not from evil or sin but from body and matter, precisely because they are unable to contemplate the One and, thus, distract the soul (4.8.4). In order to achieve contemplation, the philosopher must transcend his lower self (6.9.11) and, in so doing, this higher self that exists beyond materiality will acquire freedom. However, it is not a freedom of choice but, rather, from any necessity of choice at the level of the Νοῦς (6.8.2), a freedom to attain the true object of love, which is the One (6.9.9). This "contemplation" seems to be more of a union (6.9.11) and, perhaps, something even more.

Plotinian thought leads—and perhaps for the first time with such clarity in the history of human thought—to the differentiation between human beings' real existence in the here and now and their essence, rendering the definition of existence to be an absolute ontological deprivation, an irrevocable loss of being. A person is complete only in the realm of ideas and as pure soul, as spirit and a part of a spiritual universe. In the end, however, this celestial person encountered "another person seeking to come into being and finding us there . . . foisting and adding himself upon the person that each of us was at first."[10] The unfortunate thing is that the added presence typically nullifies the activity of the original spiritual essence, making it, in the expression of Pierre Hadot, "unconscious." The "birth" of a person, then, has to do with the profound angst of his division into a Being of essence and a Being of existence. According to Plotinus, a person's real existence means loss and reduction of Being, particularized by definition. The human soul itself is divided into a more divine soul (6.7.5) and an earthly, "poised above" soul that utilizes the body. The existence of a real being is, therefore, but a trace of life and intellect (6.7.15), indeed, the absence of real life. This 'real life' constitutes recourse to contemplation without any possibility of making up the ontological deficiency in our existence: "the good man is he who lives in contemplation." So, the angst of the loss of Being is transformed

---

9. *Enn.* 4.8.2.43–53. Translation by Arthur H. Armstrong, in Plotinus, *Enneads*, 4:405.

10. *Enn.* 6.4.14.23–26.

into the angst of contemplation. Here, contemplation is also, despite the grandeur of its horizons, the radical exclusion of actual existing being from real life (6.7.31). Contemplation means the denial of the existence, not only of subjectivism but of existing itself.

So the "alterity" of existence, as a constituent part of selfhood, must be done away with since it constitutes by nature an estrangement from God. Submerged in total transcendence, the One remains absolutely undifferentiated, neither knowing nor seeing itself (6.7.39, 6.7.41), and there is no reason, no feeling, no knowledge of itself, inasmuch as it does not even produce its selfhood (6.8.10). We desire it "of necessity" (6.9.9); Plotinic ἔρως, as Hadot perceptively remarks, is "feminine" (unlike the Platonic possessive, restless, impatient ἔρως). It is a profound passivity, a subtraction, a general expectation and readiness for a divine visitation. This passivity is, in any case, the deep characteristic of an inadequate existence which becomes self-aware and realizes the truth: human beings are not self-governed. Indeed, when they gain control over their essence, it is what causes the chasm between them and the One to deepen. Plotinus is extremely moving when he describes, almost deliriously, his philosophical paradise in the last tractate of the final Ennead. The individual, through the loss of his physical existence, is identified with Being and the One, being refracted within divinity ("one both"), finding itself within it; it becomes the One beyond essence, the real Being: "it comes not to something alien but to its very self; thus detached, it is not in nothingness but in itself . . . it becomes something not of essence but beyond essence with which it engages."[11] As such, the ecstatic self-denial of the physical on the part of individuals leads to the non-ecstatic One beyond them. The soul then becomes ecstatically amalgamated into the non-ecstatic One, into an imaginary and super-narcissistic totality (I have referred to this phenomenon in the past as "a Mythontology of Ego" to which I will dedicate few words, with Lacan's help, in the fourth section of this paper).

What is most significant at this point is that this sort of painful and dangerous ecstasis of the subject towards the One is not analogical, since the One does not appear to manifest any reciprocity. In Plotinus' words,

> The One, therefore, since it *has no otherness* that is always present, we are present with it *when we have no otherness*; and the One does not desire us so *as to be around us*, but we desire it so that we are around it. And we are always around it but do not always look to it; it is like a choral dance: in the course of its singing, the choir circles around its conductor, but it may

---

11. *Enn.* 6.9.11.38–43.

> sometimes turn away so that he is out of their sight. But when it turns back to him, it sings beautifully and is truly with him. So we too are always around him though not always turned to him. But if we were not, we would be completely dissolved into non-existence. *When we do look to him, then we have reached our goal and are at rest, not singing out of time* but truly dancing with our god, inspired to dance around him.[12]

This wonderful ecstasis described here is clearly non-analogical. The One "does not desire us," it does not move towards us, it does not want to be "around us." But let me continue with Plotinus:

> And the souls' innate love makes it clear that the Good is there, and this is why Ἔρως is coupled with the Ψυχαὶ in pictures and stories. Since the soul is other in relation to God but comes from him, *it is necessarily in love* with him, and when it is there it has the heavenly love. Here, however, love becomes vulgar.[13]

Inasmuch as the soul originates from God, this monological ecstasis seems to occur as a result of an ontological or existential necessity. Ἔκστασις is now a necessary return to an indifferent and non-ecstatic One, rather than the free, loving choice of analogical response to a divine ecstatic call on the part of the creature.

Heidegger's Parallel Ecstases

In paragraph 65 of his *Sein und Zeit*,[14] Heidegger defines ecstasis as *Dasein's* temporality, articulated as the subject's temporal outgoing within the interplay of being ahead of itself, being already in, and being alongside according to the three dimensions of time. In paragraph 68, Heidegger connects ecstasis with *Dasein's* resolve (*Entschlossenheit*), and thus with its deepest, possible authentic individualization. We read in paragraph 69 that this ecstatic temporality acquires its ultimate meaning in the act of transcendence, forming the very existential core of human being. In his mature work *Zur Seinsfrage*,[15] Heidegger speaks of three possible meanings of transcendence: (a) the relationship between beings and Being, which signals a movement

---

12. *Enn.* 6.9.8.34–45. Translation by Arthur H. Armstrong, in Plotinus, *Enneads*, 7:333–5, my emphasis.

13. *Enn.* 6.9.9.24–9. Translation by Arthur H. Armstrong, in Plotinus, *Enneads*, 7:337, modified.

14. Heidegger, *Sein und Zeit*, 323–31.

15. Heidegger, *Zur Seinsfrage*, GA 9:397–8 [225–26].

ANALOGICAL ECSTASIS   249

of the former towards the latter; (b) the relationship between beings as a movement from change to stability; and (c) the supreme Being itself. Heidegger thinks that the two latter concepts of transcendence cannot go very far, while the first forms the very essence of human philosophical activity.

In order to discuss this major form of ecstatic transcendence in Heideggerian thought, we will briefly examine his famous 1955 lecture *Was ist das—die Philosophie?* in conjunction with some of his lesser known texts, which are possibly helpful to our discussion. Why is this text so important? Because it precisely describes Being's ecstatic transcendence and man's ecstatic activity in order to reach it. In this lecture, the unconsciously Christian Heidegger follows Heraclitus (fragment 50), speaking of philosophy as a friendship of wisdom, as a homologous (*Entsprechen*) agreement with Λόγος, a human λόγος (speech, discourse) in harmony with the secret voice of Being, which calls unto the philosophers (*angesprochen*). Our speech, he argues, must then be homologous with that call: "Wenn uns dieses Entsprechen glückt, dann ant-worten wir im echten Sinne auf die Frage: Was ist das—die Philosophie?"[16] Because language is the "house of Being," this homologous speech exists in the service of language. *Denken* and *Dichten*, poetry and thought, belong together in this potentially harmonious, human response to Being's call. Heidegger laments this fall from the initial Presocratic *harmony* between Being and beings into the *appetite* for this relationship (ὄρεξις, *Streben*) in the thought Plato and Aristotle, inasmuch as *appetite* is connected with discursive thought and the intellectual representation of Being.[17] In his seminar on Heraclitus,[18] our philosopher connects *streben* with the Parmenidean Ἔρως. He focuses on this due to its mention in Plato's *Symposium*, where it is related to the *favor (Gunst)* of the nature of Being for the philosopher, who thus transforms his initial inner *harmony* with Being into a friendship/*streben*/ὄρεξις/ἔρως for the σοφόν. What is ultimately important is that, as he writes in his *Wegmarken*:[19]

> thinking initially was the human resonance (*Widerhall*) of/to Being's favor; this favor is where that which is unique becomes illuminated and allowed to happen: the fact that being *is*. This resonance is the human response (*Antwort*) to the Word of the silent voice of Being (*lautlose Stimme des Seins*). This thoughtful response is the beginning of human Word, which exclusively

---

16. Heidegger, *Was ist das—die Philosophie?*, GA11:9.
17. Heidegger, *Nietzsche*, GA6.1:51-2
18. Heidegger, *Heraklit*, GA55:132-3.
19. Heidegger, *Nachwort zu: "Was ist Metaphysik?"*, GA9:310.

causes the birth of language, as the acoustic diffusion of the Word within words.

But this is not enough. As we read in his *Identität und Differenz*[20] "Being unfolds its essence and lasts only to the point where it concerns (*an-geht*) man through its call to him, because man, being open to Being, initially permits it to come as presence."

Being calls man ecstatically and man responds as an ecstatic antiphon through his thought, *spoken by language,* as our philosopher characteristically asserts. Heidegger, in his *Gelassenheit*, wants this thought to be separated and detached from will, opposing Kant, who, together with a great part of Western philosophy, identified thought with will. Man can thus fulfil his essence as ecstasis toward a response Being's call. However, as Heidegger claims in his work *Nietzsche*,[21] whereas Being needs human ontologico-historical thought in order to be manifested, no one can guarantee that this thought really expresses Being, or *vice versa*. There is no way for man either to make sure that the content of his thought really represents Being in its fullness and truth or for Being to claim that a particular philosopher falsifies or distorts its meaning. Being's transcendence is reduced in the end to a human being's arbitrary thought, who can commit, as we have seen throughout history, indescribable atrocities, while at the same time, perhaps, praising art, poetry and philosophy, believing that he is Being's chosen one.

These are the parallel ecstases. There is no way for anyone to prove that those two ecstatic movements really and completely encounter each other and there is no way for anyone to verify their true *Entsprechung*-ὁμολογία.

Lacan's Unavoidable Ecstasis

For Lacan, ecstasis towards the Other is unavoidable, since it constitutes the very unconscious identity of the subject. Lacan's greatest discovery is that this ecstasis is constituted by an unconscious dialectic of two desires, the subject's desire and the Other's desire. The subject tries to acquire an identity from the Other, identifying his desire with the Other's desire. If this is allowed to happen in a completely unconsciously way, then the self is constituted in a mirror-like automatism of the replication of the Other's desire, which is then rendered a "relational automaton" (I have used this term elsewhere, in my *Orthodoxy and Modernization*.[22]) That is to say, a relational

---

20. Heidegger, *Identität und Differenz*, GA11:39–40.
21. Heidegger, *Nietzsche*, GA6.2:391 2:391.
22. Loudovikos, Ὀρθοδοξία καὶ ἐκσυγχρονισμός.

automaton is a radically heteronomous existence which does not "reassign its free will," as St. Maximus would say, but simply denies it. Moreover, the denial of my assumption of the Other's Desire as my own also manifests my own radical self-interest, since it is only by copying the Desire of the Other that I too can acquire a recognized-by-the-Other self. In other words, it is not really the Other that I love but his Desire for me. The Other in effect is my own fundamental deficiency, as Lacan says. The theological value of these Lacanian theses lies precisely in the discovery of the "transcendent" character of natural Desire, which parallels the "transcendent character" of the natural will in St. Maximus or the natural desire for the transcendent which de Lubac finds in Aquinas.

Of course, for St. Maximus and the Fathers, the immediate "supranatural" referentiality of the natural will/desire is God, while Lacan's secularized thought conceives of this "supranatural" referentiality as a fullness which is always coming but never arriving, realizing that union with the Other is definitively lost and unattainable in reality. What concerns us at the moment, however, is the fact that Lacan discovers the analogue of the theological *natural will*: the inclination towards a fullness that is "transcendent" or, more precisely, koinonetic, which locates an abundance of meaning and life in the definitively lost Other. As Lacan asserts, this is an inclination towards the initial unity of the Symbolic, the Imaginary, and the Real from which all the future differentiations of psychic life begin. The natural will, or natural Desire, tends to find the Other precisely through the superabundance which is implied by communion with him.

From our standpoint, the bare fact of the dialectic of desire does not imply the inevitable loss of the real Other. It can also signify the finding of the real Other precisely as superabundance of life and relation. Here, the primary and most note-worthy difference between Maximus and Lacan lies precisely in the way the Christian Maximus understands the ascetic theory of the transcendence of self-love, through which we may in the end encounter the real Other *in an intra-inter-co-being*. Following the ascetic way, we avoid becoming a remote Other for the Other, and the natural fullness of relationship is consolidated as a progressive *inter-hypostatic syn-energy*. Lacan, however, does not recognize this path, and natural fullness remains the mere imagining of a definitively lost pan-relation. It is this lack of natural fullness which matures the subject through the deep sense of the continuous *absence of the Other*. This is the so-called *symbolic castration*, through which the subject accepts this absence and, at the same time, manages to keep his ecstatic desire alive, acquiring the only possible relational maturity psychoanalysis can provide.

But Lacan's realistic contribution is valuable precisely because of this concept. Through the need for *symbolic castration,* he saves us from any *mythontological*—and, in psychoanalytic language, neurotic, or even, at times psychotic—or existential amalgamation of the self into the *Thing* (the Other or the One). He recognizes, through the Symbolic Law, both the existence and the definite distance of the Thing/Other/One from the subject. There is an inner distance of the self from the Other that makes him or her—the mother represents the Other in early childhood—extremely close but, at the same time, "strange" and "unfamiliar," constituting the unapproachable and unconscious core of the lost archaic pleasure. Thus, the Other is always absent, though his empty place is always there. A false absolute Other—such as a pagan deity, or the God of fundamentalism, or the various ideological idols—is narcissistically self-referring and prevents the subject from finding his identity through regaining meaning again and again, through the experience of his finitude and the absence of meaning in the world. According to Lacan, this signals the need for an immediate separation of the subject from the illusory, holistic, imaginary, mystical, and mythical/pantheistic merging into the absolute Other in order to find the way to the real Other, coupled with all the limitations that such a relationship entails. According to psychoanalysis, the only way for this to occur is though *transubstantiation,* an act through which the subject elevates the object of his love to the worthiness of the Thing/Other. The alternative is the repulsion or negation of the real Other for the sake of a narcissistic merging with the false Otherness of the One, ignoring any subjective deficiency or finitude, which, precisely for this reason, makes it neurotic.

This sort of ecstasis is unavoidable. The Other continually hides himself behind the Symbolic Law and is encountered only through symbolic castration. He is always there, even in his absence, and when he is finally encountered in actuality, he is always frustratingly inferior in relation to one's expectation. The Other is unavoidable, but nonetheless either non-reachable or insufficient, requiring the process of transubstantiation. In the end, psychosis is killed by frustration, or, better, castration.

Epilogue: The Quarrel of Ecstases

For St. Maximus, the fact that God created the world primarily means that *he wants the world, which means that he initially opens and offers himself to the world out of an incomprehensible ecstatic love, giving an independent identity to his created image.* In turn, he analogically agrees to receive an identity from his rational creature through man's analogical ecstasis, becoming *prime mover, mother, father, brother, love, life, providence,* etc. To use a term from modern neuropsychology, he becomes all the *primary metaphors,* expressions that describe the possible ways in which man may existentially and psychosomatically assimilate the Absolute, i.e., in terms analogous with his created existence.

According to Maximus' perspective, *subjectivity* means both to receive and to give an identity, achieving a perfect balance between autonomy and heteronomy (αὐτονομία and ἑτερονομία). This is a balance that exists prototypically in the Trinity through *consubstantiality (ὁμοούσιον),* i.e., the absolute and timeless inter-givenness of essence, which makes the divine tri-personal communion an event of perfect reciprocity.[23] *Dialogical reciprocity* of being given and giving identity can also be described as an *inter-hypostatic syn-energy* between subjects, where the mutual analogical ecstasis makes this reciprocal attribution of identity not only possible but also verifiable. The place of this dialogical identity is again human interiority. Nevertheless, this *intra-inter-co-being* does not arise as a phenomenological inter-subjectivity confined within the horizons of a solipsistic *transcendental ego.* Rather, it occurs as a continuously verifiable, diachronic, and ecstatic syn-ergy/syn-energy, which aims to achieve consubstantiality in creation and is existentially revealed as a *will-to-consubstantiality* in the likeness of Christ.

The will-to-consubstantiality is the polar opposite of the will-to-power. It is the will to overcome the horrors of all forms of solipsistic transcendental subjectivism through a progressive, syn-ergetic, and analogical opening to the real other. Psychonalysis, and especially the type we find in authors like Lacan or Heinz Kohut, has demonstrated in, perhaps, an incontestable manner the extent to which all forms of the phenomenological reduction of otherness to selfhood tend toward narcissism. Phenomenology presents itself as a medicine, but it may very well constitute an aspect of the disease if it does not take the psychoanalytic warning seriously. If phenomenology takes the psychoanalytic concern into account, it will soon discover that even this will not be sufficient to rectify its difficulties. The Maximian proposal, however, lies beyond the Plotinian monological/mythontological subject, and beyond the Heideggerian double ecstatic solipsism, both of which, according to Lacan, potentially lead to neurosis, despite the philosophers' significant attempt to provide subjectivity with a deep metaphysical foundation. Subjectivity, as it is expressed by the Confessor, would seem to be the diachronic and syn-ergetic result of a two-fold analogical ecstasis of both receiving and giving identity, linked indissolubly with a will to achieve consubstantiality as a constantly (or, if you like, anti-neurotically) and externally-verified inner co-being of all beings in the subject.

23. Loudovikos, "Possession or Wholeness?," 269–71.

Bibliography

Dionysius the Areopagite. *De coelesti hierarchia*. PG3:119A–340B.

———. *De diuinis nominibus*. PG3:585A–984A.

Heidegger, Martin. *Gesamtausgabe*. 97 vols. Frankfurt am Main: V. Klostermann, 1975–2015. Abbreviated as GA.

———. *Heraklit*. 3rd ed. GA55. Frankfurt am Main: V. Klostermann, 1994.

———. *Identität und Differenz*. In *Identität und Differenz*, 27–110. 2nd ed. GA11. Frankfurt am Main: V. Klostermann, 2006.

———. *Nachwort zu: "Was ist Metaphysik?"*. In *Wegmarken*, 303–12. GA9. Frankfurt am Main: V. Klostermann, 1976.

———. *Nietzsche*. GA6.1–2. Frankfurt am Main: V. Klostermann, 1996–97.

———. *Sein und Zeit*. 11th ed. Tübingen: Max Niemeyer, 1967. Reprinted in unchaged form since 1967 in sequentially numbered editions.

———. *Was ist das—die Philosophie?* In *Identität und Differenz*, 3–26. 2nd ed. GA11. Frankfurt am Main: V. Klostermann, 2006.

———. *Zur Seinsfrage*. In *Wegmarken*, 385–426. GA9. Frankfurt am Main: V. Klostermann, 1976.

Loudovikos, Nicholas. "Possession or Wholeness? St. Maximus the Confessor and John Zizioulas on Person, Nature, and Will." *Participatio: Journal of the Thomas F. Torrance Theological Fellowship* 4 (2013) 258–86.

———. Ὀρθοδοξία καὶ ἐκσυγχρονισμός. Βυζαντινὴ ἐξατομίκευση, κράτος καὶ ἱστορία, στὴν προοπτικὴ τοῦ εὐρωπαϊκοῦ μέλλοντος [Orthodoxy and Modernization: Byzantine Individualization, State and History, in the Perspective of the European Future]. Athens: Armos, 2006.

Loudovikos, Nikolaos. *A Eucharistic Ontology: Maximus the Confessor's Eschatological Ontology of Being as Dialogical Reciprocity*. Translated by Elizabeth Theokritoff. Brookline, MA: Holy Cross Orthodox Press, 2010.

———. Ἡ κλειστὴ πνευματικότητα καὶ τὸ νόημα τοῦ ἑαυτοῦ. Ὁ μυστικισμὸς τῆς ἰσχύος καὶ ἡ ἀλήθεια φύσεως καὶ προσώπου [Closed Spirituality and the Meaning of the Self: Christian Mysticism of Power and the Truth of Personhood and Nature]. Athens: Ellinika Grammata, 1999.

———. Ψυχανάλυση καὶ ὀρθόδοξη θεολογία. Περὶ ἐπιθυμίας, καθολικότητας καὶ ἐσχατολογίας [Psychoanalysis and Orthodox Theology: On Desire, Catholicity, and Eschatology]. Athens: Armos, 2006.

Maximus the Confessor. *Ambigua ad Iohannem*. Edited by Franz Oehler. PG91:1061–417C. Abbreviated as *AI*.

———. *Capita theologica et oeconomica* [Gnostic Chapters]. Edited by François Combefis. PG90:1084A–173A. Abbreviated as *CGn*.

———. *Quaestiones ad Thalassium*. Edited by François Combefis. PG90:244–785B. Abbreviated as *QThal*.

———. *Scholia in corpus Areopagiticum* [Scholia in Pseudo-Dionysius]. PG4:16A–184C. Abbreviated as *SchD*.

Plotinus. *Enneads*. Translated by Arthur H. Armstrong. 7 vols. Loeb Classical Library 440–45. Cambridge: Harvard University Press, 1966–88.

16

Man as Co-creator: Reflections on the Theological Insights of St. Maximus the Confessor within a Contemporary Interdisciplinary Context

Stoyan Tanev

Introduction

In a discussion of St. Maximus' understanding of the λόγοι as "predeterminations and divine acts of will," David Bradshaw points out that such understanding could explain St. Maximus' claim that God knows creatures "as his own acts of will."[1] He also points out that according to St. Maximus rational creatures are deified insofar as they move and act in accordance with their λόγοι and it is actually the free choice of human beings that makes them move either toward the state of full being, which is the Creator's intent, or towards non-being. In his reflections, Bradshaw refers to Bishop Alexander Golitzin's work on Dionysius the Areopagite where the human movement in accordance with the λόγοι is considered as a way for human beings to become their own *co-creators*:

> The λόγοι are therefore our personal and foreordained vocations to which we may or may not choose to become conformed, or better—since they remain transcendent by virtue of their source in God—to which we may choose to be ever in process of becoming conformed in order thus to share, as it were, in the eternal process of our own creation."[2]

1. Bradshaw, *Aristotle East and West*, 206.
2. Golitzin, *Et introibo ad altare Dei*, 86.

Bradshaw also refers to Jean-Claude Larchet who provides a similar reading of a long passage from the *AI* 7.16 (= PG91, 1080B).[3] It should be pointed out that St. Maximus offers multiple occasions for such interpretations. One of the most articulated examples is in his *Ascetic Life* (*LA* 979–81 = *MAS* 42.12–15) where St. Maximus emphasizes that "the Lord bestowed on us the method of salvation and has given us eternal power to become sons of God. So finally then our salvation is in our will's grasp."[4]

The reason I referred to the work of David Bradshaw is the fact that it was the first occasion for me to face the use of the term "co-creation" within a specific philosophical theological context. I happen to have a particular interest in studying co-creative phenomena since I have spent almost ten years exploring similar concepts in the fields of technology innovation management, design and marketing. In these fields value co-creation has emerged as part of a paradigm shift in the way we look at people as consumers and customers.[5] The old paradigm assigned designers, inventors and firms with the privileged role of being "the creators" of value for the rest of us, the customers, who were considered to be mere consumers. The new paradigm repositions the creation of value on the interface between the designers/inventors/firms and the customer, transforming customers into co-creators of value. Once the customer acquires the role of a co-creator, his or her contribution to the value creation process becomes personal. The most radical aspect of the new paradigm is the way it changed the dominant twentieth-century understanding of marketing where people were considered statistically, i.e., as personally indistinguishable individuals who were compartmentalized in target market segments that were to be addressed by the same product or service. The repositioning of customers as co-creators of value has also enabled the rediscovery of personhood in the social sciences.[6] This is because the technological advancements in information and communication technologies have made it possible for customers to actively participate in the definition and the *personalization* of the generic market offers that are equally available to everyone. What the technological advancements actually did was to enable the development of customer participation platforms allowing the personal contributions of individual customers. However, the growing relevance of customer *participation* in value creation was not just a technologically enabled phenomenon. It was also a reflection of an emerging trend in design studies and innovation studies fo-

---

3. Larchet, *La divinisation de l'homme*, 119–20.
4. Maximus the Confessor, *Ascetic Life*, 133, trans. Sherwood.
5. Tanev et al., "Value Co-creation Activities."
6. Smith, *What is a Person?*

cusing on the participatory role of users as contributors to the design of new products and services.[7] This trend has helped the emergence of the concepts of participatory design, participatory innovation and user innovation. It has also enabled the emergence of the unfortunate term "crowdsourcing"—a combination of the words "crowd" and "outsourcing" which was coined ten years ago by referring to a specific process used by firms to obtain innovative ideas by soliciting contributions from online user communities, rather than from traditional employees or partners. As some scholars in the business and social sciences have already realized "it is worth being careful with words because the structure of the language chosen determines the penetrative power of the resulting analysis."[8]

The emerging relevance of the various aspects of *personalization* and *participation* in our everyday lives and, respectively, in the social sciences, offers the opportunity of exploring the interdisciplinary potential of the terminological cross-examination of the co-creation concepts in philosophical theology and in the social sciences in general. It is a fact that the social sciences are in need of a refinement of the co-creation terminology since the scholarly excitement in researching co-creative phenomena has resulted in a kind of semantic pollution which is not really contributing to the relevance of the ongoing research studies.[9] The underlying motivation for such cross-examination lays in the fact that Byzantine philosophical theology in general and, more specifically, the theological anthropology of St. Maximus the Confessors offer a unique and comprehensive conceptual apparatus that could be highly valuable for the social sciences. The choice of a specific conceptual apparatus is quite important since the logic to which we rely on in a particular empirical context is directly related the conceptual apparatus that was adopted—"by changing the conceptual apparatus, we change the logic into another one."[10] This present text offers a first attempt for a terminological cross-examination with a focus on the reception of the co-creative aspects of the theological anthropology of St. Maximus the Confessor. It will continue by summarizing the contributions of several modern Orthodox theologians and philosophers who have focused on the articulation of the co-creative role of human beings in shaping their own eschatological future and conclude by discussing its potential link to Actor-Network Theory—

7. Schuler and Namioka, *Participatory Design*.
8. Spender, *Business Strategy*, 2.
9. Tanev et al., "Value Co-creation Activities."
10. The notion of conceptual apparatus was introduced by Kazimierz Ajdukiewicz. According to him, the picture of the world one has developed is not coming directly from the data of experience but depends on the specific conceptual apparatus chosen. See Ajdukiewicz, "World-Picture and the Conceptual Apparatus (1934)," 81.

a theoretical perspective which emerged in the early 1980s at the *Centre de Sociologie de l'Innovation of the École Nationale Supérieure des Mines de Paris* and which is usually associated with the names of Bruno Latour, John Law and Michael Callon.[11]

Co-creation and the Legacy of St. Maximus in the Twentieth and Twenty-First Centuries

This co-creative role of human beings as active agents in the process of their own continuous creation, salvation and deification has been emphasized by some of the key Orthodox thinkers in the twentieth and twenty-first centuries with a direct reference to the theology of St. Maximus the Confessor. For example, according to Fr. George Florovsky,

> The whole history of Divine Providence is for St. Maximus divided into two great periods: the first culminates in the Incarnation of the Λόγος and is the story of Divine condescension ("through the Incarnation"); the second is the story of human ascension into the glory of deification, an extension, as it were, of the Incarnation to the whole creation.[12]

Following a similar line of thought Fr. George points out that

> creation is not a phenomenon but a "substance." The reality and substantiality of created nature is manifested first of all in creaturely freedom. Freedom is not exhausted by the possibility of choice, but presupposes it and starts with it. And creaturely freedom is disclosed first of all in the equal possibility of two ways: to God and away from God. This duality of ways is not a mere formal or logical possibility, but a real possibility, dependent on the effectual presence of powers and capacities not only for a choice between, but also for the following of, the two ways. Freedom consists not only in the possibility, but also in the necessity of autonomous choice, the resolution and resoluteness of choice. Without this autonomy, nothing happens in creation. As St. Gregory the Theologian says, "God legislates human self-determination." "He honored man with freedom that good might belong no less to him who chose it than to him Who planted its seed." Creation must ascend to and unite with God by its own efforts and achievements.[13]

11. Latour, *Reassembling the Social*.
12. Florovsky, "Cur Deus Homo?," 70–79.
13. Florovsky, "Creation and Creaturehood," 48–49.

Another Orthodox theologian who referred to the theology of St. Maximus in order to emphasize the co-creativity of human beings in the pursuit of union with God is St. Justin Popović. According to Vladimir Cvetković,

> St. Justin relies on St. Maximus' claim that faith precedes all other virtues (*QThal* 51, 488B). . . . Taken in the context of our salvation, faith, according to St. Justin, is not only belief in the Divine salvific work, but also belief in our capacity to contribute to our salvation by acquiring the virtues. Thus, by becoming gods, human beings fulfill the purpose of their creation. Since they continue to perfect themselves throughout all eternity by love of God and other virtues, faith as the crown and the perfection of all these virtues does not stop to exist. Faith is transformed then from the belief in our salvation to the belief in the progress "from glory to glory" in the eternal union with God.[14]

The theological insights of St. Maximus have obviously helped St. Justin Popović in articulating one of the most christologically theanthropic vision of the relationship between man and God in the twentieth century. In his own words,

> In the center of the worlds stands Christ the Theanthropos. He is the axis around which all worlds, both high and low, revolve. He is the mysterious center towards which all souls that hunger for eternal truth and life gravitate. He is both the project and the source of all the creative forces of Orthodox theanthropic culture. Here God works and man collaborates; God creates through man and man creates trough God; here the divine creation is continued through man. To this end, man brings out of himself all that is divine and puts it into action, creation arid life. In this creativity, all that is divine, not only in man but also in the world around him, is expressed and brought into action; all that is divine is active, and all that is human joins in this activity. But, in order to collaborate successfully with God, man must accustom himself to thinking, feeling, living, and creating by God. . . . Man serves God through himself and all creation around him. He systematically, deliberately, brings God and the divine into all his work, all his creativity. He awakens all that is divine in nature around him, so that nature, led by man with his yearning for Christ, can serve God. In this way, all creation

---

14. Cvetković, "St Justin Popović's Reception."

participates in the universal, divine service, for nature serves man, who serves God.[15]

Fr. Nicholas Loudovikos is the Orthodox theologian who has most explicitly emphasized the dialogical natural of the relationship between man and God. His emphasis is based on an insightful reading of the Maximian teaching on the Divine λόγοι. According to Fr. Nicholas the term "λόγοι of beings" is not translatable into English.

> Λόγος means "constitutive principle.," "inner principle," "essential principle," "rationale," "reason," or simply "word" . . . The uncreated λόγοι are acts (ἐνέργειαι) of the divine loving will in constant dialogue with creation: λόγος means always διά-λογος (dialogue) in the Greek patristic tradition and particularly in St. Maximus the Confessor's thought. λόγος is uncreated but distinct from uncreated divine being. It is personal (ἐνυπόστατος) not in the sense that it is a being itself, but in the sense that it is the volitive expression of a personal being who moves his essence to act ad extra. . . . By the λόγοι . . . God creates, that is proposes to beings their own essences and an ontological dialogue follows. If essence is thus given, its "mode of existence" is only the result of this dialogue between the λόγος word of God and the λόγος-word of man. That means that the final *esse* of created beings is unknown, indeterminate, because it is the eschatological result of a long dialogue between God and man, a dialogue which culminates in the cross and the resurrection of Christ. Christ, the Divine Λόγος-Son of the Father, is himself in his incarnate composite hypostasis the ontological presupposition of this ontological dialogue. . . . So our participation in the divine energies is simply the way of our participation in the crucified and resurrected Christ.[16]

In another text Fr. Nicholas elaborates further on his dialogical theological perspective by emphasizing the generically relational and dialogical character of the Divine energies: he points out that for St. Gregory Palamas deification "is neither a sort of natural 'imitation,' nor an 'amelioration of human nature' but the assimilation of God himself through the Divine energies, which descend from the Father and become participable in Christ, through the Spirit."[17] According to Fr. Nicholas "(t)he most important thing concerning the Palamite concept of deification, as a participational ascent

---

15. Popović, *Man and the God-Man*, 49–50.
16. Loudovikos, "Ontology Celebrated," 147–48.
17. Ibid., 130.

to God through the Divine energies manifested in Christ by the Spirit, is its *relational* and finally *ecclesial* character. The energies themselves are 'relational and participational,'" which for Fr. Nicholas means that they are dialogical or analogical. And the fundamental reason for this dialogical/ analogical aspect of the Divine energies is twofold. *First*, this is the connection, on one hand, between the Divine energies and Divine will and, on the other hand, between the energies and the Dionysian or Maximian Divine processions/participations/λόγοι of beings.

> For Dionysius, as well as for Maximus, the divine processions/ participations/λόγοι, as expressions of the divine loving will, are deeply connected with the concept of analogy (while Maximus develops this concept changing it into a mimetical icon). This is a term that signifies a deep dialogue of *synergy*, or, better, *syn-energy*, since analogy for the above authors refers not to a similitude of essences but to an analogous action between two different agents in order for them to achieve union. Thus, divine energy as a participable expression of divine will, is *dialogical*, in the sense that it calls for an energetic/active response on the part of its recipients.[18]

The second dimension of the dialogical/analogical aspect of the Divine energies can be found in the ecclesial core of the Palamite understanding of participation. In the words of Fr. Nicholas,

> [i]f energy exists only as an analogical syn-energy, this synenergy does not have to do only with the vertical relation with God, but also with the horizontal relation between creatures. . . . Any real elevation to God has to happen by the grace/energy of the Holy Spirit, in Christ, and that means that man has to bring with him "every kind of creature, as he himself participates in everything and is also able to participate in the one who lies above everything, in order for the icon (image) of God to be completed." . . . In ecclesiological terms, that means that it is only in the process of the realization of the ecclesial dialogical/ analogical synergetic communion, that elevation to God can be achieved.[19]

And as Fr. Nicholas pointed out, the highest manifestation of the double participational analogy of such dialogical syn-energy can be found in the Eucharist.

18. Ibid., 131.
19. Ibid., 132.

One can see how using this dialogical participational theological perspective helps in emphasizing a very interesting aspect of the Maximian understanding of the Divine λόγοι of creation—the fact that they could explain not only the relationship between the One (Who is uncreated) and the many (who are created) but also the salvific relevance of the relationship between every one (who is created) to the rest of the many (who are created). Fr. Nicholas points out that the Divine λόγοι can be seen as the ontological expression of the entire organization of reality, a term used by Fr. Dumitru Stăniloae,[20] inasmuch as, in the words of St. Maximus, "in their substance and formation all created things are positively defined by their own λόγοι, and by the λόγοι that exist around them and which constitute their defining limits."[21]

The co-creativity of human beings therefore should be considered within the context of the multiplicity of their own λόγοι and the λόγοι that exist around them as co-constitutive principles of their existential field of action. The λόγοι of all co-existing things

> provide the basis . . . for the communication between entities, because their λόγοι interpenetrate each other and are determined by each other. The λόγος of each entity is "threefold," because "if entities have essence and potentiality and energy, it is clear that in this respect they have a threefold λόγος of being." Furthermore, we have λόγοι of races, species, and individuals, λόγοι of time and nature, without which things could not exist, and also λόγοι of bodies and of bodiless beings. We also find a special λόγος of hypostasis (substantive existence), because "nature possesses the common λόγος of being, while the hypostasis possesses the λόγος whereby something exists in itself."[22]

The multiplicity of the λόγοι is quite important in explaining the contingency of the relationship between man and God, neither in terms of some kind of agential arbitrariness or unpredictability of both, Divine activity and human existence, nor in terms of some kind of fatalistic Divine or impersonal and naturalistic form of predestination that would somewhat secretly shape the ultimate end of human destiny. It is rather in terms of the interplay between the relevance of individual human activities and the specificity, and the interdependence of the Divine providential activities

---

20. Fr. Nicholas Loudovikos refers to Stăniloae, "Introduction," 22. See Stăniloae, "The World as Gift and Word."

21. *AI* 7.19, trans. Constas, in *Difficulties*, 101.

22. Loudovikos, *Eucharistic Ontology*, 72–73.

within the creaturely context of the agency of the surrounding human and physical natural environments.

This multifold and composite format of the interactive human and worldly environments providing the context of the relationship between God and man has been also discussed by Prof. Georgi Kapriev in his recent book on St. Maximus which, unfortunately, is available only in Bulgarian. Kapriev also refers to *AI* 7.19 (= PG91, 1081B) to point out that for St. Maximus all created things are positively and entirely defined by their own λόγοι, and by the λόγοι that exist around them and which constitute their defining limits. He however emphasizes in a most explicit way that "[t]here is no one single λόγος to which each individual thing would uniquely correspond but a multiplicity of λόγοι which synthesize in a coherent way the proper λόγος of each concretely existing thing. And, in a completely symmetrical way, the λόγοι should be seen in their particularizing function due to which each particular being becomes different and independent of all other beings."[23] Kapriev points out that "from this perspective the being of the created world becomes 'intelligible' exactly because of the togetherness of its λόγοι which come from God and converge together, enter into coherence and interlink each other in a variety of ways. All differences in terms of quality depend on the different types of configurations emerging in between the λόγοι."[24]

According to Kapriev,

> [w]hen Maximus mentions a certain individual created λόγος, he always sees it in the horizon of the manifestation of another, higher or more general, λόγος, ultimately relating both of them to the highest One Λόγος. . . . The Λόγος actualizes the differentiation of the economic and creative Divine energies in a way that each individual being acquires in a concrete and specific way its individually assigned energies. . . . This is how God simultaneously sees and knows both the individual things and the entirety of the created order. When considered in itself the Λόγος is a purely dynamical reality which translates activity, i.e. energy. The dynamism of the reality consists in its in permanent correspondence with the entire energetic structure of the Divine economy.[25]

In this sense, every individual created thing should be seen as part of the logical network emerging out of the interactions of its multiple λόγοι. One should admit however that, "since it is created out of nothing, every

---

23. Kapriev, *Maksim Izpovednik*, 145.
24. Ibid., 147.
25. Ibid., 150.

single thing can deviate in a greater or lesser extent from its proper logic or 'λόγος-ness' and such deviations should be considered as an expression of its existential autonomy."[26] We should conceptualize therefore the dialogical and analogical aspects of the λόγοι in a multidimensional way, extending the uni-directional understanding of the relationship between God and man by including the interplay between the "logical" variety and consistency of the world as a gift enabling the communion between the created and uncreated order.

By referring to the understanding on the world as a gift we can now focus on discussing the theological insights of Fr. Dumitru Stăniloae who has beautifully discussed the dialogical nature of the relationship between God and man within the context of the specificity and the multiplicity of the Divine reasons/λόγοι of all created things.[27] According to him,

> The world as nature proves itself a rational unitary reality that exists for the sake of the dialogue among human beings and as a condition for the spiritual growth of humans and for the development of humankind. According to the fathers, all things have their inner principles/reasons in the divine Λόγος or the supreme Reason. ... The rationality of the world has, however, multiple values. It is malleable and contingent, and the human person is the one who makes use of these characteristics and brings them to light. ... In the human person alone does the rationality of nature's undefined possibilities acquire meaning or a purpose, or draw even closer to its fulfillment. ... By discovering and harnessing the manifold rationality of the world—freely and in cooperation with his neighbors—in order to make better use of the world's resources and to grasp its inexhaustible meanings, the human person grows in communion with these. Moreover, this process itself becomes a source that leads to the knowledge of other and still more sublime meanings.[28]

Later on, he remarks,

> Through created things God has given humans two gifts: *first*, the possibility to think and speak, for this arises from the very fact that God conceived the inner principles of things and posited them in existence, having created for them beforehand a material covering adapted to the level of humanity; and *second*,

---

26. Ibid., 151.

27. In the following section I will refer specifically to Stăniloae, "The World as Gift and Word."

28. Ibid., 27–28.

> the need to conceive and express these inner principles so as to be able to make use of them in reciprocal human relationships and in this way bring about that dialogue between themselves and God, which God himself willed to have with them, so that human beings might respond to God through their own thinking and speaking. It is precisely in this that all things find their meaning. The human person discovers ever new alternative dimensions of creative things not only through his own reason and new combinations and uses of the things themselves, but also trough the feelings and continual new thoughts his body produces in its contact with things and through the ever changing relationships between himself and his neighbors, which use created things as their medium. And this must be expressed and communicated by means of a language that is continually being enriched.[29]

This enrichment of the human language in dealing with the meaning of created reality is a creative process in itself. Interestingly, one can find similar insights in Wittgenstein's later theory of language and meaning which was articulated in some of his unpublished manuscripts. According to Hans Schneider's interpretation of the late Wittgenstein, the peculiarity of this creative process

> is not that an independent and diversely-formed preexisting reality is projected onto the plan of language, in the course of which some differentiation is inevitably lost, so that the same few forms of speech always appear, regardless of the "content." Rather an existent form of expression is used in a new context of application . . . and is this "projected" onto new kinds of objects. The starting point of projection in *this* sense is not a pre-structured reality, waiting to be articulated in language. . . . Rather, the starting point of a projection is a pre-existing grammatical form, at first necessarily specific to a *particular* area of discourse, which is then carried into *new* areas of discourse in a free, spontaneous act of creative imagination. This act was unforeseen in the in the previously available ways of speaking (i.e., available rules) of the language, but its freedom is limited, of course, by internal or external constraints of the situation and by the need to be understood.[30]

One can use the above interpretation to describe how human beings configure uniquely for themselves the world by using all of their existing linguistic

29. Ibid., 35.
30. Schneider, *Wittgenstein's Later Theory of Meaning*, 83–84.

potential to creatively discover and appropriate the meanings and the interdependencies of the λόγοι of created beings always in their ultimate relation to the Divine Λόγος. In this sense human creativity with respect to the world is always dialogical, configurational and co-creational. According to Stăniloae, in the human process of creative reconfiguration or co-creation there is always a meaning which is clearly intuited in association with every individual reality and at the same time remains unknown and undefined in the strict sense.

> The mind, or the reason as understanding, sees this higher meaning and every kind of connection between the different realities and units, and in its grasp of each unit the mind takes into account the other units as well. This shed light simultaneously upon the more complete reason of each thing. Hence there exists a general λόγος of the λόγοι of all individual realities, but one that transcends the λόγος of all λόγοι. The more general reason is the meaning or the wealth of meanings of one thing joined to the reasons and meanings of all its components and to all other things as well.... Their unique supreme meaning is the Divine Λόγος, for within this Λόγος are found the meanings of all things.... The one who believes is particularly the one who grasps this supreme meaning through a general act of intuition, that is, through his spirit.[31]

An Interdisciplinary Interlude

The conceptualization of Divine-human communion as part of a co-creative configurational process could be related to an existing theoretical movement in the social sciences and humanities which is known as Actor-Network Theory (ANT).[32] Although it is a completely secular theory, it has been already considered by Georgi Kapriev and Ivan Tchalakov as part of an interdisciplinary project focusing on using Byzantine philosophical and theological insights within the context of the contemporary sociology of action.[33] The reason to mention it here is the opportunity to discuss the interdisciplinary potential of the theological contributions of St. Maximus. It is also an opportunity to explore the analogical potential of ANT's conceptual apparatus for philosophical theology which can be found in the simi-

---

31. Stăniloae, "World as Gift and Word," 30–31.
32. Latour, *Reassembling the Social*.
33. Kapriev et al., *Le sujet de l'acteur*; Kapriev and Ivan, "Actor-Network Theory"; Tchalakov and Georgi, "The Limits of Causal Action."

larity of its linguistic format and struggles to provide a better articulation of the multiplicity of the sources of agency and the contingency of human innovative activity in the world. John Law has recently referred to ANT as a set of "tools, sensibilities and methods of analysis that treat everything in the social and natural worlds as a continuously generated effect of the webs of relations within which they are located. It assumes that nothing has reality or form outside the enactment of those relations."[34] ANT analyzes how all things—natural, conceptual, textual, social or technical, could be considered as equally or symmetrically present and equally relevant in the web of relations defining the reality around us. It "advances a *relational materiality*, the material extension of semiotics, which presupposes that all entities achieve significance in relation to others."[35] The *symmetry principle* between human and non-human entities which is promoted by ANT scholars should be interpreted as a reaction against any *a priori* assumptions about the sources and the nature of agency within a particular human context. The adoption of this principle shifts the focus away from the identity and the nature of all potential actors to the interactions, the associations, and the relationships between them. In a way, ANT dissolves the notion of social force and replaces it either by short-lived interactions or by new associations. In this way it makes it possible to distinguish between what pertains to its durability and what pertains to its substance.[36] The distinction between durability and substance allows to virtually "un-substantiate" all entities and subjects in order to focus on those aspects of agency that could lead to the emergence of durable relationships—a shift that was enabled by the introduction of the concept of "actant." An actant "is any agent, collective or individual, that can associate or disassociate with other agents. Actants enter into networked associations, which in turn define them, name them, and provide them with substance, action, intention, and subjectivity. In other words, actants are considered foundationally indeterminate, with no a priori substance or essence, and it is via the networks in which they associate that actants derive their nature.[37] On the other hand, action is not understood as springing out only from the singular intentionality, will or desire of an already-constituted subject, but rather as the effect of the hybrid association of entities of various ontologies. In ANT's version of action, humans and non-humans coalesce to achieve a kind of delocalized and distributed synergetic interaction that cannot be merely reduced to the

34. Law, "Actor Network Theory and Material Semiotics," 141.
35. Crawford, "Actor Network Theory," 1–4.
36. Latour, *Reassembling the Social*, 66.
37. Crawford, "Actor Network Theory," 1.

intention or activity of either party. ANT follows "the actors themselves" in deciding what the nature, relevance and impact of agency or activity is. The most interesting question is "not to decide who is acting and how but to shift from a certainty about action to an uncertainty about action" by asking "Which agencies are invoked? Which figurations are they endowed with? Through which mode of action are they engaged?"[38]

The main point here is that ANT offers a unique approach to conceptualizing creativity as a dialogical process which is based on the notion of configuration.[39] This approach positions creativity not only in the minds and practices of individual people but also in the effectuation of all surrounding personal human and non-human activity including the struggles and the efforts through which particular relationships emerge and through which a particular human being is constituted as such. The association of these struggles and creative efforts with the emergence of new courses of action is just one of the interesting aspects here. What is even more interesting is how the human struggles and efforts lead to the invention of new contextual configurations including new actors and new relationships. Such an understanding of creativity reminds of the definition of creation suggested by Gilles Deleuze—the act of making configurations.[40] From this perspective, studying human creativity can be only understood as the study of the way new relations or connections are established between different elements in order to make new things and situations happen. Thus, to be a creative human being is not an optional activity but a kind of necessity because the configurations that a human being builds entangle and constitute him or her as a subject.[41]

Conclusion

The brief interlude suggested here provides a hint about the opportunity for both, a theological upgrade of ANT focusing on including Divine activity as part of its relational approach to reality, and the terminological enhancement of philosophical theology through the adoption of ANT's comprehensiveness in addressing the multiplicity and contingency of agency. According to Tchalakov and Kapriev, the Byzantine philosophical tradition (such as articulated in the works of Maximus the Confessor, but also of John of Damascus and Gregory Palamas) could easily agree with many

38. Latour, *Reassembling the Social*, 60.
39. Bartels and Bencherki, "Actor Network Theory," 32.
40. Deleuze, "Qu'est-ce que l'acte de création?," 133–42.
41. Ibid..

of ANT's basic principles.⁴² It offers a unique and original language, which allows describing the way for different acting agencies to mutually influence each other in the course of action. The most important concepts here are ὑπόστασις/persona/πρόσωπον and περιχώρησις (interpenetration or co-inherence). The fact that the Byzantine concept of hypostasis has a universal meaning (every single being has a hypostasis) is of significant importance here. By emphasizing this point Tchalakov and Kapriev suggested relating the concept of hypostasis to ANT's notions of *actant* and *agency*. In turn, the fact that the concept of περιχώρησις denotes the mutual penetration and co-inherence of two (or more) different natures (together with their own properties and energies) while preserving their proper otherness, opens the possibility for the description of specific circumstances in association with composite hypostases including or combining multiple sources of agency which are grounded in multiple inhomogeneous natures but appearing as seemingly single actants. In addition, Byzantine philosophy has the ability to explicate the empirically observable differences between different hypostases (or acting agencies) having the same nature, i.e., the ability to explain how hypostatic or actant uniqueness emerges from within the same resource of natural energies. It has addressed this issue by elaborating on another Aristotelian category (in addition to ἐνέργεια)—ἕξις, which defines the personal, or rather, the uniquely hypostatic factor in the actualization of the natural energies or actions. As Tchalakov and Kapriev have pointed out, the dominant understanding of *habitus* which is currently used within the context of ANT⁴³ appears to be unable to incorporate the comprehensiveness of the Greek notion of ἕξις. Last but not least, the philosophical theology of St. Maximus in particular offers the potential of its teaching on the relationship between the Divine and created λόγοι and the multi-logi-cal nature of activity as a valuable framework that could be used for the benefits of the social sciences.

In conclusion, one should emphasize that the above reflections should not overshadow the key message in the philosophical theology of St. Maximus for whom the Incarnation is the ultimate goal of both Creation and Deification. "Because of this the whole arrangement of created things exists, they abide and were brought into being from nothing."⁴⁴

42. Tanev, "Actor-Network vs. Activity Theory."
43. Latour, *Reassembling the Social*, 210–11.
44. Sherwood, "Introduction," 28.

Bibliography

Ajdukiewicz, Kazimierz. "The World-Picture and the Conceptual Apparatus (1934)." In *The Scientific World-Perspective and Other Essays, 1931–1963*, edited by Jerzy Giedymin, 67–89. Dordrecht: Reidel, 1977.

Bartels, Gerald, and Nicolas Bencherki. "Actor-Network-Theory and Creativity Research." In *Encyclopedia of Creativity, Invention, Innovation, and Entrepreneurship*, edited by Elias G. Carayannis, 29–35. Dordrecht: Springer, 2013.

Bradshaw, David Houston. *Aristotle East and West: Metaphysics and the Division of Christendom*. Cambridge: Cambridge University Press, 2004.

Crawford, Cassandra S. "Actor Network Theory." In *Encyclopedia of Social Theory*, edited by George Ritzer, 1:1–4. Thousand Oaks, CA: Sage, 2004.

Cvetković, Vladimir. "St Justin Popović's Reception of St. Maximus the Confessor." Paper presented at the The Fourth International Conference on St. Maximus the Confessor, Tsageri, Georgia, October 10, 2011.

Deleuze, Gilles. "Qu'est-ce que l'acte de création?" *Trafic* 27 (1998) 133–42.

Florovsky, George. "Creation and Creaturehood." In *Creation and Redemption*, 43–78. Collected Works of Georges Florovsky 3. Belmont, MA: Nordland, 1976.

———. "Cur Deus Homo? The Motive of the Incarnation." In Εὐχαριστήριον. Τιμητικὸς τόμος Ἀμίλκα Ἀλιβιζάτου, 70–79. Athens, 1957.

Golitzin, Alexander. *Et introibo ad altare Dei: The Mystagogy of Dionysius Areopagita, with Special Reference to Its Predecessors in the Eastern Christian Tradition*. Analekta Vlatadon. Thessaloniki: Patriarchikon Idruma Paterikon Meleton, 1994.

Kapriev, Georgi. *Maksim Izpovednik—Bъvedenie v mislovnata mu sistema* [Maximus the Confessor: Introduction to His Thought System]. Sofia: Iztok-Zapad, 2010.

Kapriev, Georgi, and Ivan Tchalakov. "Actor-Network Theory and Byzantine Interpretation of Aristotle's Theory of Action: Three Points of Possible Dialogue." *Yearbook of the Institute for Advanced Studies on Science, Technology and Society* 57 (2009) 207–38.

Kapriev, Georgi, Martin Roussel, and Ivan Tchalakov, eds. *Le sujet de l'acteur: An Anthropological Outlook on Actor-Network Theory*. Morphomata 21. Paderborn: W. Fink, 2014.

Larchet, Jean-Claude. *La divinisation de l'homme selon saint Maxime le Confesseur*. Cogitatio fidei 194. Paris: Cerf, 1996.

Latour, Bruno. *Reassembling the Social: An Introduction to Actor-Network-Theory*. Oxford: Oxford University Press, 2005.

Law, John. "Actor Network Theory and Material Semiotics." In *The New Blackwell Companion to Social Theory*, edited by Bryan S. Turner, 141–58. Malden, MA: Wiley-Blackwell, 2007.

Loudovikos, Nikolaos. *A Eucharistic Ontology: Maximus the Confessor's Eschatological Ontology of Being as Dialogical Reciprocity*. Translated by Elizabeth Theokritoff. Brookline, MA: Holy Cross Orthodox Press, 2010.

———. "Ontology Celebrated: Remarks of an Orthodox on Radical Orthodoxy." In *Encounter between Eastern Orthodoxy and Radical Orthodoxy: Transfiguring the World through the Word*, edited by Adrian Pabst and Christoph Schneider, 141–54. Burlington, VT: Ashgate, 2009.

Maximus the Confessor. *Ambigua ad Iohannem*. Edited and translated by Nicholas P. Constas. In *Difficulties*, 1:62–450; 2:2–330. Abbreviated as *AI*.

———. *The Ascetic Life; The Four Centuries of Charity*. Translated by Polycarp Sherwood. Ancient Christian Writers 21. Westminster, MD: Newman, 1955.

———. *Liber asceticus* [On the Ascetical Life]. Edited by Peter Van Deun and Steven Gysens. CCSG 40:4–123. Abbreviated as *LA*.

———. *On Difficulties in the Church Fathers: The Ambigua*. Edited and translated by Nicholas P. Constas. 2 vols. Dumbarton Oaks Medieval Library 28–29. Cambridge: Harvard University Press, 2014. Abbreviated as *Difficulties*.

———. *Quaestiones ad Thalassium*. Edited by François Combefis. PG90:244–785B. Abbreviated as *QThal*.

Popović, Justin. *Man and the God-Man*. 1st ed. Contemporary Christian Thought Series 4. Alhambra, CA: Sebastian, 2009.

Schneider, Hans Julius. *Wittgenstein's Later Theory of Meaning: Imagination and Calculation*. Translated by Timothy Doyle and Daniel Smyth. Hoboken, NJ: Wiley-Blackwell, 2014.

Schuler, Douglas, and Aki Namioka, eds. *Participatory Design: Principles and Practices*. Hillsdale, NJ: L. Erlbaum Associates, 1993.

Sherwood, Polycarp. "Introduction." In Maximus the Confessor, *The Ascetic Life; The Four Centuries of Charity*, translated by Polycarp Sherwood, 3–102. Ancient Christian Writers 21. Westminster, MD: Newman, 1955.

Smith, Christian. *What Is a Person? Rethinking Humanity, Social Life, and the Moral Good from the Person Up*. Chicago: University of Chicago Press, 2010.

Spender, John-Christopher. *Business Strategy: Managing Uncertainty, Opportunity, and Enterprise*. Oxford: Oxford University Press, 2014.

Stăniloae, Dumitru. "Introduction." Translated by Ignatius Sakalis. In Maximus the Confessor, Φιλοσοφικά καὶ θεολογικά ἐρωτήματα. Athens: Apostoliki Diakonia, 1978.

———. "The World as Gift and Word." In *The Experience of God: Orthodox Dogmatic Theology*, translated and edited by Ioan Ionita and Robert Barringer, 2:21–63. Brookline, MA: Holy Cross Orthodox Press, 2002.

Tanev, Stoyan. "Actor-Network vs. Activity Theory: Dealing With the Changing Nature of the Asymmetry in Human-Technology Inter-actions." In *Le sujet de l'acteur: An Anthropological Outlook on Actor-Network Theory*, edited by Georgi Kapriev, Martin Roussel, and Ivan Tchalakov, 65–86. Morphomata 21. Paderborn: W. Fink, 2014.

Tanev, Stoyan, Mette Knudsen, and Wolfgang Gerstlberger. "Value Co-creation as Part of an Integrative Vision for Innovation Management." *Technology Innovation Management Review* (December 2009). http://timreview.ca/article/309.

Tanev, Stoyan, et al. "How Do Value Co-creation Activities Relate to the Perception of Firms' Innovativeness?" *Journal of Innovation Economics and Management* 7 (2011) 131–59. doi:10.3917/jie.007.0131.

Tchalakov, Ivan, and Kapriev Georgi. "The Limits of Causal Action: Actor-Network Theory Notion of Translation and Aristotle's Notion of Action." In *Yearbook 2005 of the Institute for Advanced Studies on Science, Technology and Society*, edited by Arno Bammé et al., 389–433. Technik- und Wissenschaftsforschung/Science and Technology Studies. Munich: Profil, 2005.

17

Αὐτεξούσιος Activity as Assent or Co-actuality? Compatibilism, Natural Law, and the Maximian Synthesis

Demetrios Harper

In examining the spirit and dynamics of St. Maximus the Confessor's understanding of natural law in his *Cosmic Liturgy*, Hans Urs von Balthasar poignantly observes, "the dominant mood here is Hellenic—more exactly, a Stoic—confidence in nature."[1] What von Balthasar, among other things, quite rightly notices is Maximus' tendency to utilize Stoic language and terminology as well as their pervasive sense of divine immanence to describe the intimate causal relationship between the Demiurge and created nature's destiny.[2] Creation and its τέλος are, in a certain sense, circumscribed by divine will and providence.[3] Yet, Maximus is also well recognized for his indefatigable insistence that rational beings are αὐτεξούσιος, capable of unnecessitated acts of self-determination and free will.[4] Indeed, his engagement with the topics of will and self-determination has led Gauthier, rightly or wrongly, to conclude that in Maximus we have the first description of a truly distinct faculty of free will.[5] This connection of natural law and

---

1. Balthasar, *Cosmic Liturgy*, 297.

2. Maximus' corpus quite prominently displays the deployment of a Stoic-style exemplarism and a divine voluntarism which give voice to his belief that natural law and the eschatological destiny of nature as a whole are the work of divine determinations, and indeed are pre-represented before time and creation in the benevolent "divine volitions" θεῖα θελήματα (*AI* 7, 1085A).

3. Cf. his *AI* 10, 1133C–36A.

4. Cf. especially his *TP1*.

5. See Gauthier's translation of Aristotle, *L'Éthique à Nicomaque*, 266.

eschatology to immanent divine determinations, on the one hand, and a rigorous insistence on humanity's capacity for free self-determination, on the other, might seem to suggest that the Confessor subscribed to a form of compatibilism, a view which, not coincidentally, emerges in the systems of the Stoics themselves and which ultimately limits all human determinations to internalized processes, placing all ontological realities beyond the scope of human influence. Despite Maximus' abundant use of Stoic concepts, however, I would argue that he artfully avoids a compatibilistic approach and the consequences thereof, granting rational beings the capacity to co-actualize nature in conjunction with divine determinations.[6] This is a reality that is demonstrated *par excellence* in Maximus' doctrine of the virtues, a perspective that we should seriously consider integrating into the modern Christian moral outlook.

Before moving on to Maximus' views, it is helpful to provide a very cursory overview of the basic features and consequences of a compatibilist approach, a view which has re-emerged in various forms in later philosophical systems and, often implicitly, in Christian dogma. As Jacob Klein explains, the Stoic view of divine interaction with natural laws is essentially interpreted in two ways, either as a form of divine voluntarism or, conversely, as intellectualism.[7] To very roughly summarize, the voluntarist approach considers natural law to be the result of the Creator's volitional determinations, or, as Brad Inwood puts it, "an imperative expression of what god wants men to do and what he wants to happen in nature."[8] The intellectualist interpretation suggests that the Stoics believe natural laws exist independently of the Creator, and it is only due to his superior faculty of right reason (ὀρθὸς λόγος) that he is able to perceive them and coordinate their enforcement on the natural world.[9] This so-called intellectualist perspective is manifested more explicitly in the deistic and theistic philosophical systems of the post-Renaissance Moderns.[10] Although there is variance in interpretation with regards to the origin of natural laws, their deterministic quality and their inexorable facilitation of μοῖρα, the causal fate of the

---

6. A full treatment of this topic would clearly require a rather extended discussion, including an examination of the way in which Maximus re-tools the Stoic exemplars into what Nicholas Loudovikos has termed "loving proposals" awaiting "discussion." Loudovikos, *Eucharistic Ontology*, 66–67, 92.

7. Klein, "Stoic Eudaimonism," 70–71. For a more careful treatment of this distinction, see Schneewind, *Invention of Autonomy*, 8–9, 21–23.

8. See, for example, Aëtius, *Placita* I.7; Inwood, *Ethics and Human Action in Early Stoicism*, 108.

9. Klein, "Stoic Eudaimonism," 70–71.

10. Schneewind, *Invention of Autonomy*, 8–9.

cosmos, seem axiomatic.[11] This deterministic view on the part of the Stoics gives rise to a world in which there is absolute natural necessitation, brought about by what Dorothea Frede describes as "an eternal causal nexus" where the fate of all beings is necessitated by a "network of interacting causes."[12] In addition to their deterministic views of causality, the Stoics also evaluate morality in light of nature's principles, whether or not and to what extent a given human action accords with the inherent goodness of nature and its laws.[13] As such, moral truth receives its legitimacy on the basis of ontological and naturalistic truths, a view that in this sense is also reflected in Aristotle and his intellectual progeny. Yet, unlike the Aristotelian view, natural realities are not ἐφ' ἡμῖν, or up to us, to use the Stoic expression. A rational agent cannot have any real ontological effect upon the determined natural world or work towards a higher or more virtuous state of being, inevitably restricting morality to internalized judgments and mental states. This is particularly evident in Epictetus, who, going a bit further than his predecessors, asserts there is no external action that is entirely up to us as rational agents, the act of willing consisting exclusively of an internalized dialectical process.[14] Morality and virtue are defined by the rational agent either assenting or refusing to assent to the proper mental impression that accords with nature, activities which do not affect the natural state *per se* of the agent for either good or ill.[15] As Alasdair MacIntyre has argued, the Stoics' intentions notwithstanding, this morality-as-interior-judgment approach lays the groundwork for the eventual bifurcation of ontology and morality. In disconnecting morality from the process of natural realization, MacIntyre argues, morality is not really concerned with a τέλος but rather is interiorly focused upon the will "arbitrating" and acknowledging the good. Morality is not concerned, as it would be in Aristotle, with a human being's natural transition from what he is to what he could be.[16]

This disconnection of morality from its ontological grounding would eventually find its quintessential expression in the deontological morals of Immanuel Kant and his heirs. Although Kant, who considers himself to be an heir to the Stoic paradigm,[17] and adopts aspects of their interior moral method, he takes what might be argued as a logical step and abandons their

11. Cf. Cicero, *De natura deorum* II.58, 71–153, and 154–67.
12. Frede, "Stoic Determinism," 189.
13. Irwin, *Development of Ethics*, 1:295–96, 1:305–6.
14. Epictetus, *Enchiridion* 1.1. See Frede, *Free Will*, 45.
15. Irwin, *Development of Ethics*, 1:302–3.
16. MacIntyre, *After Virtue*, 168–9.
17. Ibid., 236.

naturalistic language, overturning the Hellenistic tendency to trust nature.[18] Regarding nature and natural law in exclusively Newtonian terms and, ultimately, as that which prevents us from being moral, Kant attempts to found morality in the autonomy of the noumenal self and the human beings rational capability to will beyond his or her natural or phenomenal self.[19] The natural is not only absolutely determined but is also the ultimate enemy of a human being's moral autonomy, functioning as one of the primary mechanisms for the heteronymous enslavement of the subject.[20] Moreover, since it is only through the unreliable world of phenomena that we engage other rational creatures, we must also disregard all external heteronymous moral authority, including God's, and rely solely on our own capacity to determine an "objective" course of action.[21] Given his consignment of other rational agents to mere phenomena and his reliance on an individualistic and interiorized moral standard, it is not difficult to see why some philosophers would later regard Kant's view as tending toward moral self-directedness.[22] The "other" either exists as a phenomenal manifestation whose opinion we must ignore in order to be autonomous or as another noumenal self, which we cannot access. Given Kant's rather tenuous claims about the noumenal or metaphysical self, it is also not difficult to see why Nietzsche would later dismiss the transcendental idealist's claims about unnecessitated interior determination[23] and suggest in unequivocal terms that we should embrace the fact that reality itself resides in the necessitated world of appearances.[24]

In turning to the views of Maximus the Confessor, we find that throughout his works he frequently uses both naturalistic and compatibilistic language, a large portion of which is certainly Stoic in origin, to describe the relationship of divine causality to created nature. Moreover, Maximus is explicit in articulating the fact that God is not only the Creator and cause of all being but also the author of its eschatological end (*AI* 7, 1073C), or,

18. To quote Schneewind, *The Invention of Autonomy*, 515: "Kantian autonomy presupposes that we are rational agents whose transcendental freedom takes us out of the domain of natural causation." This is due to the fact that Kant considered nature to be a "mere phenomenon," as Collingwood argues in *The Idea of Nature*, 119, and therefore a functional barrier to aspirations toward autonomous noumenal morality.

19. Kant, *Groundwork of the Metaphysic of Morals*, 4:446–7 [97–9 in Paton's translation].

20. Ibid. Guyer, *Kant's System of Nature and Freedom*, 117.

21. Kant, *Groundwork of the Metaphysic of Morals*, 408–9 [28–30].

22. Such as Williams, *Shame and Necessity*, 94–97, for the self-directed qualities of guilt-based morality.

23. Cf. Leiter, *Nietzsche on Morality*, 80.

24. Nietzsche's views of metaphysical realities are well disclosed in *The Gay Science*, 266.

as he explains in *Ambiguum* 65, the divine λόγος of nature is the "the only source of primary, eternal, and well-being."[25] He restates this in somewhat more explicit terms in the *Gnostic Chapters*, describing God as the cause "of all being, potentiality (δύναμις) and actualization (ἐνέργεια), and of every origin, intermediary state and consummation."[26] As such, the entirety of human ontology and its activity consists of a participatory reality, including the actualizing of natural potential. Moreover, it cannot be said that natural δύναμις is absolutely intrinsic to the creature. Natural movement and actuality require constant contact with the exemplars of being,[27] an approach that certainly differs from Aristotle despite the deployment of the Aristotelian δύναμις/ἐνέργεια dichotomy.

Closely connected to Maximus' emphasis on the immanence of divine causality is his expression of the same interrelatedness of ontology and morality manifested in Aristotelians and the Stoics alike, and the constant tendency to judge human action in light of the standard of nature itself and its eschatological destiny. Pervading his corpus are references to volitional movements either according with nature and the natural law or, conversely, moving in opposition to them.[28] Indeed, even a cursory examination of Maximus' works suggests that his theological synthesis is presupposed by what we would now refer to as virtue-based or ontological ethics, an aspect of his thought that has recently attracted the attention of several Maximus Scholars.[29] References to natural law are prominent features in his synthesis and are also strongly suggestive of a univocity of the Creator's ultimate determinations for nature and humanity's moral τέλος. Perhaps the most explicit expression of this relationship can be found in Maximus' commentary on the Lord's Prayer: "Since the principle (λόγος) of nature is a law both natural and divine (ὅς [λόγος τῆς φύσεως] καὶ νόμος ἐστὶ φυσικός τε καὶ θεῖος) . . . there is nothing contrary to it when a man's will functions in accordance with this principle and it accords with God in all things."[30] As Maximus explains, any rebellion against God constitutes a violation of the generic λόγος of nature itself, which, as he also confirms in *Ambiguum*

---

25. *AI* 65, 1392D.

26. *CGn* 1.4, 1084C. Trans. according to *The Philokalia*, 2:215.

27. *AI* 10, 1133. Cf. Tollefsen, *Christocentric Cosmology*, 64–68, 77–82.

28. Though one could cite a host of references, see *TP1* 24B for one of Maximus' most concise evaluations of the actualization of human volitional powers in light of the κατὰ φύσιν/παρὰ φύσιν distinction. For a rather more complex and cosmic approach, see *AI* 65, 1392CD.

29. For example, see Blowers, "Aligning and Reorienting the Passible Self"; Louth, "Virtue Ethics."

30. *PN* 678–81. Trans. according to *The Philokalia*, 2:301.

41 (1312BC), consists of divine intentionality for the entirety of created nature. This, likewise, discloses Maximus' essentially voluntarist approach to divine determination, making the divine exemplars and laws the products of divine will and therefore posterior to the divine essence, a view which distinguishes him from not only many of the Stoics but also, if J. B. Schneewind is to be believed, from Aquinas who seems to follow Cicero in taking a more "intellectualist" approach to natural laws.[31] On the occasions where Maximus does use nature or natural law in a negative sense, it seems clear that intends such expressions to be descriptive of a fallen τρόπος or mode of existence, which, as he consistently indicates elsewhere, constitutes a παράχρησις or a misuse of nature itself and its potentiality.[32]

Many of Maximus' commentators seem to have the impression that he considered human self-determination to be exclusively the province of an interiorized moral reality. This is a position which, perhaps quite inadvertently, leads to the imposition of a compatibilist reading on Maximus' approach to divino-human relations. For example, Lars Thunburg implicitly endorses such a notion in his mammoth *Microcosm and Mediator* when he describes man's voluntary realization of καθ' ὁμοίωσιν, of his likeness unto God, as being "always of a moral and volitional character."[33] It is certainly true that man's volitional and moral dimensions are inherent to this process. However, Thunburg gives no indication that this καθ' ὁμοίωσιν realization also has an ontological dimension, giving the impression that a rational being's "in the likeness" is composed exclusively of behavioral patterns. Polycarp Sherwood, in a similar fashion, reads a rigid distinction between moral and ontological realities into Maximus' texts. In reviewing the five modes of contemplation in the tenth *Ambiguum*, Sherwood asserts that the latter two (κράσις and θέσις, 1133A), modes that are dependent upon human self-determination, are of an exclusively moral character, while the first three

---

31. Schneewind, *Invention of Autonomy*, 23.

32. *TP1* 24B. An example of the Confessor's use of natural law in relation to creation's fallen mode of existence appears rather prominently in *AI* 31, where Maximus seeks to interpret Gregory Nazianzen's reference to Christ "loosing the laws of nature." These laws were brought about by humanity's lapse into sin and are in fact παρὰ φύσιν. However, it is essential to note that Maximus juxtaposes the corrupting laws of nature with what he terms the "spiritual laws of nature," which are renewed and realized in Christ such that the natural world again aspires to its proper end or πέρας (1276BC). In short, natural law is meant here to suggest the state in which nature exists, whether or not it is moving towards its divinely ordered end. This use of law (νόμος) in relation to an existential mode is represented again in *TP1* in more positive terms, where Maximus refers to our positive response to the λόγος of virtue as the "actualized law of natural powers that accords with nature" (24B).

33. Thunberg, *Microcosm and Mediator*, 330.

modes of contemplation are exclusively the province of divine causation inasmuch as they are ontological categories.³⁴ Sherwood takes this yet a step further, arguing that one of the key errors of Origen was his tendency to conflate moral and ontological realities, a distortion, Sherwood tells us, that Maximus corrects.³⁵

Although Maximus certainly utilizes the language of Stoic determinism as one of his tools of articulation and indeed sees divine providence as being involved in all dimensions of human ontology, it is certainly inaccurate to characterize his views of human self-determination as pertaining exclusively to a disconnected "moral" sphere, and therefore limited to an internal psychological process. The most immediate refutation of such a hermeneutic rather obviously comes via Maximus' view of the Fall. In assessing the causal realities associated with post-lapsarian humanity, Maximus not only assigns volitional culpability to man for his lapsed state but also causality for the *natural* fragmentation thereof (*QThal* epist., 256B). Despite Maximus' extensive corrective of Origen and an extended criticism of his anthropology, he nonetheless chooses to appropriate Origen's tendency to cast humanity's self-determinations in terms of a dialectic between divinely-authored being and the abyss of non-being. In Question 61 of the *Ad Thalassium*, a passage that is infrequently mentioned, Maximus explains that in falling into sin (ἁμαρτία) Adam complied and was complicit with the devil's desire to "dissolve" (διαλῦσαι) creation, and in so doing, "forced the nature of created things (ὠθοῦσα τὴν φύσιν τῶν γεγονότων) unto death and toward the undoing of creation (πρὸς ἀπογένησιν κατὰ τὸν θάνατον)."³⁶ This dialectic of being/nonbeing also appears several times in the *Ambigua* with reference to humanity's eschatological end. In *Ambiguum* 65, speaking of those who reject and violate the λόγος of nature, Maximus says that they shall assume a τρόπος of woe-being, receiving "non-being in place of the containment of well-being because of their opposition to it" (1392D). In short, a rejection of God's determinations for being result in the human agent turning towards the abyss of nothing from which he or she was taken and, to the extent possible, "participating" in the dark oblivion of non-being. As Maximus clearly indicates, though created being and its eternal existence are an irrevocable gift,³⁷ evil constitutes the recalcitrant attempt to undermine created ontology and achieve its complete dissolution, which,

---

34. Sherwood, *Earlier Ambigua*, 37.

35. Ibid., 193–94. This is repeated by Cooper in his otherwise excellent book *The Body in St Maximus the Confessor*, 86–87.

36. *QThal* 61, 633B.

37. *CChar* 3.28, 1025B; 4.11, 1048C.

though unsuccessful, nonetheless results in a real fragmentation of nature, both universally and particularly.

When, therefore, Maximus says that well-being (εὖ εἶναι) and a proper response to the natural law are up to us, he is not referring to some interiorized moral assent on the part of a rational agent, but to a concrete and more Aristotelian sense of natural actualization according to which a human agent co-actualizes with the λόγοι of nature toward created nature's τέλος (*AI* 7, 1073C; and 65, 1392). Indeed, this is a progressive realization that constitutes a well-coordinated and cooperative process between ethical and ontological realities, an approach that is well captured in Maximus' doctrine of natural will in his *Opusculum* 1. As he explains, θέλημα or θέλησις in its natural state "holds together the essence (of a being)" (*TP1* 12C), which is suggestive of a participatory cooperation with the aforementioned "generic" λόγος of nature (*AI* 41, 1312BC). This maintenance role on the part of the will, however, is a more primitive function, inasmuch as its ultimate purpose is to serve as the natural impetus for the achievement of what he terms in the *Opusculum* as "complete being" (πλήρης ὀντότης, 12CD), but which Maximus arguably refers to elsewhere as well-being (εὖ εἶναι).[38] In short, the natural will is a rational desire to realize in particular the call to well-being or, to use Terence Irwin's term, to "mature nature,"[39] a call that is issued by the Λόγος himself through the law of nature. This achievement of mature being, though actualized by a particular agent's gnomic determinations and connected to his or her moral habituation, is by no means an event limited to particular significance, but constitutes an active participation in the universal constitution of human nature itself; it is a diachronic transition from what Nicholas Loudovikos has described as mere natural "sameness" to a functional "consubstantiality" of created nature.[40] This participatory consubstantializing on the part of rational creatures is strongly affirmed by a passage from Question 39 of Maximus' *Ad Thalassium*. Anagogically interpreting the sojourning multitudes interaction with Christ in Matthew 15:32 as an interaction with the three laws of the Λόγος, the Confessor provides the following description: "In lieu of the natural law (ὑπὲρ δὲ τοῦ φυσικοῦ [νόμου]), the sojourning multitudes receive unfailing actualization of the passions in a way that accords with nature (τὴν ἄπταιστον τῶν κατὰ φύσιν ἐνέργειαν) by which a reciprocal relationship between each other is established (καθ' ἣν ἡ ἀλληλοῦχος σχέσις συνίσταται), such that *every*

---

38. *AI* 7, 1073C; 65, 1392AB; and *CChar* 4.11, 1049C.
39. Irwin, *Development of Ethics*, 1:146.
40. Loudovikos, "Possession or Wholeness?," 265–66.

dispersive otherness (ἑτερότητα) *and division is removed from nature.*"[41] Man's volitional δύναμις and moral determinations are responsible for the actualization of a given rational agent's natural potential, yet also provide the means for a gradual transition from a being in solipsistic isolation to one that participates in the community of nature constituted by the οἰκονομία of the Incarnate Λόγος. Conversely, involuntarily actualizing and gnomically constituting oneself in opposition to the natural law of the Λόγος, a rational agent turns towards the solipsistic isolation of non-being and, as Maximus affirms throughout his corpus, divides the divinely-intended unity of created nature.

Mankind, therefore, does not merely possess psychological freedom but also a form of natural freedom, the ability to answer the λόγοι of being in ontological terms. However, if God authors the beginning, end, and middle states of the diachronic flow of being, what is it that a rational agent constitutes and actualizes? What is within the power of the human subject such that he or she is able to disrupt participation in the consubstantiality of creation and exist in the solipsism of bare being? The answer to this query is woven into many of Maximus' carefully-crafted theological engagements, but is, perhaps, most explicitly represented in the following from *Opusculum* 1 when he affirms that "the λόγος of virtue is up to us," which, when utilized, is "the actualized law of existent natural powers." [42] In other words, ontological freedom is the capacity to realize natural destiny and co-actualize with the divine predestinations (προορισμοί) through the virtues; this means that virtue, in a functional sense, is the maturation and realization of nature itself, and is indeed what enables a being to be a participant in the aforementioned consubstantial community of nature.

To the modern mind-set—an outlook that involuntarily transmits the criteria of deontological notions of morals—the idea of virtue being something that defines the difference between natural freedom and the lack thereof might seem strange or inconsequential. Maximus, however, regarded the virtues not only as the hallmarks of a transition to complete and natural functionality but as also disclosing the very existential characteristics of divinity. As he explains in the *Quaestiones et Dubia*, we attain a likeness to God by imitating his divine character, by acquiring, to the extent possible,

---

41. *QThal* 39, 393AB.

42. *TP1* 24B. The context of the passage is as follows: "If man is the only one amongst all other animals who is by nature capable of freely electing, and if the ability to freely elect consists in being able to cause things that are within our power and up to us, those things whose ends are yet uncertain, and the λόγος of virtue is up to us, that is, the actualized law of existent natural powers." Maximus is building rhetorically here on what he takes to be ontological givens.

his virtues.[43] This is also affirmed by *Ambiguum* 7 where Maximus identifies the acquisition of virtue with participation in the Eucharistic reality distributed by the Incarnate Λόγος, which, *inter alia*, also discloses the close connection between natural eschatology and grace in Maximus' thought and, thus, between the laws of grace and nature (1081C).[44] Yet, the most powerful testimony of his belief in the inherent ontological significance of virtue comes via his doctrine of love. Departing from both the Aristotelian ethical tradition and Evagrian ascetic teaching, Maximus establishes love as not only the primary virtue but the very mechanism of the human attainment of a consubstantial mode of being. This is daringly affirmed in the *Ad Thalassium* when he says, "the most general principle of all the virtues is love, the λόγος of the all virtues, the most general and constitutive power of nature."[45] This approach is clarified and grounded by Maximus in his famous *Epistle* 2 where he announces that all forms of the virtues are fulfillments of the "power of love," actualizing and leading towards the establishment of nature in a complete and unified mode (*Ep2* 400AB). Here ontology and ethics synchronize perfectly in Maximus' expression. Every authentic virtue is a manifestation or, better, a particular actualization of love, which is itself the unitary λόγος of virtue and simultaneously the λόγος of created nature's well-being. All true manifestations of virtue constitute an expansion—a διαστολή, if you will—of the monad of love.[46] In their contraction, their συστολή, they aspire to and converge in the λόγος of love (cf. *AI* 21, 1249B), progressively leading toward humanity's proper eschatological state: a mode in which nature consists of a functional community, enabling genuine reciprocity between each rational being and between the Incarnate Λόγος and his creatures.

In closing, I would draw attention to the significance of Maximus' approach for current interconfessional discussions concerning ethics and human self-determination, discussions that follow in the wake of the impasses created by the epistemological retreat of thinkers like Kant. In the Confessor's corpus we have an invaluable resource, namely, a form of natural law and divine determinism that allows, no, insists on the immanent and personal character of divine οἰκονομία. Yet, his theological and philosophical vision also permits rational creatures self-determination that is not merely limited to the establishment of an internal disposition, but allows for the exercise of real ontological freedom. Most pertinently, because of his

---

43. *QD* 3, 1. Cf. the translation of Despina Prassas, *Questions and Doubts*, 156–57.
44. Cf. Blowers, *Exegesis and Spiritual Pedagogy in Maximus the Confessor*, 117–18.
45. *QThal* 40, 397B.
46. Cf. *QThal* 55, 541BC for the μονάς/μυριάς of virtue.

inherently other-directed approach to both ontology and virtue, Maximus offers us a philosophical vision of real unity and real engagement with the other upon the field of universal nature. Other rational beings cease to be abstractions or, worse, obstacles to moral autonomy, becoming instead co-actualizers of the divine gift that is human nature.

Bibliography

Aristotle. *L'Éthique à Nicomaque*. Edited by René Antoine Gauthier and Jean Yves Jolif. Vol. I.1–II.2. Aristote: Traductions et Études. Leuven: Peeters, 2002.

Balthasar, Hans Urs von. *Cosmic Liturgy: The Universe According to Maximus the Confessor*. Translated by Brian E. Daley. A Communio Book. San Francisco: Ignatius Press, 2003.

Blowers, Paul Marion. "Aligning and Reorienting the Passible Self: Maximus the Confessor's Virtue Ethics." *Studies in Christian Ethics* 26 (2013) 333–50.

———. *Exegesis and Spiritual Pedagogy in Maximus the Confessor: An Investigation of the Quaestiones ad Thalassium*. Christianity and Judaism in Antiquity. Notre Dame: University of Notre Dame Press, 1991.

Cooper, Adam G. *The Body in St Maximus the Confessor: Holy Flesh, Wholly Deified*. Oxford Early Christian Studies. Oxford: Oxford University Press, 2005.

Frede, Dorothea. "Stoic Determinism." In *The Cambridge Companion to the Stoics*, edited by Brad Inwood, 179–205. Cambridge: Cambridge University Press, 2003.

Frede, Michael. *A Free Will: Origins of the Notion in Ancient Thought*. Edited by A. A. Long. Sather Classical Lectures 68. Berkeley: University of California Press, 2011.

Guyer, Paul. *Kant's System of Nature and Freedom*. Oxford: Oxford University Press, 2005.

Inwood, Brad. *Ethics and Human Action in Early Stoicism*. Oxford: Clarendon, 1985.

Irwin, Terence. *The Development of Ethics: A Historical and Critical Study*. 3 vols. Oxford: Oxford University Press, 2007.

Kant, Immanuel. *Groundwork of the Metaphysic of Morals*. Translated by Herbert James Paton. New York: Harper & Row, 1964.

Klein, Jacob. "Stoic Eudaimonism and the Natural Law Tradition." In *Reason, Religion, and Natural Law*, edited by Jonathan A. Jacobs, 57–82. Oxford: Oxford University Press, 2012.

Leiter, Brian. *Nietzsche on Morality*. New York: Routledge, 2002.

Loudovikos, Nicholas. "Possession or Wholeness? St. Maximus the Confessor and John Zizioulas on Person, Nature, and Will." *Participatio: Journal of the Thomas F. Torrance Theological Fellowship* 4 (2013) 258–86.

Loudovikos, Nikolaos. *A Eucharistic Ontology: Maximus the Confessor's Eschatological Ontology of Being as Dialogical Reciprocity*. Translated by Elizabeth Theokritoff. Brookline, MA: Holy Cross Orthodox Press, 2010.

Louth, Andrew. "Virtue Ethics: St. Maximos the Confessor and Thomas Aquinas Compared." *Studies in Christian Ethics* 26 (2013) 351–63.

MacIntyre, Alasdair. *After Virtue*. 2nd ed. London: Duckworth, 1981.

Maximus the Confessor. *Ad Marinum presbyterum (Theologica et polemica i)* [To Marinus the Very Pious Priest]. Edited by François Combefis. PG91:9A–37D. Abbreviated as *TP1*.
———. *Ambigua ad Iohannem*. Edited by Franz Oehler. PG91:1061–417C. Abbreviated as *AI*.
———. *Capita de caritate* [Four Centuries on Charity]. Edited by François Combefis. PG90:960A–1080D. Abbreviated as *CChar*.
———. *Capita theologica et oeconomica* [Gnostic Chapters]. Edited by François Combefis. PG90:1084A–173A. Abbreviated as *CGn*.
———. *Epistula ii* [Epistle 2, To John the Chamberlain]. Edited by François Combefis. PG91:392D–408C. Abbreviated as *Ep2*.
———. *Orationis dominicae expositio* [On the Our Father]. Edited by Peter Van Deun. CCSG 23:27–73. Abbreviated as *PN*.
———. *Quaestiones ad Thalassium*. Edited by François Combefis. PG90:244–785B. Abbreviated as *QThal*.
———. *Quaestiones et dubia* [Questions and Doubts]. Edited by José H. Declerck. CCSG 10:3–170. Abbreviated as *QD*.
———. *St. Maximos the Confessor's Questions and Doubts*. Edited and translated by Despina D. Prassas. DeKalb: Northern Illinois University Press, 2010.
Nietzsche, Friedrich. *The Gay Science*. Translated by Walter Kaufmann. New York: Random House, 1974.
Schneewind, Jerome B. *The Invention of Autonomy: A History of Modern Moral Philosophy*. Cambridge: Cambridge University Press, 1997.
Sherwood, Polycarp. *The Earlier Ambigua of Saint Maximus the Confessor and His Refutation of Origenism*. Studia Anselmiana, philosophica theologica. Rome: "Orbis Catholicus"/Herder, 1955.
The Philokalia: The Complete Text; Compiled by St. Nikodimos of the Holy Mountain and St. Makarios of Corinth. Translated and edited by G. E. H. Palmer et al. 4 vols. Boston: Faber and Faber, 1979–.
Thunberg, Lars. *Microcosm and Mediator: The Theological Anthropology of Maximus the Confessor*. 2nd ed. Chicago: Open Court, 1995.
Tollefsen, Torstein. *The Christocentric Cosmology of St. Maximus the Confessor*. Oxford Early Christian Studies. Oxford: Oxford University Press, 2008.
Williams, Bernard. *Shame and Necessity*. Sather Classical Lectures 57. Berkeley: University of California Press, 1993.

18

Creation Anticipated: Maximian Reverberations in Bonaventure's Exemplarism

Justin Shaun Coyle

From Augustine to Anselm, the long Christian tradition has adopted and adapted the broadly Platonic grammar of exemplarism, or the divine ideas, to explain creation as an act of divine self-multiplication. Consider, on this point and for example, dramatic literary expressions like the lilting song of Aslan, the tonality of which generates Narnia; or the heated verse of Dylan Thomas, for whom the Creator glories in his "shapeless maps";[1] or else Piers Plowman's vision of the Word's parchment, upon which he inscribes creation.[2] Among the theological archive, perhaps the most dramatic theological performances of the divine ideas are staged in the thought of Maximus the Confessor in the form of his doctrine of the λόγοι, and in the thirteenth-century Franciscan schoolman Bonaventure of Bagnoregio's cosmic theory of exemplarism.[3] Maximus and Bonaventure, more than any others, embed

---

1. Thomas, "Foster the Light," 69.

2. Langland, *Piers Plowman,* Passus 9, 36–42: "As who saith, 'More must hereto *(be)* than my word one: / My might must help now with my speech.' / Right as a lord should make letters, and him lacked no parchment, / Though he could write never so well, if he wield no pen, / The letter, for all the lordship, I lieve were never y-made! / And so it seemeth by him, as the Bible telleth, there he said / *Faciamus hominem ad imaginem nostram.*" Modern English translation by Ben Byram-Wigfield at http://www.ancientgroove.co.uk/books/PiersPlowman.pdf. For an interesting study on Bonaventure's influence on Langland, see Clopper, *Songes of Rechelesnesse.*

3. This essay is intended as a contribution to the fresh scholarship cataloguing the similarities between Maximus the Confessor and Bonaventure. Tikhon Alexander Pino, for instance, notes that the synthesis of Maximus the Confessor with the Dionysian corpus issues in a "unique harmony with the thirteenth-century scholastic thought of Bonaventure." See his forthcoming "Scholastic and Patristic Thought," 81; Kappes et

a theology of the Word within the drama of salvation history, gathering the classical doctrine of exemplarism tightly around the person of Christ. For both, the Word stands for creation as its creative source, centermost depth, and final embrace. I consider these three stages in Maximus first and Bonaventure next, situating them within their respective historical episodes and calling attention to resemblance and dissimilitude throughout.

A brief and preliminary word on method. My interest here is strictly theological in scope, which is to say that I tender no claims about whether or not Bonaventure in fact read Maximus. The question is interesting, though, insofar as both of their projects can be seen as decisive episodes in the reception of Dionysius the Areopagite. Bonaventure had before him the Dionysian corpus, as is known, translated into Latin first by Eriugena and mediated to the Franciscans through the canons regular at St. Victor; that Bonaventure's reading of Dionysius bears a close family resemblance to that of Maximus—especially as regards the divine ideas—renders an objective Maximian connection seductive, if highly speculative. In any case, the cursory thoughts that follow intend to draw attention to conceptual similarities rather than those textual with the hope that they might occasion deeper theological engagement with Maximus and Bonaventure both.

Maximus the Confessor

In his *Ambiguum 7*, Maximus' doctrine of the λόγοι is couched within a refutation of what amounts to a specious reading of a difficult passage from Gregory Nazianzen. Indeed, the animus of Maximus' treatment may be seen as principally exegetical; at issue is the Origenist interpretation of Gregory's description of the human creature as "a portion of God that has flowed down from above."[4] What then is to be said about the human person as a "portion of God," and to what does this "flow" refer? Maximus' answer reveals an elegant (if tangled) pattern of thought into which his doctrine of the

---

a1. "Palamas among the Scholastics." In 2001, Delio in *Simply Bonaventure*, 91 observed to a "Christic element" common to the Greek Fathers (she mentions Gregory of Nyssa and Maximus) and Bonaventure.

4. *AI* 7.1. All translations from *The Ambigua* come from *Difficulties*, translated and edited by Nicholas Constas. I am deeply grateful to Fr. Maximos (Nicholas Constas) who introduced me to the relevant texts, commented on an earlier instantiation of this paper, and whose hospitable and critical theological eye has received me both patiently and graciously. For the contextual insight regarding Maximus' refutation of Origenism, I am indebted to Sherwood's *Earlier Ambigua*, 90–102. Sherwood is helpful in pointing up how Maximus' doctrine of the λόγοι need not be delimited to just a revision of Origenist cosmogony; it is *at least* that, but the Maximian doctrine also renders possible a positive, fresh reading of Christian Neoplatonism.

λόγοι is deeply threaded. The following reflections attempt to sketch a brief representation of that pattern, with special attention given to the exegetical revisions proffered by Maximus. For the present purposes, the doctrine of the λόγοι will be displayed through the Confessor's threefold break with the Origenist system: Maximus denies (1) that στάσις preceded both κίνησις and γένεσις; (2) that κίνησις is intimately, if not inextricably, bound to evil; and (3) that γένεσις entails the enfleshment that attends the fall of preexistent souls. These will be treated in reverse order in view of illuminating the doctrine of the λόγοι, reflecting Maximus' rearward reconfiguration of the Origenist narrative structure—that is, γένεσις, κίνησις, and στάσις.

Γένεσις

The logic of creation is keyed to what Maximus calls διαφορᾶς τὸν λόγον (*AT* 5.20), the principle of difference. To be a creature is as such and in sum to have "a constitutive and determinative difference"[5]—constitutive, because difference fixes a creature's existence as this or that; and determinative because difference functions to distinguish this *from* that. But upon what is this difference grounded? Here Maximus introduces his doctrine of the λόγοι,[6] the ontological basis for the grammar of difference: "And if the many are different, it must be understood that their λόγοι, according to which they essentially exist, are also different, since it is in these, *or rather because of these* λόγοι, that different things differ."[7] It is because of the λόγοι, he thinks, embedded as they are in creation, that each among the ensemble of beings is both guaranteed to be what it is and thereby differentiated from all others as such.[8]

Beginning with *creatio ex nihilo* as the propositional axiom of Christian theologizing allows Maximus to deny the Origenist doctrine of preexisting minds even as it opens a yawning interval between the Creator and his good creation (*AI* 7.3, 7.15). Differently put, Maximus' refusal of an emanationist metaphysic on one front threatens to reintroduce the problem

---

5. *AI* 67.9. This section follows closely—and is therefore deeply indebted to—the work of Perl, "Methexis."

6. For the historical development of Λόγος/λόγοι theories, see Tollefsen, *The Christocentric Cosmology*, 21–63; Thunberg, *Microcosm and Mediator*, 73ff, 157.

7. *AI* 22.2, emphasis mine.

8. *AI* 17.7: "What are the intelligible principles (λόγοι) that were first embedded within the subsistence of beings, according to which each being is and has its nature, and from which each was formed, shaped, and structured, and endowed with power, the ability to act, and to be acted upon, not to mention the differences of and properties in terms of quantity, quality, relation, place, time, position, movement, and inclination."

of the One and the many on another. Yet just here Maximus' doctrine of the λόγοι holds together the denial of γένεσις as the fall of preexisting souls with the participation of creation in God as origin and cause:

> We believe ... that a λόγος of angels preceded and guided their creation ... a λόγος of human beings likewise preceded their creation ... (and) the creation of everything that has received its being from God ... (who), by virtue of his infinite transcendence, is ineffable and incomprehensible, and exists beyond all creation and beyond all differences ... this same One manifested and multiplied in all the things that have their origin in him, in a manner appropriate to the being of each. (*AI* 7.16)

Ingredient to this compressed passage are the key tenets of the doctrine of the λόγοι, the first of which concerns the preexistence not of rational beings, but rather of the λόγοι in God.[9] The λόγοι as the "defining limits" prescribe how this or that creature participates in God according to a manner appropriate and proportionate to each (*AI* 7.16, *AI* 7.19). These exist in God eternally as a kind of "creation in potency," so to speak.[10] Yet Maximus pushes the logic further still, insisting that the λόγοι are identical with God: "one Λόγος is many λόγοι and the many are One."[11] And because

---

9. "For there exists absolutely none among beings whose principle (λόγος) did not preexist in God, and the principles of substance of these beings likewise preexist in God" (*AI* 42.15).

10. "For God is eternally an active creator, but creatures exist first in potential, and only later in actuality" (*AI* 7.19).

11. *AI* 7.20. The paradox looming, of course, is that the λόγοι are simultaneously fixed (united unconfusedly in the Λόγος) and embedded in the multiplicity of the created order. If the λόγοι are the one Λόγος and the one Λόγος the many λόγοι, as Maximus affirms, then what is to be made of difference? The point may be thematized by suggesting that the doctrine of the λόγοι repays a view from two vistas. The first is from the horizon of creation, wherein creatures see the λόγοι as the "constitutive and determinative difference" between beings; from here, the λόγοι give themselves as the immanent presence of the Creator in the created order. (Recall that in *Ambiguum* 22 it is the λόγοι that account for and even cause the difference of beings.) But the λόγοι can be glimpsed from another vista, too—that of God—in whom "preexist the principles (λόγοι) of all good things, as if from an ever-flowing spring, in a single, simple, unified embrace" (*AI* 10.120). For Maximus the λόγοι are God, remember, and thus the doctrine of the λόγοι can be seen to shore up a theology of radical transcendence. From this perspective, it must be that God knows all things by his own acts of knowledge and will, here the λόγοι. But just here looms a difficulty: how is it possible from the creaturely perspective for God to possess knowledge of the λόγοι of all beings before the λόγοι themselves cause that difference?

Here lies the paradoxical center of Maximus' doctrine of the λόγοι, that is, the question of difference's origin. The epistemological problem rehearsed in outline above translates to one ontological insofar as this "reciprocal causality of differentiation" leads

these λόγοι are not self-subsisting entities like Origen's preexisting minds, they lay in potency until actualized by their Creator.[12] On this score, the λόγοι are perhaps best described as blueprints or schematics—Balthasar suggests "outlines"[13]—of creation which are multiplied as creation is performed by and through the one Λόγος. One differs from another in their being circumscribed "by their own λόγοι"; and that they are circumscribed at all accounts for their difference from the one Λόγος who is, as Maximus reiterates with almost liturgical frequency, "beyond all being" (*AI* 7.19–20).

The principle of difference is not therefore an artifact of the fall, but rather the very center of what could be called the erotics of incarnation; such is the character of a God who wishes, in Maximus' programmatic phrase, "always and in all things to accomplish the mystery of his embodiment" (*AI* 7.22). This is, then, the second apposite tenet of the doctrine of the λόγοι, intimately related to the first. For Maximus, γένεσις is less a result of divine seepage (as in Neoplatonism) or a concession for an antecedent fall (as in Origenism) than a gratuitous gift, an ornament of divine "lavishness" (*AI* 7.35—7; 42.13—16). Indexed to the theology of *creatio ex nihilo*, the sheer gratuity of creation styles God as the great Lover whose kisses engender the very possibility of love in the created order. When God sang the world into being, "He did so on the basis of these λόγοι" (*AI* 7.15), the principles

---

to a two-sided reduction. See Perl, "Methexis," 176. From the creaturely vista, the λόγοι are the cause and guarantors of difference; from the divine, they are the one indivisible Λόγος, the thought and will of God. A neat reduction to either vista is untenable, too, as in the latter the λόγοι collapse into God, issuing in monism, where the former rules out the preexistence of the λόγοι in the Λόγος. A Maximian theory of the λόγοι would seem to leave us with a statement of identity only—that the λόγοι are the one Λόγος somehow multiplied in the created order—that threatens to erase difference without remainder. And so, as Perl has it, "if God must be differentiated in order for creatures to exist, and creatures must exist in order for God to be differentiated," then whence the grammar of difference? See Perl, "Methexis," 177. Perl and Thunberg both suggest that the origin of difference is found in the hypostatic principle, wherein difference (natures) is secured in unity without erasure (hypostasis). It is there in the incarnation of the Lord, then, Maximus thinks, that the grammar of difference is secured: "For the union," he writes, "by excluding division, does not impair the distinction" (*AT* 5.20). But Maximus pushes this logic further still; the grandeur of Christ is gorgeously displayed in "the generation of opposites (ἐναντίων γενέσει)" (*AT* 5.14). Thunberg sees the causality working the opposite way by suggesting that the incarnation is primarily a unifying event, whereas the logic of *AT* 5 seems to run from unity into difference; here the union actually generates opposites even as it secures them within what I'll call an erotics of incarnation. See Thunberg, *Microcosm and Mediator*, 77–79.

12. This is not divine capriciousness, notice, as "according to the ineffable wisdom of God . . . all things are brought into being at a time that has been foreknown," *AI* 42.14.

13. Balthasar, *Cosmic Liturgy*, 16.

of delimiting difference grounded in the one Λόγος. For Maximus, creation is not the result of satiety (as it was for the Origenists), but rather of divine ἔρως.

Κίνησις

The second principle of Origenism which Maximus denies is that κίνησις is intimately, if not inextricably, bound up with evil (*AI* 7.29). Recall that Origenist grammar links motion to Gregory's "flowing down"; κίνησις is therefore keyed to the turning of the preexisting minds' gaze away from their divine source which are thereby "variously dispersed" (7.2). Motion, on that account, is always and everywhere deprivative. And yet Maximus' revision of κίνησις aims to recast it not only as not deprivative, but even salutary: it is no less than the vehicle, Maximus thinks, of divinization. Principal among Maximus' revisions, then, rewrite motion as properly passive and appetitive.

That last first. Κίνησις is, when it "is impelled toward its proper end . . . either a 'natural power,' or else a 'passion'" (7.7). This is to say that motion is inherently appetitive, tending toward the Good or else toward darkness—that is, toward nothing whatever. And tending toward or desiring God happens by attending to the λόγος, which, as noted, delimits the mode of motion proper to each creature; whoever so acts may be said to move, Maximus notes, "in God in accordance with the λόγος of well-being that preexists in God, since he is moved to action by the virtues" (*AI* 7.22). Here the virtues are closely tethered to the λόγοι, as both belong properly to God in an undifferentiated sense: the λόγοι are the one Λόγος, the virtues his divine attributes. To the extent we "love and cleave affectionately to the aforementioned λόγοι," Maximus writes hotly, we "love and cleave affectionately to God himself, in whom the λόγοι of beautiful things are steadfastly fixed" (*AI* 7.22).

But that motion is appetitive does not rule out its being abused or otherwise misdirected. No, it is of course possible for those who (freely) turn their gaze from their λόγοι to be "irrationally swept away toward nonbeing," that is, into "a condition of unstable deviations" (*AI* 7.23). Here motion would be properly termed a πάθος, or a passion, and it is in this sense that Maximus rewrites Gregory's language about "flowing down," shifting the meaning from a cosmological syntax to moral description.[14]

---

14. *AI* 7.30. On this point, Maximus is careful to underline the freedom of the will: "For though such a person had it *well within his power* to direct the footsteps of his soul to God, he *freely chose* to exchange what is better and real for what is inferior and nonexistent," or later, "In each case, *the voluntary decision* to move either in accord with

Motion is also passive. This is directly attendant upon Maximus embedding his doctrine of the λόγοι within the grammar of *creatio ex nihilo*; for him, "no being in principle is devoid of motion," for only "that which is self-caused transcends the nature of beings, since it exists for the sake of nothing else" (*AI* 7.6, 7). Motion belongs then to the order of creation, as God alone remains uncaused and therefore lacks nothing, operating outside of desire whether virtuous or vicious (*AI* 7.7, 7.9, 15.6). To be created is, Maximus might say, to be moving and to be moved[15]—perpetually, too, as no created being has yet attained rest (*AI* 7.7, 7.14, 7.28). Negatively put, this treatment upends the Origenist scheme in which preexistent minds enjoy a primordial rest in and with the *henad*. In a more positive key, however, passivity names a constitutive principle of created being, one that renders all creatures ultimately dependent upon God for their coming to be.[16] Passivity is, then, a direct concomitant of having received one's λόγος from without; from, that is, its Lord. And such passivity anticipates, too, with the restive anxiety of a young bride in her bridechamber, its consummation with that Lord.

Ἔκστασις

But what does motion come to? Again, Maximus reverses and thickens the narrative structure of the Origenists by situating στάσις at the end rather than at the beginning. If the Origenist grammar of στάσις is static, eventually dissolved by satiety of the minds, rest for Maximus is vividly dynamic, or ek-static. Rest is an indexical, too; as a "relative concept," it refers to "the end of the potential activity in the origin of created things . . . the cessation of motion" (*AI* 15.10). A Maximian lexicon imagines στάσις to entail, *inter alia*, both the attenuation of knowledge and the ecstasy of self abandon.

In *Ambiguum* 7, Maximus composes an epistemological model by which to describe the movement of creatures from being to their end in well-being (*AI* 7.10). This can and should be seen as a *reditus* in some sense, as the giving of the λόγοι, inscribed upon creatures, precipitates motion by way of which creatures can chart their course back to God, the beginning

---

the will and λόγος of God or against it prepared each person to hear the divine voice." *AI* 7.23, 7.24, emphasis mine.

15. *AI* 7.9: "For all things that have come to be passively experience being moved, since they are neither motion itself nor power itself."

16. Each creature has a pattern of motion proper to it: "No being in principle is devoid of motion (including beings that are inanimate and merely objects of sense perception) . . . all things move in either a linear, circular, or spiral manner. All motion, in other words, unfolds in simple and composite patterns" (*AI* 7.6).

and the end.[17] And this happens first by knowing the object of desire, then by loving it, and finally by moving "until it is wholly present in the whole beloved, and wholly encompassed by it." The affective communion between the knower and the known finds its terminus in an ascetical unknowing, "for the soul has nothing left to think about," purged as it is of desire for things created (*AI* 15.8, 71.7). And the extent to which this is possible is precisely the extent to which the soul burns for union with God, "in which all things that are in motion will come to rest."

Maximus hastens to add, rehearsing the Dionysian *via negationis*, that God is "not an object of knowledge or predication" and as such subsists "beyond all thought"—even "beyond all being."[18] How then can there exist any final intimacy between God and his creatures? Maximus charts an eschatological middle term between the Scylla of the Neoplatonic model, whereby difference yields to erasure in God, and the Charybdis of Origenism, in which the gap that yawns between Creator and creation is fundamentally insurmountable.[19] Maximian ecstasy therefore holds together ontological identity and difference by grounding στάσις in an erotic moment of self abandon wherein "being wholly circumscribed, (the creature) will no longer wish to be known from its own qualities, but rather from those of the circumscriber," like air to light or iron penetrated by fire.[20] Sounding his eschatological antiphon, Maximus announces that "just as a soul permeates its body," so also will God's glory "permeate" the saints (*AI* 7.26).

This is perichoretic language, notice.[21] Notice, too, how this account of divinization strikes a sonorous Pauline chord; recall Paul's assertion that

---

17. *AI* 7.10: "For from God come both our general power of motion (for he is our beginning) and the particular way we move toward him (for he is our end)."

18. *AI* 15.8, 7.10. The razor of Maximian apophaticism may be felt in *AI* 10.92: "When we say the divine 'exists,' we do not say it exists in a certain way. And for this reason we say of God that he 'is' and 'was' in a simple, infinite, and absolute sense. For the Divine is beyond closure in language or thought, which is why when we say that the Divine 'exists,' we do not predicate of it the category of being, for though being is derived from God, God himself is not 'being' as such. For God is beyond being."

19. This because Origenism posits an infinite regress of fallen worlds: If the unity yoking minds in primordial rest was not strong enough to forestall their fall, Maximus argues, then no rest will be.

20. *AI* 7.10. It is difficult here to quiet the deafening incarnational resonances to *Ambiguum* 5, where Maximus says of the divine and human natures: "both the difference of the energies and their union are preserved intact, the former understood to be 'without division' in the natural principle of what has been united, while the latter are 'known without confusion' in the unified mode of the Lord's activities" (*AI* 5.11).

21. *AI* 7.26: "In this way, man as a whole will be divinized, being made God by the grace of God who became man . . . beyond which nothing more splendid or sublime can be imagined." Thunberg notes that here "The interpenetration of divine and human

"it is no longer I who live, but it is Christ who lives in me" (Gal 2:20 NRSV). Upon becoming God, the λόγος of the creature does not suffer erasure but rather its "consummation" in which God fully actualizes what remained in potency here below (*AI* 7.27). Still, according to his λόγος, "man will remain wholly man in soul and body . . . but will become wholly God in soul and body owing to the grace and the splendor of the blessed glory of God" (*AI* 7.26). Where the στάσις of the Origenists proves ephemeral and vulnerable to the acids of satiety, the Maximian vision imagines στάσις as the consummate quietus of creation, ecstatically charged with "pleasure, passion, and joy" (*AI* 7.27).

Bonaventure

If Maximus' doctrine of the λόγοι is polished in the heat of polemics against Origenist cosmology, Bonaventure's theory of exemplarism is forged as a defense against the looming threat of radical Aristotelianism at Paris.[22] That defense is gathered around two intimately related anxieties: Bonaventure is concerned first to challenge the notion of a wholly autonomous philosophy, a pattern of thought trafficked among the so-called Latin Averroists, and second to defend God's knowledge of the world against the Aristotelian axiom that God cannot know particulars but only himself.[23] As a corrective, Bonaventure displays his theory of exemplarism in the form of a scholastic *reductio*, or distillation of metaphysical inquiry, to three questions only: (1) why there is something instead of nothing; (2) how the created order reflects the divine ideas thereof; and (3) how do things return to their source. If the metaphysician be true, she will offer an account of emanation, exemplarity, and consummation; if not, not.[24]

---

in Christ is thus reflected in man's mystical union with God." See Thunberg, *Microcosm and Mediator*, 426.

22. One thinks immediately of Boetius of Dacia and Siger of Brabant, both of whom were censured in the Condemnations of 1277 and the last of whom Dante (curiously or ironically) places in Paradise next to Thomas Aquinas.

23. For Maximus on the same, see *AI* 10.101.

24. *Hexaemeron* 1.13 (Quaracchi 5:331). Unless noted otherwise, all quotations from Bonaventure are from Bonaventure come from *Doctoris Seraphici Sancti Bonauenturae S.R.E episcopi cardinalis Opera omnia* (referred to as "Quaracchi"); the English citations reflect my own translation.

Emanation

For Bonaventure the grammar of difference begins already in the very life of the Trinity in the form of emanation.[25] Emanation is itself a drama in two acts—intratrinitarian and extra—with the Son as the leading player (where the first is the necessary and sufficient condition of the second).[26] Both acts presuppose the Dionysian axiom that the supremely good tends to be supremely self-diffusive,[27] and so both for Bonaventure represent an emanation of the divine goodness. That Dionysian pattern of thought, threaded together with the trinitarian theology of Richard of St. Victor, which posits love as the highest good, renders the Trinity the first site in which the "highest diffusion" necessarily unfolds.[28] This the supremely affective definition of self-diffusion demands, of course, as the intimacy God and the world share is grounded first in the intimacy between the persons of the Most Holy Trinity.[29] The intratrinitarian self-diffusion is nothing other than the Father's act of self-knowing,[30] an act that generates the Son. That act

25. It hardly bears saying that Bonaventure stands at a safe distance from historical Origenism, of course; he exhibits no anxiety about using the term *emanatio* to describe both the generation within the Trinity and the creation of the universe.

26. This section owes a debt of gratitude to Bowman's brilliantly detailed piece "The Cosmic Exemplarism."

27. *Itinerarium mentis in Deum* 6.2 (Quaracchi 5:310–311). Cf.:"This essential Good, by the very fact of its existence, extends goodness into all things"; or later, in 4.20: "Perfect goodness reaches out to all things and not simply to immediate good neighbors. It extends as far as the lowliest of things"; Luibhéid's translation, in *Pseudo-Dionysius: The Complete Works*. In *Itinerarium* 5.2, Bonaventure calls the Good the "primum nomen Dei." He continues, noting that while "Damascenus igitur sequens Moysen dicit, quod qui est primum nomen Dei . . . Dionysius sequens Christum dicit, quod bonum est primum nomen Dei" (Quaracchi 5:308).

28. Bonaventure, Disputed Questions on the Mystery of the Trinity, 15–16.

29. *Itinerarium* 6.2: "Summa autem diffusio non potest esse, nisi sit actualis et intrinseca, substantialis et hypostatica, naturalis et voluntaria, liberalis et necessaria, indeficiens et perfecta. Nisi igitur in summo bono aeternaliter esset productio actualis et consubstantialis, et hypostasis aeque nobilis, sicut est producens per modum generationis et spirationis . . . Hoc est Pater et Filius et Spiritus sanctus; nequaquam esset summum bonum, quia non summe se diffunderet" (Quaracchi 5:310–311).

30. Hence Bonaventure ascribes the name "fontalem plenitudinem" to the Father in *Breviloquium* 1.3.7 (Quaracchi 5:212). *In 1 Sent.*, d. 27, 1, a.u., q. 2 connects this name to the *Book of Causes* (which Bonaventure erroneously attributes to Aristotle): "whatever is more prior is more fecund" (Quaracchi, 1:473). In his translation of the *Breviloquium*, Dominic V. Monti, O.F.M. argues that Bonaventure's view of the Father as the fontal source has less to do with Augustine's note on the Father's primacy (*De Trinitate* 4.20.29) than it does with a typically Greek Trinitarian theology, namely Dionysius's in *Divine Names* 2.7: "The Father is the originating source of the Godhead and the Son and the Holy Spirit are, so to speak, divine offshoots, the flowering and transcendent

is exhaustive, too, insofar as the Son receives the expression of the Father without remainder: for "whatever is possessed is given," Bonaventure notes, "and given totally."[31] The Son is, then, the perfect image of the Father.[32] But this similitude is of a unique sort, he hastens to add, insofar as it is in fact identical to the original.[33]

Yet in the Word the Father speaks not only himself but indeed all things,[34] and so for Bonaventure the Son can be called "exemplar," "idea," "word," and "art."[35] As the exhaustive Word of the Father, "it is necessary that (the Son) possesses the Ideal Form, or rather the Ideal Forms."[36] The Word is therefore the site of the eternal reasons, the exemplary causes of each and every created things that are themselves uncaused (as with Maximus), inextricably bound as they are to the divine essence itself.[37] Following Dionysius and Augustine,[38] Bonaventure thinks of these *rationes* as "the origin, the definition, and the termination of what it is to be an instance."[39] And the *rationes* are expressive, too, insofar as creation is performed through them.

---

lights of the divinity." See *Breviloquium*, 35.

31. *Itinerarium* 6.3: "(E)t quia totum communicatur, non pars; *ideo ipsum datur, quod habetur, et totum*," emphasis mine (Quaracchi 5:311).

32. *Hexaemeron* 1.16: "Pater enim, ut dictum est, similem sibi genuit, scilicet Verbi coaeternum, et dixit similitudinem suam, et per consequens expressit omnia, quae potuit" (Quaracchi 5:332). See also *Hexaemeron* 1.13: "Pater enim ab aeterno genuit Filium similem sibi et dixit se et similitudinem suam similem sibi, et cum hoc totum posse suum" (Quaracchi 5:331).

33. Gilson, *Philosophy of St Bonaventure*, 143. Cf. *Hexaemeron* 3.4 and *Breviloquium* 1.3.8 (Quaracchi 5:343–344, 5:212). This is, of course, the fundamental difference between Christian exemplarism on the one hand and that of Plotinus (*Enneads* 5.3.15, 5.4.1) and Philo (*De opificio mundi* 4.5) on the other. For an interesting study on the development of exemplarism in the Christian West, especially in Augustine, see Kondoleon, "Divine Exemplarism," 181–95.

34. *In 1 Sent.* d. 32, a. 1, q. 1, arg. 5: "Sed Pater verbo suo, quod ab ipso procedit, seipsum dicit" (Quaracchi 1:516).

35. *Breviloquium* 1.8.2 (Quaracchi 5:216). Cf. *Hexaemeron* 1.13 (Quaracchi 5:331).

36. *Hexaemeron* 12.3 (Quaracchi 5:385).

37. *De scientia Christi*, q. 2, co: "But since these eternal Ideas are not distinct from the Creator, they are not the true essences or quiddities of created things . . . Therefore, the Ideas must be the exemplary forms and hence the representative likenesses of created beings." All quotations of this work taken from *Disputed Questions on the Knowledge of Christ*, translation and introduction by Zachary Hayes. Gilson summarizes nicely: "The relation of the ideas to the divine substance, considered in its metaphysical origin, is therefore one with the relation of the Son to the Father." See Gilson, *The Philosophy of St. Bonaventure*, 147.

38. His grammar of *rationes* is, Bonaventure makes plain, directly taken from *Divine Names* 5.3 and *Confessiones* 1.6.9, respectively. See *De scientia Christi*, q. 2, co.

39. Mackey, "Singular and Universal," 153.

It follows, then, that these name the mode by which the Most Holy Trinity knows the world. While we arrive at knowledge because of a similitude from without—we know the Brandenburg Concerto No. 2 in F major, for example, first by the vibrations it affects in our inner ear and second by the impression it leaves in our mind—concerning God this gets it exactly backward. If our act of knowing is discursive and representative, God's is generative, which is to say whatever he knows comes to be simply by his thinking it.[40] His knowledge is therefore unbounded, representing all possible configurations of the ensemble of creatures.[41] Against the Anselmian exemplarism of his teacher Alexander of Hales,[42] Bonaventure thinks that in the *rationes* God has knowledge of particulars, too. Still, the plurality of the *rationes* in the created order is logical only, not ontological;[43] they are according to "thing" one, Bonaventure says, but according to knowing many.[44] A final concomitant of this view is that for Bonaventure creatures exist more fully and more properly in God than they do in their concrete existence in creation.[45] This last sounds the death knell for the Aristotelian axiom that God knows only himself.

Performed within the first act—that is, the self-diffusion of the Father in the Son—is the first step from unity to multiplicity.[46] Yet the inertia of God's movement outside himself does not stop in the exemplarism of the Son and its consummation in the Spirit, but rather "explodes outward into

---

40. *In 1 Sent.* d. 35, a.u., q. 1, co. (Quaracchi 1:601).

41. *In 1 Sent.* d. 35, a. u., q. 5 (Quaracchi 1:612). Cf. *Hexaemeron* 3.7 (Quaracchi 5:344).

42. *In 1 Sent.* d. 35, a.u., q. 4 (Quaracchi 1:610). See Wood's detailed analysis on the question of divine ideas among the early Franciscans in "Distinct Ideas."

43. *De scientia Christi*, q. 3, co: "God has a knowledge of all things within the divinity itself as in a likeness that expresses all things, so that in God the ideal causes of things are multiplied not really but only logically." See also Bonaventure's distinction between the ideas themselves and the things ideated, *In 1 Sent.* d. 35, a.u., q. 4 (Quaracchi 1:610).

44. *In 1 Sent.* d. 35, a.u., qq. 3: "Et quoniam cognoscens est unum, et cognita sunt multa; ideo omnes idaea in Deo sunt unum secundum rem, sed tamen plures secundum rationem intelligendi sive dicendi. Unde concedendae sunt omnes rationes in Deo esse unum quid; sed non unam ideam, sive rationem, sed plures" (Quaracchi 1:608).

45. Perhaps more subtlety is needed here. There are for Bonaventure three ways of existing in a thing: (1) in the divine exemplar; (2) in a created intellect; and (3) in the world itself. According to thing in themselves, they exist more truly in a diverse manner; according to their similitudes in God, they more truly *are* than their being in the world. See *In 1 Sent.* d. 36, a. 2, q. 2, co (Quaracchi 1:625) and *De scientia Christi* q. 3, co.

46. Bettoni, *Saint Bonaventure*, 47.

a thousand forms."[47] The *rationes* are therefore enshrined in a world which bears the marks of its Trinitarian origin, analogous to the Image the Son bears to the Father. This is, then, the first scene of the second act; God's necessary self-diffusion is here extended contingently as the creation of the world is performed. The cosmic symphony of creation, we might say, is for Bonaventure the liturgical *responsus* to the hymnody the Trinity chants.

Exemplarism

If emanation affords a vision of self-diffusion glimpsed from the divine perspective, then exemplarism gazes upon the same with sight darkened by sin. Emanation and exemplarism are, to use a warmed-over conceit, two sides of the same coin. Still, it was clear enough to see how, in the Trinitarian phase of Bonaventure's drama of self-diffusion, the Son comes to represent the Father; less obvious, however, is how creatures come to resemble the Trinity. How, then? Here I highlight two aspects of Bonaventure's theory of exemplarism, his grammar of analogy, and the world as *hierarchia signorum*, before returning to the problem of the One and the many.

That the Word is the Exemplar of God and of creatures both trades on the scholastic notion of exemplary causality.[48] As everywhere, the key to this scholastic pattern of thought lies with a distinction, here between *similitudo imitativa,* or likeness of imitation, and *similitudo exemplativa,* or exemplary likeness.[49] If the first belongs to the creature's mode of reflecting the Creator, the second belongs to the resemblance the Son bears to the Father, and, it follows, to the likeness Word bears of the world—it is both "expressing and expressive."[50] Important for our purposes here (and by way of comparison with Maximus) is the active and passive dimensions of this distinction; the Exemplar, bearing a *similitudo exemplativa* to his creation, stands on the active side of expression, whereas the image, bearing a *similitudo imitativa* to its Exemplar, receives its imprint passively.[51] To bear an image is then to be passive to the Exemplar's gift of analogous relation, "the law according to which creation is effected."[52] And because analogy names

47. Bowman, "Cosmic Exemplarism," 183.
48. Ibid, 184.
49. *De scientia Christi*, q. 2, co.
50. *De scientia Christi*, q. 2, co. Cf. Cullen, *Bonaventure*, 74; Bettoni, *Saint Bonaventure*, 48; Gilson, *Philosophy of St. Bonaventure*, 151–52; and, perhaps most importantly, Reynolds "Bonaventure's Theory of Resemblance."
51. Bowman, "Cosmic Exemplarism," 184.
52. Gilson, *Philosophy of St. Bonaventure*, 209.

a relation of two beings that differ essentially, Bonaventure can affirm with Maximus that insofar as the image bears the mark of the Exemplar, "the creature is said to be the similitude of God, and conversely that God is the Similitude of the creature."[53]

Bonaventure thematizes this analogous relation between Creator and created by drawing on two familiar conceits, both known to Maximus: the world is at once a mirror and a book.[54] The world is, then, ornamented with reflections and words, to be gazed upon and lingered over not for its own sake, but for the sake of the Creator. Insofar as all creatures issue forth according to their *rationes* in the Exemplar Word, they exist in him and so equally;[55] yet insofar as they are ideated, ensconced in matter of various densities, they are ordered and arranged hierarchically. Such ordering results in a *hierarchia signorum* of three basic levels: *vestigium*, *imago*, and *similitudo*.[56] While all nonrational creatures—the magnolia, the Giant Sequoia, and the honeybee alike—stand as *vestigium* of the Trinity, the *imago* belongs to human creatures alone; humans as *imagines* possess a special receptivity to God. But the descriptor *similitudo* is reserved for *soli deiformibus*, only those deiform. Before the devastation of the world by sin, the image sufficed to both represent and discern the penmanship of the Word. Here in the devastation, however, we have lost our acumen for unity; movement through the theophanous prose of creation is—like mine through Maximian Greek—stilted and stumbling.

A renewed reading of the *hierarchia signorum* will, Bonaventure thinks, reveal Christ as the "highest and most noble perfection."[57] In the incarnation the principles of matter, intellect, and the divine ideas are taken up into the person of Christ: the Exemplar becomes the Image.[58] Christ therefore stands

---

53. *In 1 Sent.* d. 35, a.u., q. 1, co: "et hoc modo dicitur creatura similitudo Dei, vel e converso Deus similitudo creaturae" (Quaracchi 1:601). The linguistic resonance with Maximus' statement in *AI* 7.3 is worth note: "Φασὶ γὰρ ἀλλήλων εἶναι παραδείγματα τὸν Θεὸν καὶ τὸν ἄνθρωπον."

54. For the mirror trope, see *Hexaemeron* 1.27: "Et sic patet, quod totus mundus est sicut unum speculum plenum luminibus praesentantibus divinam sapientiam, et sicut carbo effundens lucem" (Quaracchi 5:340). For the world as a book, see *Breviloquium* 2.12.1: "Ex praedictis autem colligi potest, quod creatura mundi est quasi quidam liber, in quo relucet, repraesentatur et legitur Trinitas fabricatrix secundum triplicem gradum expressionis" (Quaracchi 5:230). Cf. *Itinerarium* 2.1 (Quaracchi 5:299). For Maximus on the same, see *AI* 10.31.

55. *In 1 Sent.* d. 35, a. u., q. 6 (Quaracchi 1:613).

56. *Breviloquium* 2.12.1 (Quaracchi 5:230).

57. *De reductione artium ad theologiam* 20 (Quaracchi 5:324).

58. Bowman, "Cosmic Exemplarism," 188; Delio, "Theology, Spirituality," 374.

as the "book written within and without,"⁵⁹ the very center of Bonaventure's exemplarism—indeed, the center of the universe. He is himself the coincidence of opposites, and this not only in his incarnation but also in his life, death, and resurrection.⁶⁰ So it is that philosophical inquiry cannot glimpse the hidden depths of the world alone, then, because it is Christ is himself the starting point of true metaphysical inquiry; there can be no autonomous philosophy where Christ stands as "the totality of our metaphysics."⁶¹

Consummation

Uniting the Eternal Art to its dynamic reflection in the book of the world through the coincidence of opposites, Christ reveals the very purpose of creation: "so that the world might serve as a mirror and a footprint to lead humankind to love and praise God, its Artist."⁶² This final phase of the journey into the loving embrace of the Most Holy Trinity is for Bonaventure a twofold process: it entails an intellectual union with the *rationes* as they are in the Word himself first and a volitional (and ecstatic) consummation with the flame of divine love last.

The theophanic structure of the universe is for Bonaventure pedagogical; we are, then, to read the world of signs as ordered to that Signified.⁶³ Yet movement in and through creation affords, as in Maximus, the clinging toward or turning from the Exemplar; use of nature can and often does become abuse. The temptation, Bonaventure thinks, is to fix our gaze upon the surface of creation rather than plumbing its depths. To so fix our gaze upon creation's mirror is to make of all creation a lie, he cautions;⁶⁴ and to glimpse in the mirror only the reflection of one's self, rather than that of

---

59. *Breviloquium* 2.11.2 (Quaracchi 5:229).

60. The first collation of the *Hexaemeron* considers Christ the center: in his eternal generation (between Father and Spirit); in his incarnation (between created and Creator); in his crucifixion (between the depths and the heights); in his resurrection (between immortality and mortality); in his ascension (between darkness and light); in his judgment (between beauty and justice); and in his eternal beatification (between the natural and the supernatural). For more on this topic, see Cousins, *Bonaventure*. Maximus uses this language, too, but indexes it to the incarnation only.

61. *Hexaemeron* 1.17: "Et haec est tota nostra metaphysica." (Quaracchi 5:332).

62. *Breviloquium* 2.11.2 (Quaracchi 5:229).

63. *Itinerarium* 2.11: "They are divinely given signs ... so that through sensible things ... they might be lifted to the intelligible things which they do not see, moving from signs to that which is signified" (Quaracchi 5:298).

64. *Hexaemeron* 3.8: "Omnis creatura mendacium est" (Quaracchi 5:344).

the Word, is to fall like Satan.⁶⁵ This is not to say, notice, that the problem lies with God's creation. No, the problem lies instead with the acids of sin, rendering the analogous resemblance between Exemplar and image to our eyes more dissimilar than not.⁶⁶

We must come to know things, then, in the light of their Exemplar. This is of a piece with Bonaventure's anxieties about the Aristotelian insistence that things find their true existence in themselves and not in the transcendent reality of the *rationes*;⁶⁷ for Bonaventure, as Gilson notes, "all light springs from exemplarism and all darkness from the denial of it."⁶⁸ Because God's knowing is generative in the person of the Son, it remains the condition of ours. All knowledge is therefore guaranteed by the preexistence of the *rationes* in the Divine Art. We know, that is to say, by participating in the *rationes* as they subsist in the Exemplar by which, through which, and in which creation is exercised. Here, where the order of being(s) and the order of knowing are intimately bound,⁶⁹ true knowledge—*plena resolutio*—is glimpsed in light of its cause.⁷⁰ Such is the consummate height of the cognitive faculty: to gaze into the mirror of the world only to discern the face of God, the vestige of the Most Holy Trinity, gazing back.⁷¹

But knowledge yields to desire.⁷² While this awareness of the "simultaneity of form"⁷³ in the Exemplar and the image restores our vision, it is for Bonaventure penultimate. Unity with the God whose effusive love engendered creation does not terminate in intellection, but rather in a *stuporem admirationis,* that is, an awestruck stupor.⁷⁴ Stoked by the white-hot flame of

65. *Hexaemeron* 1.17: "Si vero declinamus ad notitiam rerum in experientia, investigantes amplius, quam nobis conceditur; cadimus a vera contemplatione et gustamus de ligno vetito scientia boni et mali, sicut fecit lucifer" (Quaracchi 5:332). Cf. Bowman, "Cosmic Exemplarism,"188.

66. Cullen, *Bonaventure,* 76.

67. *Hexaemeron* 6.2 (Quaracchi 5:361).

68. Gilson, *Philosophy of St. Bonaventure,* 141.

69. *Hexaemeron* 1.10 (Quaracchi 5:331).

70. *Itinerarium* 3.4 (Quaracchi 5:305).

71. Space here precludes a foray into Bonaventure's difficult (and hotly contested) illuminationist epistemology; I note it nevertheless, as it remains inextricably linked to his theory of exemplarism. For a brilliant, if controversial, study of Bonaventure's illuminationism, see Schumacher, *Divine Illumination.*

72. *Itinerarium* 3.4: "Desiderium autem principaliter est illius quod maxime ipsum movet . . . nihil igitur appetit humanum desiderium nisi quia summum bonum" (Quaracchi 5:305).

73. Bowman, "Cosmic Exemplarism," 189.

74. *Itinerarium* 6.3 (Quaracchi 5:311). This is due principally to the fact that for Bonaventure, as a dutiful student of Dionysius, it is quite impossible "comprehendere incomprehensibilem."

Christ's passion,[75] the heart is cauterized even as the mind passes over *sensibilia* and *intelligibilia* both,[76] resting finally in the tomb of Christ.[77] "Let us die, then, and walk into the darkness," Bonaventure famously exhorts at the narrative climax of his *Itinerarium mentis in Deum*, "let us cross over with the crucified Christ from this world to the Father."[78] Mystical participation in Christ's cross, then, is the quietus of the human creature.

If Maximian ecstasy is perichoretic, then Bonaventurian ecstasy is affective. And this follows directly, I think, from their respective accounts of creation's origin in the Word; for Maximus, creation is itself described in incarnational terms. The embedding of the λόγοι in creation remains for him inseparable from the Λόγος becoming flesh in history, and these from the incarnation of divine attributes in the faithful. (Here Maximus too speaks of intellection's end in a "apophatic indeterminateness" by means of a spiritual crucifixion[79]; his rhetorical thrust, however, suggests this mystical death as a condition for Christ's incarnation in the form of virtue.) For Bonaventure, creation unfolds in love from the start insofar as it is attendant upon and consequent to an ecstatic explosion of intratrinitarian love. Where in the Maximian drama the minds of the blessed are emptied so that "God, the intelligible *sun of righteousness*, rises in the intellect," for Bonaventure knowledge is scorched by the smoldering flame of desire[80]—here there is no sun, only divine darkness.[81]

Conclusion

The differences here canvassed—Bonaventure beginning exemplarism with the Father and Maximus the Son, for example, or their respective emphases

---

75. *Itinerarium* 7.6 (Quaracchi 5:313).

76. *Itinerarium* 7.4. This perfect rest requires, too, since "oportet quod relinquantur omnes intellectuales operationes, et apex affectus totus transferatur et transformetur in Deum" (Quaracchi 5:312).

77. *Itinerarium* 7.2 (Quaracchi 5:312).

78. *Itinerarium* 7.6: "Moriamur igitur et ingrediamur in caliginem . . . transeamus cum Christo crucifixio ex hoc mundo ad Patrem" (Quaracchi 5:313).

79. *AI* 47.2.

80. *In 2 Sent.* d. 23, a. 2, q. 3, ad 4: "Amor enim . . . multo plus se extendit quam visio" (Quaracchi 2:545).

81. This reading of Bonaventure is not uncontested; I direct those interested to the sharp exegetical disagreement between Karl Rahner and Hans Urs von Balthasar on Bonaventure's eschatology. See Rahner, *Experience of the Spirit*, 104–34; Balthasar, *Glory of the Lord*, 2:228–308. For an overview of the broader disagreement with mention of Bonaventure, see Fields, "Balthasar and Rahner on the Spiritual Senses."

in the ecstatic moment—do not finally destroy the lines of continuity between the dynamic metaphysics of the Word in Maximus and Bonaventure both. Against specious readings of Gregory the Theologian, Maximus develops his robust doctrine of the λόγοι, reversing and rewriting the narrative myth of the Origenists. Γένεσις precipitates motion, which in turn finds its end in ecstatic union with the one Λόγος. More, Maximus grounds creation in what I have called an erotics of incarnation; here the creative multiplication of the λόγοι in the ensemble of creatures remains inextricable from the Word made flesh in Christ. Bonaventure, some 600 years later, wields a strikingly similar theological corrective to the errors of the radical Aristotelians. His cosmic exemplarism compresses metaphysical inquiry into three questions which are, in turn, embedded within the drama of salvation history. For Bonaventure, all of creation finds its paradigm in the self-diffusive generation of the Word God speaks; the divine artistry he expresses; and the ecstatic love he displays on the cross. By enfolding the mystery of creation into the Word as its creative source, centermost depth, and final embrace, Maximus and Bonaventure incant the Christic liturgy written into the very structure of the world.

Bibliography

Balthasar, Hans Urs von. *Cosmic Liturgy: The Universe According to Maximus the Confessor*. Translated by Brian E. Daley. A Communio Book. San Francisco: Ignatius Press, 2003.

———. *The Glory of the Lord: A Theological Aesthetics*. Vol. 2, *Studies in Theological Style: Clerical Styles*. Translated by Andrew Louth, Francis McDonagh, and Brian McNeil. Edited by John Riches. San Francisco: Ignatius Press, 2014.

Bettoni, Efrem. *Saint Bonaventure*. Translated by Angelus Gambatese. Notre Dame: Notre Dame University Press, 1964.

Bonaventure of Bagnoregio. *Breviloquium*. Translated by Dominic V. Monti. Works of Saint Bonaventure 9. St. Bonaventure, NY: Franciscan Institute, 2005.

———. *Disputed Questions on the Mystery of the Trinity*. Translated by Zachary Hayes. Works of Saint Bonaventure 3. St. Bonaventure, NY: Franciscan Institute, 1979.

———. *Doctoris Seraphici Sancti Bonauenturae S.R.E episcopi cardinalis Opera omnia*. Edited by the Fathers of the Collegium S. Bonaventurae. Vols. I–IX. Quaracchi: ex Typographia Collegii S. Bonaventurae, 1882–1902. Abbreviated as Quaracchi.

Bowman, Leonard J. "The Cosmic Exemplarism of Bonaventure." *The Journal of Religion* 55 (1975) 181–98.

Clopper, Lawrence M. *Songes of Rechelesnesse: Langland and the Franciscans*. Ann Arbor: University of Michigan Press, 1998.

Cousins, Ewert H. *Bonaventure and the Coincidence of Opposites*. Chicago: Franciscan Herald, 1978.

Cullen, Christopher. *Bonaventure*. New York: Oxford University Press, 2006.

Delio, Ilia. *Simply Bonaventure: An Introduction to His Life, Thought, and Writings.* Hyde Park, NY: New City, 2001.

———. "Theology, Spirituality, and Christ the Center." In *A Companion to Bonaventure*, edited by Jay M. Hammond, J. A. Wayne Hellman, and Jared Goff, 361–402. Brill's Companions to the Christian Tradition 48. Leiden: Brill, 2014.

Dionysius the Areopagite. *Pseudo-Dionysius: The Complete Works.* Translated by Colm Luibhéid in collaboration with Paul Rorem. Classics of Western Spirituality. New York: Paulist, 1987.

Fields, Stephen. "Balthasar and Rahner on the Spiritual Senses." *Theological Studies* 57 (1996) 224–41.

Gilson, Étienne. *The Philosophy of St. Bonaventure.* Translated by Illtyd Trethowan and F. J. Sheed. London: Sheed & Ward, 1938.

Kappes, Christiaan W., et al. "Palamas among the Scholastics: A Review Essay Discussing D. Bradshaw, C. Athanasopoulos, C. Schneider et al., *Divine Essence and Divine Energies: Ecumenical Reflections on the Presence of God in Eastern Orthodoxy*." Λόγος: *A Journal of Eastern Christian Studies* 55 (2014) 175–220.

Kondoleon, Theodore. "Divine Exemplarism in Augustine." *Augustinian Studies* 1 (1970) 181–95.

Langland, William. *William's Vision of Piers Plowman.* Edited by Ben Byram-Wigfield. Ancient Groove Music, 2006. Electronic publication. http://www.ancientgroove.co.uk/books/Piers_Plowman.pdf.

Mackey, Louis. "Singular and Universal: A Franciscan Perspective." In *Peregrinations of the Word: Essays in Medieval Philosophy*, 147–80. Ann Arbor: University of Michigan Press, 1997.

Maximus the Confessor. *Ambigua ad Iohannem.* Edited and translated by Nicholas P. Constas. In *Difficulties*, 1:62–450; 2:2–330. Abbreviated as *AI*.

———. *Ambigua ad Thomam.* Edited and translated by Nicholas P. Constas. In *Difficulties*, 1:2–58. Abbreviated as *AT*.

———. *On Difficulties in the Church Fathers: The Ambigua.* Edited and translated by Nicholas P. Constas. 2 vols. Dumbarton Oaks Medieval Library 28–29. Cambridge: Harvard University Press, 2014. Abbreviated as *Difficulties*.

Perl, Eric David. "Methexis: Creation, Incarnation, Deification in Saint Maximus Confessor." PhD diss., Yale University, 1991.

Pino, Tikhon Alexander. "Continuity in Scholastic and Patristic Thought: Bonaventure and Maximos the Confessor on the Necessary Multiplicity of God." *Franciscan Studies* 73 (2014) 107–28.

Rahner, Karl. *Experience of the Spirit: Source of Theology.* Translated by David Morland. Theological Investigations 16. New York: Seabury, 1979.

Reynolds, Philip L. "Bonaventure's Theory of Resemblance." *Traditio* 58 (2003) 219–55.

Schumacher, Lydia. *Divine Illumination: The History and Future of Augustine's Theory of Knowledge.* Malden, MA: Wiley-Blackwell, 2011.

Sherwood, Polycarp. *The Earlier Ambigua of Saint Maximus the Confessor and His Refutation of Origenism.* Studia Anselmiana, philosophica theologica. Rome: "Orbis Catholicus"/Herder, 1955.

Thomas, Dylan. "Foster the Light." In *The Collected Poems of Dylan Thomas*, 69. Augmented ed. New York: New Directions, 1957.

Thunberg, Lars. *Microcosm and Mediator: The Theological Anthropology of Maximus the Confessor.* Acta Seminarii Neotestamentici Upsaliensis 25. Lund: Gleerup, 1965.

Tollefsen, Torstein. *The Christocentric Cosmology of St. Maximus the Confessor.* Oxford Early Christian Studies. Oxford: Oxford University Press, 2008.

Wood, Rega. "Distinct Ideas and Perfect Solicitude: Alexander of Hales, Richard Rufus, and Odo Rigaldus." *Franciscan Studies* 53 (1993) 7–31.

19

The Oneness of God as Unity of Persons in the Thought of St. Maximus the Confessor

Vladimir Cvetković

Since the appropriation of Théodore de Régnon's[1] distinction between Greek patristic and Latin scholastic Trinitarian doctrine on the basis of the priority given to the diversity of persons and unity of nature respectively, modern Orthodox theology is caught in long-lasting debates over the nature of the Holy Trinity. Throughout the years these debates have moved their focus from the original scope of Régnon's differentiations applied to the Cappadocians and Augustine, to reflection on the Mystery of the Trinity in other patristic authors, including Maximus the Confessor. This is apparent in the recent polemic between Metropolitan John (Zizioulas) of Pergamon[2] and J.-C. Larchet[3] over the roles that the notions of nature and person play in Maximus' thought. This paper attempts to contribute to a better understanding of Maximus' Trinitarian mystery, by investigating the reasons of his identification of the oneness of God with the unity of divine persons. Maximus' development of the idea of one God on the basis of the unity of divine persons is worth being explored as it stands in contrast with the modern Trinitarian perspective that roots the oneness of God in the concept of common essence.

Nicholas Madden aptly remarks that Maximus' doctrine of Trinity is so fundamental to his Christian vision that his Christology and anthropology would be senseless without it.[4] This remark may be turned around

---

1. de Régnon, *Études de théologie positive sur la Sainte Trinité*.
2. Zizioulas, "Person and Nature."
3. Larchet, *Personne et nature*, 207–396.
4. Madden, "Maximus Confessor on the Holy Trinity and Deification," 103.

and it may be said that Maximus' Christology and anthropology are keys for understanding his Trinitarian theology. This is evident in Maximus' treatment of Trinitarian mystery always in the larger context of the so called fourfold definition of God: God as essence, God as energy, God as the Holy Trinity and God as the Incarnate Λόγος. By close comparison of Maximus' fourfold definition of God with Dionysius the Areopagite's *Divine Names* 2.1–5, one may conclude that Maximus heavily relies on Dionysius, who defines God in terms of "united unity," which refers to the Godhead, "differentiated unity" pertaining to the Goodness, "united differentiations" which relates to the Holy Trinity and "differentiated differentiations," which is a clear reference to the Incarnation. Maximus slightly departs from Dionysius, when he identifies the Truth with the divine essence, the Goodness with the divine energy, the Oneness of God with the Holy Trinity and God's uniqueness with the fact of his Incarnation.[5] It would be then pertinent to ask, not in the context of some modern Orthodox Trinitarian debates, but in the context of Maximus' own thought, why, in his view, the Oneness of God is based on the unity of the Holy Trinity, and not on one essence, which in Dionysius' scheme corresponds to undifferentiated "united unity."

In order to respond to this question I intend to investigate Maximus' argumentations on three levels: (*a*) *historical*, against the backdrop of tritheism, which occurred in the seventh century in connection with monoenergism; (*b*) *philosophical*, in connection with a possible resemblance to the Neoplatonic process, which begins in a simple and ineffable Monad and ends in the appearance of the Son of God in body; and (*c*) *epistemological*, in regard to the hypothesis that human reasoning is structured to acknowledge God not on the basis of his essence, but rather on the mode (τρόπος) of his subsistence.

The Historical Aspect

One of the first appearances of Maximus' fourfold definition of God is in his *Centuries of Charity* 2.26–30, a work composed around 624–25, and not later than 626.[6] The passages 2.26–28 deal with divine essence and divine energies. The passage 2.29 is dedicated exclusively to the Holy Trinity, while the passage 2.30 deals with the Incarnation and its consequences on humanity. In the passages 2.26–28, Maximus reflects on the capacities of mind

---

5. *Myst* 420–421: "τῷ Θεῷ ἀληθινῷ τε καὶ ἀγαθῷ καὶ ἑνὶ καὶ μόνῳ ἑνωθήσεται." For the translation, see *SelWrts*, 193.

6. The dating of Maximus' works is according to Sherwood, *Annotated Date-List*, 26.

and reason to pursue contemplative and active life. The active life consists of discernment between virtue and vice, while the contemplative life leads to the knowledge of the λόγοι of the incorporeal and corporeal creation. The mind progresses toward the divine essence, whose nature is incapable to reach, and towards the divine energies represented by divine eternity, immensity, infinity, goodness, wisdom and power, reaching a level at which the human being departs for God ("πρὸς Θεὸν ἐκδημεῖ"). As Polycarp Sherwood suggests, the term "ἐκδημία" pertains to a state of being abroad, and the context in which this term is used here refers to a process of reducing the contemplated λόγοι to One Λόγος, and of entering the realm of mystical theology.[7] However, the next passage 2.29 does not deal with the Λόγος of God, but with the topic of the Trinity. This long passage is a combination of four Trinitarian arguments pertaining to Gregory the Theologian, which Maximus uses in order to counter Tritheists. Gregory Benevich rightly remarks that although the *Centuries* are written long before the Monoenergist crisis, they somehow anticipate the problem of Monoenergism, which goes along with Tritheism. This remark seems to be confirmed by the case of John Philoponus, against whom Maximus appears to direct his arguments.[8] In both heresies it is evident the tendency to ascribe to each hypostasis of the Trinity its characteristic hypostatic property, which combined with the teaching of "particular substances" leads to Tritheism, while in the case of Monoenergism it implies hypostatic energy or will. Since this issue has been convincingly discussed by Benevich, the following discussion builds on his results. Maximus presents two Trinitarian models that inadequately portray the relations among persons and the relation between essence and hypostases respectively. The first Trinitarian model is Tritheistic and it supposes that the existence of three persons in the Trinity implies the existence of three Gods and three origins. Thus, the "1+1+1" divine person would not be one God but obviously three gods.[9] In this model the Father, the Son and the Holy Spirit are seen as three different hypostases, belonging to the same genus and differing among themselves by characteristic properties. As Benevich argues, the problem is that this model transforms the hypostatical properties, which connect the persons, such as the generation of the Son and the procession of the Holy Spirit from the Father, into distinctive properties of each divine person, while it maintains the formal unity of the Trinity through passive essence seen as common genus.[10] The generation of the Son

---

7. See Sherwood's note in his translation of Maximus, *The Ascetic Life; The Four Centuries of Charity*, 89, 248n6.

8. Benevich, "Maximus Confessor's Polemics," 596–97.

9. Ibid., 602.

10. Ibid., 604.

and the procession of the Spirit become individual characteristic properties of the persons that do not relate any more to other divine persons. Therefore, although he quotes Gregory almost *verbatim*, Maximus avoids Gregory's identification of hypostases with properties.[11] Instead of Gregory's formulation of God as "three in properties, and indeed in hypostases" Maximus proposes to confess one God in "three hypostases, each with its characteristic properties."[12] The second Trinitarian model seems to be fully transposed from Gregory the Theologian's *Oration* 20, where he criticizes Eunomius' denial of Son's eternal generation. Although this model preserves the oneness of God, because one God the Father originates one Son and one Spirit, it also may imply that the Holy Trinity is a secondary reality, unfolded from God the Father.[13] In this model the ontological connection among persons, such as the generation of the Son and the procession of the Holy Spirit from God the Father, is preserved, but by distinguishing the primordial divinity of the Father from the derivative divinity of the Son and the Holy Spirit, this model endangers the sameness of the divine nature of the three persons.[14]

Maximus ends the passage 2.29 by claiming that it is necessary to preserve the "one God," who is, according to Gregory the Theologian, "divided without division" and "united with distinction."[15] For Maximus both the division and the union are paradoxical, and they do not resemble in any way the union and divisions among human beings suggested by Gregory of Nyssa's analogy between human and divine persons. By challenging Nyssa's analogy and by proclaiming his Trinitarian model "paradoxical," it seems that Maximus points to the proper understanding of the Trinity. It may mean, as Benevich suggests, that the oneness of human nature, as well as divine, does not secure a single essence.[16] For Benevich the "hypostatic properties correspond to the mutually connected and eternally established existence of the persons of the Trinity."[17] This means that the hypostatic properties are the basis for the distinctions among the persons, but not for

11. Ibid., 509. See also Gregory of Nazianzus, *In sancta lumina* (*Or. 39*), 345.41-42: "τρισὶ μέν, κατὰ τὰς ἰδιότητας, εἴτουν ὑποστάσεις" (three in properties, and indeed in hypostases).

12. *CChar* 2.29: "Χρὴ γὰρ καὶ τὸν ἕνα Θεὸν τηρεῖν καὶ τὰς τρεῖς ὑποστάσεις ὁμολογεῖν, κατὰ τὸν μέγαν Γρηγόριον, καὶ ἑκάστην μετὰ τῆς ἰδιότητος." The English translation from Benevich, "Maximus Confessor's Polemics," 599.

13. Benevich, "Maximus Confessor's Polemics," 603.

14. Ibid.

15. *CChar* 2.29: "Καὶ γὰρ 'διαιρεῖται' μέν, ἀλλ' 'διαιρέτως,' κατὰ τὸν αὐτόν, καὶ 'συνάπτεται' μέν, 'διῃρημένως' δέ."

16. Benevich, "Maximus Confessor's Polemics," 607.

17. Ibid., 606.

divisions because the generation of the Son and the procession of the Holy Spirit from the Father have mutually connected and eternally established the existence of the persons of the Trinity. Although Benevich's reflection is appropriate, it is read into the text. However, in my view, Maximus refers to something else.

The passage 2.30, which deals with abolishing the human differences in one Λόγος, might offer an answer to the question of oneness of God. The "paradox" of Trinitarian union deeply relates to the mystical theology seen above by Sherwood as a process of reducing the multitude of λόγοι to One Λόγος. Therefore, Christology truly becomes the key for understanding the Trinitarian theology as it has been claimed in the beginning of this paper. Maximus employs a Λόγος–λόγοι dialectics. The opposite terms such as faithful and unfaithful, slave and freeman, male and female are at the same time relational terms, i.e., there is no faithful without unfaithful, no slave without freeman, nor male without female. It is impossible to establish identity solely on something that requires something else for its affirmation. Fatherhood is not possible without having an offspring, nor is manhood possible without the distinction from women. In both cases one identifies oneself in relation to others and not in relation to oneself. These are hypostatic characteristics by which one may identify oneself as a person distinct from other humans (*TP26* 276B). If the one single human nature is taken in consideration, then one "considers all equally and is disposed equally towards all."[18] Here, Maximus argues that, by abolishing through love differences among themselves, by recognizing one single human nature and by being directed toward the Λόγος, the human beings are not divided among themselves any more. Thus, if "1=1=1= . . ." by their interrelatedness, common nature and direction toward the Λόγος as their origin and end of their movement, it is possible to conclude that the multiplicity of human beings is one Λόγος, in the same way in which the Holy Trinity is one God.

The Philosophical Aspect

Maximus' fourfold definition of God, seen from a dynamic perspective as a process that begins in the simple and ineffable Monad and ends in the appearance of the Son of God in body, may resemble the Neoplatonic internal activity of the One, which has as consequence the production of various levels of reality, including the corporeal one. However, the main philosophical problem that stands behind the superficial analogy between Maximus'

---

18. *CChar* 2.30. Maximus the Confessor, *Four Centuries of Charity*, 158, trans. Sherwood.

and the Neoplatonic framework is whether the Incarnation of Λόγος is ontologically bound to the Mystery of the Holy Trinity and, consequently, whether we can achieve knowledge of the Holy Trinity from the fact of the Incarnation. This problem, discussed especially in the context of the mystery of Christ from *Ad Thalassium* 60, divided Maximus' scholars into two competing camps. The majority of Maximus' experts, from Epifanovich[19] and Balthasar[20] to Blowers[21] and Tollefsen,[22] consider that the Incarnation of Λόγος is foreordained from eternity as part of the original divine plan. Their opponents, such as Vladimir Lossky[23] and Larchet,[24] argue that the Incarnation of Λόγος is inseparable from the context of the fall and salvation of humanity.

I am inclined to give a credit to the first approach, not only to do justice to a correct interpretation of *Ad Thalassium* 60, but also because the mystery of Christ is an all-pervading theme in Maximus' thought. Maximus is more than explicit in stating that the mystery of Christ as the mystery of his Incarnation, which circumscribes "all ages of time and beings within those ages,"[25] is essentially (κατ' οὐσίαν) held by the Holy Trinity (*QThal* 60, 49–50). Since the Incarnation of Λόγος is part of the original plan of the Holy Trinity for the creation and it includes the action not only of the Son of God, but also of the whole Holy Trinity, it is possible to distinguish two plans that pertain to the oneness of the Trinity: one that points to the unity of actions of the Holy Trinity in the economy of salvation, and another that refers to the hypostatical unity of λόγοι in one Λόγος which is analogous to the tri-hypostatic unity of God. Maximus provides us with frequent examples that the Incarnation as great counsel of God the Father ("Μεγάλη βουλὴ τοῦ Θεοῦ καὶ Πατρός," *CGn* 2.23, 1136A) is accomplished by approval (εὐδοκίαν) of the Father, self-realization (αὐτουργίαν) of the Son and cooperation (συνεργίαν) of the Holy Spirit (*QThal* 60, 49–50). Therefore, Maximus claims that the Λόγος made flesh teaches theology by revealing the Fathers and the Son (*PN* 87). Theology here pertains to the relationship between the persons within the Holy Trinity, and thus is synonym for Trinitarian theology.

19. Epifanovich, *Prepodobny Maksim Ispovednik*, 87–88.
20. Balthasar, *Kosmische Liturgie*, 270.
21. Blowers, *Drama of the Divine Economy*, 267–68.
22. Tollefsen, *Activity and Participation*, 120.
23. Lossky, *Mystical Theology*, 136–37.
24. Larchet, *La divinisation de l'homme*, 84–104, especially 87.
25. *QThal* 60, 49–50. Cf. also the English translation in *CMofJCh*, 125.

The second plan deals with the unity between Λόγος and λόγοι that is modeled by and thus analogous to the unity of the Holy Trinity. This actually means that the subsistence of the created nature reflects the hypostatical subsistence of the Λόγος, and the Holy Trinity in general. The creation reflects the life of the Holy Trinity both by their principles (λόγοι) of nature and by modes (τρόποι) of subsistence. By natural λόγοι, creatures preserve identity in themselves as differentiated processions, while through the τρόποι of subsistence creatures enter in unity with other differentiated processions. Thus, the differentiated processions are distinct if they preserve their identity in accordance with the natural λόγος. Moreover, if they tend toward unification in the higher level of being they subsist in accordance with their τρόπος. If, however, the creatures cease to find unity in the higher levels of processions, then they act against their natural λόγος and contrary to the mode (τρόπος) of subsistence. As a consequence of this, the distinctions that are introduced through the differentiations become divisions. The creatures attain the higher level of unity of the created differentiations by subsisting in accordance to the proper τρόπος. By exercising the appropriate τρόπος they end up in the ultimate unity with the Λόγος of God. The created beings united in one Λόγος preserve the identity of substance by their natural λόγοι in the same way in which the consubstantiality of divine persons safeguards the identity of divine substance. Similarly, the hypostatical τρόπος of subsistence of the created beings united in one Λόγος demonstrates their inseparableness among themselves and oneness with the Λόγος, in the same way in which the hypostatic mode of subsistence of the Holy Trinity indicates the inseparableness of divine persons and the oneness of God.[26] Maximus claims, not only that the Incarnate Λόγος is the teacher of theology, but also that being becomes the teacher of theology (meaning here Triadology or Trinitarian theology), because it teaches the created beings to return from the things caused to the cause (*AI* 10:19, 1133C).

The Epistemological Aspect

There is one substantial difference between the unity of the Λόγος with λόγοι and the unity of the tri-hypostatic God. Although the movement from the multitude of λόγοι to the one Λόγος, and the corresponding movement from

26. *PN* 232–234: "Εὐθὺς καθηκόντως θεολογίας ἐν τούτοις ἀπάρξασθαι διδάσκει τοὺς προσευχομένους ὁ κύριος καὶ τὴν πῶς ὕπαρξιν τῆς τῶν ὄντων ποιητικῆς αἰτίας μυσταγωγεῖ, κατ' οὐσίαν τῶν ὄντων αἴτιος ὤν." Trans. Berthold, *SelWrts*, 106: "First of all the Lord, by these words, teaches those who say this prayer to begin as is fitting by 'theology,' and he initiates them into the mystery of the mode of existence of the creative Cause of things, since he himself is by essence the Cause of things." Cf. also *Myst* 23, 834–839.

three persons to one God take place in us, and not in the created order or God, the first movement is structured according to the contraction of expansion ("κατὰ διαστολῆς συστολήν"), while the second is not (*AT* 1.23–6, quote in 1.24). In the first *Ambiguum* to Thomas, Maximus explains that the alleged movement within Trinity from Monad into Triad, argued by Gregory the Theologian in his sermons (*AT* 1.1–7),[27] constitutes our knowledge (*AT* 1.36–38). Deeply concerned to avoid the negative implication of Gregory's expression "movement of a Monad," Maximus transposes the movement from the immovable Trinity to the human process of acquiring knowledge about God. According to Maximus, the human cognitive capacity is structured to acknowledge first the existence of something, before understanding how it exists or subsists.[28] Thus, before God is understood as subsisting in Trinitarian mode (τρόπος), he is acknowledged as one God by the fact of one Λόγος of his essence (*AT* 1.32–3; *AI* 67, 1400D–1401A).

Maximus differentiates between the processes of acquiring knowledge of human and divine realities. Both processes include understanding of common nature and different hypostases. In the case of created nature Maximus distinguishes between nature and hypostases, stating that the nature has the λόγος of being that is common (λόγον κοινόν), while hypostasis in addition has the λόγος of being that belongs to itself, i.e., it shows a someone (*TP21* 264AB). Due to the λόγος of its own being, the hypostasis is not identical, nor reducible to nature. At the same time if the hypostasis, as acting subject (*TP16* 205BC), attempts to ignore the nature it remains just individual as someone distinct from other human beings by virtue of their own, natural properties (*TP26* 276A). An individual becomes a hypostasis, when directing himself toward the λόγος of God, his own λόγος binds with the λόγοι of nature, such as λόγοι of specific species (εἰδικώτατα εἴδη), of species (εἴδη), of intermediate genera (γενικώτερα γένη), of highest genus (γενικώτατον γένος), and finally with the most general Λόγος of being (*AI* 10, 1177C). The hypostasis appears as the result of merging the individual or particular character of being itself, revealed by its own λόγος, with the consubstantial character of being with others, revealed by the λόγοι of nature (*Ep15* 553B). The consubstantiality for human beings is not just being in union with other hypostases of the same human nature by complying with the λόγος of specific species, but also being in union with other created beings, by complying with the λόγοι of the higher genera and with the most general λόγος of being. The human or created consubstantiality should be

---

27. *De Filio III* (*Or.* 29) 2.11–12.

28. *AT* 1.36–8: "ἡ δι' ἐκφάνσεως γινομένη περὶ τε τοῦ εἶναι αὐτὴν καὶ τοῦ πῶς αὐτὴν ὑφεστάναι." The term manifestation (ἔκφανσις) corresponds to Dionysian term procession (πρόοδος).

understood not in terms of sameness, but rather in terms of achieved oneness.[29] Affirming his or her own natural consubstantiality with other created beings is a dynamic process that presupposes the contraction of expansion ("κατὰ διαστολῆς συστολήν"), whose final result is in attaining the fullness of its capacity in the communion with the Λόγος.

In the case of the Holy Trinity, the divine essence is usually referred to as the Monad, while the three divine hypostases pertain to the Triad. The Monad should be understood as the enhypostasized reality of the consubstantial Triad ("ἐνυπόστατος ὀντότης ὁμοουσίου τριάδος") and the Triad as the mono-substantial existence of the three-hypostasized Monad ("ἐνούσιος ὕπαρξις τρισυποστάτου μονάδος," AT 25–28). I am inclined to understand the term ἐνυπόστατος in line with Lampe[30] and Andrew Louth[31] not in the sense of personal existence or existence in person, but simply as existence or existent, that is opposed to ἀνυπόστατος, which means non-existent. Maximus confirms this sense of ἐνυπόστατος in his *Opuscula theologica and polemica* 21, by claiming that nature which is not hypostasized or without hypostasis (οὐκ ὑπόστασιν) is ἀνυπόστατον (*TP21* 264A). Similarly to nature, which is always hypostasized (ἐνυπόστατος) and it does not exist without hypostasis (ἀνυπόστατον), hypostasis exists only by being in essence (ἐνούσιος) and there is no hypostasis without essence (ἀνούσιον).[32]

However, the process of the contraction of the expansion lacks in the Trinity, because the divine persons do not need to achieve consubstantiality with higher levels of beings before entering in the loving relationship among themselves. Each of the divine persons already possesses the fullness or wholeness of their nature or essence that allows them to enter the communion with other persons exclusively out of love.[33] There is no need therefore like in case of human individuals to comply with the wholeness of natural order in order to achieve a hypostatic way of being suitable for union with the Λόγος. Pierre Piret rightly remarks that the human oneness or union is itself union and difference, because of nature and individuality of human hypostases. In contrast to human oneness, the divine oneness or union is a union of divine hypostases in the difference to their hypostatic properties.[34] Moreover, the divine ὁμοουσία is identical to divine ἑτεροϋποστασία,

---

29. Loudovikos, "Possession or Wholeness?," 258–86.
30. Lampe, *Patristic Greek Lexicon*, 485–86.
31. Louth, *Maximus the Confessor*, 214n5.
32. *TP16* 205B. Cf. also *Ep15* 557D.
33. Loudovikos, "Possession or Wholeness?," 267.
34. Piret, *Christ et la Trinité*, 138.

because it directly refers to the divine Persons in their otherness.³⁵ Therefore, although human rational capacity tends to understand something first by acknowledging its λόγος of essence, and then its mode of subsistence, in God the divine essence is the expression of the Trinitarian mode of being: the wholeness of divine essence is in every divine person and every divine person reveals other divine persons by being substantially related to them.

By way of conclusion, Maximus almost always reflects on the question of the Holy Trinity in the larger context of apophatic and cataphatic theology, Christology and anthropology. Due to historical circumstances, in which he countered the heresy of Monoenergism, Maximus' Trinitarian reflections are largely dealt with in the context of christological problems. However, Maximus develops the theological language that is applicable both to Trinitarian and christological issues, showing that Christology is deeply imbedded in Trinitarian theology. The oneness of God based on consubstantiality and mutually related hypostatic properties serves as a model for the oneness of the created nature in one Λόγος. Thus, the analogy between ὑπόστασις, nature and essence of Christ and the Holy Trinity is not just a useful methodological tool, but rather the key for understanding the structure of reality. In this structure the unity of divine and human hypostases safeguards the oneness of nature, what Maximus demonstrates by offering the examples of the relationship between Λόγος and λόγοι and inter-Trinitarian relations between divine persons. The fact of divine Incarnation pertains equally to the unity of the Holy Trinity as unity of divine activity and to the way of subsistence of created human beings in the Λόγος of God as fashioned in accordance with the subsistence of divine persons in the Holy Trinity. The oneness of both humanity and divinity is not conceived in relation to the λόγος of nature, but rather as a result of the mode of subsistence. Maximus reconsiders some concepts and expressions used by the Fathers. He explains that the proper understanding of the tri-hypostasized Monad, does not suppose the movement of expansion of contracted divine essence into the Holy Trinity, as Gregory the Theologian previously hinted. This movement originates in our cognitive apparatus, which cannot perceive the mode of subsistence in Trinity, before acknowledging that God exists as one. Finally, by differentiating between human dynamic and achieved hypostatic existence and divine hypostatic existence, which wholly possesses its essence and eternally interrelates within, Maximus demonstrates that the loving unity of consubstantial hypostases, as expression of divine essence, secures the oneness of God.

---

35. *Ep15* 549B. Cf. Madden, "Holy Trinity and Deification," 107–8.

Bibliography

Balthasar, Hans Urs von. *Kosmische Liturgie. Das Weltbild Maximus des Bekenners.* 2nd "völlig verändert" ed. Einsiedeln: Johannes, 1961.

Benevich, Grigory. "Maximus Confessor's Polemics against Tritheism and His Trinitarian Teaching." *Byzantinische Zeitschrift* 105 (2012) 595–609. doi:10.1515/bz.2012.0022.

Blowers, Paul Marion. *Drama of the Divine Economy: Creator and Creation in Early Christian Theology and Piety.* Oxford: Oxford University Press, 2012.

Epifanovich, Sergey L. *Prepodobny Maksim Ispovednik i vizantiyskoe bogoslovie.* Kiev: Petr Barskiy v Kieve, 1917.

Gregory of Nazianzus. *In sancta lumina (Or. 39).* Edited by J.-P. Migne. PG36:336A–60A.

Lampe, G. W. H., ed. *A Patristic Greek Lexicon.* 5 vols. Oxford: Oxford University Press, 1961–68.

Larchet, Jean-Claude. *La divinisation de l'homme selon saint Maxime le Confesseur.* Cogitatio fidei 194. Paris: Cerf, 1996.

———. *Personne et nature: La Trinité—le Christ—l'homme; contributions aux dialogues interorthodoxe et interchrétien contemporains.* Théologies. Paris: Cerf, 2011.

Lossky, Vladimir. *The Mystical Theology of the Eastern Church.* Translated by Members of the Fellowship of St. Alban and St. Sergius. London: J. Clarke, 1957.

Loudovikos, Nicholas. "Possession or Wholeness? St. Maximus the Confessor and John Zizioulas on Person, Nature, and Will." *Participatio: Journal of the Thomas F. Torrance Theological Fellowship* 4 (2013) 258–86.

Louth, Andrew. *Maximus the Confessor.* Early Church Fathers. London: Routledge, 1996.

Madden, Nicholas. "Maximus Confessor on the Holy Trinity and Deification." In *The Mystery of the Holy Trinity in the Fathers of the Church: The Proceedings of the Fourth Patristic Conference, Maynooth, 1999*, edited by Vincent Twomey and Lewis Ayres, 100–117. Irish Theological Quarterly Monograph Series 3. Dublin: Four Courts, 2007.

Maximus the Confessor. *Ambigua ad Iohannem.* Edited by Franz Oehler. PG91:1061–417C. Abbreviated as *AI*.

———. *Ambigua ad Thomam.* Edited by Bart Janssens. CCSG 48:3–34. Abbreviated as *AT*.

———. *The Ascetic Life; The Four Centuries of Charity.* Translated by Polycarp Sherwood. Ancient Christian Writers 21. Westminster, MD: Newman, 1955.

———. *Capita de caritate* [Four Centuries on Charity]. Edited by Aldo Ceresa-Gastaldo. In *CSC*, 48–238. Abbreviated as *CChar*.

———. *Capita theologica et oeconomica* [Gnostic Chapters]. Edited by François Combefis. PG90:1084A–173A. Abbreviated as *CGn*.

———. *De duabus unius Christi Dei nostri uoluntatibus (Theologica et polemica xvi)* [On the Two Wills of the One Christ Our God]. Edited by François Combefis. PG91:184C–212B. Abbreviated as *TP16*.

———. *De qualitate, proprietate et differentia, seu distinctione, ad Theodorum presbyterum in Mazario (Theologica et polemica xxi)* [On Quality, the Proper and Difference, to Theodore Priest in Mazaria]. Edited by François Combefis. PG91:245D–57A. Abbreviated as *TP21*.

———. *Epistula xv* [Epistle 15, To Cosmas the Deacon, of Alexandria]. Edited by François Combefis. PG91:544D–76D. Abbreviated as *Ep15*.

———. *Mystagogia*. Edited by Christian Boudignon. CCSG 69:3–74. Abbreviated as *Myst*.

———. *On the Cosmic Mystery of Jesus Christ: Selected Writings from St. Maximus the Confessor*. Translated by Paul Marion Blowers and Robert L. Wilken. St. Vladimir's Seminary Press Popular Patristics Series. Crestwood, NY: St. Vladimir's Seminary Press, 2003. Abbreviated as *CMofJCh*.

———. *Orationis dominicae expositio* [On the *Our Father*]. Edited by Peter Van Deun. CCSG 23:27–73. Abbreviated as *PN*.

———. *Quaestiones ad Thalassium*. Edited by Carl Laga and Carlos Steel. CCSG 7:3–539; 22:3–325. Abbreviated as *QThal*.

———. *Selected Writings*. Translated by George C. Berthold. Classics of Western Spirituality. New York: Paulist, 1985. Abbreviated as *SelWrts*.

Maximus the Confessor and Anonymous. *Ex quaestionibus a Theodoro monacho illi propositis (olim Theologica et polemica xxvi)* [From the Things Asked Him by the Monk Theodore]. Edited by François Combefis. PG91:276A–80B. Abbreviated as *TP26*.

Piret, Pierre. *Le Christ et la Trinité selon Maxime le Confesseur*. Théologie historique 69. Paris: Beauchesne, 1983.

Régnon, Theodore de. *Études de théologie positive sur la Sainte Trinité*. Paris: Victor Retaux, 1892.

Sherwood, Polycarp. *An Annotated Date-List of the Works of Maximus the Confessor*. Studia Anselmiana, philosophica theologica 30. Rome: "Orbis Catholicus"/ Herder, 1952.

Tollefsen, Torstein Theodor. *Activity and Participation in Late Antique and Early Christian Thought*. Oxford: Oxford University Prtess, 2012.

Zizioulas, John. "Person and Nature in the Theology of St Maximus the Confessor." In *KPC*, 85–114.

20

Seeking Maximus the Confessor's Philosophical Sources: Maximus the Confessor and Al-Farabi on Representation and Imagination

Georgios Steiris

It has been repeatedly stated that Maximus the Confessor's (c. 580–662) thought is of eminently philosophical interest, and his work has been approached from a philosophical point of view in a number of monographs. However, no dedicated collective scholarly engagement on Maximus the Confessor as a philosopher has been produced. Although Maximus' treatises reflect a strong philosophical background, prior research has failed to determine with clarity his specific philosophical sources and predilections.[1] Recently, Marius Portaru has systematically attempted to shed light on Maximus' philosophical influences, focusing predominantly on Aristotle and Platonism.[2] Nevertheless, we still cannot fully integrate Maximus in a coherent history of late antique or Byzantine philosophy. Maximus primarily used philosophical insights in order to further elaborate and strengthen his theological views. Besides apologetic purposes, he referred occasionally to purely philosophical topics, which are more adequate to reveal Maximus' philosophical education and knowledge. Among these topics are representation and imagination, which have a significant role in epistemology.

---

1. Gauthier, "Saint Maxime le Confesseur et la psychologie"; Lackner, "Studien zur philosophischen Schultradition"; Völker, "Zur Ontologie des Maximus Confessor"; Moreschini, *Storia della filosofia patristica*; Moreschini, "Sulla presenza e la funzione dell'aristotelismo in Massimo il Confessore"; Roueché, "Byzantine Philosophical Texts of the Seventh Century."

2. See Portaru, "Classical Philosophical Influences."

Maximus' epistemology[3] proves his dependence on ancient Greek philosophy, especially Aristotle, Stoicism and Alexandrian Neoplatonism. A few centuries later, Abu Nasr Muḥammad ibn Muḥammad Al-Farabi (c. 870–c. 950), the founder of medieval Arabic philosophy, dealt with the same topics in his epistemology. He had a good knowledge of ancient Greek philosophy, as it was presented in late antique commentaries. Namely, the principal sources of his philosophy are to be sought in the Greek tradition, in the original writings of Plato and Aristotle, in Neoplatonism and in the Aristotelianism of Alexandria.[4] Most significant is his turn towards the much undervalued Middle Platonism.[5] Al-Farabi followed in the footsteps of the late antique Alexandrine school of philosophy, which blended Platonism and Aristotelianism. Al-Farabi's philosophy has been studied extensively and we have a good idea about his possible sources. There are several indications that Al-Farabi and Maximus the Confessor share common insights, for they resort to the same ancient Greek tradition. In this paper, I attempt to compare Maximus' and Al-Farabi's epistemology in order to reveal affinities and differences that permit us to analyze and assess Maximus' philosophical education.

Maximus the Confessor on Representation and Imagination

Maximus the Confessor's epistemology was influenced, besides Christian thought, by Aristotelian, Stoic, and Neoplatonic philosophy. According to Maximus, representation has a significant role in sensation. While Aristotle discerns representation, sensation and reasoning as cognitive functions (*De anima*, 427a18–429a9), Maximus frequently combines them and refers to sensible representation (φαντασία αἰσθητική). The Mind perceives sensibles through representation.[6] Maximus holds that mental images do not consist of true and indisputable knowledge.[7]

According to Maximus, knowledge originally comes from the senses. Sense knowledge is a divine gift that enables humans to acquire knowledge

    3. Aquino, "The Philokalia and Regulative Virtue Epistemology"; Aquino, "Maximus the Confessor"; Miquel, "Πεῖρα. Contribution à l'étude du vocabulaire de l'expérience religieuse dans l'œuvre de Maxime le Confesseur."
    4. Fakhry, "Al-Farabi and the Reconciliation of Plato and Aristotle"; Gutas, "Fārābī iv: Fārābī and Greek Philosophy"; Vallat, *Al Farabi et l'école d'Alexandrie*, 11–28.
    5. Mahdi, "The Editio Princeps of Fārābī's *Compendium Legum Platonis*," 3; Mahdi, *Al-Farabi and the Foundation of Islamic Political Philosophy*, 2.
    6. Cattoi, "Liturgy as Cosmic Transformation," 422.
    7. Betsakos, "Τα πάθη της φύσης και του προσώπου"; Sextus Empiricus, *Aduersus mathematicos* 7.253–262.

of their Creator (*CChar* 4.10, 1049B–C). Nature, from its part, participates in the formation of sense knowledge since it corresponds to the human sensitive faculty. Maximus supports the idea that nature has its own sense virtue. The soul, according to Ps-Maximus, is inextricably connected with the body and the sense organs. Namely, there are the gates through which the soul receives sense impressions and transforms them into mental images (*Ps59* 17, 251–8 = PG90, 868C). The soul unites the reasons of beings, which are identical with the archetypes found in God's Mind (*AI* 21.8 = PG91, 1248C). Despite Aristotelian teleology according to which the goal of each being lies inside it, Maximus holds that the reasons and goals of beings are in God. Only the voluntary identification of beings' movement with the natural reason of their creation would lead them in their true essence.[8]

According to Maximus, representation has a significant role in sensation. He did not hesitate to combine sense and representation. Moreover, he interchangeably refers to sense or material representation. Representation is a relation (σχέσις), not a process; it connects imaginative (φανταστικόν) and imagined (φανταστόν), while their interaction creates imageries (φαντάσματα).[9] Maximus reproduces Nemesius of Emesa's *De natura hominis*, where Nemesius summarizes key elements of Stoic psychology.[10] Moreover, Pseudo-Plutarch's *De placitis philosophorum* could also serve as Maximus' source.[11] While Al-Farabi describes in detail the cognitive functions of the soul and their implications,[12] Maximus avoids doing the same. He examines representation as far as it concerns the possession of full scale knowledge, which is not fragmented and partial. Sense gathers powers and actions from nature and, with the cooperation of reason (λόγος), imagines nature. Sense representation of the visible transforms the sensibles into

---

8. Betsakos, "Τα πάθη της φύσης και του προσώπου."

9. "Σχέσις γάρ ἐστι τοῖς ἄκροις δι' ἑαυτῆς μεσιτεύουσα, 'ἄκρα δέ,' φημί, τό τε φανταστικὸν καὶ τὸ φανταστόν, ἐξ ὧν διὰ μέσης τῆς φαντασίας, σχέσεως οὔσης τῶν ἄκρων, τὸ φάντασμα γίνεται, πέρας ὑπάρχον ἐνεργείας καὶ πάθους, ἐνεργείας μὲν τοῦ φανταστικοῦ, πάθους δὲ τοῦ φανταστοῦ, τῶν διὰ μέσης τῆς φαντασίας, σχέσεως αὐτῶν ὑπαρχούσης περὶ αὐτό, ἀλλήλοις συναπτομένων ἄκρων." *AI* 19.3 = PG91, 1236A. ("For the imagination itself is a relation that mediates between two extremes. By 'extremes' I mean the capacity to imagine something and that which is imagined, from which, through the mediation of the imagination (which is the relation of two extremes), an image is produced, being the end product both of the activity of he imagining subject and the passivity of the imagined object, in which the two extremes have converged through the relational medium of the imagination"; trans. Constas).

10. Nemesius of Emesa, *De natura hominis* 6.1–73 = 6.55.9–57.15 Morani; Bakker, "Maximus and Modern Psychology," 536–40.

11. Ps.-Plutarch, *De placitis philosophorum* 900B–901A.

12. Al-Farabi, *Mabadi' ara' ahl al-madinah al-fadilah*, chs. 13–14.

meanings so that reason apprehends the reasons (λόγοι) of beings.[13] Sense and representation permits the intellect (νοῦς) to receive data from outside. Sense transfers data to the passive intellect, which receives and transforms the imageries. Sense acts in a way similar to the intellect, since it collaborates with intelligence (νόησις).[14] Maximus combines and reformulates Aristotle's *De anima*[15] and *Analytica Posteriora* (67a39–b11).

Representation refers to the present[16] and the past, never to the future, because it receives natural things in the soul.[17] Under the influence of Platonism, he supports that the product of representation is not true knowledge but a true opinion (δόξα)[18] of beings, their accurate attribution in discursive reason (διάνοια). According to Maximus' spurious work *Capita Diversa*, that kind of knowledge is called divisive ignorance (διαιρετικὴν ἄγνοιαν).[19] Humans receive the product of sense knowledge as an autonomous imagery. Irrational senses provide the soul with a fable image of beings, since they do not have an integrative power. Only rational apprehension (κατάληψις) could lead to truth, because it connects beings and reveals their relations. Imagining the visible helps the intellect to grasp the intelligibles (νοητά). Yet, man reaches genuine knowledge when he finds the truth which is concealed in the reasons of beings (*QThal* 27.83–91 = PG90, 356A–B). The alignment of senses, imageries and meanings does not constitute truth. Representation provides forms and shapes of the sensibles. As a result, it remains in a superfluous level of the being. Only mind (νοῦς), with the assistance of the spirit, could reach the existential depth of beings, the reasons of nature, the connections of beings and their unique reference to God. At the same time, the soul is overwhelmed by the divine light and achieves true knowledge.[20] It is obvious that Maximus reappraises Philoponus' commentaries,[21] when he as-

13. *AI* 10.13 = PG91, 1116D; De Angelis, *Natura, persona, libertà*, 34–36; Törönen, *Union and Distinction*, 160; Matsoukas, *La vie en Dieu selon Maxime le Confesseur*, 89–98; Tollefsen, *Christocentric Cosmology*, 64–81.

14. *AI* 10.11 = PG91, 1116A.

15. Aristotle, *De anima* 3.7, 431a15–17; 3.7, 431b2–9; 3.8, 432a1–14; 3.12, 434b4–7; Themistius, *In libros Aristotelis De anima paraphrasis* 116.10–24, 109.27—110.1.

16. Biondi, *Aristotle, Posterior Analytics II.19*, 172.

17. Cf. *AI* 19.2–3 = PG91, 1233C–36A.

18. Balthasar, *Cosmic Liturgy*, 104.

19. *CDiv* 1384A; Berthold, "Christian Life and Praxis," 404–5.

20. Plested, "Ascetic Tradition," 168; de Andia, "Pseudo-Dionysius the Areopagite," 188–89; Louth, *Maximus the Confessor*, 25–26, 41; Bradshaw, *Aristotle East and West*, 211–13; De Angelis, *Natura, persona, libertà*, 44–54.

21. John Philoponus, *In Aristotelis De anima libros commentaria* 192.21—195.32, 254.23–31.

sociates δόξα and διάνοια. Pseudo-Simplicius' commentary on Aristotle's *De anima* could also have been Maximus' source.[22] In addition, his emphasis on κατάληψις proves his dependence on Stoic epistemology.[23] Although Maximus seems to have been inspired by ancient Greek philosophy, I support that he does not rely on original philosophical texts or commentaries. His wording and the superficial analysis of challenging philosophical subjects indicates that Maximus resorts predominantly in compendia and synopses, like Nemesius of Emesa's *De natura hominis*. Nemesius and Maximus share common insights and their approach on imagination and the formation of knowledge is similar.[24]

Maximus held that will (βούλησις) confers a new triad to volition (θέλησις): imagination (φαντασία), intellection (διάνοια) and end (τέλος) replacing the triad: power (δύναμις), being (οὐσία) and λόγος.[25] While λόγος mobilizes volition, volition is mobilized by the end. Volition reaches the end through imagination and intellection. Will is nothing less than a designated volition ("ποιὰ φυσικὴ θέλησις"). Volition is a kind of overall appetite (ὄρεξις) and drive (ἔφεσις). Volition designates this uncertain volition, which from its part is moved by λόγος aiming at a certain end. λόγος moves natural volition, while mode (τρόπος) alters volition and turns it to intention (βούλησις) with regard to an end-goal.[26]

Imagination is a potentiality of overcoming the power and the personal designation of volition (θέλημα) through the end. Imagination, in other words, is man's potentiality to bring forward goals which exceed his powers. Through these goals, man alters his volition, a rather positive outcome, even though Maximus seems not to appreciate imagination.[27] In his *Epistle 2* to John the Cubicularius, Maximus speaks about how during the Fall the one human nature was fragmented in many opinions and imaginations. He therefore links the imagination of the individual to the individual gnomic will and to the fact that this fragmented gnomic will (γνώμη) and opinion (δόξα) is "post-lapsarian," namely it is a condition following the fall. This condition of the multiple fragmented φαντασίαι seems to be contrary to the

---

22. Simplicius, *In libros Aristotelis De anima commentaria* 285.1–19, 321.5–32.

23. Sextus Empiricus, *Aduersus mathematicos* 7.150–56.

24. Nemesius of Emesa, *De natura hominis*, 6.1–73 = 6.55.9–57.15 Morani, 13.1–65 = 13.68.15–69.18 Morani.

25. TP1 13B–16A; Skliris, "Πρόσωπο, ἄτομο καὶ γνώμη"; Bathrellos, *Byzantine Christ*, 117–28; Madden, "The Authenticity of Early Definitions of Will."

26. Skliris, "Πρόσωπο, ἄτομο καὶ γνώμη," 81–82; Blowers, "The Anagogical Imagination."

27. TP1 13B–16A; Blowers, *Maximus the Confessor*, 161; Manoussakis, *For the Unity of All*, 70.

universality of the human nature. In any case, it is worth mentioning that, according to Maximus, the Fall took place (almost) simultaneously with the creation of the human being (ἅμα τῷ γενέσθαι), so a perfect universality of human nature did not last in the past as a reality. This universality of human nature is to be sought rather in Christology and in eschatology as a final eschatological goal of human nature. Nevertheless, my point here is that the multiplicity of different individual imaginations is linked to the multiplicity of different opinions (δόξαι) and thus to the γνῶμαι and to the fallen mode of existence that is contrary to universality.[28]

According to Maximus, the man who is living within the limitations of the temporal realm can never fully grasp the naked truth of the Word: "Even if he be perfect in his earthly state both in action and in contemplation, he still has knowledge, prophecy, and the pledge of the Holy Spirit only in part, not in their fullness."[29] The fullness of the truth will only be known when he obtains his eternal glory. According to the Scholiast of *Ad Thalassium* 25, God is the source of pure prophecy.[30] Man seeks truth through prayer while prophecy is simply a way to communicate truth.[31] Although Maximus seems to be cautious when he refers to prophecy, he admits that some men occasionally receive mental images without the mediation of the senses. For example, they hear things spiritually (πνευματικῶς). Their imagination is activated "παραδόξως τὲ καὶ ὑπερφυῶς," without any sense perception. Maximus hastened to illustrate that these mental images refer to the present and the past, never to the future (*AI* 19.3 = PG91, 1236A). As a result, I support that Maximus describes a visionary and not a prophet in the classical sense. The visionary could perceive divine truths and not future events.

Like Al-Farabi later, Maximus distinguishes between real and false prophecies. According to Maximus, prophecy requires the ability of distinguishing spirits, so that one may know the true nature of prophecy. Without the proper discernment of spirits, no prophecy should be understood and accepted. Such knowledge comprises the origins of prophecy, its content, the spirit it belongs to, and its goal. Otherwise, it may simply be idle talk. In this case, it may be the outcome of misjudgment on the part of the speaker, or a self-caused impulse, a trait of ingenious, experienced and learned men, or even from an evil and demonic spirit. Maximus reminds us of the sayings

28. *Ep2* 396D–397A; Nichols, *Byzantine Gospel*, 176.
29. *CGn* 2.87, 1165BC. Trans. Berthold, in *SelWrts*, 166.
30. *QThal* sch. 25.12.54–66 = PG90, 340BC.
31. See *QThal* sch. 25.12.56–9 = PG90, 340 B: "τοῦ δὲ φυσικοῦ προσευχὴν φησιν εἶναι τὴν περὶ τῶν ὄντων ἐπιστημονικῆς γνώσεως αἴτησιν, προφητείαν δὲ τὴν ταύτης κατὰ τὴν ἀληθῆ διδασκαλίαν εἰς ἄλλους μετάδοσιν."

of Montanus and those like him. In addition, some people reproduce the sayings of others and speak with great airs, out of vanity to gain admiration and acknowledgment. Their aim is that others might think that they are wise (*AI* 68.2 = PG91, 1404D–5C).³² In order to enforce his views, Maximus resorted to Saint Paul, who claimed that "let two or three prophets speak, and let the others weigh what is said" (1 Cor 14:29 NRSV). Prophecy without interpretation is useless and dangerous, since people would think of the prophet as a mad man. Maximus dissociated the prophet from the interpreter and supported that the gift of prophecy is superior in comparison to that of interpretation.

Al-Farabi on Representation, Imagination, and Revelation

Al-Farabi's epistemology is heavily influenced by the philosophy of Aristotle, its Middle Platonist and Neoplatonist interpretations and variations. Besides Aristotle, Al-Farabi seems to be influenced by Stoic philosophy, especially Stoic psychology. According to Al-Farabi, representation (*takhayyul*) is associated with appetite. In addition to the combination and division of sense–impressions, representation preserves them. According to Al-Farabi, the faculties of the soul are five and not three as Aristotle suggested: the nutritive, the faculty of sense perception, the faculty of representation, the faculty of reason and the appetitive faculty.³³ With the exception of the nutritive faculty, all the others are connected to a desire (δύναμις ὀρεκτική). Al-Farabi followed the general pattern of Alexander of Aphrodisias' psychology, which was heavily influenced by Stoic and Middle Platonist philosophy. While Aristotle never discussed the mimetic activity of imagination, Alexander and Al-Farabi turned their attention to mimesis.³⁴

The faculty of sense depends on the five senses. According to Al-Farabi, the faculty which rules the senses resides in the heart.³⁵ Al-Farabi's terminology, when he refers to the ruling faculty of sensation or to the common sense, is similar to that of Galen, Alexander of Aphrodisias and Themistius.³⁶ In addition, Al-Farabi reproduced common trends of ancient Greek

---

32. *AI* 68.2 = PG91, 1404D–5C.

33. Al-Farabi, *Mabadi* IV.10.1. Walzer, *Al-Farabi on the Perfect State*, 382.

34. Ibid., 383; Rahman, *Prophecy in Islam*, 21; Leaman and Nasr, *History of Islamic Philosophy*, 848.

35. Al-Farabi, *Mabadi* IV.10.3.

36. Galen, *De placitis Hippocratis et Platonis* 8.8.5.1–8.9.19.8; Alexander of Aphrodisias, *De anima Liber cum mantissa* 78.6–21; Themistius, *In libros Aristotelis De anima paraphrasis* 87.1–16.

philosophy when he mentioned a ruler and auxiliaries within the faculty of sense.[37] Namely Plato, Galen, the Stoics, Plotinus and Themistius shared the same description.[38] In the heart there is also the faculty of representation, which is not dependent on bodily organs. Nowhere in his works did Aristotle locate representation in the heart. Alexander of Aphrodisias, under the influence of the Stoics, established the existence of representation in the heart.[39] Representation retains the sensibles, controls them and judges them. Moreover, the faculty of representation arranges the sensibles: it separates and combines them in various ways, even contrary to reality and the sensibles derived from it. The chief goal of representation is the formation of a totalized perception. Its main role is to bridge the gap between perception and reason. It is worth noticing that, while representation remains subordinate to intellect, it has its own independent status. The faculty of representation is associated, as all the other faculties besides appetite, with an appropriate desire, a δύναμις ορεκτική.[40] The Stoics and Alexander of Aphrodisias held similar views.[41]

Al-Farabi held that representation acts in three major ways. First, it represents man's hopes and expectations, past facts, even wishes. Second, it uses and transforms sensibles according to inner motivations. Finally, it be activated by the rational faculty.[42] It is obvious that representation presupposes sense perception, since all its manifestations are based on sensibles. Al-Farabi, contrary to Aristotle, clearly separates sensation (common sense) and representation. Instead, he preferred the views of the philosophical school of Alexandria. Representation receives forms from both common and particular sense perception, whereas common sense only from the particular sense.[43]

Al-Farabi discussed representation because he associated it with divination and prophecy, which from their part are of critical importance for Al-Farabi's epistemology and politics. It was a common trend in Late Greek philosophy to discuss precognition. Besides Plato and Aristotle, where we can find certain indications concerning the possibility of divination, the

37. Al-Farabi, *Mabadi* IV.10.3.

38. Plato, *Timaeus* 70b; Galen, *De placitis Hippocratis et Platonis* 1.8.1.10–1.9.3.5; Chryssipus, *Fragmenta Logica et Physica* 879; Plotinus, *Enneads* 5.3.3–6; Themistius, *In libros Aristotelis De anima paraphrasis* 87.4–16.

39. Alexander of Aphrodisias, *De anima Liber cum mantissa* 97.8–100.17.

40. Al-Farabi, *Mabadi* IV.10.4

41. Walzer, *Al-Farabi on the Perfect State*, 387.

42. Al-Farabi, *Mabadi* IV.10.8.

43. John Philoponus, *In Aristotelis De anima libros commentaria*, 507.16–508.25.

Stoics would be Al-Farabi's chief source.⁴⁴ The faculty of representation lies between the faculty of sense and the rational faculty. In most cases, the faculty of representation deals with the sensibles brought by the senses or is kept busy by the rational faculty and the appetitive. When the rest of the faculties reach their first perfection, e.g. during sleep, the faculty of representation is relieved and turns to the imprints which are preserved in it, connecting or disconnecting them freely.⁴⁵ Furthermore, it displays *mimesis*, reproductive imitation. In this case, the faculty of representation imitates the preserved sensibles, including desiderative forms. For example, when the body inclines towards sexual desire, the faculty of representation simulates the corresponding to the sexual act bodily humor. As a result, the sexual organs are stimulated not by a desire towards a real object. Instead, they are stimulated by an imaginary desire, without any reference to a real object.⁴⁶ Similar views were expressed by Sextus Empiricus,⁴⁷ Plutarch⁴⁸ and Alexander of Aphrodisias.⁴⁹ Proclus mentioned a passage from Porphyry, where the latter connects imagination with bodily reactions.⁵⁰ Moreover, John Philoponus' description of the relation between sense perception, representation and imagination reminds us of Al-Farabi's description.⁵¹ Plutarch held similar views when he divided φαντασία into representation and imagination. Representation provides reason with material from sense perception, while at the same time the rational faculty provides material to imagination, which, in turn, translates into visible and sensible images.⁵² The faculty of representation has to process sensibles and is obliged to transform the temperaments of the body and intelligibles. Moreover, the Active Intellect acts upon the faculty of representation, bridging representation with theoretical and practical reason. The Active Intellect provides the faculty of representation with intelligibles from the theoretical reason and with particulars in the form of sensibles from the practical reason. The particulars reach the faculty of representation without the mediation of delib-

---

44. Plato, *Timaeus* 71d; Plato, *Phaedrus* 248d; Aristotle, *De insomniis* 460b28–61a8; Aristotle, *De diuinatione per somnum* 463b25–431, 464a15; Dodds, "Supernatural Phenomena in Classical Antiquity."

45. Al-Farabi, *Mabadi* IV.14.1.

46. Al-Farabi, *Mabadi* IV.14.2–5.

47. Sextus Empiricus, *Aduersus mathematicos* 7.402–432.

48. Plutarch, *Quaestiones conuiuiales* 705C-705F.

49. Alexander of Aphrodisias, *De anima Liber cum mantissa* 76.18–77.23.

50. Proclus, *In Timaeum* 1.395.22–29.

51. John Philoponus, *In Aristotelis De anima libros commentaria* 507.16–509.3.

52. John Philoponus, *In Aristotelis De anima libros commentaria* 515.12–515.29; Walzer, "Al-Farabi's Theory of Prophecy and Divination," 211.

eration. This is the reason true visions arise from the particulars through the intervention of the Active Intellect. On the other hand, divinations originate from the intelligibles.[53] Visions and divinations concern very few people, especially when they occur in waking state. In addition, the majority of them, which occurs during sleep, stem from particulars and not intelligibles. According to Al-Farabi, the perfection of the faculty of representation enables it to control and process the sensibles. As a result, the faculty of representation is able to represent particulars or intelligibles by visible sensibles.[54] The man who perfects his faculty of representation receives present and future particulars, and imitations of the intelligibles. This awareness of future events and of divine things is prophecy (*nubuwwa*).[55] Al-Farabi supported that, besides those who perfected their faculty of representation, there are others who see or receive all this fragmentarily and others who see or receive only parts of them. People differ in quality.[56] Al-Farabi's views are closer to Plutarch's philosophical explanation of prophecy than to Marinus', who described Proclus' intuitive insights in a purely theurgic mode.[57] Al-Farabi distances himself from Neoplatonist philosophy which accepts the mystical union and rejects any kind of union of the human mind and the Active Intellect.[58] Al-Farabi did not follow Al-Kindi (c. 801–73) who thought of the prophet, the man who receives immediate and valid intuition, as superior to philosophers.[59] Al-Farabi concluded that the ability of prophesying is not always permanent. Some people lose it somehow. Furthermore, Al-Farabi illustrated that many who claim that they are prophets and they can see things divine, are insane and fraud.[60]

The ruler of the state should have reached the perfection of his faculty of representation in order to receive from the Active Intellect the sensibles and the intelligibles. After the perfection of his Passive Intellect, the ruler acquires a superior actual Intellect, the Acquired Intellect (νοῦς θύραθεν, νοῦς ἐπίκτητος).[61] The Passive Intellect is the substratum for the Acquired Intellect, while the latter is the substratum for the Active Intellect. With

53. Al-Farabi, *Mabadi* IV.14.7.
54. Al-Farabi, *Mabadi* IV.14.8.
55. Al-Farabi, *Mabadi* IV.14.9.
56. Al-Farabi, *Mabadi* IV.14.10.
57. Walzer, *Al-Farabi on the Perfect State*, 421–22.
58. Walzer, "Al-Farabi's Theory of Prophecy and Divination," 210.
59. Walzer, *Al-Farabi on the Perfect State*, 523.
60. Al-Farabi, *Mabadi* IV.14.11.
61. Alexander of Aphrodisias, *De anima Liber cum mantissa* 82.1, 90.19, 108.22–109.4, 110.4–25.

the proper collaboration of these Intellects, a man could become wise, a philosopher and visionary prophet. This man is most perfect and the ideal ruler.[62] Furthermore, Al-Farabi discerned prophecy from revelation (*waḥy*), while, at the same time, he connected the latter with philosophy and not religion. Revelation is the union of perfected philosophical knowledge with authentic prophecy.[63] Only the authentic philosopher could attain it. As Rahman states, "The Stoics distinguished the prophecy by divine possession or inspiration which comes without learning on the one hand, and divination by means of rational interpretation of signs[64] accepted only prophecy by inspiration."[65]

Besides this upper class of prophets, there are several others who perceive the aforementioned things partially or in a feeble and corrupted state. Al-Farabi separates the mentally ill who visualize things that do not exist. It is obvious that the Arab philosopher holds that the highest stage of human perfection is attainable through imagination and not reason, which deals with the universals. This evaluation of prophecy approaches Plato's stance as expressed in *Timaeus* (72a), *Phaedrus* (248d) and the *Republic* (9, 571c). According to Walzer, "Al-Farabi represents in this respect, as elsewhere, what is ultimately a Hellenistic or Middle Platonic tradition which may have been drawn upon by Porphyry . . . But the details in his theory presuppose not only Alexander of Aphrodisias' *De anima*, but also the Neoplatonist metaphysics of emanation."[66]

Conclusions

In sum, it is proven that Maximus the Confessor and Al-Farabi had access to various ancient Greek and Roman sources. Namely, Al-Farabi was heavily influenced by the Alexandrian school of neo-Aristotelianism. He promulgated neo-Aristotelianism as the one true philosophical doctrine. His understanding of the identity of the philosophies of Plato and Aristotle is not dogmatic, as it is in Porphyry, but nuanced in favor of Aristotle, as espoused by the school of Ammonius. He created a philosophical system of his own on the basis of principles which he inherited from neo-Aristotelianism and by using the entire array of Greek philosophical thought as his material. Particularly, on the issue of φαντασία, he blended Aristotelianism, Stoicism

62. Al-Farabi, *Mabadi* V.15.8–11.
63. Walzer, "Al-Farabi's Theory of Prophecy and Divination," 207.
64. Cicero, *De diuinatione* 1.18.1–19; Iamblichus, *De mysteriis* 10.3–4.
65. Rahman, *Prophecy in Islam*, 66.
66. Walzer, "Al-Farabi's Theory of Prophecy and Divination," 207.

and Neoplatonism. Al-Farabi did not challenge the primacy of philosophy, although he accepted prophecy and revelation. The latter is subordinated to reason, since Al-Farabi confined them to imagination. In other words, he attempted the rationalization of a key element of the major religious traditions at his times.

On the other hand, despite Maximus the Confessor's preference of Neoplatonism, his writings, especially on cognition, prove the influence of Aristotelianism and Stoicism. I suggest that Maximus does not study in detail the original philosophical texts and their commentaries. Instead, he resorts to compendia and paraphrases like the works of Nemesius of Emesa and Pseudo-Plutarch. Moreover he relies on ascetic writers like Macarius and Evagrius.[67] While Al-Farabi describes in detail, in a purely philosophical manner, the cognitive functions of the soul and their implications, Maximus avoids doing the same. It is worth noticing that Al-Farabi and Maximus present their views on representation in works whose main subject was not epistemology, since their thought is oriented towards metaphysics. Furthermore, they do not simply reproduce ancient Greek philosophy. Instead, they adapt it to their philosophy and theology in order to reinforce their views.

The crucial difference in their projects is the role of imagination and prophecy. Ancient philosophers, like Cicero, Plutarch, Pseudo-Plutarch, Iamblichus and several others discussed prophecy and divination thoroughly.[68] Al-Farabi attempts to rationalize and integrate prophecy in an epistemological and metaphysical tree, despite the fact that he accepts the possibility of foreknowledge. In addition, Al-Farabi connects prophecy with an innate faculty of the soul and does not describe it as a state of possession by supernatural powers. Prophecy permits Al-Farabi to explain rationally the way humans attain high knowledge. His epistemology does not need any kind of mystical union.

On the contrary, Maximus does not need imagination and prophecy in order to establish the road to truth. He prefers the combination of sense, reason and faith, although he does not hesitate to discuss prophecy and diminish it in the status of visions concerning the past and the present, not the future. Maximus seems to follow aspects of Stoic rationalism in combination with Neoplatonist mysticism. While he discusses prophecy, he fails to analyze it on purely philosophical grounds. Although he rejected mystical union, Maximus' theory lies closer to Al-Farabi's revelation and his sources would comprise the later Stoics, Pseudo-Plutarch and Plutarch. We also have to bear in mind that both Maximus and Al-Farabi combine the faculties of

67. Plested, "Ascetic Tradition," 173–74.
68. Walzer, "Al-Farabi's Theory of Prophecy and Divination," 217.

the soul with ὄρρεξις,[69] another proof of their common sources. The original idea was Aristotle's, but it was Plotinus and later the Neoplatonists who discussed ὄρεξις and connected it with the faculties of the soul.[70] Finally, Maximus and Al-Farabi discern the difference between representation and imagination, although the Greek word φαντασία is ambiguous in the context of epistemology. It is obvious that, despite their different perspectives, Maximus and Al-Farabi resorted primarily to the same Middle Platonic and Neoplatonic tradition on representation, imagination and prophecy.

Bibliography

Al-Farabi. *Mabadi' ara' ahl al-madinah al-fadilah*. Edited and translated by Richard Walzer. In Richard Walzer, *Al-Farabi on the Perfect State*. Oxford: Clarendon, 1985.

Andia, Ysabel de. "Pseudo-Dionysius the Areopagite and Maximus the Confessor." In *OHMC*, 177–93. doi:10.1093/oxfordhb/9780199673834.013.8.

Aquino, Frederick. "Maximus the Confessor." In *The Spiritual Senses: Perceiving God in Western Christianity*, edited by Paul L. Gavrilyuk and Sarah Coakley, 104–20. Cambridge: Cambridge University Press, 2011.

———. "The Philokalia and Regulative Virtue Epistemology: A Look at Maximus the Confessor." In *The Philokalia: Exploring the Classic Text of Orthodox Spirituality*, edited by Brock Bingaman and Bradley Nassif, 240–51. New York: Oxford University Press, 2012.

Bakker, Michael. "Maximus and Modern Psychology." In *OHMC*, 533–47. doi:10.1093/oxfordhb/9780199673834.013.27.

Balthasar, Hans Urs von. *Cosmic Liturgy: The Universe According to Maximus the Confessor*. Translated by Brian E. Daley. A Communio Book. San Francisco: Ignatius Press, 2003.

Bathrellos, Demetrios. *The Byzantine Christ: Person, Nature, and Will in the Christology of Saint Maximus the Confessor*. Oxford Early Christian Studies. Oxford: Oxford University Press, 2004.

Berthold, George C. "Christian Life and Praxis: The Centuries on Love." In *OHMC*, 397–413. doi:10.1093/oxfordhb/9780199673834.013.20.

Betsakos, Vasileios. "Τα πάθη της φύσης και του προσώπου στον Αριστοτέλη και τον Μάξιμο Ομολογητή." *Synaxi* 93 (2005) 16–29. http://www.myriobiblos.gr/texts/greek/betsakos_aisthisis.html.

Biondi, Paolo C. *Aristotle, Posterior Analytics II.19: Introduction, Greek Text, Translation and Commentary Accompanied by a Critical Analysis*. Zêtêsis. Québec: Les Presses de l'Université Laval, 2004.

Blowers, Paul Marion. "The Anagogical Imagination: Maximus the Confessor and the Legacy of Origenian Hermeneutics." In *Origeniana Sexta: Origène et la Bible/ Origen and the Bible; Actes du Colloquium Origenianum Sextum, Chantilly, 30*

---

69. Balthasar, *Cosmic Liturgy*, 264.

70. Blumenthal, *Plotinus' Psychology*, 31–37; see also Blumenthal's notes in Simplicius, *On Aristotle's "On the Soul 3.1-5"*, 131.

août–3 septembre 1993, edited by Gilles Dorival and Alain le Boulluec, 639–54. Bibliotheca Ephemeridum Theologicarum Lovaniensium 118. Leuven: Peeters, 1995.

———. *Maximus the Confessor: Jesus Christ and the Transfiguration of the World*. Oxford: Oxford University Press, 2016.

Blumenthal, Henry J. *Plotinus' Psychology: His Doctrines of the Embodied Soul*. The Hague: M. Nijhoff, 1971.

Bradshaw, David Houston. *Aristotle East and West: Metaphysics and the Division of Christendom*. Cambridge: Cambridge University Press, 2004.

Cattoi, Thomas. "Liturgy as Cosmic Transformation." In *OHMC*, 414–38. doi:10.1093/oxfordhb/9780199673834.013.21.

De Angelis, Bernardo. *Natura, persona, libertà: L'antropologia di Massimo il Confessore*. Quaderni dell'Assunzione. Rome: Armando, 2002.

Dodds, Eric Robertson. "Supernatural Phenomena in Classical Antiquity." In *The Ancient Concept of Progress and Other Essays on Greek Literature and Belief*, 156–210. Oxford: Clarendon, 1973.

Fakhry, Majid. "Al-Farabi and the Reconciliation of Plato and Aristotle." *Journal of the History of Ideas* 26 (1965) 469–78.

Gauthier, René Antoine. "Saint Maxime le Confesseur et la psychologie de l'acte humain." *Recherches de théologie ancienne et médiévale* 21 (1954) 49–100.

Gutas, Dimitri. "Fārābī iv: Fārābī and Greek Philosophy." In *Encyclopaedia Iranica*, edited by Ehsan Yarshater et al., vol. 9, fasc. 2, 219–23. London: Encyclopædia Iranica Foundation. Last updated January 24, 2012. http://www.iranicaonline.org/articles/farabi-iv.

Lackner, Wolfgang. "Studien zur philosophischen Schultradition und zu den Nemesioszitaten bei Maximos dem Bekenner." PhD diss., Karl-Franzens-Universität Graz, 1962.

Leaman, Oliver, and Seyyed Hossein Nasr, eds. *History of Islamic Philosophy*. Routledge History of World Philosophies 1. London: Routledge, 1996.

Louth, Andrew. *Maximus the Confessor*. Early Church Fathers. London: Routledge, 1996.

MacArthur, John. *First Corinthians*. MacArthur New Testament Commentary. Chicago: Moody, 1984.

Madden, John D. "The Authenticity of Early Definitions of Will." In *Maximus Confessor: Actes du Symposium sur Maxime le Confesseur, Fribourg, 2–5 septembre 1980*, edited by Felix Heinzer and Christoph Schönborn, 61–79. Fribourg: Éditions Universitaires, 1982.

Mahdi, Muhsin S. *Al-Farabi and the Foundation of Islamic Political Philosophy*. Chicago: University of Chicago Press, 2001.

———. "The Editio Princeps of Fārābī's *Compendium Legum Platonis*." *Journal of Near Eastern Studies* 20 (1961) 1–24.

Manoussakis, John Panteleimon. *For the Unity of All: Contributions to the Theological Dialogue between East and West*. Eugene, OR: Cascade, 2015.

Matsoukas, Nikolaos A. *La vie en Dieu selon Maxime le Confesseur: Cosmologie, anthropologie, sociologie*. Translated by Maurice-Jean Monsaingeon. Néthen: Éditions Axios, 1994.

Maximus the Confessor. *Ad Marinum presbyterum (Theologica et polemica i)* [To Marinus the Very Pious Priest]. Edited by François Combefis. PG91:9A–37D. Abbreviated as *TP1*.

———. *Ambigua ad Iohannem*. Edited and translated by Nicholas P. Constas. In *Difficulties*, 1:62–450; 2:2–330. Abbreviated as *AI*.

———. *Capita de caritate* [Four Centuries on Charity]. Edited by François Combefis. PG90:960A–1080D. Abbreviated as *CChar*.

———. *Capita theologica et oeconomica* [Gnostic Chapters]. Edited by François Combefis. PG90:1084A–173A. Abbreviated as *CGn*.

———. *Epistula ii* [Epistle 2, To John the Chamberlain]. Edited by François Combefis. PG91:392D–408C. Abbreviated as *Ep2*.

———. *Expositio in Psalmum lix* [On Psalm 59]. Edited by Peter Van Deun. CCSG 23:3–22. Abbreviated as *Ps59*.

———. *Quaestiones ad Thalassium*. Edited by François Combefis. PG90:244–785B. Abbreviated as *QThal*.

———. *Selected Writings*. Translated by George C. Berthold. Classics of Western Spirituality. New York: Paulist, 1985. Abbreviated as *SelWrts*.

Miquel, Pierre. "Πεῖρα. Contribution à l'étude du vocabulaire de l'expérience religieuse dans l'œuvre de Maxime le Confesseur." In *Studia Patristica VII*, edited by F. L. Cross, 355–61. Texte und Untersuchungen zur Geschichte der Altchristlichen Literatur. Berlin: Akademia-Verlag, 1966.

Moreschini, Claudio. *Storia della filosofia patristica*. Brescia: Morcelliana Edizione, 2004.

———. "Sulla presenza e la funzione dell'aristotelismo in Massimo il Confessore." *Koinonia* 28–29 (2004–5) 105–24.

Nichols, Aidan. *Byzantine Gospel: Maximus the Confessor in Modern Scholarship*. Edinburgh: T. & T. Clark, 1993.

Plested, Marcus. "The Ascetic Tradition." In *OHMC*, 164–76. doi:10.1093/oxfordhb/9780199673834.013.7.

Portaru, Marius. "Classical Philosophical Influences: Aristotle and Platonism." In *OHMC*, 127–48. doi:10.1093/oxfordhb/9780199673834.013.5.

CDiv   Pseudo-Maximus the Confessor. *Diuersa capita ad theologiam et oeconomiam spectantia deque uirtute et uitio (xxvi-d)*. Edited by François Combefis. PG90:1188A9–392A.

Rahman, Fazlur. *Prophecy in Islam: Philosophy and Orthodoxy*. London: Allen & Unwin, 1958.

Roueché, Mossman. "Byzantine Philosophical Texts of the Seventh Century." *Jahrbuch der Österreichischen Byzantinistik* 23 (1974) 61–76.

Simplicius. *On Aristotle's "On the Soul 3.1–5"*. Translated by Henry J. Blumenthal. The Ancient Commentators on Aristotle. London: Duckworth, 2000.

Skliris, Dionysios. "Πρόσωπο, ἄτομο καὶ γνώμη στὴ σκέψη τοῦ ἁγίου Μαξίμου τοῦ Ὁμολογητή." *Theologia* 84 (2013) 65–123.

Tollefsen, Torstein. *The Christocentric Cosmology of St. Maximus the Confessor*. Oxford Early Christian Studies. Oxford: Oxford University Press, 2008.

Törönen, Melchisedec. *Union and Distinction in the Thought of St. Maximus the Confessor*. Oxford Early Christian Studies. Oxford: Oxford University Press, 2007.

Vallat, Philippe. *Al Farabi et l'école d'Alexandrie: Des prémisses de la connaissance à la philosophie politique*. Études musulmanes 38. Paris: Vrin, 2004.

Völker, Walther. "Zur Ontologie des Maximus Confessor." In . . . *und fragten nach Jesus: Beitrage aus Theologie, Kirche und Geschichte; Festschrift fur Ernst Barnikol zum 70 Geburtstag*, edited by Udo Meckert et al., 57–79. Berlin: Evangelische Verlagsanstalt, 1964.

Walzer, Richard Rudolf. *Al-Farabi on the Perfect State*. Oxford: Clarendon, 1985.

———. "Al-Farabi's Theory of Prophecy and Divination." In *Greek into Arabic: Essays on Islamic Philosophy*, 206–19. Oriental Studies 1. Oxford: B. Cassirer, 1962.

APPENDIX

Philosophy and Theology—the Byzantine Model

Statement on the Round Table
"Revisiting the Theology-Philosophy Divide"

Georgi Kapriev

The "theology-philosophy" differentiation regarding Byzantine culture does not need so much revising, but rather adequate defining according to the criteria of this culture. I will take the opportunity to express some basic positions, leading to such definitions.

At first, a denial should be stated; a denial of the scholastic division of philosophy and theology, which is not valid even for the early Latin Middle Ages, but is nevertheless applied by the first generation of scholars of Byzantine philosophical culture (Erhard, Beck, Hunger). This leads on to declaring that Byzantine theology is once for all competent in the field of metaphysics. According to such claims, philosophy itself lacks any creativity whatsoever. Podskalsky's thesis that the criterion for differentiating philosophy and theology should be methodology, and not the issues discussed, is the first step in searching for the peculiarity of philosophy and theology in Byzantium. But there are more steps to be taken.

What is theology, from the Byzantine point of view? In order to answer, one should make a distinction, which, in its most rough form, allows delineating at least two types of theology. In the first place, theology is self-revelation of God, accessible in the form of personal spiritual and mystical experience within the sacramental life of the Church. The fundamental manifestation of this unutterable *per se* experience is dogmatic theology, which in turn necessarily rests on the discursive tradition of Christian mentality. Speculative theology, determined explicitly as part of the first philosophy by Photios at the latest, opens up a different perspective. Although Eastern Christian thought, from the Cappadocians to Photios and his heirs, is characterized by the simultaneous development of both these perspectives, the beginning of the eleventh century marks the formation of two really antagonistic lines, which can be labeled as theocentric and anthropocentric. Each of them claims to be perfectly true in regard to both theology and philosophy, and blames the other one of incompetence.

The question "what is philosophy" does not have a clear answer either. Several usages of the term are to be distinguished here. In relation to theology as a mystical experience one should mention first "practical philosophy," in the sense implied by Symeon the New Theologian and Nicetas Stethatos. Starting point of this philosophy are the ascetic virtues and the overcoming of fleshly thoughts. The spiritually illuminated person ascends to true and subtle knowledge of being, of things divine and human, as well as to a right comprehension of doctrines. According to this philosophy, to philosophize before one is born of the Spirit and to rely on one's own reason only, especially in regard to divine and spiritual matters, is inadequate and blameworthy—in this life and beyond.

On the contrary, theoretical philosophy is based on human reason and its standpoint is the scientific knowledge (episteme) of being and of the principles and causes of the world. This philosophy is considered pivotal also for theology, accessible to human reason. It claims the ability to correctly formulate theological positions and to articulate them adequately through universally valid conceptual framework. The conflicts between representatives of both trends throughout history are well known.

The decisive step to reconcile this futile strife is taken by Gregory Palamas and his contemporaries. For both, the systematic hesychasts of the fourteenth century, as well as their opponents, the difference between true and correct thinking is already obvious. In view of the solid and extremely subtle conceptual framework of theology by that time, Palamas constructs a rational approach to systematic conceptualizing and philosophical validation of mystical experience. The model, formed by the two trends, is not destroyed but asserted on a different level. This tendency asserts itself and culminates with the work of Georgios Scholarios.

Until very recently, theoretical philosophy in Byzantium was interpreted as a unified tradition. It was only newly that one started to actively discuss the real plurality of different philosophical "projects," "the multifaceted profile" of Byzantine philosophy. To be sure, the awareness of plurality should not hinder the systematization and classification of the different programs. In my view, a primary, basic systematization is the one stemming from the differentiation between "philosophy in Byzantium" and "Byzantine philosophy."

By "philosophy in Byzantium" I mean the totality of all philosophical projects in Byzantine culture. With "Byzantine philosophy," on the contrary, I describe the programs which consciously focus their philosophical interest on the act, using the energy-concept as a pillar. In my consideration this peculiar nuance of metaphysical speculation is a specific contribution of philosophical culture in Byzantium—more radical than that of other programs. It should be immediately stated that "Byzantine philosophy" is not necessarily identical with the theocentric line in Byzantine mentality.

The contemporary approach to theology and philosophy in Byzantium should take into consideration their post-Byzantine fate. It seems that theology has been preserved; it must be admitted, however, that until as late as the twentieth century, theology was deprived of the creativity it had been marked by before the sixteenth century. In the course of time it adopted biased conservatism, empty formulae and enthusiastic rhetoric, sparking itself by superficial confrontation with the theological and philosophical culture of the West. Opening of gaps at any costs and the complacent self-isolation, falsely seen as uniqueness, are now typical. Even worse is the fate of philosophy: it simply disappeared. Around the middle of the eighteenth century, the attempts to philosophize according to the model of what is herein called "Byzantine philosophy" were completely abandoned, being replaced by the Western philosophical paradigms.

In the twentieth century one can identify two equally tendentious lines. The first line declares itself for self-sufficient non-communicative theology, intentionally renouncing philosophy. Still widespread is the approach, this is namely the second line, which deprives the philosophy from the innate theological issues and debates. Attempts are being made to discuss its tools and conceptual framework, apart from its context and motivation.

The task of the present day, our task is to overcome the prejudice and to renounce any shibboleths, any ideological identifications and oppositions. Our duty is to produce the dioptric for seeing theology and philosophy in their proper levels, as well as to specify the points of confrontation, but also of co-operation between them, always keeping in mind the context of Byzantine culture, with its historical dynamics and peculiarities.

—Translated from Bulgarian by Smilen Markov

Index

Al-Farabi, 325–27, 330–40
Anaxagoras, 35–42, 44, 46, 55–56
Aristotelianism, 6, 9, 16, 18, 301,
    326, 335–36
Aristotle, 4, 5, 6, 8, 9, 14, 15, 21, 26,
    30, 33, 36, 41, 60–61, 67–78,
    92–93, 100, 112, 126, 138,
    139, 175, 181–82, 191, 195,
    255, 261, 276, 277–79, 281,
    283, 286, 288–89, 301–2,
    304, 308, 325, 337–39
Augustine, 3–4, 13, 51, 144, 291,
    302, 303, 311, 313

Bonaventure, 291–92, 301, 302,
    303–11
Brague, Rémi, 70, 75, 136, 137, 144
Byzantine, 3–4, 14, 18, 21, 67, 68,
    105, 112, 136, 137, 171–72,
    176, 182, 184, 195, 197, 199–
    201, 207, 230, 233, 260, 263,
    273, 275–77, 325, 329, 330,
    337, 339, 342–44

Cappadocian, 5, 100–101, 112, 162,
    175, 179, 186
cause, 11, 15, 24, 26, 29, 38–44, 72,
    75, 79, 80, 82, 84–87, 89–91,
    93, 105, 139–40, 189, 240,
    248, 282–83, 287, 294, 296,
    308, 319
Chalcedon, 103, 163–64, 180, 205,
    206
change, 37, 39, 42, 51, 66, 69, 70–72,
    77, 78, 79, 85, 92, 105, 119,
    122, 164, 174, 209, 210, 237,
    241, 242, 255, 263

communion, 11, 30, 31, 60, 65, 73,
    81–84, 85, 87–89, 91–93,
    104, 182, 188, 250, 257, 259,
    268, 271, 273, 300, 321
contemplation, 29, 63, 64, 66, 117,
    122, 136, 138, 139–44, 151,
    165, 169, 227, 252, 253, 284,
    285, 330
contraction, 27, 29, 164, 288, 320,
    321
created, 7, 10–11, 19, 25–29, 32–33,
    41, 43–44, 48, 51, 54–55,
    60–65, 67, 70, 73, 74, 78, 80,
    82–86, 90, 92, 100, 103–104,
    116, 121, 124–26, 129, 143,
    149, 153, 156–57, 167, 169,
    184, 188, 193, 200, 226, 229,
    238, 239, 247, 250, 258,
    259, 264, 266, 269–73, 276,
    279, 282, 284–88, 294, 296,
    299–301, 303–4, 306–7,
    319–22, 335
createdness, 79, 82, 83, 84, 89, 93
creatio ex nihilo, 72, 293, 296, 299
creation, 11–12, 14, 25, 27, 31–32,
    36, 39, 49, 51, 54, 59–62,
    64–67, 70, 72–74, 78, 82,
    84, 86, 87, 89, 92–93, 101–8,
    110, 118, 123, 125, 162–63,
    165–69, 235–239, 241,
    248–49, 259, 261–66, 269,
    273, 275, 278–79, 284–85,
    287, 291–94, 296, 298–310,
    315, 318–19, 327, 330
Crucifixion, 11–14, 16, 18

Damascene, John, 163, 181

338 INDEX

deification, 55, 60, 62–63, 74, 91–92, 102, 111, 194, 264, 266
dialectic, 6, 8–9, 11–12, 14, 18–20, 103, 116, 122, 124, 125, 127, 132–33, 154, 178, 256, 257, 285
difference, 29–32, 42, 46, 53, 59, 72, 78, 92, 93, 102, 103–4, 106, 114, 116–17, 120–21, 123, 126–27, 132–33, 138, 144, 177–79, 181, 186, 190, 194, 206, 213–15, 236, 241–43, 257, 287, 293–96, 298, 300, 302–3, 319, 321, 336, 337, 343
division, 12, 16, 20, 27, 59, 66, 72, 100, 102, 104, 164, 177, 207, 214, 239, 240, 242–43, 252, 287, 296, 300, 316, 331, 342

eighth day, 14
eschatology, 6–14, 17, 18, 19, 41, 46, 78, 93, 99, 106–7, 109, 110–11, 130, 194, 235, 241, 243–44, 263, 266, 279, 282–83, 285, 288, 300, 309, 330
essence, 19–20, 25, 27, 28, 30–31, 59, 60, 62, 73–74, 78, 86–87, 101, 117–18, 121, 123–24, 127, 129, 145–46, 148–49, 151, 153, 155–57, 163–64, 166, 173–77, 179–86, 188, 189, 226, 229, 247, 252–256, 259, 266, 269, 274, 284, 286, 303, 313–16, 319, 320–22, 327
ever-moving repose, 78, 84, 88–89, 91–92
στάσις ἀεικίνητος, 78, 84, 88, 91
evil, 7, 8, 12, 14, 49, 53, 65, 83, 189, 191, 217, 227, 237, 238, 252, 285, 293, 298, 330
existence, 10–11, 17, 26, 27, 28, 40, 48, 49, 51–53, 55, 60–62, 64–67, 73, 77, 79, 80–83, 85–90, 92, 93, 100, 119, 121, 122, 125, 127, 140, 143, 152, 153, 154, 155, 163–67, 169, 173, 175–76, 180, 181–86, 188–90, 192–95, 209, 214, 236–39, 241, 243, 250–54, 257–59, 266, 269, 271, 284–85, 293, 302, 304, 308, 315–17, 319–22, 330, 332

faculty, 4, 11, 138, 215, 279, 280, 308, 327, 331, 332, 333, 334, 336
felix culpa, 12–13

Garrigues, Jean-Miguel, 3, 4, 21, 186, 200, 230
Gnosticism, 6
Gregory of Nyssa, 8, 26, 43, 78, 93, 95, 100, 102–4, 112–13, 146, 148, 150–51, 153, 157, 172, 198, 206, 236, 237, 238, 242, 292, 316

Hadot, Pierre, 140–42, 144, 252–253
Heidegger, Martin, 36, 41, 52, 56, 101, 112, 114, 134, 146–47, 156–58, 191, 195, 247, 254, 255–56, 260
Heraclitus, 37, 42, 255
history, 4–9, 11–13, 18, 36, 40, 44, 46, 49, 52, 54–55, 61–67, 75–76, 99, 106, 110–12, 140, 144, 147, 150, 179, 189, 192, 193, 222, 252, 256, 260, 264, 290, 292, 309–11, 325, 331, 338, 343
History, 59
holomerism, 26, 28
humanity, 12, 17, 19, 31, 33, 40, 46, 55, 67, 83, 105, 111, 117, 118, 122, 123, 129, 142, 148–49, 177, 193, 195, 205, 216, 240, 248, 271, 280, 283–85, 288, 314, 318, 322
hypostasis, 6, 11, 18, 25, 31, 59, 61, 116, 117, 119–23, 127, 129, 130, 133, 163, 165, 173–75, 177–81, 184, 185–86, 188–92, 194–95, 200, 206,

208–14, 217, 266, 269, 276, 296, 302, 315, 320–21
hypostatic, 10–11, 13, 62, 66–67, 103, 104, 111, 116, 119–21, 123, 127, 130–33, 163, 173, 177–80, 186, 189, 190, 192–94, 209–10, 251, 257, 259, 276, 296, 315–17, 318, 319, 321, 322
ὑπόστασις, 120–21, 130, 163, 166, 175, 177, 179–84, 189, 190, 276

intellect, 7, 11, 15, 17, 63–64, 66, 90, 129, 137–39, 142–44, 152–53, 185, 224, 225, 226, 227, 228, 229, 249, 252, 304, 306, 309, 328, 332

Kant, Immanuel, 39, 75, 147, 256, 281–82, 288, 289
Kierkegaard, Søren, 35–37, 40, 42, 44, 46, 48–56, 58
knowledge, 17, 37, 40, 63–65, 82, 86, 87, 111, 124–27, 129–31, 137–38, 140–41, 147, 151, 153, 220, 223–26, 228, 240, 242, 250, 253, 271, 294, 299, 300–301, 304, 308, 309, 315, 318, 320, 325, 326, 327, 328, 329, 330, 335, 336, 343

Lacan, Jacques, 19, 247, 253, 256, 257, 258, 259
language, 7, 35, 44, 54, 77, 79, 85, 87–89, 99–106, 110, 121, 125, 130, 137, 140, 147, 152–54, 163–64, 182, 211–14, 216, 218, 219–20, 229, 237, 255–56, 258, 263, 272, 276, 279, 282, 285, 298, 300, 307, 322
Late Antiquity, 4–6, 140
Lossky, Vladimir, 149, 157, 318, 323
Loudovikos, Nikolaos, 4, 9–10, 19, 21, 73, 75, 78–80, 82–84, 86–87, 94, 171–72, 196, 247, 250–51, 256, 259, 260, 266, 269, 277, 280, 286, 289, 321, 323
Louth, Andrew, 72, 76, 80–81, 83, 94, 114, 120, 134, 158, 162, 166, 169, 237–42, 244, 283, 289, 310, 321, 323, 328, 338
love, 11, 15, 16, 17, 48, 64–65, 67, 73, 85, 86, 105, 111, 178, 182–83, 185, 227, 248–50, 252, 254, 257, 258, 265, 288, 296, 298, 302, 307–10, 317, 321

MacIntyre, Alasdair, 281, 289
metaphysics, 5, 6, 8, 15, 16, 17, 18, 20, 27, 28, 32–33, 35–36, 38–39, 49, 67, 100, 103, 126, 193, 218, 307, 310, 335, 336, 342
methodology, 41, 201, 342
mode, 9–11, 13–16, 19–20, 59, 62, 67, 69, 81–82, 87, 92, 93, 100, 105, 116, 119–22, 131, 140, 147, 163–64, 166–69, 184–86, 189–90, 193–95, 207, 215, 227, 236–238, 240–41, 243–44, 250–51, 266, 275, 284, 288, 298, 300, 304–5, 314, 319–20, 322, 329–30, 334
Monothelitism, 7, 8
motion, 9, 27, 38–42, 44, 46, 48, 52, 54–55, 69–74, 77–93, 99, 101–2, 104, 106, 119, 149, 167–68, 247–49, 298–300, 310

nature, 4–7, 9, 10–11, 13–16, 18, 28–29, 30–32, 42–43, 46, 54–55, 60, 63–64, 66–67, 70–73, 79, 81–86, 88–93, 99, 104–5, 115–19, 121–27, 129–38, 141, 151–52, 154, 162–201, 207, 214–16, 221–22, 226, 228–29, 235–36, 237–43, 247–48, 253, 255, 264–66, 269, 271, 274–76, 279–86, 287–89, 293, 299,

307, 313, 315–23, 327–29, 330
Neoplatonism, 6, 9, 16, 18, 22, 292, 296, 326, 336
Neoplatonic, 8, 26, 35, 48–49, 215, 218, 243, 300, 314, 317–18, 326, 337

ontology, 1, 7, 9, 13, 19, 21–22, 27, 29, 31–32, 35, 40–41, 44, 59–63, 65, 67, 68–69, 72–75, 78–80, 82–84, 86–87, 93–95, 102–3, 105, 114, 120, 122, 125, 147–48, 162, 172, 183, 188, 196–97, 201, 244, 247, 250–52, 254, 260, 266, 269, 277, 280–81, 283–86, 288–89, 293, 295, 300, 304, 316
Origen, 35, 48–49, 51–52, 54–55, 58, 60, 73–75, 111, 175, 285, 296, 337
Origenism, 22, 35, 36, 46, 49, 54, 58, 113, 135, 170, 243, 290, 292, 296, 298, 300, 302, 312
origination, 77, 79–80, 89–90, 163
Orthodox, 4, 21, 23, 75, 94, 145, 148, 172, 174, 192, 196–97, 231, 260, 263–66, 277, 278, 289, 313–14, 337

Palamas, Gregory, 4, 22, 105, 112, 172, 181, 197, 266, 275, 292, 311, 343
particulars, 25–32, 83, 221, 301, 304, 333, 334
perception, 29, 65, 122, 129, 228, 249, 299, 330, 331, 332, 333
Plato, 39, 41, 43, 48, 58, 71, 73–74, 77, 100, 112, 137, 141, 147, 148, 151, 157, 162, 255, 326, 332, 333, 335, 338
Plotinus, 6, 7, 8, 21, 22, 41, 49, 51, 60, 217, 247, 251, 252, 253, 254, 260, 303, 332, 337, 338
Porphyry, 6, 26, 27, 33, 60, 68, 126, 208, 217, 333, 335
psychology, 4, 171, 251, 327, 331

relational, 30, 61, 63, 125, 142, 143, 178, 181, 182, 183, 184, 186, 256, 257, 266, 268, 274, 275, 317, 327
Roman Empire, 5

secularization, 9, 247
sexual, 66, 235, 236, 237, 238, 239, 240, 242, 243, 333
Sherwood, Polycarp, 8, 16, 22, 35, 54, 58, 78, 80, 95, 104, 113, 118, 135, 163, 170, 186, 199, 203, 234, 262, 276, 278, 284, 285, 290, 292, 312, 314, 315, 317, 323, 324
Socrates, 39, 40, 41, 42, 43, 53, 54
Sorabji, Richard, 4, 99, 113

teleology, 5, 6, 7, 9, 11, 14, 15, 16, 18, 39, 62, 327
Thunberg, Lars, 29, 33, 104, 113–14, 120–23, 125, 127, 135, 140, 144, 200, 234–35, 240, 244, 284, 290, 293, 296, 300–301, 312
transcendence, 20, 85, 102, 106, 115, 117, 120–22, 125, 127, 130–33, 253, 254, 255, 256, 257, 294

universals, 25, 26, 27, 28, 31, 335

voluntarism, 4, 18, 279, 280

Yannaras, Christos, 4, 11, 23, 83, 95, 156, 157, 158

Zizioulas, Metropolitan John of Pergamon, 11–13, 23, 172, 196, 198, 200–201, 234, 260, 289, 313, 323, 324

κίνησις, 35–38, 40–42, 44, 46, 51–52, 55, 63, 69–70, 74, 77–78, 80–81, 83, 85, 90, 293, 298
λόγος, 4, 9–16, 18, 19, 25, 26, 27, 28, 29, 30, 31, 43, 61–63, 79, 80–81, 85–87, 100, 118, 120,

122, 140, 144, 153, 162–69,
176, 184–86, 188–92, 194,
236, 237, 240–43, 247, 249,
255, 266, 269–71, 273, 280,
283–88, 294, 298–99, 301,
319, 320, 322, 327, 329
λόγοι, 10–12, 14, 16, 19, 25–33,
41–43, 62, 73, 81, 83, 85,
91, 102, 111, 118–19, 126,
139–40, 142–44, 162–63,
165–66, 168–69, 186, 188,
190, 193, 236, 241, 243,
249–50, 261, 266, 268–71,
273, 276, 286–87, 291–96,
298–99, 301, 309–310, 315,
317–20, 322, 328
Λόγος, 10–11, 16, 25, 27, 29, 32,
43–44, 49, 61, 73, 99, 102–3,
111, 121, 126, 162, 186,
193–94, 243, 255, 264,
266, 270–73, 286, 287–88,
293–94, 296, 298, 309–311,
314–15, 317–22
πρόσωπον, 165–66, 173, 175, 177,
179, 181–82, 223, 227–29,
276
τρόπος, 4, 9–13, 15, 18–19, 59–61,
67, 118, 120, 122, 162–69,
184–86, 188–90, 192–94,
237, 243–85, 314, 319–20,
329

www.ingramcontent.com/pod-product-compliance
Lightning Source LLC
Chambersburg PA
CBHW032012300426
44117CB00008B/1006